ACCESS® 365
PROJECT BOOK

Publisher: David Pallai
MERCURY LEARNING AND INFORMATION
121 High Street, 3rd Floor
Boston, MA 02110
info@merclearning.com
www.merclearning.com
800-232-0223

Julitta Korol. *Access® 365 Project Book: Hands-On Database Creation*
ISBN: 978-1-68392-094-6

The publisher recognizes and respects all marks used by companies, manufacturers, and developers as a means to distinguish their products. All brand names and product names mentioned in this book are trademarks or service marks of their respective companies. Any omission or misuse (of any kind) of service marks or trademarks, etc. is not an attempt to infringe on the property of others.

Library of Congress Control Number: 2023945502

232425321   Printed on acid-free paper in the United States of America.

Our titles are available for adoption, license, or bulk purchase by institutions, corporations, etc. For additional information, please contact the Customer Service Dept. at 800-232-0223(toll free).

All of our titles are available in digital format at *academiccourseware.com* and other digital vendors. *Companion files for this title are available by contacting info@merclearning.com.*
The sole obligation of MERCURY LEARNING AND INFORMATION to the purchaser is to replace the disc, based on defective materials or faulty workmanship, but not based on the operation or functionality of the product.

CONTENTS

PART VI   COMPACT, SPLIT AND SECURE THE DATABASE   407

Chapter 12 Compacting, Splitting, and Securing an
Access Database..409

INTRODUCTION

Microsoft Access has been the top database management solution for individuals and businesses for over two decades. Many of today's database systems started as small Access databases or were ported from Microsoft Excel spreadsheets. With Microsoft's commitment to continuing the development of the product, Access keeps getting better with each new update. Across all types and sizes of organizations, people continue to utilize Access to collect, track, and analyze data from multiple sources and build useful forms and reports. Non-developers are creating various Access databases because with Access they can quickly move forward and get their job done without requiring much support from the IT (Information Technology) department.

Access 365 Project Book: Hands-On Database Creation is a hands-on database project that guides you through the process of building a traditional Access desktop database that is later split into two files: a back-end database that contains tables with data, and a front-end database that contains forms, reports, queries, macros, and code modules. By separating the data from the rest of the database, the Access database can be easily shared by multiple users over a network. When you build a so-called "split database," you can provide a faster experience to your database users, and later the database can be migrated to another database system with fewer issues and fewer objects that need to be redone.

In this book, instead of working through some random examples, you will walk through a series of steps that will teach you the essential skills you need to acquire to develop a desktop database from beginning to end. The focus of this book is the creation of the Employee Training Database (ETD) database. If you are looking for a "tell it all" Access reference, this is not a book for you. This book is not meant to provide a complete guide to all Access features because no project requires the use of all the capabilities of a particular software. There are numerous books on the market that will give you an in-depth look into Microsoft Access, but they do not walk you through a complete project of building an Access database from beginning to end.

This book does not explain all the details of working with Access. Instead, it focuses on topics that are essential in the process of building and enhancing your database. The required Access features and capabilities are introduced exactly when you need them to complete a particular task in your database project. If you are looking for a book you can work with for full engagement and to get a sense of accomplishment when completed, this is the right place to start.

The book's approach is to learn by doing. For most people new to database topics, there's no better way than step by step. Simply turn on the computer, open this book, launch Access, and work through all the guided Hands-On exercises. But before you get started, allow me to give you a short overview of the things you'll be learning as you progress through this book.

This book is divided into the following six parts:

    I. Plan, Design, and Create a Database

    II. Create and Work With Database Tables

    III. Create and Work With Queries

    IV. Create and Work With Forms

    V. Create and Work With Reports

    VI. Compact, Split, and Secure the Database

Each part of this book builds on previous parts. Each chapter will draw from material covered in previous chapters and introduces you to new techniques that are necessary for completing each new phase of the database project.

Part I focuses on introducing you to some database concepts. Access databases are created by using Access objects. These are tables, queries, forms, reports, macros, and modules. You must understand these and numerous other terms before you can create meaningful databases for yourself and others. In this part of the book, we determine the purpose and scope of our database project and examine the database planning, designing, and data normalization processes. We also begin setting up the database we'll be working with throughout this book project.

Chapter 1: Planning and Designing a Database
In this chapter, you learn about Access and its various database objects. You will find out details about Access tables, the importance of primary keys, and the role of foreign keys and table relationships. This chapter explains how database planning phase plays a vital part in building and designing a successful database, and how the process known as normalization can ensure the correct flow and storage of data.

Chapter 2: Creating a Desktop Database
You start this chapter by creating a blank Access database. You learn about Access database files and naming conventions. You also learn how to design your first table and enter, modify, delete, and save your data. You get to know various properties that allow you to control how the data is formatted and displayed. You find out about default field values and learn how to control user's input with validation rules and validation text. You get comfortable working in Table Design and Datasheet view. You also learn how to copy, export, and delete a table. You finish this chapter by generating and printing your first table structure.

Part II introduces you to several techniques of implementing database tables. As tables consist of fields, you will learn about data types that the fields can hold to correctly store your data. You also learn how to set up primary keys, indexes, and create relationships between your tables, and explore several methods of filling in Access tables with data from various file formats.

Chapter 3: Creating Access Tables
In this chapter, you learn how to use the Tables group on the Ribbon's Create tab to create Access tables. Any other object you create later in this database will depend on these tables. As tables consist of fields, you learn about various data types that the fields can hold to correctly store your data. The available data types are discussed and implemented throughout the book.

Chapter 4: Setting Up Primary Keys, Indexes, and Table Relationships
In this chapter, you learn how to add primary keys and indexes to your database tables using Access built-in tools. You also learn how to create relationships between your tables using both the Edit Relationship dialog box and the Data Definition Language SQL commands.

Chapter 5: Populating Access Tables With Data
This chapter deals with several ways of filling in Access tables. Here you learn how to import data from spreadsheets, text and XML files, and other Access databases.

Part III teaches you essential database operations such as adding, updating, and deleting records. You learn how to use the Query Design view to create and run various types of database queries that will help you analyze data and locate records based on supplied criteria. You also learn how to calculate, group, and summarize data.

Chapter 6: Creating and Working With Select Queries
Database queries are essential in all sorts of database operations. You can use Access wizards or Query Design view to create your queries. Queries are questions

you pose to the database to get you a set of data you need or to perform certain operations on the data. In this chapter, you learn various methods of creating basic Select queries that retrieve data from one or more tables with or without criteria, sorted in ascending or descending order. You also learn how to use various expressions, aliases, and aggregate functions. You practice creating more advanced Select queries that can use parameters to set a query's criteria at runtime and crosstab queries that summarize data in a familiar row/column format. You will spend quite a bit of time in this chapter learning the SQL language behind queries.

Chapter 7: Performing Database Operations With Action Queries
In this chapter, you are introduced to other types of queries that allow you to perform database operations such as updating, deleting, and appending records to our database tables. You learn the functionality of each type of action query starting from making a new table, appending new records to an existing table, modifying values in specific fields in a table, and deleting data from a table.

Part IV focuses on creating and working with Access forms. You learn about designing various types of forms that can be used for data input and viewing.

Chapter 8: Designing and Using Forms
You start this chapter by creating a form using the Form Wizard. Next, you learn how to start from a blank form. You work in Design or Layout view and learn how to use various form properties to set up your forms. Various form controls (text boxes, combo boxes, buttons, hyperlinks, etc.) are discussed and used in this chapter. You also learn about the Visual Basic Editor window and use various built-in functions to create complex expressions.

Chapter 9: Form Customization
In this chapter, you spent quite a bit of time on form design and learn how you can customize a form by adding advanced controls such as a combo box and a list box, and how these controls can interact with each other. You work here with various control properties that will give your form a more polished look. You learn how to use events to ensure that a control refreshes whenever the value in another control changes. You are also taught how you can use domain aggregate functions in your form controls, specifically DLookup() and DCount(), to display data from other tables based on given criteria.

Part V guides you in the process of creating reports that provide your data for analysis, presentation, and printing.

Chapter 10: Designing and Using Reports
In this chapter, you learn about different options for creating reports. You are introduced to report wizards that help you create various reports. You also learn about report and report control properties that can make your reports more visually appealing. You find out about various report parts and learn how to add page breaks and use expressions in reports.

Chapter 11: Report Customization
In this chapter, you work with numerous report and control properties and learn about report sections and their customization. You create a report completely from scratch and go through various stages of the report design process step by step. In this chapter you also discover how forms can provide a handy user interface for your reports. You learn how to convert the Wizard-generated embedded macro into Visual Basic and learn how to modify it to extend it to other form controls quickly. You learn new VBA keywords and constructs like Select Case. You advance your knowledge of building more complex expressions by using functions such as Intermediate IIF and Switch.

Part VI focuses on making your desktop database capable of running well in a network environment.

Chapter 12: Compacting, Splitting, and Securing the Database
In this chapter, you are introduced to topics that allow you to run your Access database in a multi-user environment. You learn the steps that you need to follow in the process of splitting an Access database into a front-end file and back-end file and find out how to work with the Linked Table Manager to manage the linked tables in the front-end database. You also learn how to use the Compact and Repair Database, Database Backup, and Encrypt with Password features that are built-into Access. You find out why you cannot use the User-Level security in the ACCDB databases and what resources you can use when you decide to migrate your Access database back-end to SQL Server.

Appendix: Microsoft Access File Formats
This appendix provides more information about various Access file formats that are available in various versions of MS Access.

SUMMARY OF FEATURES

- Understand the concepts of database planning, information gathering, and database normalization.
- Discover various methods of building database tables and establishing table relationships.
- Learn about database keys, indexes, and NULL values.
- Populate tables by bringing data from different file formats (Text, XML, Excel, and Access).
- Create Select queries and learn the SQL language behind the queries.
- Learn how to perform important database tasks such as inserting, appending, and deleting data.
- Create simple and complex expressions that use various built-in functions that help you retrieve data and make decisions.
- Learn various methods of creating forms and making required changes by controlling form and form controls' properties, and use domain aggregate functions in your form controls: specifically DLookup() and DCount().
- Create a custom data entry form and learn how to synchronize combo box and list box controls.
- Learn how to work with report wizards to generate quick, out of the box reports.
- Create a custom multipart report and use various report and report section settings to get the desired look and feel.
- Learn about report section events and how to convert embedded macros into Visual Basic code and then modify the code to suit your needs.
- Customize the behavior of forms and reports by working with events in Form and Report code modules.
- Learn how to use the Compact and Repair and the Backup features to maintain your database.
- Split an Access database and secure it for a multi-user access.

WHO IS THIS BOOK FOR?

This book is a practical introduction to building and managing Access desktop databases. Instead of simply explaining the inner workings of Microsoft Access, which you will find in many reference books, this book makes sure that you, the reader, can complete with ease all the required tasks related to the creation, use, and management of an Access database. The focus of this book, learn by doing, will give you the skills you need to feel comfortable working with Access databases.

For success with this book, the assumption is that you have basic familiarity with Access user interface. This book also touches upon several programming techniques via the Access built-in language, Visual Basic for Applications (aka VBA). For VBA basics, you may want to work through the examples presented in my recent book titled *Access 2021 Programming Pocket Primer* (Mercury Learning and Information, 2022).

To follow along with the database project in this book, you will need a stand-alone version of Microsoft Office Professional 2021 or Microsoft 365 edition. If you don't have access to this software, Microsoft offers a free trial.

COMPANION FILES

The example files for all the hands-on activities in this book are available in the companion files included with this book. Replacement files may be downloaded by contacting the publisher at *info@merclearning.com*. Digital versions of this title are available at *academiccourseware.com* and other digital vendors.

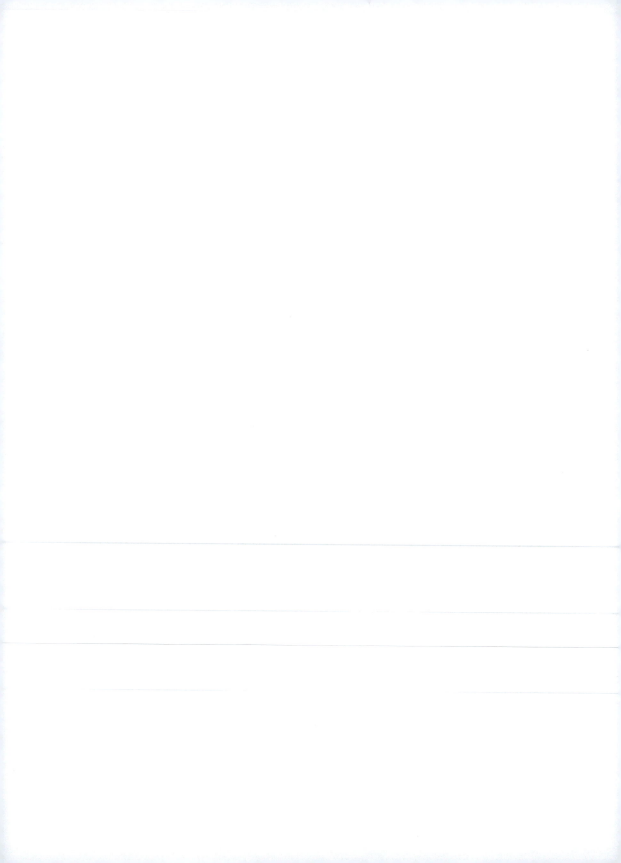

ACKNOWLEDGMENTS

I would like to express my sincere gratitude to everyone who helped me in the process of writing this book. Without their support and guidance, this book would not have been possible.

First and foremost, I would like to thank my publisher, David Pallai, for believing in my vision for this Access 365 Project Book, and giving me the opportunity to share it with the world. Many thanks to Eugene Zheleznov, my dear colleague, friend and mentor, for his support, advice and encouragement. Eugene offered his expertise and time in assisting me in the database design process and provided many useful suggestions to make this book more helpful to you. I am especially grateful to my project manager, Jennifer Blaney, who was always there to answer my questions, provide feedback, and keep me on track. She is a true professional and a pleasure to work with.

I would also like to thank the IBI Copy Editing team member who meticulously reviewed every word and sentence in this book correcting my errors and improving my style and clarity.

Finally, I would like to thank my compositor, SwaRadha Typesetting, who transformed my manuscript into a beautiful and easy to follow book. They did an amazing job with the layout, design, and typography. They also handled the technical aspects of the production with ease and efficiency.

I hope that you will enjoy working and learning from this book as much as I enjoyed writing it. Thank you for your interest and support.

Julitta Korol
October 2023

Part **I**

PLAN, DESIGN, AND CREATE A DATABASE

Part I introduces you to database concepts. Access databases are created by using Access objects: tables, queries, forms, reports, macros, and modules. You must understand these and numerous other terms before you can create meaningful databases for yourself and others. In this part of the book, we determine the purpose and scope of our database project and examine the database planning, designing and data normalization processes. We also begin setting up the database you'll be working with throughout this book project.

Chapter 1

PLANNING AND DESIGNING A DATABASE

In general terms, a database is a collection of information concerning a certain topic and is composed of one or more tables. While it is considerably easy to get started with a Word document or an Excel spreadsheet, creating a database requires a lot of preliminary thinking and information gathering. Even if you are already familiar with the concept of database tables, please do not skip this chapter. The initial steps which you must take prior to designing your database will determine whether your efforts will meet with a success or failure. This chapter gives you some background knowledge about Access, including the planning and design tasks that you need to complete outside of Access before you are ready to mold the information you have gathered into a working and user-friendly database application.

ABOUT ACCESS DATABASES

Microsoft Access stores data in related tables, hence it's called a *relational database*. Most databases include many related tables. By using multiple tables, you can decrease the input of redundant data and simplify data entry. We will expand on this concept known as *normalization* as we progress through this chapter.

In a relational database data in one table is related to data in another table by a common field. A classic example are Customers and Orders tables, where the Customers table stores information about customers such as their ID, Name, Address, Phone and so on, and the Orders table contains information about each order placed by a customer. Each row (record) in the Orders table must include a column (field) that identifies the customer who placed the order. The customer information is stored only once in the Customers table and by including the CustomerID field in the Orders table we can easily retrieve Customer data when needed without entering it again. Instead of storing customer data together with the order data like you would do in a spreadsheet, in a relational database you will split data into multiple tables. This approach will greatly simplify data entry and reporting and prevent duplication of data. Figure 1.1 illustrates table relationships using the sample Northwind.mdb file shipped with earlier versions of Microsoft Access.

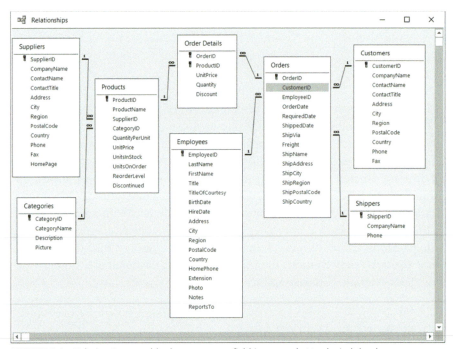

FIGURE 1.1.   Relating Access tables by a common field in a sample Northwind database.

Each box in the above diagram represents a single Access table. The data in each table is stored in fields A *field* is like a column in an Excel spreadsheet. A field can hold a specific type of data such as text, number, logical value (true or false) and so on. Some fields are designated as *primary key* fields. These fields uniquely identify each record in a table. In database terms, we will refer to rows as records. In the above relationship diagram, the CustomerID field in the Customers table has a primary key symbol next to it. Each CustomerID is unique;

there are no two customers with the same ID. In the related Orders table, the CustomerID key is known as a *foreign key*. Primary and foreign keys are used for joining tables, so that you can extract related data. A customer can have many orders. Each order has one customer. This type of a relationship is known as *one-to-many* and is depicted by 1 and the infinity symbol at the end of the joining line as you can observe in Figure 1.1. You will learn the details of fields and relationship types as you begin the process of designing your database.

ABOUT ACCESS OBJECTS

Microsoft Access databases are built, maintained, and automated using *Access objects*. An *object* is a thing that is specifically designed to enable a specific feature that you will need to create and work with in your database. The six main Access objects and their short descriptions are listed in Table 1.1.

TABLE 1.1 Microsoft Access Objects

Access Object Name	Object Description
Table	Used for storing data in the database. Tables store data in a tabular format, divided into columns referred to as fields and rows referred to as records. Tables may be related to each other by a common field.
Query	Used for locating specific information in a field or fields in your database and performing other database actions such as inserting, updating, and deleting data in tables.
Form	Used for entering new information into the database tables and providing user friendly presentation of existing information.
Report	Used for presenting details and summaries of database data for display on screen and for printing.
Macro	Small procedure that gathers all the required steps for automating various database tasks. Macros can be created with the built-in macro designer without the knowledge of computer programming.
Module	Sheets that look like Word documents but are used solely for creating and storing procedures and functions written in Visual Basic for Applications (VBA)—a built-in programming language of Access and other Microsoft 365 applications. Modules allow you to implement complex logic in your databases.

You will get many chances of working with Access objects listed in Table 1.1 as you design, work, automate, and maintain your database. Just by looking at the objects listed in Table 1.1, it is easy to notice that Microsoft Access provides a complete programming environment that, in addition to creation of database tables, allows you to build your data entry screens and reports, and includes multiple ways of accessing and automating your database via queries, macros and programming code written in modules.

THE EMPLOYEE TRAINING DATABASE (ETD)

The database you will be designing, creating, and working with in this book is called the Employee Training Database (ETD). This database will aim at addressing the needs of any company or organization that is looking for a simple and reliable system of scheduling and keeping track of employee training. The training management is poorly executed in many companies. Frequently, the employee training data is stored in spreadsheets, on various scraps of paper, or in other systems that were not designed to handle the training needs. As employee training is ongoing, it makes sense to spend time and design a dedicated database system that will eliminate wasted time, resources and money lost in attempting to keep track of this process. Think of how much frustration can be avoided daily if the employee training data has its own system that is easy to work with and maintain.

The ETD database will be a welcome solution to someone like Frank, who was seeking a nice customizable template to track employee training but found none. When he tried to create one himself in Microsoft Access, he realized that he was lost in the myriad of features that Access offers out of the box. Which features should he use first? How will he connect them into a meaningful system of storing and presenting data? Will it be usable when he's done?

By following easy, step-by-step instructions in this book, you can avoid many of the pitfalls that Frank had encountered and learn how to go about the process of building a simple and maintainable Training Management System.

PLANNING YOUR DATABASE

A primary purpose of a database is effective data storage and easy information retrieval. The database planning phase plays a crucial role in ensuring that the database you design will serve its intended purpose. Without a solid plan, your database project may prove to be nothing else but a costly waste of time and other resources that were provided. So, where do you start? The steps you need to take will depend on the size of the database project. Complex databases will require a great number of elements to consider and thus, will take longer to plan. However, no matter how big your project is, it is a good idea to start by setting up a meeting with the stakeholders—people that are most interested in bringing the database project to its successful completion. These individuals should be your starting point of reference. Find out what is expected of the new system, how it will benefit its users, and what is the expected delivery time.

Some Database Design Questions to Ask

1. Is there currently any other system in use that serves a similar need?
   If some of the information you need is already available in another system (documents, spreadsheets, or other databases), find out who you can contact to obtain samples of the data and discuss how that data is being used. It is beneficial to get the names and types of columns (fields) used, as well as any diagrams presenting the flow of data. Ask if you can link directly to other databases to provide data lookups in your database forms.

2. Make a list of all the resources you were able to identify; state their format (i.e., text file, Excel spreadsheet, SQL, MySQL, or other database table, another Access database, diagram, JSON, or XML/HTML file). Don't forget to include information that may have been shared with you via email, text, or Zoom.

3. List the names of identified fields/columns.
   - Make a list of proposed names for the database.
   - Make a list of proposed tables.

4. Ask for examples of the use cases for the database.
   Identify groups of users who will use the database on a regular basis. Ask what type of information they will need to store and retrieve. How would they like their data entry forms to look like? And what about the reports? How many reports they need and what kind of details they want to include? Will the reports be run manually or must be scheduled to run automatically at specific time intervals?

5. Ask various people to prepare mock-up forms and reports on paper or in a computer program they are comfortable with. The idea is to get as much end-user input as possible in this initial planning stage. Be sure to take a careful note of the specific wants of those individuals so you can include their requests early in the database design.

6. Schedule regular follow-up meetings with stakeholders and end-users to keep them informed about your progress and listen to their feedback. Your goal is to have a well-planned and useful database, and that requires a well-coordinated team effort.

Business Rules for the Database

It is important to determine what kind of logic you will need to implement in the database. *Business rules* are policies, procedures, or standards that a company has adopted which need to be enforced by the database system you design.

The following are some examples of business rules you could implement in your database:

- An employee can only register for one course in one quarter.
- An employee cannot take the same course more than once in a year.
- An employee must fill out a feedback form after each course.
- A course cannot be given in the same room in the same period while another course is taking place.
- Each course may have one or more prerequisite courses.

Business rules restrict the allowable data values for a database object in one way or another. They are often implemented via *constraints* which are rules that are placed on a database object such as a table or a column. Later in this book you will learn about types of constraints, including *referential constraints*, that enforce relationships between database tables; *NOT NULL constraints*, that specify whether null values are permitted for the field; and *CHECK constraints*, that use logical statements to validate whether a value is permitted in a field.

Creating a Database Diagram

After you have gathered substantial amount of information about the requirements for your database, decide what tables you will need and what data will go into each table. Because your tables will be in various relationships with one another, you will need to give a lot of thought to the primary key fields that uniquely identify each record in a table. When you perform a database search by this key, you should only get one record in return. Sometimes one key field is not enough to ensure the uniqueness of the data. You may need to combine two or more fields to meet this condition. We will talk about the selection of keys in Chapter 2.

It is important to make a preliminary diagram of a database showing the tables and listing the fields that they should have. Highlight the proposed relationships between the tables by drawing the lines between them. This diagram will be very helpful to you in the design phase.

Figure 1.2 depicts a table relationship diagram for the ETD database you will be building in this book.

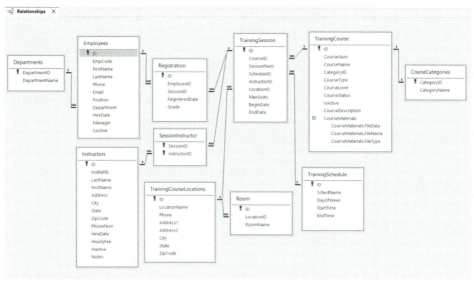

FIGURE 1.2. Table Relationships in the Employee Training Database (ETD)

Action Item 1.1

The Companion files include an Excel workbook named **etd_Fields.xlsx**. You will find there the Fields worksheet with a listing of the fields as well as field data types of the data collected during the planning stage. Add a new worksheet to this workbook for each table depicted in Figure 1.2 and assign each field from the etd_Fields worksheet to an appropriate table. When done, check your work against the **etd_Tables.xlsx** file in the Companion files.

DESIGNING THE DATABASE

The first law of database design is to accurately define the requirements. You must conduct a thorough analysis of what you want to do and how you want to do it. In our Employee Training database all employees can sign up for offered training sessions but only some employees should be allowed to administer the database. These admin users in addition to reading the data; could insert, update, and delete data. In database terms, they can perform Create, Read, Update, Delete (CRUD) operations. The database should be able to keep track of all the training offerings and employees who enroll in them. It should contain forms that allow for easy data entry as well as reports that provide detailed summaries of completed training for the company management needs.

With the database planning phase completed, you are now ready to call on Microsoft Access to help you implement your database design. Access offers many built-in tools, known as Wizards, to make this process as much enjoyable and efficient as possible. The design process you are embarking on will continue throughout the book as you create tables, define relationships between them, set up primary and foreign keys and indexes, include validation and business rules, design your forms and reports, create statements to retrieve, insert, update, and delete data. You will enhance your design skills by learning how to automate certain database tasks via programming code. The skillset required to create even a simple database is enormous and the only way to get the hang of it is simply by doing. As you are working in Access it will be easier to find out any mistakes made in your initial mockup design. Corrections are also easier to make when the only user is the database designer. So, where do you start?

You cannot have a database unless you've got at least one table, so let's create one.

Guidelines for Creating Tables

Decide which table you are going to create first. Look at the diagram shown earlier and pick a table that seems central to your database design. As the ETD database will track employee training, it is wise to start by creating a table for employees. In your real-life database project, you may decide to create a link to the Employees table that already exists in your Human Resources database instead of creating a new table. However, to keep this database entirely stand-alone, we'll build our own Employees table from scratch. In later chapters you will fill in this table with the existing HR data.

When creating tables pull out the spreadsheet from Action Item 1.1 earlier in this chapter and look over the fields that were identified for the database. Are all those fields needed? Cross out the ones that you are not planning to include in your forms, reports, or calculations. Make sure that each field you keep goes into one table. Each piece of information in a database should be kept only in one place so that the process of updating data is quick and efficient. The data that may be needed for calculations can be stored in a database field, but you must avoid storing any data that can be calculated (or derived) from existing fields. Take for example the age of an employee. If you are already storing the birth date, skip the age field. Access has many built-in math functions that can get you the answers you need for your forms and reports, or any decision-making process you need to implement.

Most databases rely on so called lookup tables. These tables usually contain a code and a description. For example, States table can have two fields: one with a state code and the other with the full name of the state. Lookup tables are very helpful as they prevent errors that may result from erroneous data entry in multiple places. The code description can be easily looked up simply by storing only a code field in the tables you need.

Understanding Table Relationships

When you need to display data from more than one table you will need to understand how to connect tables with one another so data can be easily retrieved. This process called *joining* is essential to understanding the relational databases. There are three basic types of relationships between tables:

- one-to-one
- one-to-many
- many-to-many

The *one-to-one* relationship indicates that for every record in the first table only one record exists in the second table. Notice that in our ETD database (see the diagram in Figure 1.2), there is no one-to-one relationship. These types of relationships are very rare. Often time there are used in situations when you simply don't want to store certain information in the same table for security reasons. For example, the knowledge of some personal data may be confidential and restricted to a small group of authorized individuals, so keeping that data in a separate table would absolutely make sense. Take the Employees table. To keep the Social Security number of each employee restricted to only authorized persons, you could create an ESSN table that is joined to the Employees table by the EmployeeID field. The ESSN table would only have two fields: EmployeeID and SSN. Only authorized people should be able to query the ESSN table. The relationship between the Employees table and the ESSN table would be a one-to-one.

While the one-to-one relationships are rare, the *one-to-many* relationships are the most common type of the relationships in database systems. In our ETD database there are several such relationships. For example, the Employees table is related to the Registration table as a one-to-many relationship. This tells Access that for each Employee in the Employee table there can be many registration entries in the Registration table as any employee can register in multiple training sessions. In other words, many registration records can be associated with a single employee.

The third type of a relationship, *many-to-many*, serves all those situations where each record in both tables can be related to none, one, or multiple records in the other table. This type of relationship requires a separate *join table*. The join table, also called a *junction table* or an *intermediate table*, will have at least two fields: a primary key field from one table and a primary key field from another table. To better visualize this scenario, look at the OrderDetails table depicted in Figure 1.1. Notice that the OrderDetails table has both the OrderID field from the Orders table and ProductID field from the Products table. Without the join table it would be impossible to connect Orders and Products tables to get the details of each order placed. As there are many products and there are many orders, it is said that these tables are in a *many-to-many relationship*.

In our ETD database, you will create a join table named SessionInstructor. This table will join the Instructor and TrainingSession tables as depicted in Figure 1.2. These tables are in a many-to-many relationship as there are many instructors and many training sessions. By creating a join table SessionInstructor, you will be able to determine which sessions are taught by which instructor and vice versa..

About Primary Keys

As mentioned earlier, a *primary key* is a field that uniquely identifies each record in a table. To find that key, ask yourself a question: *If I choose this field as a primary key, can I be certain that this field is different for every record in a table?* For example, if you are creating a bookstore database, the International Standard Book Number (ISBN) printed on the back of the book cover can be used as a primary key in the Books table because each book has a unique ISBN number. *How about the Social Security number for the Employees table?* Although SSNs are unique, for privacy reasons, it is not recommended that you use them as primary keys. When deciding on a primary key keep in mind the following:

- A primary key must be unique; you cannot have a duplicate value in this key.
- A primary key cannot contain a Null value; the value for that field must exist when the record is created.
- Once created, the primary key cannot be changed.
- Default order of data displayed in an Access table is by primary key, so selection of your key is important.

The keys play fundamental role in establishing relationships between tables. Unless you find a unique key, you will not be able to relate (or connect) your tables.

Sometimes finding a unique key will seem like a daunting task. If one field cannot guarantee the uniqueness of data, try to identify two or more fields that together have values that are different for any given record. These types of primary keys are known as *composite primary keys*. If none of these methods work, you can assign each record in a table a unique number. This is easily done with Microsoft Access autonumbering feature. Access will number the record as you enter it, thus making it unique.

Primary key fields speed up searching for records as Access automatically creates an index for each primary key field. Indexes are discussed in Chapter 4. Keep in mind that Access will allow you to have a table without a primary key, but you will not be able to set up relationship with other tables unless you add that key.

About Foreign Keys and Null Values

When you include the primary key from one table as a field in a second table to form a relationship between the two tables, the key in the second table is called a *foreign key*. While primary keys are used to ensure the integrity of the records within a table by guaranteeing their uniqueness, foreign keys are used to protect the integrity of data spread over multiple tables. Each value in a foreign key field must exist as values in the primary key field of the table being referred to. This concept is called a *referential integrity rule*. This rule prevents us from entering a child record when there is no parent record in the first table. A foreign key can be used as a check constraint by limiting a column to the defined set of values in the parent table. Foreign key columns almost always contain repeating values. Unlike primary key columns, it is possible for a foreign key column to contain *Null values*. In database terms, Null refers to data that's either missing or is unknown at the time of data entry. Keep in mind however that if the foreign key contains a Null value, you won't be able to relate the foreign key records to the records in the parent table uniquely identified with a primary key. To protect the integrity of your data, you should require a value in foreign key fields. You will learn how to check for Null values and how to use Null later in your database project when you start working with Access expressions and functions.

You will work with foreign keys while creating table relationships in Access.

What Is Database Normalization?

Normalization is a process of organizing the data in a database. The Normalization process includes creating tables and establishing relationships between those tables. During the normalization process you apply a set of rules to your unnormalized data. These rules help eliminate data redundancy and protect data integrity. The normalization rules were first proposed in 1971 by Edgar F. Codd, an English computer scientist, as part of his relational model (RM) for database management. While studying various relations (tables), Codd discovered that unnormalized relations present some problems when attempts are made to update, insert, or delete data from a relation. He called these problems anomalies.

Figure 1.3 illustrates an update, insertion, and delete anomaly as presented in Wikipedia: *https://en.wikipedia.org/wiki/Database_normalization.*

Employees' Skills

Employee ID	Employee Address	Skill
426	87 Sycamore Grove	Typing
426	87 Sycamore Grove	Shorthand
519	94 Chestnut Street	Public Speaking
519	96 Walnut Avenue	Carpentry

An **update anomaly**. Employee 519 is shown as having different addresses on different records.

Faculty and Their Courses

Faculty ID	Faculty Name	Faculty Hire Date	Course Code
389	Dr. Giddens	10-Feb-1985	ENG-206
407	Dr. Saperstein	19-Apr-1999	CMP-101
407	Dr. Saperstein	19-Apr-1999	CMP-201
424	Dr. Newsome	29-Mar-2007	?

An **insertion anomaly**. Until the new faculty member, Dr. Newsome, is assigned to teach at least one course, their details cannot be recorded.

Faculty and Their Courses

Faculty ID	Faculty Name	Faculty Hire Date	Course Code
389	Dr. Giddens	10-Feb-1985	ENG-206
407	Dr. Saperstein	19-Apr-1999	CMP-101
407	Dr. Saperstein	19-Apr-1999	CMP-201

DELETE

A **deletion anomaly**. All information about Dr. Giddens is lost if they temporarily ceases to be assigned to any courses.

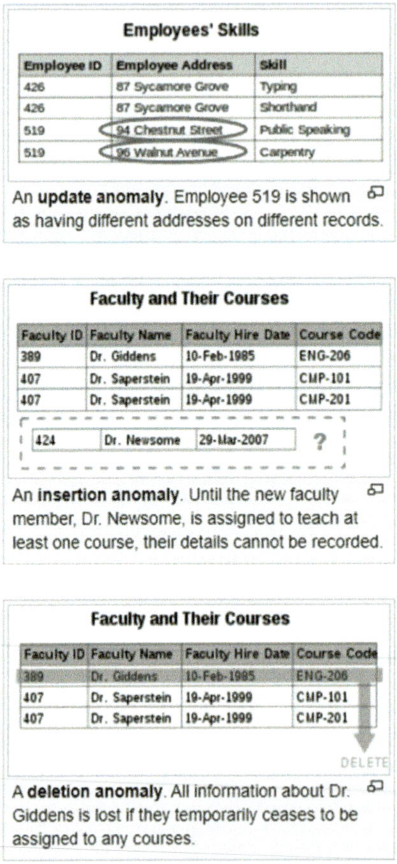

FIGURE 1.3. Database Normalization – Wikipedia, The Free Encyclopedia[12,3]

[1.] Nabav, "Example of a relational database table that suffers from an update anomaly", 2012-02-17, accessed March 23, 2023, *https://en.wikipedia.org/wiki/Database_normalization#/media/File:Update_anomaly.svg*

[2.] Nabav, "Example of an insertion anomaly in a relational database", 2007-08-07, 2008-02-13, accessed March 23, 2023, *https://en.wikipedia.org/wiki/Database_normalization#/media/File:Insertion_anomaly.svg*

[3.] Nabav, " Example of a relational database table that suffers from a deletion anomaly", 2008-08-08, 2008-01-23, accessed March 23, 2023, *https://en.wikipedia.org/wiki/Database_normalization#/media/File:Deletion_anomaly.svg*

The Update anomaly refers to a situation where an update of a single data value requires updates of multiple rows of data. As Figure 1.3 illustrates, to update employee's address we may need to change one or more records. Update anomalies often result in inconsistent data as it is easy to miss some of the data that should have been included in the update but weren't. To avoid update anomaly, it is important to store only one copy of the data and refer to it wherever required instead of duplicating it.

The Insert anomaly refers to a situation where a row of data cannot be inserted into a table because information that should be kept in two separate tables is kept in one. As Figure 1.3 illustrates, because we don't know the course code for Dr. Newsome, his personal information cannot be inserted. To avoid insert anomaly it is important to keep data related to different categories in separate tables. The faculty information should not be embedded in the Courses table.

The Delete anomaly is the opposite of the insert anomaly. Because Faculty and Courses data are kept in one table, deleting a row of data for Dr. Giddens (see Figure 1.3) will result in loss of his personal information as well as the information about courses he was assigned to teach.

Data Normalization Rules

The normalization rules are formally known as *normal forms*. Each rule is called a *normal form*. Each normal form has rules that must be satisfied before you can go to the next form. How far you should normalize depends on whether you want to optimize your database storage and updates or get more efficient querying capabilities. Too much normalization increases the complexity of your queries as multiple tables must be accessed to retrieve data. To achieve the highest level of normalization, start with unnormalized data and organize your data into tables in such a way that it complies to first normal form, then second normal form, until the data satisfies at least the third normal form. This is a progressive process in which each step must be completed before higher level of database normalization can be achieved. The Action Item 1.2 at the end of this chapter provides a link to a 5-minute overview and examples of normal forms. The three normal forms will cover most cases encountered while designing today's database information systems.

Benefits of Data Normalization

By following specific normalization rules, it is possible to determine the most efficient way to divide the information into tables so that each piece of data is stored only once in the database and all related information can be easily retrieved. As Codd stated, by normalizing the database you can avoid undesirable insertion, update, and deletion dependencies and reduce the need to restructure the database as new types of data are introduced. Changes made to a fully normalized database should only minimally affect the applications that interact with that database. A properly normalized database saves time and money, while the unnormalized database will lead to maintenance headaches in the future.

What Is Database Denormalization?

Normalization leads to creating more tables and joins. Sometimes you will need to denormalize the database. Suppose your database users report serious performance issues while running complex queries that retrieve company's asset data. You have tried to eliminate these issues by tuning your database, and even upgraded your computer hardware, but the issues seem to persist. At this point, denormalization may be the solution you need to consider. You may improve the performance of your database by storing some redundant and summarized data in tables and combining some tables that were split during the normalization process. Keep in mind that denormalization should be your last resort. By denormalizing data, you will reintroduce data anomalies that you tried to eliminate in the process of normalization, thus you will end up with a database application that is faster but less accurate. You need to decide which outcome will be most beneficial to you.

Action Item 1.2

Get familiar with the normalization concepts before proceeding to the next chapter. Spend the next five minutes reading Microsoft documentation at: *https://docs.microsoft.com/en-us/office/troubleshoot/access/database-normaliza-tion-description*

When you are done reading, don't miss the opportunity to download the Office Products Troubleshooting PDF file that will serve you as a go to reference on Microsoft Access and other Microsoft 365 products. You should see the download PDF link in the left scroll area. And, in case you missed it, use this link:

https://docs.microsoft.com/en-us/office/troubleshoot/opbuildpdf/clienttoc/toc.pdf?branch=live

SUMMARY

In this chapter, you began your journey into the exciting world of Access database development. As you have seen, properly designing a database, even a small one, is a big job. To get good results you must have a clear understanding of the underlying data and its various relationships. You were introduced to the required database terminology and basic database concepts that should help you working with the remaining chapters of this book. If some of these concepts still feel foreign to you, don't panic. You will have plenty of time to assimilate this new knowledge as you progress through this book and learn how these concepts are implemented piece by piece in Access. If you picked up this book because of its hands-on approach, get ready for the next chapter where we begin building the Employee Training Database.

	CREATING A
Chapter 2	DESKTOP DATABASE

Now that you are familiar with the basic database terms and you've gathered your company's requirements for the training database, it's time to begin the implementation phase by building an Access desktop database.

ABOUT ACCESS DATABASE FILE FORMATS

Depending on your needs, Access databases can be created in various file formats. In this book you will use the ACCDB format to create the Employee Training database. The ACCDB file format, which is recognized by its .ACCDB extension in the file name, was first introduced in Access 2007 and has been the default file format for desktop databases since then. In earlier versions of Access, the MDB file format was used. For a complete listing of Access file formats and their differences, please see Appendix A.

CREATING AN ACCESS DESKTOP DATABASE

When you launch Microsoft Access, you are given options for creating a new database or for opening an existing Access database (see Figure 2.1). On this screen you will also find various predefined templates that Microsoft includes with Access free of charge. These templates provide examples of prebuilt Access applications that you can use as a starting point in your database development or as a handy learning tool. The search box available on this screen enables you to search for additional templates that are available online. This book's focus is on creating a database from scratch, so templates are not covered. However, it is recommended that you take time to download and explore some of these templates to get familiar with the structure of various databases.

NOTE	*Files for the Hands-On project may be found in the Companion files.*

(⊙) Hands-On 2.1   Creating a Blank Database

1. Launch Microsoft Access and choose New (blank database) as shown in Figure 2.1.

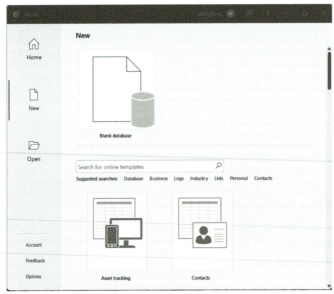

FIGURE 2.1. Creating a desktop database (Step 1).

Access displays the blank database dialog box (see Figure 2.2) where you can specify the location and database name. The default database name is shown automatically in the File Name and so is the default file location.

2. Click the file folder image next to the File Name box in Figure 2.2.

FIGURE 2.2. Creating a desktop database (Step 2).

Access displays the File New Database dialog box (see Figure 2.3).

3. Select the folder where you would like to save the database and enter **ETD** as the database name as shown in Figure 2.3. Notice that you can create a new folder for your database by clicking the New folder button in this window. For easy reference all objects and files created in this book will be stored in the **AccessProjectBook1** folder. A database file is like any other computer file, so it can be moved or copied later to another preferred folder.

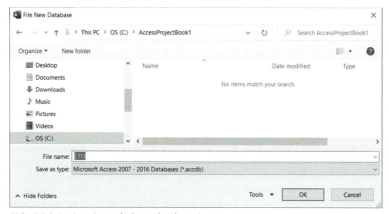

FIGURE 2.3. Creating a desktop database (Step 3).

When you click OK in the File Name Database dialog, you will be returned to the blank database screen where all the default options are replaced with your selections as shown in Figure 2.04.

4. Click the `Create` button to create the ETD database in the AccessProjectBook1 folder.

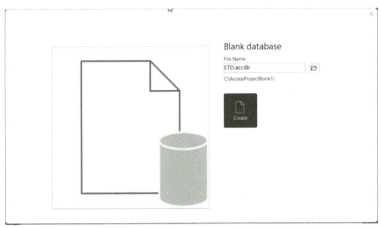

FIGURE 2.4. Creating a desktop database (Step 4).

Access automatically opens the newly created ETD database for you. This database contains a blank table named Table1 with one field named ID (Figure 2.5). This is the starting point in building any Access table. The asterisk denotes an empty record. Notice that when the table is in the Edit mode the Table Fields is selected in the Ribbon menu.

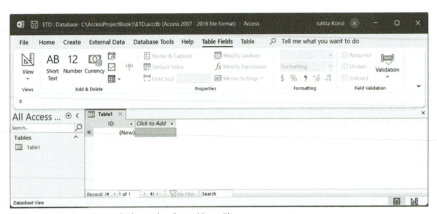

FIGURE 2.5. Creating a desktop database (Step 5).

COMPLETING THE INITIAL TABLE STRUCTURE

Creating all the required tables is the next logical step in designing your database. In the next few chapters of this book, we will work extensively with various tables and their options. Because we cannot have a database without at least one table, let's continue with Access Table1 that has already been started for us.

⊙ **Hands-On 2.2   Creating a Table Manually**

NOTE	*Please complete Hands-On 2.1 before you continue with steps below.*

1. Click the drop-down arrow in the `Click to Add` column and select `Short Text` (Figure 2.6). Use this data type whenever you plan to enter up to 255 alphanumeric characters as a value in an Access field. Refer to Table 2.3 later in this chapter for the summary of data types that are available in Access.

    Access will add a new field to the table named **Field1**.
2. While Field1 name is highlighted type **EmpCode** as the new name for the field and press **Enter**.
3. To add another field to the table, again click the drop-down arrow in the `Click to Add` column and select the data type for the field. Then rename the field by typing a new name in the highlighted area. Using the same technique, complete the table structure as shown in Table 2.1 starting with FirstName. To speed up the data entry, press the Tab key to move to another field.

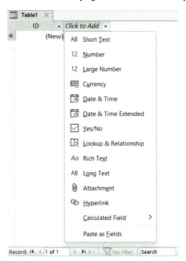

FIGURE 2.6. Field types.

TABLE 2.1 The Structure of the Employees Table

Field Name	Field Data Type
ID	AutoNumber
EmpCode	Short Text
FirstName	Short Text
LastName	Short Text
Phone	Short Text
Email	Hyperlink
HireDate	Date/Time
Position	Short Text
Department	Number
Manager	Short Text
Inactive	Yes/No

When you have entered all the fields in the table using the field names and data types listed in Table 2.1, your screen should match Figure 2.7. Notice that all the fields are displayed here in the spreadsheet-like format, with each field being a separate column.

FIGURE 2.7. Employees Table fields. Notice that the table still bears the default name Table1, because the changes have not yet been saved.

Access calls this layout the *Datasheet View*. In the Datasheet View it is easy to work with multiple records. Another view, called *Design View*, allows you to add new fields to a table as well as configure field properties. You will work in Design View later in this chapter.

Naming Conventions in Access

While creating your first table you had to name individual fields and assign to them appropriate data types. Let's look at the Access rules that you must keep in mind when performing these tasks.

When you create a database, you must decide on the naming convention you will use for your database objects. Access allows up to 64 characters for the names of your objects so you can give your tables, queries, forms, and reports descriptive and informative names. However, longer names take longer to enter and can be easily misspelled. When deciding on the names, keep in mind that your users will not see the formal names of your database objects as Access provides a way for a developer to assign different names in the User Interface (UI). Some developers prefer to add the prefix of the object type to the object name. For example, instead of naming a table Employees, they use tblEmployees (see Table 2.2 for the popular prefixes that are in use).

TABLE 2.2 Popular Prefixes for Access Database Objects

Database Object	Prefix	Example
Table	tbl	tblEmployees
Query	qry	qryEmployeesPay
Form	frm	frmEmployeeRegistration
Report	rpt	rptNewHires
Macro	mcr	mcrReformatDates
VBA module	bas mod	basNewProcedure modNewTestSettings

When using multiple words in object names, the *camel case* is preferred. Camel-case names are easier to read and remember than compound names written all in lowercase or uppercase characters. Spaces in object names should be avoided because they can cause problems when porting Access databases to other database environments.

Naming a Field

It is important to name the field so it can be easily identified by anyone using Access. Field names can be from 1 to 64 characters long and can include letters, numbers, and special characters except for the following: period (.), exclamation point (!), accent grave (`), and brackets ([]). While field names can include spaces, you should avoid spaces for the same reasons already mentioned in the previous section. Also, field names cannot begin with a blank space.

What Is the Data Type?

When you add fields to your table you must specify what type of data each field will hold. Access offers many data types as shown in Table 2.3. The Number data type should not be used for fields that will not be used in performing arithmetic operations. For example, don't store data like phone numbers, zip codes, or social security numbers in numeric fields. It's important to remember that numeric fields do not store the leading zeros. Always select the smallest data type/field size that will satisfy your field storage requirements. Before deciding on the field size, determine the largest value you will ever want to store in that field. Field types must be selected with caution for another reason. Binary type fields, such as Long Text or OLE Object can't be sorted or indexed. While we discuss sorting and indexing in later chapters, remember that numeric types will sort differently from text data. When dealing with dates, use the Date/Time data type if your data output requires chronological order. The Large Number data type was added to Access to support compatibility with other databases such as SQL Server. This data type is not compatible with older versions of Access and should be used sparingly.

Access allows you to specify the exact size of the Short Text data field in the Field Size property area. You will learn about field properties when we discuss the table Design View further on in this chapter.

TABLE 2.3 Data Types Available in Desktop Databases in Microsoft Access 2013 and Later.

Data Type	Type Description	Size
Short Text (Previously called Text)	Alphanumeric characters (Letters, numbers, and punctuation)	255 characters or fewer
Long Text (Previously called Memo)	Alphanumeric characters (Letters, numbers, and punctuation)	1 GB characters or less
Number	Numeric values	Integers 1, 2, 4, or 8 bytes. 16 bytes when used for Replication ID (GUID)
Large Number	Numeric values Introduced in 2019 for compatibility with other databases.	8 bytes
Date/Time	Date and time values	8 bytes
Date/Time Extended	Date and time values Compatible with SQL Server datetime2 data type.	Encoded string of 42 bytes
Currency	Monetary values	8 bytes
AutoNumber	Automatic number increments	4 bytes 16 bytes when used for Replication ID (GUID)
Yes/No	Logical value: Yes / No True /False	1 bit (0 or -1)

Data Type	Type Description	Size
OLE Object	Picture Graph Sound Video	Up to 2GB depending on available disk space
Hyperlink	Link to Internet resources	Up to 8,192 (each part of a Hyperlink data type can contain up to 2048 characters)
Attachment	Used for attaching external files such as pictures, documents, spreadsheets, or charts.	Up to 2 GB
Calculated	Stores calculation based on values in other fields in the table	Depends on the setting of the Results Type property
Lookup & Relationship	Brings up the Lookup Wizard that allows you to get the values for the field from another table or query or enter your own values.	Depends on the data type of the lookup field.

Saving the Table

When you try to close the table using the Close (x) button in the Datasheet View tab, Access will ask you to save the table if the changes you made have not yet been saved. During this time, you will be given a chance to change the name of the table from Table1 to whatever name you want. Let's save our table as **Employees**.

(◉) Hands-On 2.3 Saving a Table

1. Right click the **Table1** tab name as shown in Figure 2.8 and choose Save from the shortcut menu.

FIGURE 2.8. Saving the Employees table (Step 1).

Access displays the Save As dialog box as shown in Figure 2.9.

FIGURE 2.9. Saving the Employees Table (Step 2).

2. Enter **Employees** in the Save As dialog and click **OK**.
   Access renames the Table1 to Employees and lists the table in the Navigation pane at the left of the screen as shown in Figure 2.10. The Navigation pane is divided into several categories that can be accessed via the drop-down list at the top. Currently All Access Objects category is shown. If you need more room in the main screen for your table, you may use the shutter bar Open/ Close button (<) above the Search box.

FIGURE 2.10. Saving the Employees Table (Step 3).

3. Right click the **Employees** tab name and choose `Close`. You can also click the **Close** button (**x**) any time you want to close an Access object.

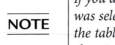	*If you accidently clicked OK in the Save As dialog when Table1 was selected, Access saved the table as Table1. You can rename the table by right clicking its name in the Navigation pane and choosing `Rename`.*

WORKING IN THE TABLE DESIGN VIEW

In the previous sections, you created a new Access table using the Datasheet View. This view does not provide all the features you may want to have available while building Access tables. Access offers another view called the Design View which is a special developer tool for creating new tables and setting various table and field properties. You can activate this view in one of several ways:

- If the table you want to modify is already open in the Datasheet View, right click the name of the table in the tab and select Design View from the pop-up menu.

- If the table is currently closed, right click its name in the Navigation pane on the left side of the screen and select Design View from the pop-up menu.

- If you want to create a new table in the Design View, choose Create in the Ribbon and click the Table Design button.

Access will display the current table in the Design View, or it will create a new table for your input called Table1. Let's examine and configure the Employees table which you have just built.

Hands-On 2.4   Working in the Design View

1. In the Navigation pane on the left, right click the **Employees** table name and choose `Design View`.
   Access shows the table design with the ID field selected (see Figure 2.11).

FIGURE 2.11. Employees Table opened in the Design View.

Property Sheet which appears on the right-hand side of the screen, is not a part of the Table Design View. It may be missing on your screen if you never turned it on. To make it visible, click the **Property Sheet** button on the Ribbon. The Property Sheet lists settings (also known as attributes) for the specific selection. In Figure 2.11, we are looking at various table properties. Access allows you to change many of these settings by either typing in a new setting, choosing an option from a drop-down list or by configuring your setting through the built-in Expression Builder indicated by the ellipsis (...). The latter two controls automatically appear when you click in the second column to edit the current value. You will work with Property Sheet for various Access objects throughout this book.

The Table Design View consists of the following two parts:

- **Field Entry Area** at the top of the screen allows you to enter field names, their data types and optionally description of the field's purpose. While optional, field description can be useful for explaining the type of data that the field expects. You can enter up to 255 characters to describe the purpose of the field.

- **Field Property Area** at the bottom of the screen gives you access to various field properties such as field size, field format, input mask, default value, caption, and other properties. The available properties depend on the field's data type. Notice that the Field Property Area is divided into two tabs. The General tab lists all the properties that can be configured for the selected field data type. Figure 2.11 displays properties for the selected ID field. The Lookup tab allows you to specify the type of control to use to display the field on forms. Again, the type and availability of lookup controls depends on the selected field type. There are no settings to select in the Lookup tab when the field type is AutoNumber.

In Design View. you can specify which field or fields in the table constitute primary key and which fields are indexed. The primary key fields are indicated by the key symbol to the left of the field name, as you can see in Figure 2.11. Here, the ID field has been automatically designated by Access as primary key for the Employees table. This field is also indexed. Indexes speed up searches and sorting on the field but may slow down updates of the data. In the Field Properties area, setting the Indexed property to "Yes - No Duplicates" will prohibit duplicate values in the field. Access displays a helpful descriptive text in the field property area when you attempt to specify or change a property value. Now, let's work with some of these properties.

2. With the **ID** field selected in the Field Entry Area (see Figure 2.11), click the `Indexed property` in the Field Property Area.

   Access will highlight the current Indexed property value – **Yes (No Dupli-cates)** and will reveal a drop-down list in this field. Notice the informational text that appears for the selected property.

3. From the drop-down list, choose **No**.

   Access displays the informational message notifying you that removing or changing the index would require a removal of the primary key. You are also advised how to go about making that type of change.

   You can learn a lot about the inner workings of Access by paying close attention to the messages that pop up on the screen when you make various selections.

4. Click **OK** to close the message dialog.

   Access just told you how to remove a primary key. Let's try this out.

5. Click the `ID` field in the Field Entry Area and then click the **Primary Key** button on the Ribbon.

   Notice that Access removes the key symbol from the ID field and sets the Indexed property to No. Now that you know how to do this, let's restore the previous settings.

6. While the ID field is still selected, click the **Primary Key** button on the Ribbon. Again, your screen should resemble Figure 2.11.

7. Let's look at the `New Values` property.

   This property is used with the AutoNumber field type, and it tells Access how new values should be generated for the AutoNumber field. The Increment setting will assign a Long Integer value (see the Field Size property of the ID field) to the field beginning at 1 and increment this value each time a record is added to the table. Another setting for this property is Random. When the Random setting is selected, a random number is generated for each new record. You may have only one AutoNumber field in a table.

8. Click the **Caption** property for the ID field and enter **EmpID**.

   This will indicate that we want to use EmpID as the field label when we display employee records in the Datasheet View.

NOTE	*Access also allows you to set the field's Caption property in the Query Design View that will be covered in another chapter. Because that Caption property can contain a different text than the one set in the Design View you must be very careful not to confuse Caption properties for different objects.*

9. Press **Ctrl+S** or click the **disk** image in the title bar of the Access Application window to save the recent changes to the table design.
Leave the Design View open as we are not done working with the field properties.

Modifying a Field Size

The Short Text fields use the default 255 characters field size. Access will only store the actual number of characters that are entered. However, you can limit the number of characters for the Short Text field by entering a new value in the Field Size property. Let's take a few minutes to make some modifications.

(⊙) Hands-On 2.5   Modifying Field Size of the Short Text Data Type

1. In the Field Entry area of the Employees table Design View, click the First Name field. The properties of this field should now appear in the lower portion of the screen.
2. Enter **100** in the Field Size property.
3. Select the Last Name field and change its Field Size property to **200**. Do the same for the Manager's field.
4. Select the Phone field and change its Field Size property to **12**.
5. Press **Ctrl+S** or click the **disk** image in the title bar of the Access Application window to save changes to the table design.

Specifying the Field Format and Input Mask

When data is entered into an Access table you can specify how this data should be formatted. There are many types of formats you can apply to your data. For example, the text data types can be formatted as uppercase or lowercase characters; dates and numeric values can assume many display formats. You can assign a predefined format via the Input Mask property to get consistent formatting of phone numbers, zip codes, social security numbers, dates, and so on.

(⊙) Hands-On 2.6   Assigning Specific Formats to Fields

1. Click the **HireDate** field and set the Format property of this field to Short Date as shown in Figure 2.12.

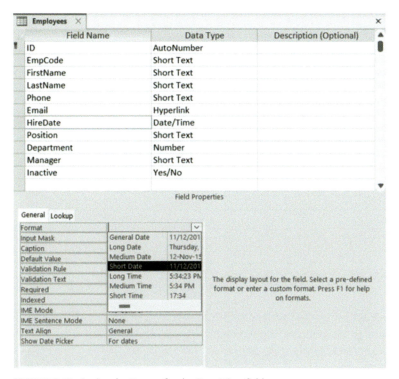

FIGURE 2.12. Setting the Format for the Date/Time field.

2. In the list of fields, click the **Phone** field and then click in the blank column next to the Input Mask property. When you see the Builder button (**...**), click it to specify the format for the Phone field. When Access prompts you to save the table first, click **Yes**. You will be presented with the Input Mask Wizard dialog as shown in Figure 2.13.

Input Mask Wizard displays the name of predefined input masks and the examples of how the data will look like when you select that mask.

3. With the phone number selected in the Input Mask Wizard, click the **Try It** text box and enter any phone number to see how the data entry will look.

Access displays the following input mask:

(___) ___-____

With this mask, when you enter your phone number, the data will appear as follows:

(718) 345-2345

FIGURE 2.13. Using the Input Mask Wizard to specify the data entry format for a field.

4. Click the **Next** button to proceed to the next screen in the Input Mask Wizard. If you want to change the input mask, you can specify your custom format using this screen (see Figure 2.14).

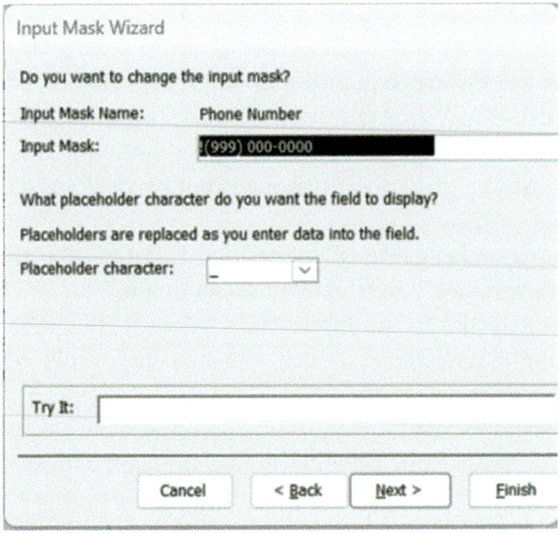

FIGURE 2.14. Using the second screen of the Input Mask Wizard to specify the custom format for the input mask.

Access allows you to specify a different placeholder symbol in your input mask. Placeholders are replaced as you enter data into the field. You can specify the following symbols: underscore (_), " ", #, @, !, %, and *. Table 2.4 displays the listing of all characters that can be used to construct a custom string in the Input Mask box.

TABLE 2.4 Input Mask Characters

Input Mask Character	Description
!	Exclamation point. Indicates that characters in the input mask are filled from right to left.
.	Period. Serves as the decimal placeholder.
,	Comma. Serves as thousands separator.
:	Colon. Serves as the date and time separator.
;	Semicolon. Used as a separator character.
-	Dash. Used as a separator character.
/	Forward slash. Used as a separator character.
\	Back slash. Displays the next character as a literal.
<	Less than sign. Converts all characters to lowercase.
>	Greater than sign. Converts all characters to uppercase.
&	Permits any character or space (required).
C	Permits any character or space (optional).
?	Question mark. A letter from A to Z is optional.
L	A letter from A to Z is required.
a	A character or digit is optional.
A	A character or digit is required.
0	Indicates that a digit is required. Plus (+) and minus (–) signs are not permitted.
9	Indicates that a digit is optional. Plus (+) and minus (–) signs are not permitted.
#	Indicates optional digit or space. Spaces are removed when the data is saved in the table.

5. Using the Table 2.4 as a reference, modify the Phone input mask so it requires the user to enter the area code. Try the modified input mask by entering a phone number without an area code in the Try it box and then press **Next**. Access should display a message that the value you entered isn't appropriate for the input mask.

6. Click **OK** to the message and now enter the phone number with the area code in the Try it box and then click the **Next** button.

   Access displays the next Input Mask Wizard screen as shown in Figure 2.15.

FIGURE 2.15. Using the third screen of the Input Mask Wizard after specifying the custom format for the input mask.

7. Click the first option button to indicate that the data should be stored in the table with all symbols in the mask, and then click **Next**.

8. Access displays the last screen of the Input Mask Wizard as shown in Figure 2.16.

9. Click the **Finish** button to create the input mask.

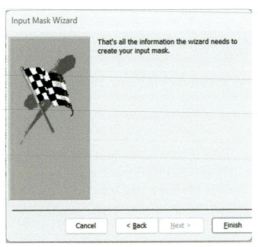

FIGURE 2.16. Last screen of the Input Mask Wizard.

Access fills the Input Mask property with the mask you created as shown in Figure 2.17.

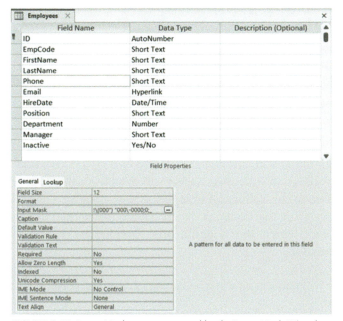

FIGURE 2.17. Input Mask property created by the Input Mask Wizard.

The Input Mask that Access has created based on your input in the Wizard Screens looks like this:

!\(000") "000\-0000;0;_

You can see here three sections, separated by semicolons:

- The first section contains the mask itself. For example: !\(000") "000\-0000. The mask is comprised of characters listed in Table 2.4.

- The second section indicates whether Access will store the data with the symbols in the input mask or without. Zero (**0**) indicates the first option button in the Input Mask Wizard screen as shown in Figure 2.15. If you should choose the second option button, you will see **1** in this section.

- The third section indicates the placeholder character you selected to tell the user how many characters are expected in the input area.

Specifying the Default Value for a Field

Default Value is the initial value that will be automatically provided for the specified field every time a new record is created. This value can be a number, a text string, or an expression, and can be changed during data entry. Default Value must be appropriate for the field's data type. The Default Value for Number and Currency data types is set to 0 by default. Once specified, the Default value is available in the Table Datasheet View, in queries and on forms.

Specifying Validation Rule and Validation Text

The validation properties allow you to enforce specific requirements for data input into a field.

For instance, you can use the Validation Rule property to prevent anyone from entering date greater than today in the HireDate field. When data fails validation, you can display a custom message in the Validation Text property. The maximum length of the Validation Text property value is 255 characters. If you don't enter the Validation Rule text, Access will display a generic message when the rule specified in the Validation Rule property is violated. The Validation Rule property is a string that contains the expression that should be used to test user's input. Let's implement the validation properties for the HireDate field in the following Hands-On.

(◉) Hands-On 2.7.   Implementing Validation Properties for a Table Field

1. In the Design View of the Employees table, click the **HireDate** field.
2. Click in the empty column next to the Validation Rule property and click the Builder button (…).
   Access displays the Expression Builder dialog as shown in Figure 2.18.

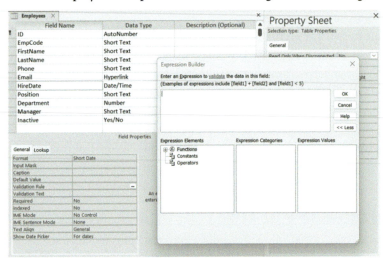

FIGURE 2.18. Getting started with a Field Validation rule.

Notice that the Expression Builder provides an example of an expression and an area where you can build your expression. The lower part of the screen has three panes where you can access the expression elements, categories and values that can be used to create the expression.

3. Click the plus sign next to the Functions in the Expression Elements pane and select **Built-in Functions**.

Access fills the second and third pane with the list of all function categories and function names that are available (see Figure 2.19). *Functions* are programs that perform specific actions and return results. Some functions require additional data input before they can be executed. This extra data is called *parameters* or *arguments*. If the function requires arguments, they will be listed inside the parentheses after the function name. Functions that don't require additional input will have a pair of empty parentheses.

4. Click the **Date/Time** in the Expression Categories pane to narrow down the list of functions to those that are date related.

5. In the Expression Values pane, select the Date function as shown in Figure 2.19.

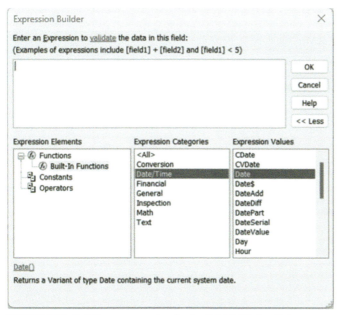

FIGURE 2.19. Building an expression for the Field Validation Rule.

Access displays the name and description of the selected function at the bottom of the Expression Builder screen. Date is a built-in function that returns the current system date.

For the HireDate field we want our expression to say that the date shouldn't be greater than today. Let's build this expression right now.

6. Double-click the selected Date function in the Expression Values pane. Access enters the function name in the upper pane of the Expression Builder. Notice a pair of empty parentheses after the function name.

    You can use operators and constants to create the Validation Rule expressions.

7. In the Expression Elements pane, click the **Operators** entry. Access will populate the Expression Categories pane with the following types of operators: Arithmetic, Comparison, Logical and String. Click each category to check out the available operator values. To enter the specific operator in the upper pane, double-click it. You can also enter the required operator by typing it yourself.

8. Modify the Evaluation rule expression as shown in Figure 2.20 by entering: < **Date() + 1.**

9. Click **OK** to exit the Expression Builder. Notice that Access enters your expression in the Validation Rule property.

10. In the Validation Text property enter the following text: **Invalid Date. Please enter the date that is not greater than today**.

11. Press **Ctrl+S** to save changes you have made to the Employees table.

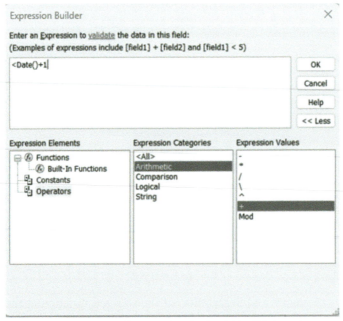

FIGURE 2.20. Completing the Expression for the Field Validation rule.

Keep in mind that every time you need to use a constant date in an Access expression, you will need to surround it with pound signs (#). For instance, to limit the HireDate to the period between January 1, 2020 and today, you would enter the following expression:

```
Between #1/1/2020# and Date()
```

The # is commonly called a *delimiter*. There are many other delimiters that you will learn while working with this book.

Data validation rules are extremely important during the data entry as they prevent bad data from getting into your database. You will test the rule you entered when you add the first record to the Employees table. For now, let's continue working in the Table Design View to find out what else you can do here.

Changing a Table Design

So far, you used the Table Design View to add and modify field properties. If the table does not contain any data, it is safe to modify its design. However, when there is already data in the table you must be careful not to make changes that would affect the existing data. For instance, changing the size of text and number fields may cause data no longer to fit into the field and be truncated. Access will not allow you to make certain changes to the table design if it finds that they could cause serious issues. You will see some of these issues in action once you are done with the process of creating your tables and populating them with data.

Modifying the Field Data Type

Sometimes it is necessary to change the data type of a field. If your table is empty (has just been created) this is an easy task to perform. However, when the table already contains some data or is related to other tables in the database, the change of data type may not be allowed or may cause loss of existing data. This is an advanced topic which will not be discussed here. Access has specific data type conversion rules that must be followed to address these types of issues.

You may wonder why in the Employees table the Department field data type has been set to Number instead of Short Text. To prevent data entry errors, we will store the department names in a separate table. The number data type will allow us to establish a relationship in a later chapter between the Employees and Departments tables.

◉ Hands-On 2.8.   Modifying a Decimal Places Property for a Number Data Type

1. In the Design View of the Employees table, locate the **Department** field and in the lower pane, specify zero (**0**) for the **Decimal Places** property. The default value is Auto.
2. Press **Ctrl+S** to save changes you have made to the Employees table.

Changing a Field Name

While a table is empty and has no relationships with other tables in the database you can easily change a field name by selecting the field name in the Table Design View and entering a new name.

Action Item 2.1

Take a moment now and change the Inactive field name to **IsActive**.

Changing a Field Location

The order your fields appear in Design View determines the order in which the fields will be displayed in the Datasheet View. If you need a different order of fields, you should drag the field to a different location in Design View. To do this, click the field selector (the grey square to the left of the field name) and drag the selected row to another location.

Action Item 2.2

Take a moment now and drag the **HireDate** field to position it just before the **Manager** field.

Inserting a New Field

To add a new field to a table design, simply enter the new field definition (the Field Name and the Data Type) in the empty row below the last field. To insert a new field in a specific location, click the existing field, and choose the **Insert Rows** button in the Ribbon. You can also right click the field and choose Insert Rows from the shortcut menu. Access will add a new row to the table pushing the existing fields down. Enter the new field definition in the new row. Inserting a new field to a table that already contains data does not cause any issues. The new field will not be automatically added to other Access objects such as queries, forms, or reports. You must revise those objects if you need to include any new fields that were added to the table after you have created these objects.

Action Item 2.3

Take a moment now and insert a field called **CreatedDateTime** with the **Date/ Time** datatype to the Employees table. Use any of the methods previously described. Set the **Format** property of this field to **General Date**.

Deleting a Field

To delete a field right click the field name and choose Delete from the shortcut menu. You can also delete the field by selecting it and clicking the Delete Rows button in the Ribbon. There is also a third method that allows you to select the field and press the Delete key on the keyboard. When the field already contains data Access will warn you that you will lose data in the table for that field. Access does not automatically delete the field from queries, forms, reports, and other Access objects. You will have to remove the field yourself when you work with those objects. If the field you want to delete is a part of a relationship, Access will warn you that you must first remove the relationship. Again, Access is quite informative when it comes to performing a task that could create problems in other areas of your database. The relationships will be covered in another chapter.

Action Item 2.4

Take a moment now and delete a field called **CreatedDateTime** that you created in the previous *Action Item*. Use any of the methods described above.

ENTERING DATA IN A TABLE

There are many ways in which you can get the data into your Access tables. By the time you finish this book project you will know how to accomplish this task efficiently depending on the available resources. For starters, the easiest way is to use the Datasheet View and enter the data manually. This is like entering data into an Excel spreadsheet. You simply type the value in each column (field). You can skip the values only for the fields that were not marked as having a Required property in the Table Design View. Let's enter a few records in the Employees table so we can complete this chapter with a feeling of accomplishment.

(◉) Hands-On 2.9   Entering Data in the Datasheet View

1. Press **Ctrl+S** to save any recent changes you have made to the Employees table.

2. In the Ribbon, click the **View** button to activate the Datasheet View.

   Notice that the Department field has a default value of zero (0) and the IsActive field has a check box.

3. Enter the data shown in Figure 2.21 for the first three employees. You will skip entering data for the following columns: EmpID, EmpCode, Department, and Manager. These fields will be filled in later in this book project. You do not need to enter data in the EmpID field as it has been designated as an AutoNumber field and we be provided automatically by Access. Each new record will have a (New) entry in the EmpID field as you start inputting your data.

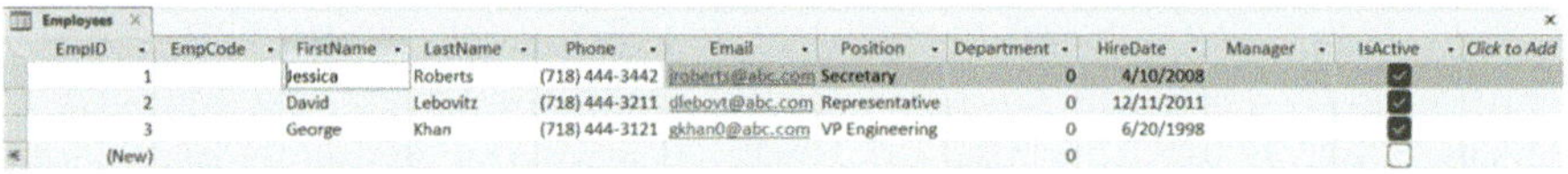

FIGURE 2.21. Initial data for the Employees table.

As soon as you start typing Jessica in the First Name field, Access places the record in the Edit mode which is easy recognized by the placement of a tiny pencil image in the record selector as shown in Figure 2.22. At the same time, the EmpID field is automatically filled with 1 to indicate the first record.

FIGURE 2.22. Activating the data entry mode by typing a value in a field.

To enter a value in the next field, simply press the Tab key to activate the Last Name, enter Roberts, and press Tab again. As soon as you start typing the phone number Access displays the Input mask for the phone which you had set up in an earlier Hands-On. Enter the phone number as indicated by the input mask (Figure 2.23) and press the Tab key to move to the next field.

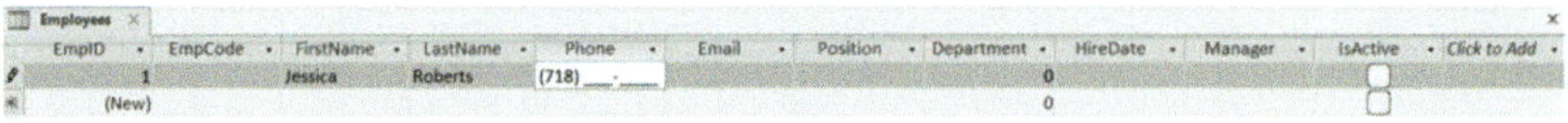

FIGURE 2.23. Entering phone number with the Input Mask guidance.

It looks like Access is complaining about the Phone field size as you try to Tab over to the next field (Figure 2.24).

FIGURE 2.24. Entering phone number with the Input Mask guidance -Access Warning Message.

Errors in Table Design do happen, and you need to know from the very beginning how to correct them. Click OK to the message and delete the phone number you have entered as Access will not accept it until the problem is corrected. You can press Backspace to delete the digits you entered. Press Ctrl+S to save the changes to the table so you don't lose values you entered in the first and last fields. Next, click the View button in the Ribbon to activate the Table Design View, then select the Phone field. Enter 14 characters for the Field Size property. Press Ctrl+S to save your changes and press the View button to return to the Datasheet View. Enter the phone number for the first record and press Tab. Access should not complain as you have fixed the issue with this field. Continue entering values for the first record. Notice that in the HireDate field Access provides you with a Calendar control where you can choose the date. You can also enter the date manually. When you get to the IsActive field, click the check box or the Spacebar to mark this employee as an active member of your organization. When you are done entering all values for the first record, press Enter, or Tab and Access will activate the next row.

NOTE	*Access saves the new record automatically while you're typing it. During the data entry you can press Ctrl+Z to undo your work. You can also delete the record by right clicking the record selector to the left of the first field and choosing Delete from the shortcut menu. Notice that at the end of each row there is a field called Click to Add which you can use to add a new field to the table without going back to the Table Design View.*

Enter the next two records in the Employees table as shown in Figure 2.21.

4. Close the Employees table by right clicking the Employees tab and choosing `Close`, or simply click the x next to the table name. If the data needs to be saved, Access will prompt you to do so before closing.

At any time, you can reopen the table and make changes to the data. Later in this book you will learn how to design forms to make data entry quicker and easier for the end user.

COPY, EXPORT, AND REMOVE TABLES

Now that you created your first Access table, let's perform some operations on the tables. The first thing that comes to mind is how to make a copy of a table. It is sometimes a good idea to use a copy of the table to try out various Access features without worrying that you may break something in the original table.

Hands-On 2.10   Copying a Table

1. In the Navigation pane of the ETD database, right click the **Employees** table and choose Copy from the shortcut menu as shown in Figure 2.25 below.

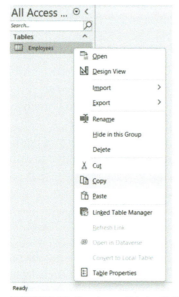

FIGURE 2.25. Copying an Existing Table (Step 1).

2. Right click anywhere in the blank area of the Navigation pane and choose Paste from the shortcut menu as shown in Figure 2.26.

FIGURE 2.26. Copying an Existing Table (Step 2 – Paste operation).

Access displays the Paste Table As dialog box as depicted in Figure 2.27. Here you can replace the suggested table name by typing your own text. Notice that there are three paste options to choose from. The selected default option (Structure and Data) will create the exact copy of the table. The structure only option will not copy the existing data. You will get a blank table that has the same structure as your original table. The last option button when selected will allow you to copy the existing data from one table to another. You'll be asked to select a table to paste the data to from any existing tables.

3. With the Structure and Data option selected, click **OK** in the Paste Table As dialog box.

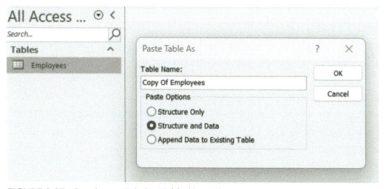

FIGURE 2.27. Copying an Existing Table (Step 3).

The copied table appears in the Navigation pane as shown in Figure 2.28. You can rename this table by right clicking its name and choosing Rename and then entering a new name.

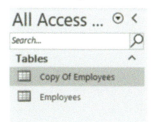

FIGURE 2.28. Copying an Existing Table (Step 4).

4. Double click the **Copy of Employees** table and verify that its content and structure is the same as in Employees table. It is a good idea to always check what was copied, especially when there are several selections to choose from prior to performing a specific Access task.

5. Close the **Copy of Employees** table.

Sometimes you may be asked to provide a copy of an Access table to some-one else in Microsoft Excel file format, in a text file, or another format. The next Hands-On walks you through the process of exporting your data to an Excel spreadsheet.

Hands-On 2.10   Exporting a Table

This Hands-On requires that you have Microsoft Excel installed on your computer or can access it online.

1. In the Navigation pane of the ETD database, right click the **Employees** table and choose **Export**.

Access displays a long list of file formats you can use (see Figure 2.29). Depend-ing on the format you select, various additional screens will be displayed.

2. From the list of file formats, choose **Excel**.

Access displays the Export – Excel Spreadsheet dialog box where you need to se-lect the destination for the data you want to export. It also suggests the location and name for your data file. The default location is your user folder, like this:
C:\Users\yourname\Documents\Employees.xlsx

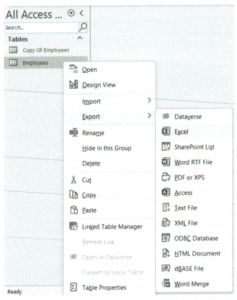

FIGURE 2.29. Exporting a table to another file format (Step 1).

3. Click the **Browse** button (Figure 2.30).

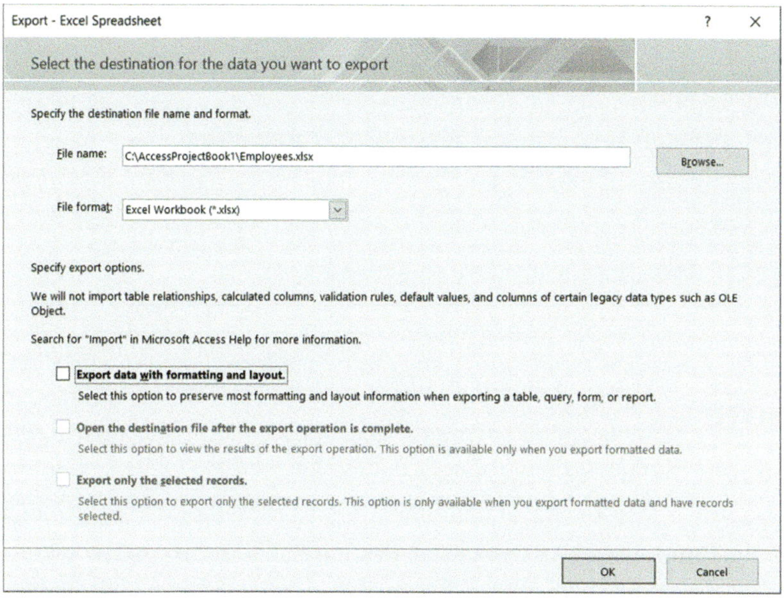

FIGURE 2.30. Exporting a Table to an Excel spreadsheet (Step 2). Note: The folder name is changed via Step 4 in this Hands-On.

4. In the File Save dialog box that appears after clicking the Browse button in Figure 2.30, select and activate the project folder: **AccessProjectBook1**. Then click the **Save** button, to save the **Employees.xlsx** file.

Notice that the dialog box also allows you to select other Excel workbook formats such as an older (*.xls) workbook or the binary format (*.xlsb). You can specify export options that tell Access whether you want to export data with formatting and layout or whether all data or only selected records should be exported. Some options become available when certain conditions are met before export (like selecting appropriate data rows in the Table Datasheet View).

5. Back in the Export – Excel Spreadsheet dialog box, click the **Export data with formatting and layout.**

When you make this selection Access will make the next choice available where you can tell it to open the exported file.

6. Select the **Open destination file after Export operation is complete** option and click **OK** to proceed with the Export operation.

Figure 2.31 displays the Employees data as an Excel workbook.

FIGURE 2.31. Exporting a table to an Excel spreadsheet (Step 3).

NOTE	*Now that you have your data in the Excel worksheet, you could ask someone else to enter more employees into the worksheet and then import this worksheet back to Access. When you start working with other applications in addition to Access you can simplify some tasks that can be tedious for someone to perform in Access. Always use the best tool you are familiar with for the task at hand.*

7. Close the **Employees.xlsx** workbook, exit Excel, and return to Access.

Access displays Export – Excel Spreadsheet screen (Figure 2.32) that notifies you that the Employees table was successfully exported to the selected destination file. Also, you are given the opportunity to save these export steps, so next time you can quickly repeat the same operation without using the wizard.

8. For now, click **Close** without choosing to save the export steps.

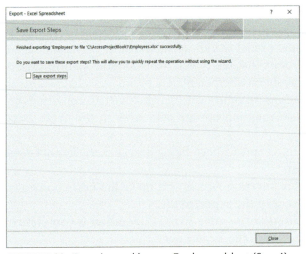

FIGURE 2.32. Exporting a table to an Excel spreadsheet (Step 4).

It is a good idea to keep your Access database file clean. Objects that you no longer need should be removed so they don't clutter the Navigation pane. Let's remove the Copy of Employees table created in Hands-On 2.9.

Action Item 2.5

In the Navigation pane of the ETD database, right click the Copy of Employees table and choose Delete. Click Yes in response to the Access informational message that deleting this object will remove it from all groups. After you complete this Action Item your Navigation pane should only display the Employees table.

PRINTING A TABLE DESIGN

With Access, you can use its built-in Database Documenter to generate and print a report of table fields, its properties, indexes, and other settings. Let's see how this is done in the next Hands-On.

Hands-On 2.11   Using Access Documenter

1. In the **Database Tools** tab of the Ribbon, click the **Database Documenter** button. Access displays the Database Documenter dialog as shown in Figure 2.33.

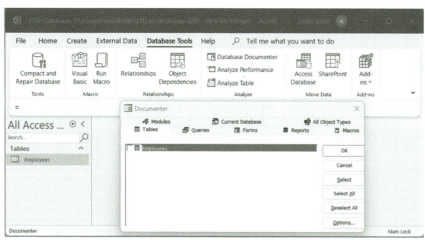

FIGURE 2.33. The Documenter Dialog Box.

2. Click the check box next to the **Employees** table and click **OK**.

Access opens the Object Definition report in the Print Preview (Figure 2.34). The Print Preview Ribbon has buttons for printing, formatting, and exporting the report to another file format.

3. Click the **PDF or XPS** button to export the document to the PDF or XPS Document file.

Access displays the Publish as PDF or XPS dialog where you can specify the File name and location for this report (Figure 2.35).

4. Accept the default options and click the **Publish** button.

Access publishes the report and opens the published PDF file. The file details the names, data types and sizes for each field in the Employees table. It also specifies the fields that were marked as indexed and primary keys, and their sort order.

5. Close the **doc_rptObjects.pdf** file.

6. Back in Access, close the Export PDF dialog box without saving export steps.

7. Click the **Close Print Preview** button to close the Object Definition.

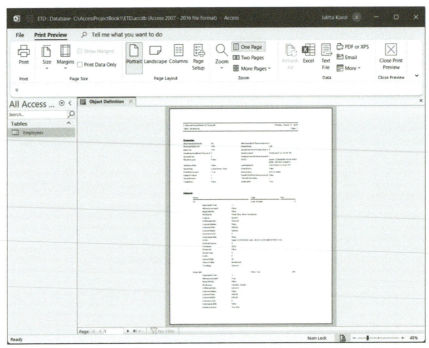

FIGURE 2.34. The Object Definition report for the selected object displayed in Print Preview.

FIGURE 2.35. Exporting the Object Definition report to the PDF or XPS Document.

SUMMARY

You started this chapter by creating a blank Access database. You learned about MS Access default ACCDB file format and hopefully took time to review other Access formats listed in Appendix A. You manually created your first table and entered some sample data. You got to know various properties and tools that allow to control how the data is formatted and displayed. You worked with default values for your fields and learned how to control user's input with validation rules and validation text. You worked in Table Design and Datasheet View. You tried copying, exporting, and removing a table from a database. You finished this chapter by learning how you can use Database Documenter to generate and print or export your table structure to a PDF file.

In the next chapter, you will add the remaining required tables to the ETD database using various other methods.

Part II

CREATE AND WORK WITH DATABASE TABLES

P art II introduces you to several techniques of implementing database tables. As tables consist of fields, you will learn about data types that the fields can hold to correctly store your data. You also learn how to set up primary keys, indexes, and create relationships between your tables. Empty tables are pretty much useless, so before you can display and perform operations on data, you need to get the data into your database. In the last chapter of Part II, you explore several methods of filling in Access tables with data in various file formats.

Chapter 3

CREATING ACCESS TABLES

I n the previous chapter, when you created the ETD database, Access auto-
matically created and opened a blank table for you in the Datasheet View.
You worked in this view for a while adding all the required fields to the table.
Next, you switched to Design View and worked with various field properties.
In Design View Access, it does not display data. You must switch to Datasheet
View to view or enter new data. Design View shows only the structure of a table
and allows you to set various properties that define the fields.

In this chapter, you will need to create all the remaining tables in the ETD
database. Any other object you create later in this database will depend on these
tables. You could use the skills you already have to create tables, but this would
be very repetitive and boring. Luckily, Access provides many ways of performing the same task, so we can keep things interesting while we are getting these
tables ready. Let's get started.

CREATING A TABLE IN DESIGN VIEW

Design View and Datasheet View are two main ways to add new tables to an
Access database. In this section, we will use Design View to build our next table
that will keep track of course registrations.

Action Item 3.1

The Companion files include an Excel workbook named **etd_Tables.xlsx** (see Figure 3.1). Keep this file open as you work through this chapter's Hands-On exercises.Each worksheet lists table fields and their data types.

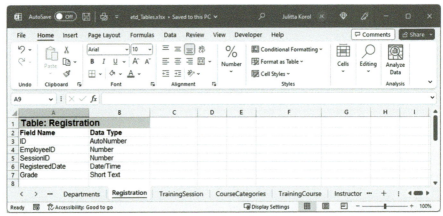

FIGURE 3.1. A list of field names and data types for each table in the ETD database.

NOTE	*Files for the Hands-On project may be found in the Companion files.*

⦿ Hands-On 3.1   Creating a Table in Design View

1. Open the ETD database and in the Tables group of the Create tab click the Table Design button as shown in Figure 3.2.

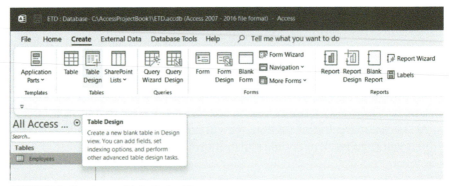

FIGURE 3.2. Creating a table in Design View.

2. Use the upper area of Design View to enter the field names and data types for the Registration table as shown in Figure 3.1. Each field is a separate row, and you must enter the type of data for each field. Start by placing the cursor in the field name column. Enter the field name and press Enter or Tab to move to the Data Type column. Select the field's data type from the drop-down list. The Description column is optional, and we will skip it for now. However, keep in mind that you should aim to fill in this column for important fields in a table as it is an effective way to document your database. The Description column is helpful to users of the database because Access displays it in the status bar when the field is selected in Datasheet View or in a form, thus guiding the user in the data entry.

   Use the down arrow to move between rows or click on any row you want to work with. Access will save your entry automatically when you move the cursor to another row. If you miss a field while completing the table, do not worry. You can click the Insert Rows button in the Tools area of the Design Tab to insert a blank row just above the row that you are currently on.

   Enter all the fields in the Registration table before continuing to the next step.
3. Click in the row with the and press F6. This will switch the focus from the top to the bottom of the Table Design View where you can work with the field's properties.

   With the ID field selected, the General tab in the Properties area on the bottom displays all properties that can be set or modified for the field. Access sets some properties by default; others are left blank for you to decide when you need a particular behavior or format for the table.
4. Click the **Indexed** property of the **ID** field and change its value to **Yes (No Duplicates)**. This setting is used for data that should be unique within the table. We will set the ID field as the primary field later in this Hands-On activity. Fields that are indexed speed up queries, as well as sorting and grouping operations.
5. In the Fields area, click the **RegisteredDate** field and in the Properties set the Format property to **Short Date**.
6. In the Fields area, click the **Grade** field and set the **Size** property to **25** (see Figure 3.3). The default value for Short Text data type is 255 characters, which can be letters, numbers, or punctuation. Access uses variable length field to store text data. This means that if you designate 25 characters for your field size and then enter fewer characters in this field, Access will only store the number of characters you entered.

> | **NOTE** | *To find out more information about a field property, click on the row that shows the property name and press F1. This will launch your browser and activate Microsoft documentation on the topic if it is available.* |
> |---|---|

With the table fields entered, data types selected, and some field properties set, let's save the table.

7. Right click the default table name (**Table1**) and choose **Save**. Access will display the Save As dialog. Type **Registration** for the name of the table as shown in Figure 3.3 and click OK.

   Access complains that there is no primary key in the table you are attempting to save (Figure 3.4). Although it is not necessary to have a primary key, a table that will be used in relationships with other tables should include one. So, let's have Access create it for us.

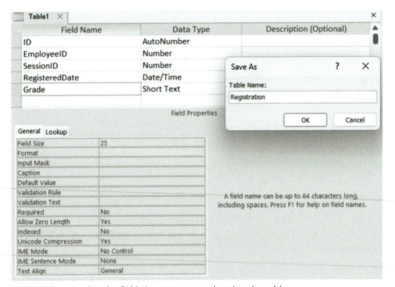

FIGURE 3.3. Setting the field size property and saving the table.

FIGURE 3.4. Access displays various informational messages to guide you in the process of creating various database objects.

8. Click **Yes** in response to the warning message.

You should see Registration table listed below Employees table in the Navigation pane of your database window. What happened to the primary key? Was it created?

Notice a small key icon to the left of the ID field (Figure 3.5). This is the primary key indicator. Another way to spot a primary key is the big primary key button that is highlighted in the Tools group of the Table Design tab of the Ribbon. If you click this button while the ID field is selected, you will remove the primary key setting from the field. Click the button again, to put it back. Access provides many such toggle buttons that allow you to turn on and off certain features of various Access objects.

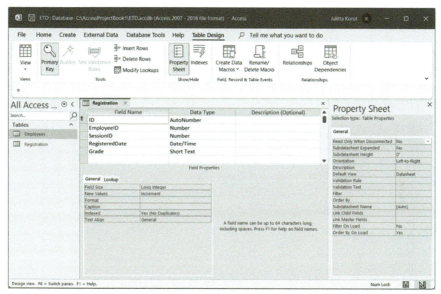

FIGURE 3.5. Primary key field can be set in Design View by using the primary Key button.

9. Close the Registration table.

There are now two tables in the ETD database that were created using two main methods of creating Access tables: the Datasheet View and Design View. Let's learn about and apply the third method to create the Instructors table.

CREATING A TABLE USING APPLICATION PARTS

Access includes many built-in tools to make it easier for you to create the database. One of these tools is an application part which is available in the Create tab by choosing the Application Parts button. Application Parts allow you to insert or create portions of a database or an entire database application. By using Application Parts, you can build your database faster. An application part can be a single Access object, like a form, or a set of database objects, for example, a table, or related forms and reports. Let's see how we can use the application part to build the Instructors table.

⊙ Hands-On 3.2   Building a Table With an Application Part

1. With the ETD database open, click the Create tab on the Ribbon, and then click the Application Parts button in the Template group (see Figure 3.6).

    Access displays a gallery of ten form types under the Blank Forms category. There are also five Application Parts under the Quick Start category.

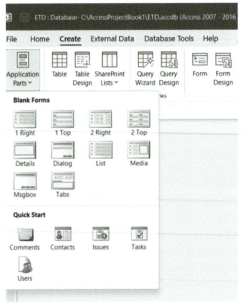

FIGURE 3.6. Using the Application Parts button you can create many common types of database objects.

2. Click **Contacts** in the Quick Start list.

    Access displays the Create Relationship dialog.

3. Select the option **There is no relationship** as shown in Figure 3.7 and click **Create**.

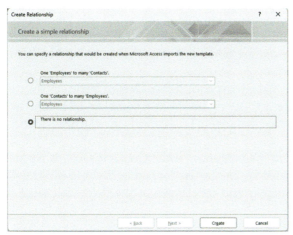

FIGURE 3.7. Creating a table structure using the Application Parts method.

Access goes to work and creates the Contact table with many related objects. In addition to the Employees and Registration tables, the Navigation view should now display the Contacts table, the ContactExtended query, three contact forms, and four types of contact reports (Figure 3.8).

FIGURE 3.8. The Application Part command builds a complete table and its supporting objects (queries, forms, and reports).

We will delete all the supporting objects the Application Part command created so you can just focus on the Contacts table.

4. In the Navigation Pane, highlight the query **ContactExtended** and press Delete. Click **OK** in the confirmation dialog box when you are prompted to delete the object. Continue to select and delete the remaining three forms and four reports. When you are done, only three tables should be left in the Navigation pane.

5. Right click the **Contacts** table name and choose **Design View**.

As you can see in Figure 3.9, Access has built a complete table structure for a Contacts table. This table includes 20 fields with the ID field defined as a primary key.

Let's now do some field maintenance on the Contacts table so we are only left with fields that we need for the Instructors table. Refer to the etd_Tables.xlsx workbook for the names and data types of the fields you need in the Instructors table.

Field Name	Data Type	Description (Optional)
ID	AutoNumber	
Company	Short Text	
LastName	Short Text	
FirstName	Short Text	
EmailAddress	Short Text	
JobTitle	Short Text	
BusinessPhone	Short Text	
HomePhone	Short Text	
MobilePhone	Short Text	
FaxNumber	Short Text	
Address	Short Text	
City	Short Text	
StateProvince	Short Text	
ZIPPostal	Short Text	
CountryRegion	Short Text	
WebPage	Hyperlink	
Notes	Long Text	
Attachments	Attachment	
ContactName	Calculated	
FileAs	Calculated	

FIGURE 3.9. The Contacts table structure created by Access can be modified to address your specific needs.

6. Select the **Company** field in the Contacts table and type **InstrRefID** for the field name. Leave the **Short Text** as this field's data type.

7. Right click the **EmailAddress** and choose Delete Rows. Proceed to delete **JobTitle, BusinessPhone, MobilePhone, FaxNumber, CountryRegion, WebPage, Attachments, ContactName** and **FileAs** fields in the same way. If you inadvertently delete incorrect field row, press **Ctr+Z**.

8. Rename **ZipPostal** to **ZipCode**.

   Notice that ZipCode data type is set to Short Text. Even though this field will store numbers, setting this field to Short Text will allow you to store leading zeros (so that 03458 does not appear as 3458) and include other characters such as dashes and parentheses. Remember that you can use the Input Mask Wizard to define Zip codes, phone numbers, Social Security numbers and dates, as well as other codes you may want to use in your database. Fields that allow Input Mask will display the Input Mask property in the General tab of the Field Properties at the bottom of the Design View when the field is selected.

9. Rename **StateProvince** to **State**.

10. Rename the **HomePhone** field to **PhoneNum**.

11. Click and hold the gray record selection area to the left of the PhoneNum field name. You should see the dark line above the PhoneNum field. While holding the left mouse button drag this line down and release it when it is positioned between ZipCode and Notes field. Press **Ctrl+Z** if you need to get back and repeat this move operation.

12. Right click the Notes field and choose **Insert Rows**. Access adds an empty row above the Notes field. Using the empty row, enter **HireDate** for the name of the field and choose **Date/Time** in Data Type column.

13. Right click the Notes field and choose **Insert Rows**. Enter **HourlyFee** for the field name and choose **Currency** in the Data Type column.

   Currency data type is used for storing numbers with a currency sign in front of them. Like number fields, currency fields cand do calculations. It's important to point out that calculations with Currency fields are faster than those with numbers.

14. Right click the Notes field and choose **Insert Rows**. Enter **Inactive** for the field name and choose **Yes/No** in the Data Type column.

   You have not completed the modification of the Contacts table. Let's save our changes so we can proceed to rename this table.

15. Click the **Save** button located on the Quick Access Toolbar in the left-hand corner of the database title bar. You can also save the table by right clicking the table tab (currently named Contacts) and choosing Save.

16. Close the table by clicking on the x in the table tab or right click the **Contacts** tab and choose **Close**.

17. In the navigation pane, right click the **Contacts** table and choose Rename. Enter **Instructors** for the table name.
18. Right click the **Instructors** table and choose **Design View**. If you find that Access has kept the fields you deleted earlier, delete them again making sure that you match the table structure as shown in Figure 3.10.
19. Save and close the Instructors table.

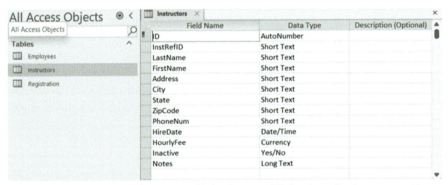

FIGURE 3.10 Access generated Contacts table has been modified and saved as Instructors table.

As you have seen in the previous Hands-On, using the built-in Application Parts to build your tables will often require that you change field names and properties a bit, delete the fields you don't need and add additional fields. Some users find this feature more convenient and easier than starting from scratch, others prefer to stick to the Datasheet or Design View for creating new tables. Which method you use depends strictly on your preference.

But we are not finished yet. There are still few other ways in which you can create an Access table.

CREATING A TABLE USING A MAKE TABLE QUERY

While you still have a long way to go before you learn how to create and work with Access queries, there is a very neat feature of queries you can use right now, and it is not very hard to grasp even when you have never worked with queries before. If you have already a table that has fields that are required in your new table, you can use the Make Table query to save some time. With the Instructors table already created, the next table we can create with similar fields is the TrainingCourseLocations table. Let's find out how this can be achieved.

⊙ Hands-On 3.3   Building a Table With the Make Table Query

1. Make sure that the ETD database is open.
2. On the Create tab, click the Query Design button.

    Access opens a Query grid as shown in Figure 3.11. This grid includes an empty area on the top where you add tables, and the lower area is the grid for the fields you will select in just a moment. Notice that the Query Design tab of the Ribbon displays many types of queries you can create. Select query type is the default option and it is currently selected.

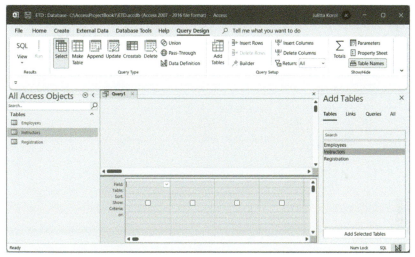

FIGURE 3.11 Access Query Design View.

3. In the Query Type group of the Query Design tab, click the **Make Table** query.

    Access displays the Make Query dialog box asking you for the new table name and its location.

4. Enter **TrainingCourseLocations** for the Table Name as shown in Figure 3.12 and click **OK**.

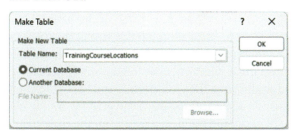

FIGURE 3.12 Specifying a new table name in the Make Table dialog box.

Notice that nothing has changed in the Query Design View or the Navigation pane of the main database window, but now the Make Query button is selected in the Design tab of the Ribbon.

The next step is to specify the table whose fields we want to get into our new table.

5. If the Add Tables pane is shown (see Figure 3.11), drag the **Instructors** table name and drop it in the empty gray area of the Query Design. If the Add Tables pane is not visible, right click the empty gray area of the Query Design and click **Show Table** from the pop-up menu.

Access will then open the Add Tables pane on the right-hand side of the query window. The names of all the existing tables in your database are listed.

The table Instructors should appear in the Query Design as shown in Figure 3.13.

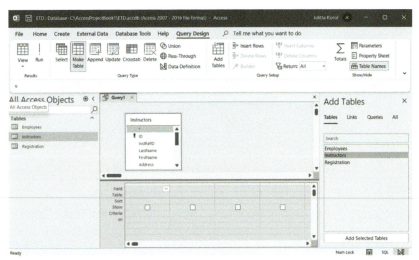

FIGURE 3.13 Adding a table to the Query Design View.

If you wanted fields from more than one tables, you could add other tables to this view in the same way. Notice that there is an asterisk above the ID field in the table Instructors. If you want to bring all the fields from the table Instructors to your new table, it's enough to double click the asterisk to make all these fields available. However, we must select only the fields we will need.

6. Double click the **ID** field and notice that Access fills the first column of the Query grid. You can bring all the desired fields to the grid by double clicking their name in the table or by dragging the field name from the table to another empty column of the grid. You can also select the field name from the drop-down list of an empty column of the Field row.

7. Use any of the techniques described in the previous step to bring the following fields to the Query grid: **InstrRefID**, **PhoneNum**, **Address**, **City**, **State** and **ZipCode**.

NOTE	*Press Ctrl+Z to undo if you make a mistake. If you need to delete a field from the grid, place the mouse over the column you want to delete until you see a black down arrow, then click to select the column and press Delete.*

The completed grid is shown in Figure 3.14.

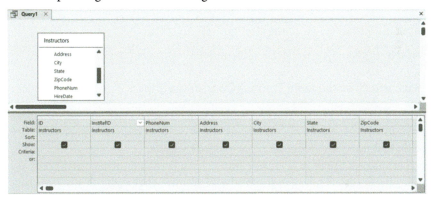

FIGURE 3.14 Selecting fields for a new table in the Query Grid.

With the required fields selected, it's time to generate the table.

8. Quick the Run button in the Results group of the Query Design tab of the Ribbon.

   Access displays a message that you are about to paste 0 row(s) into a new table. As you know, we don't yet have any records in the table Instructors, therefore Access can only create a new table structure. If there was any data in the existing table, Access could bring it to the new table. The Make Table query is often used to make a new table that contains a copy of the data in a table or query.

9. Click **Yes** to the message and notice that Access added **TrainingCourseLocations** table to the Navigation pane.

10. Close the Query1 without saving it. We don't need this query for anything else. The next step is to check the newly created table structure.

11. Right click the table **TrainingCourseLocations** in the Navigation pane and choose **Design View**.

    It's time to modify the table structure Access has created for us.

12. Use any technique you learned so far to make changes in the table TrainingCourseLocations so that it matches Figure 3.15. Make sure to set ID as the primary key for this table.

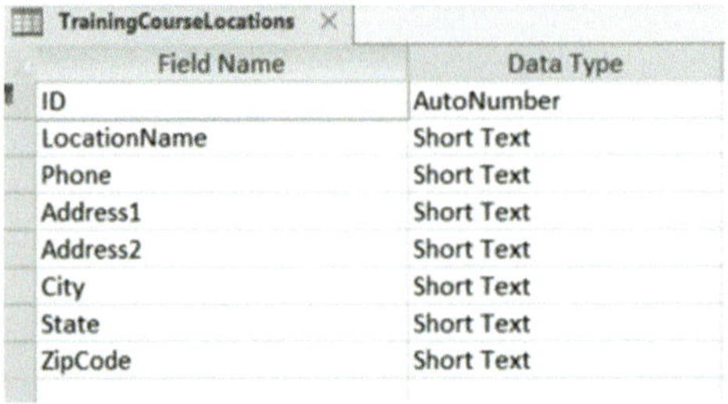

TrainingCourseLocations ✕	
Field Name	**Data Type**
ID	AutoNumber
LocationName	Short Text
Phone	Short Text
Address1	Short Text
Address2	Short Text
City	Short Text
State	Short Text
ZipCode	Short Text

FIGURE 3.15 Modifying the table structure after running a Make Table query.

13. Save and close the table TrainingCourseLocations.

Great, you have now mastered another quick way of creating Access tables. This method can be handy if you already have several tables in your database with fields that are good candidates for your new table.

Let's take a break now before embarking on yet another method of creating tables in Access. This new method will require that you put on your new programming hat. We'll call it – Quick SQL and we'll tackle with it the creation of the table TrainingSession.

CREATING A TABLE WITH A DATA DEFINITION QUERY

Another built-in Access feature that you may find useful in the process of creating tables is the Data Definition query window. To work with this window, you will need to learn a couple of SQL statements. SQL stands for *Structured Query Language*. This is a language that relational database management systems use to perform various tasks. When you build queries, Access automatically generates SQL statements (special instructions) in the background to perform its processes. If you are planning your career around database systems, it is vital that you acquire SQL skills. The easiest way to get started is by analyzing the SQL statements that Access generates as you create various queries. Refer to Part III of this book for more information on this topic. SQL is usually an advanced topic introduced later in the learning path. However, by learning some SQL foundations early you will be more prepared to perform more advanced operations that your database calls for later. Some database operations that you may want to perform may require more than the Access user interface. Are you ready for some quick SQL?

Let's use it to create our next table.

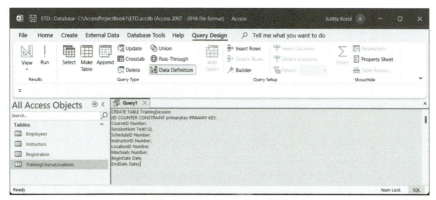

Hands-On 3.4 Building a Table With Data Definition query

1. Open the ETD database and choose **Query Design** from the **Create** tab.
2. In the Query Type group of the Query Design tab, double click **Data Definition**.

Access opens the Data Definition query widow also known as the SQL View. The blank area of the Query1 is where you need to enter specific SQL instructions that will tell Access to create a table. These instructions are referred to as statements.

3. In the blank area of the Query1, type in the following Create Table statement (also shown in Figure 3.16):

```
CREATE TABLE TrainingSession
(ID COUNTER CONSTRAINT primaryKey PRIMARY KEY,
CourseID Number,
SessionNum Text(12),
ScheduleID Number,
InstructorID Number,
LocationID Number,
MaxSeats Number,
BeginDate Date,
EndDate Date);
```

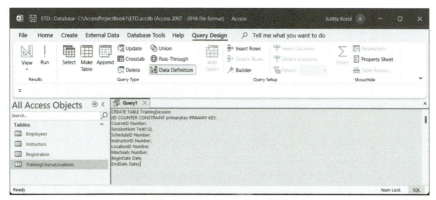

FIGURE 3.16 Entering Create Table statement in the Data Definition query window (SQL View).

Let's first examine the statement in Figure 3.16. The CREATE TABLE statement is used to create the structure (also called the *schema*) of a table. This statement creates an empty table. As your table needs a name, you must follow the CRE-ATE TABLE with the table name as depicted in the first line of the statement. It is not necessary to break the statement into multiple lines. You can enter the entire statement on a single line; however, it is much easier to troubleshoot any mistakes in the statement you might make when you see it clearly line by line. After you specify the name for your table you must list all the fields you want to create followed by their data types. The list of fields must appear between the parentheses. Each field is separated from the next one by a comma. To specify the field size for the text fields, place the number of characters you want for that field in parentheses following the field data type. In the statement, we specified that the SessionNum is a text field, and it should accept a maximum of 12 characters. If the field size is omitted, Access will use the default field size that is specified in the database.

The following are some rules you must follow when manually entering SQL statements.

- If you need to enter a column with a name that includes spaces or a non-alphanumeric character, you must put brackets around the field name when writing your SQL statement. For example, if the column you want to create is Begin Date with a space between Begin and Date, then you must enter it as [Begin Date].

- Each SQL statement ends with a semicolon, but if you forget one Access will automatically add it when the query compiles. The first time you run the query, the Access Jet Engine will check for proper syntax and will "compile" the query into a binary form. The compilation will result in a special plan that Access will use to run your query.

When creating a table using the CREATE TABLE statement, just like in the Design View, you can specify the field that should serve as the primary key for the table. Use the COUNTER keyword to have Access create the AutoNumber field. The CONSTRAINT statement is then used to specify the field as PRIMARY KEY. The CONSTRAINT statement is always followed by the constraint name and constraint type. You can enter any name for the constraint. In this case we entered primaryKey but you could name it pKey or any other name as long as it does not conflict with Access naming conventions and is not a reserved keyword that Access uses for its internal operations.

NOTE	*About Constraints*

Constrains are rules or conditions that are applied to the data within a table to ensure that data is consistent and follows business rules. By using constraints, you can define limitations and requirements that the data must meet, thereby preventing the entry of invalid or inconsistent data. There are different types of constrains available in Microsoft Access, such as:

NULL/NOT NULL: Used to indicate if a field can be left blank when records are entered into a table.

PRIMARY KEY: Used to uniquely identify every record in a table.

FOREIGN KEY: Used to link records of a table to the records of another table.

UNIQUE: Used to ensure that every value in a column is different.

CHECK: Used to define a criterion for the data entered in a column.

NOTE	*Refer to the **AddConstraints.txt** file in the Companion files for more information on using constrains in the Access SQL view. To find out how you can implement a business rule on the Registration table, please see the BusinessRule_RegistrationTable. txt file and its accompanying image file - BusinessRule_DataMacro_Registration.tif.*

4. Right click the **Query1** name and choose **Save**.

   Access will display the Save As dialog box where you can enter the name for your query. The default name is Query1.

5. Type **CreateTable_TrainingSession** as the name for your query and click **OK**.

   Access goes to work and checks your query for syntax errors. If you wrote your statement correctly, Access will save your Data Definition query in the Queries category of the Navigation pane (Figure 3.17).

NOTE	*If you made a mistake while typing the Create Table statement, you will see a message informing you that there is a syntax error in field definition. Click OK and Access will position the cursor where it identified the issue. You must figure out what Access is looking for. You will not be able to save the query until you correct all the errors in your statement.*

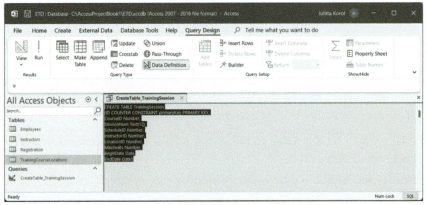

FIGURE 3.17 Data Definition query for creating an Access table is saved in the Queries category of the Navigation pane.

6. Close the CreateTable_TrainingSession query which is still open after you've saved it in the previous step.

   Notice that Access has not yet created the new table. The query you just created and saved is one of the Action queries that performs a specific task. Access will execute the statement entered in the Data Definition query when you run this query.

7. In the Navigation pane double click the query **CreateTable_TrainingSession**.

   Access displays the message shown in Figure 3.18.

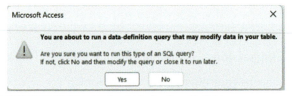

FIGURE 3.18 Running (executing) a Data Definition query.

8. You do want to run this query, so select **Yes**.

   Access runs the query and adds a new table named TrainingSession to the Navigation view.

   Let's check this table's structure.

9. In the Navigation pane, right click the table name **TrainingSession** and choose **Design View**.

   You should see the table structure depicted in Figure 3.19. As you can see there is no difference between what you would have manually entered for the fields in this table and what Access has created for you after you have entered a simple SQL statement. If you found it easier and quicker to work with the SQL, welcome to the Programmers Club. If you'd rather utilize other methods for creating tables that you acquired earlier in this chapter, welcome to the Power Users Club. Whichever club you're in, you now have skills that will enable you to speed up the process of developing any Access database. The sooner you're done with the creation of tables, the quicker you can get started with getting your data into these tables.

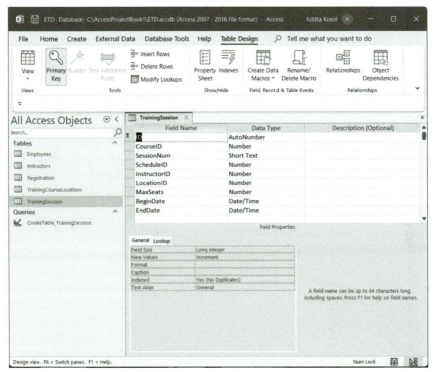

FIGURE 3.19 The TrainingSession table structure shown in Access Design View was created via the Data Definition query using an SQL Create Table statement.

10. Close the table **TrainingSession**.

   Let's keep the CreateTable_TrainingSession query in our database so you can always review the SQL statement when you need to create another table using the same technique. If you try to run this query again, Access will display a message that you are trying to run a query that will modify the data. If you click Yes to the message, Access will tell you that the table you want to create already exists. Sometimes you may want to add additional fields in the table you created with the Data Definition query or modify the existing fields. In this case, you should first delete the table you are trying to modify, then open your saved Data Definition query in Design View, modify your CREATE TABLE statement and save and run your modified query.

CREATING REMAINING TABLES IN THE ETD DATABASE

Are we done yet with table creation methods that you can use in Access? There are still methods of creating Access tables using VBA (Visual Basic for Applications) code which we will not be able to cover here as they require understanding of various data access technologies that Access offers to programmers. VBA is the common language that Access and many other Microsoft 365 applications use for programming. You will have a chance to write some code in this language later in this database project. For now, let's continue building the remaining tables using any of the methods already introduced. Use whatever method makes you most productive or comfortable. However, I challenge you to use the technique you feel the least comfortable with. Give it another chance and remember the adage: *Practice makes perfect.*

Action Item 3.2

On your own, create the following tables in the ETD database:

- Departments
- CourseCategories
- TrainingCourse
- SessionInstructor
- Room
- TrainingSchedule

Refer to the Excel workbook named **etd_Tables.xlsx** (see Figure 3.1) in your Companion files for the list of fields and their data types.

SUMMARY

In this chapter, you were introduced to various ways of creating Access tables. For the beginner user Access provides two easy ways to create tables: Datasheet View and Design View. However, if you are looking to speed up the process of creating tables, other options are also available. We have discussed how by using Application Parts you can create a blueprint of a table and modify it to your liking. We also worked with two types of queries that can help you in the process of creating tables. One was a Make Table query and the other was a Data Definition query. We walked through the steps necessary to apply each of the table creation methods. Finally, you were given an opportunity to practice on your own and use any of the table creation methods to create the remaining tables in the ETD database. Your Navigation pane should now show eleven tables. We will connect these tables with one another in the next chapter where we dig deeper into primary and foreign keys, indexes, constraints, and create table relationships.

Chapter 4

SETTING UP PRIMARY KEYS, INDEXES, AND TABLE RELATIONSHIPS

One of the goals of good database design is to divide data into many subject-related tables so that each data item can be stored only once. In the previous chapter, you created all the tables that will store employee training data. In many of these tables you specified the ID field with the AutoNumber data type to uniquely identify each record in the table. When you saved the table design, Access suggested that you designate the primary key if you'd like later to create relationships between the table and other tables in the database. When you went along with this recommendation, the ID field with the AutoNumber data type was marked as primary key field. Access allows only one AutoNumber field in a table. In the next chapter when you start entering data into your tables, you will see how Access automatically generates the key for each record. Once generated, the key cannot be changed. Access stores AutoNumber fields as a Long Integer data type. This type occupies 4 bytes and can accommodate up to 4,294,967,296 unique numbers, and that's more than what you'll ever need for most tables.

The next logical step in the database design is to ensure that you can easily combine the data from your different tables and display it on a form or in a report. In other words, you need to implement relationships between the different tables of data.

RELATING TABLES

It is important that you define table relationships before you create other database objects such as queries, forms, reports, or macros. Relationships are necessary for pulling data from multiple tables via queries for display on screen or in reports. Right now, your ETD database has eleven defined tables. You started this project by creating the Employees table, so let's see how this table can be connected to other tables in your database. Recall that you added the Department field with the Number data type to the Employees table. You also created the Departments table that will store a list of your company departments. Let's make sure that you can retrieve the Department Name instead of its ID field when you need to pull out data for any employee.

Action Item 4.1

In Chapter 1 of this book, you were briefly introduced to table relationships. Take a few minutes now to reread the topic "Understanding Table Relationships."

NOTE	*Files for the Hands-On project may be found in the Companion files.*

◉ Hands-On 4.1   Relating Employees and Departments

1. Open the ETD database.
   After working through Chapter 3, you should have eleven tables listed in the Navigation pane.
2. Click the **Relationships** button in the Relationships group of the Database Tools tab.
   Access opens an empty Relationships View. The Add Tables pane on the right-hand side of the Relationship window lists the names of all the tables in the database. If the Add Tables pane is missing, click the Add Tables button in the Relationships group of the Relationships Design tab.
3. In the Add Tables pane, click on the **Departments** table and holding down the **Shift** key click the **Employees** table to select both tables for the first relationship.
4. Click the **Add Selected Tables** button to add selected tables to the Relationships View (Figure 4.1).
   Notice that each table added to the Relationship View is represented by a box. If you picked the wrong tables, click the Clear Layout button in the

Relationships Design tab of the Ribbon to clear the boxes from the Relationships View, and go back to Step 4.

Each table box consists of two parts. The top part serves as the title bar, which not only identifies the table, but is also used to select and reposition the box. To select the table box, simply click the mouse anywhere in the title box. Once the box is selected, you can move the box to another area of the Relationships View by simply pointing to the title bar and dragging. To make the table box bigger or smaller you can click and drag any of its borders. Below the title bar, Access lists all the fields that are available in a table. The primary key is indicated with the key icon to the left of the field name. If the table contains many fields, you may want to expand its borders so you can see all of them at once without having to use the scrollbars.

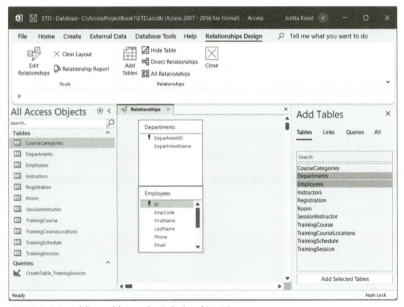

FIGURE 4.1. Adding tables to the Relationships View.

5. In the Relationships Design View, click the title bar of the Employees table and drag it to position the table to the right of the Departments table. Point to the lower border of the Employees table, click, and drag down to resize it so you can see the names of all the fields.

With the two tables placed conveniently in the Relationships View, you are now ready to create your first relationship. Each employee belongs to one and only one department while each department can have more than one employee. This means that the relationship between the employees and departments table is *one-to-many*. The "one" table is the master table and the "many" table is often referred to as a detail table.

As you recall from Chapter 1, the one-to-many relationships are the most common relationships in database systems. Once you've defined the type of relationship you have, you must determine the fields that should be used to connect both tables. The detail table must have a foreign key field (or fields) that match the primary key field(s) in the master table. In this case, the Primary Key in the master table (Departments) is DepartmentID. The foreign key in the detail table (Employees) is Department. The Department field could have been named DepartmentID to make it less confusing, but it is not necessary for the related fields in both tables to have the same names. What matters though is that the types, lengths, and contents of the fields match.

6. Drag the **DepartmentID** field in the Departments table over to the Employees table dropping it on the Department field. You will see a small plus icon when you move to the Employees table and when you release the mouse Access displays the Edit Relationships dialog box (Figure 4.2). This dialog shows the linking fields from both tables side by side. Be sure the linking fields that are shown match exactly Figure 4.2. If the drop operation did not produce the intended result, simply select the correct name of the field(s) in the Edit Relationships dialog or click Cancel in the dialog and try again.

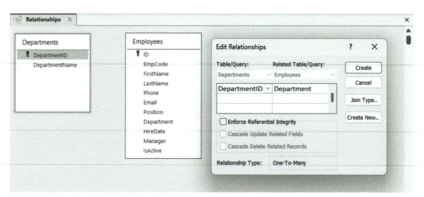

FIGURE 4.2. Creating a relationship by linking fields from both tables.

Notice that the type of relationship between Departments and Employees is displayed at the bottom of the Edit Relationships dialog. There are also a couple of options you can set here that determine how your table relationships work. While creating table relationships you can apply referential integrity rules to protect data from loss or corruption. Whenever a new record is added, updated, or deleted, Access can check the key fields (primary or foreign) to see if a value in a key field invalidates the relationship.

7. Select the **Enforce Referential Integrity** check box.

When this check box is selected, Access won't allow you to enter a record in the Employees table with the DepartmentID that does not exist in the Departments table. The referential integrity is used to prevent orphan records, that is, records in one table with no matching records in related table.

Notice that after selecting Enforce Referential Integrity, two other options become available:

- Cascade Update Related Fields—When this option is checked Access updates detail records automatically when you change the matching master record.

- Cascade Delete Related Records—When this option is checked Access deletes detail records when you delete the master record. This is a rather dangerous feature, so think twice before you activate this option as Access will delete the detail records without asking you for confirmation.

8. Click **Create** to create the relationship between the two tables you selected.

Access goes to work, and it looks like it will not allow you to create the relationship until you make some changes. You've got a very detailed message in which Access is telling you what could be wrong and how you can fix the issue (Figure 4.3).

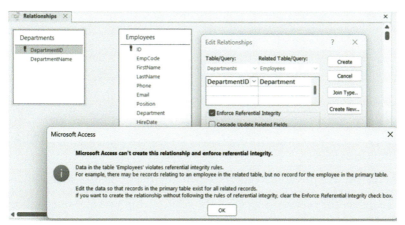

FIGURE 4.3. Access alerts you when creating a relationship and enforcing referential integrity is not possible.

Recall that in Chapter 2 you entered a few records into the Employees table, but you don't yet have any records in the Departments table. When you create table relationships it is important to examine the records in both related tables before asking Access to apply referential integrity rules. We will address this issue in Chapter 5.

—— **NOTE**	*Access may display an entirely different message depending on the issue it finds. For example, if the data types of the two joining fields don't match you would need to go back to the Design View of the appropriate table and change the field's data type and / or its size.*

9. Click **OK** to dismiss the message, and then clear the **Enforce Referential Integrity** check box, and click the **Create** button.

   Notice that in the Relationships View Access displays a relationship line that connects the two tables, linking the primary key of the Departments table with the foreign key in the Employees table (Figure 4.4). This type of line indicates that the relationship does not enforce referential integrity rules. Later, when you create queries, Access will know how to join these two tables so you will be able to access data from both.

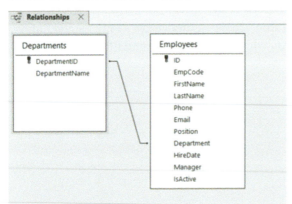

FIGURE 4.4. The relationship between Departments and Employees table does not enforce the referential integrity rules.

Once created, it is possible to edit or delete the relationship.

- To delete the relationship, click the relationship line and once it becomes bold to indicate that it is selected, simply click the Delete key, and then click Yes, to confirm the deletion of the relationship.
- To Edit the relationship, double click the relationship line.

Remember that to remove any table from the Relationships view, you first need to delete the relationship line. When you delete the table from the Relationship View, you only change the relationship diagram; the table is not deleted from the database. The Relationship View simply helps you see how tables are related to each other. However, the Relationship View serves as a tool for creating relationships and specifying the relationship rules between your tables. With the two tables now joined, let's exit the Relationship Design View.

10. Click the **Close** button on the Ribbon or right click the Relationships tab and choose Close.

    Access displays a message asking you if you want to save changes to the layout of Relationships.

11. Click **Yes**.

    Congratulations! You've mastered another important feature of Access. Let's continue with setting up relationships for other tables in the ETD database.

(⊙) Hands-On 4.2   Relating Employees and Registration Tables

1. Click the **Relationships** button in the Relationships group of the Database Tools tab.

    Access opens the Relationships View just as you left it in the previous Hands-On.

2. Right click anywhere in the gray area of the Relationships view and choose **Show Table**.

3. This option simply activates the Add Tables pane if it was not yet activated.

    In the Add Tables pane, double click the **Registration** table until it appears in the Relationships view or add it using the **Add Selected Tables** button.

4. Close the Add Tables pane to make more space on the screen and drag the **Registration** table to the right of the **Employees** table.

    Think of the type of relationship these two tables are in and what common keys they have. We want to allow each employee to enroll in multiple courses. Therefore, the Registration table can have many records for one employee. Again, we are dealing with the one-to-many relationship.

5. Drag the **ID** field from the Employees table and drop it onto the **EmployeeID** field of the Registration table.

    Make sure that the Edit Relationships dialog box displays the correct fields under Table/Query and Related Table Query columns.

6. Click the **Enforce Referential Integrity** check box and click **Create**.

    Notice that Access draws a line between the Employees and the Registration table, but now the line has some extra symbols (Figure 4.5). When a relationship enforces referential integrity, you should see a 1 on one end of relationship line and an infinity symbol at the other end of the line.

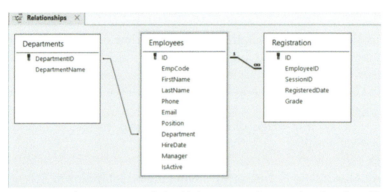

FIGURE 4.5. The one-to-many relationship between Employees and Registration table enforces the referential integrity rules.

7. Right click the **Relationships** tab and choose **Save** to save the Relationships layout before continuing to the next Hands-On.

The Registration table is now related to the Employees table. It must also be related to the TrainingSession table so that you can retrieve the information about various training sessions. Let's join these two tables together in the next Hands-On.

⊙ Hands-On 4.3   Relating Registration and TrainingSession Tables

1. Click the **Relationships** button in the Relationships group of the Database Tools tab.

    Access opens the Relationships View as you saved it in the previous Hands-On.

2. Right click anywhere in the gray area and choose **Show Table**.

3. Double click the **TrainingSession** table until it appears in the Relationships View or add it using the Add Selected Tables button in the Add Tables pane.

4. Close the Add Tables pane to make more space on the screen and drag the **TrainingSession** table to the right of the **Registration** table.

    Think of the type of relationship these two tables are in and what common keys they have. For each row in the Registration table, we need to specify the session information the Employee has registered for. Again, we are dealing with the one-to-many relationship; the "many" side being the Registration table, and the "one" side being the TrainingSession table.

5. Drag the **ID** field from the **TrainingSession** table and drop it onto the **SessionID** field of the **Registration** table.
   Make sure that the Edit Relationships dialog box displays the correct fields under Table/Query and Related Table Query columns.
6. Click the **Enforce Referential Integrity** check box and click **Create**.
7. Make any necessary changes to the Relationship View layout so it matches Figure 4.6.

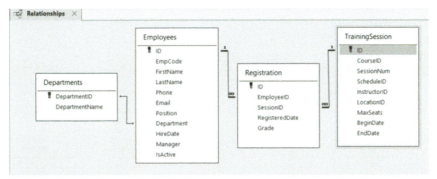

FIGURE 4.6. The relationship between Registration and TrainingSession table enforces the referential integrity rules.

8. Right click the **Relationships** tab and choose Save to save the Relationships layout before continuing to Action Item 4.2.

Action Item 4.2

On your own, create two additional relationships between TrainingSession and TrainingCourse tables, and TrainingSession and TrainingSchedule tables. The TrainingSession should be the many side of these two relationships. Link the foreign keys (CourseID and ScheduleID) of the TrainingSession table to the primary keys of the TrainingCourse and TrainingSchedule table.

NOTE	*When you attempt to enforce the referential integrity rules, Access will present the warning message as shown in Figure 4.7. Click OK and cancel the Edit Relationships dialog box. Next, use the Navigation pane to open the TrainingSession table in Design View and modify the Field Size properties of both foreign keys. It should be set to Long Integer, instead of Double. Save and close the modified table and return to the Relationships View to continue setting up the relationships.*

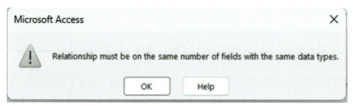

FIGURE 4.7. When enforcing the referential integrity rules between the tables always check the joining fields data types and sizes.

Make the appropriate adjustments to the Relationships View so it matches Figure 4.8.

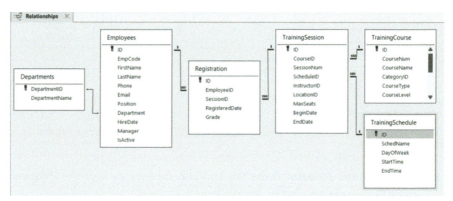

FIGURE 4.8. The one-to-many relationships between TrainingSession, TrainingCourse, and TrainingSchedule tables enforce the referential integrity rules.

Action Item 4.3

On your own, add the TrainingCourseLocations and Room table to the Relationships View and create a one-to-many relationship between TrainingSession and TrainingCourseLocations table and TrainingCourseLocations and Room table.

NOTE	*If Access complains, refer to important message in Action Item 4.2 for guidance.*

The resulting relationships are shown in Figure 4.9.

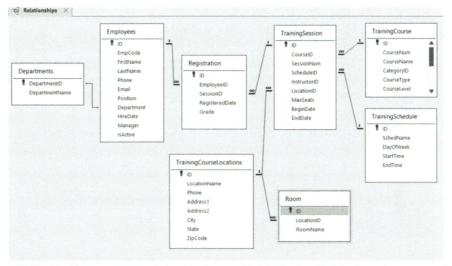

FIGURE 4.9. The one-to-many relationships between TrainingSession, TrainingCourseLocations, and Room tables enforce the referential integrity rules.

Still a bit more to go to complete our Relationships diagram and we can call it a day. In Hands-On 4.5, we will connect the table Instructors with the table TrainingSession. But before we do so, let's examine another type of table relationship.

CREATING MANY-TO-MANY RELATIONSHIPS

When a row in one table can have many matching records in another table, and vice versa, we have a *many-to-many* relationship. To create this type of relationship, you need to define a third table, called a *linking* or *junction* table, whose primary key consists of the foreign keys from both tables you want to relate. For example, the table Instructors and the table TrainingSession have a many-to-many relationship. This relationship is defined by setting up a one-to-many relationships to the junction table SessionInstructor. Let's first ensure that the junction table has a primary key.

◉ Hands-On 4.4   Specifying a Primary Key in a Junction Table

1. In the Navigation pane, right click the **SessionInstructor** table and choose **Design View**.

    Notice that this table doesn't have a primary key defined. You need a primary key in any table that is going to participate in relationships with other tables. Each field in the SessionInstructor table is a link to another table, so both fields must be selected in order to create a primary key.

2. To quickly select both fields, click on the **SessionID** field and press **Ctrl+A**. Or you can click the gray selection bar to the left of the **SessionID** field and click the **InstructorID** field while holding the **Ctrl** key.

3. With the two fields selected, click the **Primary Key** button on the Table Design tab of the Ribbon.

   Both fields should now be marked with a key icon as depicted in Figure 4.10. The Field Size property of each of these fields should be set to Long Integer.

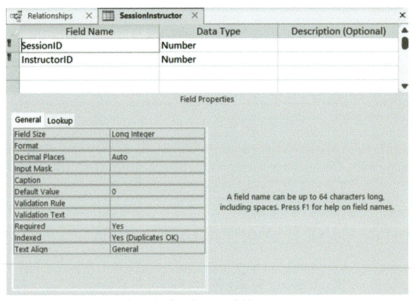

FIGURE 4.10. Creating a primary key based on two fields.

4. Save and close the **SessionInstructor** table.

Hands-On 4.5 Relating Intructors, SessionInstructors and Training- Session Tables

1. Click the **Relationships** button in the Relationships group of the Database Tools tab.

   Access opens the Relationships View.

2. Add the **Instructors** and **SessionInstructor** tables to the Relationships View.

   Access may position the tables out of the view, so use the scrollbars to find the tables and move them up so that SessionInstructor table is positioned just below the Registration table, and the Instructors table is below the Employees table. You may have to move other tables to make room for these two tables.

NOTE	*You can quickly move a whole bunch of tables in the diagram by clicking in the gray area and dragging the mouse around the tables you want to include in the selection as if you were drawing a rectangle. Once the tables are selected, point to any selected table title bar, and start dragging.*

3. Drag the **ID** field from the table Instructors and drop it onto the **InstructorID** field of the table SessionInstructor.
4. In the Edit Relationship dialog, check the **Enforce Referential Integrity** and click **Create**.
5. Drag the **ID** field from the **TrainingSession** table and drop it onto the **SessionID** field of the SessionIstructor table.
6. In the Edit Relationship dialog, check the **Enforce Referential Integrity** and click **Create**.

   The completed relationship diagram is depicted in Figure 4.11.

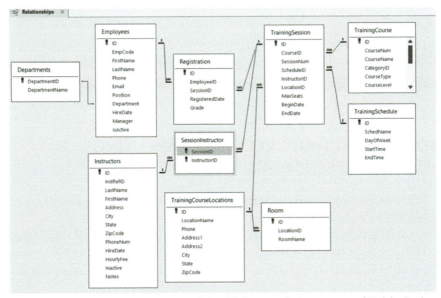

FIGURE 4.11. Creating a many-to-many relationship between the Instructors and TrainingSession requires a junction table (SessionInstructor).

<table>
<tr><td>NOTE</td><td>Access may mess up your relationship layout when you return to Relationships View after having performed other database operations. You will notice that the tables jump to other areas and the relationship lines cross each other. Adjust your layout and be sure to always save it before doing anything else.</td></tr>
</table>

7. Close Relationships View saving the recent changes you made in its layout.

As you have seen in the previous Hands-On, many-to-many relationships are more complicated than the one-to-many relationships because they require a third table that sits in the middle of the two tables. It is a recommended practice for the join table to have a name that reflects the association. In our example, we have named the join table SessionInstructor to indicate that it references TrainingSession and Instructors tables. A join table usually has no more than three fields. One would be a unique key to identify each record, and two other fields would reference each side of the association. In this exercise we only used two fields in the join table, and we used these fields to set up a multi-field primary key.

A primary key that consists of two or more fields is often called a *composite* primary key.

Action Item 4.4

On your own modify the Relationship Diagram to include the CourseCategories table.

ESTABLISHING TABLE RELATIONSHIPS USING DATA DEFINITION LANGUAGE

As mentioned earlier in this book, Access provides more than one way of performing a database task, and you guessed it, Relationships View, is not the only way to link the tables. In Chapter 2, you learned some Data Definition Language (DDL) commands that enabled you to create a table. In the next Hands-On, you will learn commands that are used to remove an existing relationship and create a new one while enforcing the referential data integrity rules.

Hands-On 4.6   Using the Data Definition Query to Create Table Relationships

NOTE	*This Hand-On assumes that you have linked all the tables as instructed in this chapter. The following steps will demonstrate how to delete and recreate a relationship between the table TrainingCourseLocations and the Room table.*

1. In the ETD database window, click the **Query Design** button in the **Create** tab.
2. Double click the **Data Definition** button located in the Query Type group of the Query Design tab.
3. In the **Data Definition Query** window that appears, enter the following statement, also shown in Figure 4.12:

```
ALTER TABLE Room DROP CONSTRAINT [TrainingCourseLocationsRoom];
```

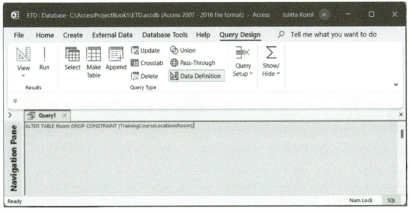

FIGURE 4.12. Data Definition query window with the statement that deletes a relationship between TrainingCourseLocations and Room tables.

The previous statement tells Access to remove the relationship between the table TrainingCourseLocations and the Room table. Recall that the Room table has a foreign key that references the TrainingCourseLocations table primary key – ID.

To remove a relationship between two tables, we start with the ALTER TABLE statement, which tells Access to make some changes in a table definition. This statement can be used to modify table fields and other constraints like primary keys, foreign keys, or indexes.

The `ALTER TABLE` statement must be followed by the name of the table that you are trying to modify. To remove the relationship, you must specify the child table name, which in this case is the Room table. Next, you use the `DROP CONSTRAINT` statement to tell Access to remove some constraint that was defined in the table but no longer applies. In this case you want to drop the relationship line that connects the two tables. Access expects that you provide it with the name of the constraint (relationship) you want to remove. But, how do you know the name of the relationship that Access creates in the Relationships View? Well, you don't. Whatever you do manually using the built-in interfaces in Access, is basically hidden from your view. Several system tables store information related to different Access objects you create and modify. You can look inside these tables to get the information you need. See the section following this Hands-On for the details.

4. Click the **Run** button on the Query Design tab of the Ribbon to run the statement you entered in the previous step. If there is an error somewhere within the statement, Access will display an error message, otherwise it will perform the requested operation.

5. To verify that indeed there is no relationship between the two tables, choose the **Relationships** button on the Database tab. There should be no line between the TrainingCourseLocations and Room tables in Relationships View.

    Let's recreate this relationship in the next step.

6. Leave Relationship View open and go back to the query window.

7. Type the following statement in the query window overwriting the previously entered statement. Enter it on one line.

```
ALTER TABLE Room ADD CONSTRAINT RelLocations FOREIGN KEY
(LocationID) REFERENCES TrainingCourseLocations (ID);
```

The previous statement modifies the Room table using the `ALTER TABLE` statement. To create a relationship between any two tables, you need to use the `ADD CONSTRAINT` statement followed by the relationship name. Here you are in charge, so you can use any name you like if it's not a word reserved by Access internal operations. Here we named the relationship RelLocations. After specifying the name for the relationship, you must use the `FOREIGN KEY` command and indicate in parentheses the name of the foreign key in the child table. In this case it is the LocationID key in the Room table. Next, use the `REFERENCES` command to specify the parent table name and the primary key that the foreign key will reference. The primary key must be enclosed in parentheses. The entire statement ends with the semicolon.

8. Run the statement you entered in Step 7 by clicking the **Run** button on the Query Design tab of the Ribbon.

9. Return to the Relationships View to verify the state of the relationship. Notice that there is no line between the TrainingCourseLocations table and Room table. You must refresh the view to see the latest change.
10. Right click anywhere in the gray empty area of the Relationships window and choose **Show All Relationships**.
    Now Access displays the connecting line between the two tables.
11. Close all the tabs that you may have open. You do not need to save the Query 1.

DISPLAYING THE SYSTEM OBJECTS

As mentioned in the previous Hands-On, Access creates several system tables for its own use while you are performing your database work. By default, these tables are hidden from the Navigation pane. You can review the tables Access creates after making them visible. Follow the steps outlined in Action Item 4.5 and examine the content of the MSysRelationships table.

Action Item 4.5

To enable the visibility of Access system tables:

- Choose **File | Options | Current Database**.
- Click the **Navigation Options** button below the Navigation Category.
- In the Navigation options window, ensure that the **Show System Objects** is checked, and click **OK** until you return to the database window.
- In the Navigation pane, you should see several **MSys** tables displayed in light font. One of them, **MSysRelationships**, stores the relationship information. Open this table in Datasheet View and review its data.

  The relationship name is shown in szReferencedObject column (see Figure 4.13).

NOTE	*When entering statements in the query window you must use the brackets when specifying the relationship name, for example: [TrainingSessionRegistration].*

- To view how Access stored the action you performed in the query window (See HandsOn 4.6), look at the last record in the MSysRelationships table. Notice that the last column of this row shows the relationship name you assigned in Step 7 of that Hands-On.
- Close the **MSysRelationships** table after previewing it.

- To remove Access system tables from the Navigation pane, choose **File | Options | Current Database | Navigation Options**.
- Clear the **Show System Objects** check box and click **OK** until you return to the main database window. All system tables will no longer appear in the Navigation pane.

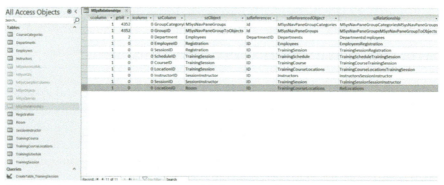

FIGURE 4.13. Examining an Access system table that stores information about various table relationships.

Now that you know more than one way of creating table relationships, you can feel confident that you have the skills needed for relating your Access tables. To certify that you've successfully mastered this topic, let's produce the Relationship report.

CREATING THE RELATIONSHIP REPORT

While working in the Relationships View you may have noticed several buttons in the Ribbon. One of them, the Relationship Report, will open a Print Preview window with your relationship diagram.

Action Item 4.6

- Activate the Relationship View and click the **Relationship Report** in the Tools group of the Relationships Design tab.
- Access loads a relationship report into a new tab.
- In the Page Layout group of the Print Preview tab, click the **Landscape** button to ensure that all the tables fit on one page (Figure 4.14).

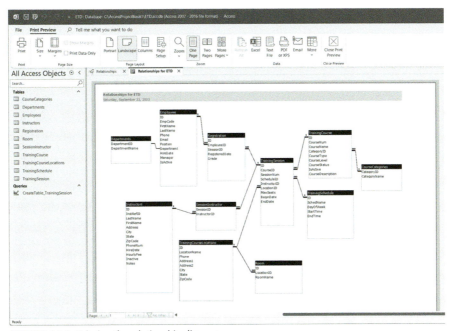

FIGURE 4.14. Printing the relationship diagram.

- If you have a printer available, click the **Print** button to print the diagram.
- If you don't have a printer, click **PDF or XPS** button to save it for printing later. You should enter the desired name and location for your file and click the **Publish** button. Access will generate a PDF file and open it in your PDF viewer. Close the PDF file and close the Export-PDF window that was opened by Access.
- Now close all open tabs. One of the tabs should be **Report1**. When prompted to save the report, click **Yes**. Save the report as **Relationships for ETD** and click **OK**.

You should now see the report listed under the Reports category in the Navigation pane.

You've worked hard in this chapter, and you deserve a break, even though we are not completely done. Take your time, and when you're ready, let's proceed to the next section that introduces you to the process of indexing.

INDEXING FIELDS

When you design Access tables you can specify which field in a table should be indexed. A table index is just like an index in a book. It helps Access put the records in a table in a specific order so you can find them quickly. For example, the primary key in each table you have defined earlier is an index that will put the records in order by the ID field. Primary key fields are always indexed. Access automatically adds indexes to your foreign key fields when you create relationships.

If you often search a table, query, sort or filter its records by a particular field, you can speed up these operations by creating an index for the field. Indexing is done by setting the `Indexed` property in the Properties pane of the Table Design View. Any field that has No selected next to `Indexed` property, has no index for that field. You can change that by clicking on the drop-down menu and choosing one of the two options—Yes (Duplicate OK) and Yes (No Duplicates). Access will then either allow or prevent duplicate entries in your table.

It's important to remember that the `Indexed` property is available only for fields that can be indexed. Access does not allow indexing of the fields with the following data types: *calculated*, *attachment*, *hyperlink*, and *OLE object*.

The more records you have in a table, the more you'll benefit by setting up the index on the field you want to search by. Without an index, Access must scan every record in a table to return the requested results and this can slow performance significantly. For certain database operations that update, append, or delete records, indexes can adversely affect the performance, as Access may need to update the indexes as the operation is performed. Therefore, you should add indexes only when you need them and when you have verified that you can get faster results after having added the index.

You will gain a better understanding of indexes once you start working with the data in the chapters devoted to queries.

In the next Hands-On, you'll learn how to create an index on the LastName field in the Employees table to speed up future searches on this field.

⊙ Hands-On 4.7   Creating an Index

1. In the Navigation pane of the ETD database, open the Employees table in the Design View.
2. Click in the LastName field and notice in the Field properties area at the bottom of the Design View, that the `Indexed` property is currently set to No (Figure 4.15).

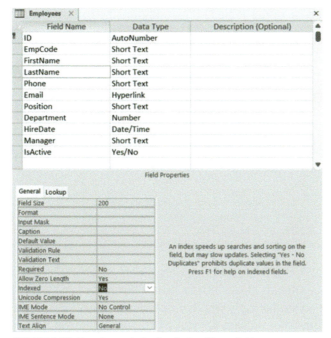

FIGURE 4.15. Creating an index for the LastName field.

3. Set the `Indexed` property value to **Yes (Duplicates OK)** by choosing it from the drop-down list.

   This will tell Access to index the LastName field and allow duplicate entries in this field, as we need to allow for the scenario when there is more than one employee with the same last name. Yes (Duplicates OK) is the most common choice. You should use it whenever the records can have the same value in this field.

   Always check that you set the `Indexed` property for the intended field. To remove the existing index from the selected field, choose No in the drop-down list. To make a permanent change to the index setting, press Ctrl+S to save.

   You can set up an index at any time. The table can be empty or already contain records. Access may take longer to create the index if your table contains thousands of records.

   Unlike a primary key, which gets upon its creation a special key icon to the left of the field name, Access does not provide any visual clue in the Fields section that the field is indexed. You must look at the Field Properties. There is, however, another area where you can view and adjust indexes for a table.

4. In the Show/Hide group of the Table Design tab, click the **Indexes** button.

Access brings up the Indexes window displaying all the indexes created for this table (Figure 4.16).

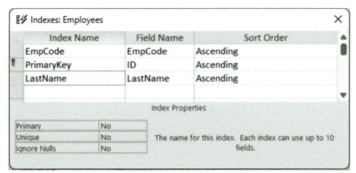

FIGURE 4.16. The Indexes window displays all indexes for the table and can be used to add, modify, and delete an index.

Notice that there are already three indexes in the Employees table. As mentioned earlier, Access automatically sets an index for a primary key field. Access may also create some other indexes for you when you design your table. The EmpCode index was added by Access, and LastName index you've just created by setting the `Indexed` property is also listed here. Each index is assigned an Index Name in the first column, specifies the Field Name is refers to in the second column, and displays the default Ascending (A–Z) Sort Order in the third column. For each index field you are allowed to specify your own index name and the sort order.

The bottom area of the Index popup window displays the Index properties as follows:

- Primary: Yes indicates that the field is the primary key for the table, No otherwise.
- Unique: Yes when the value of the field must be unique, No otherwise.
- Ignore Nulls: Yes when the nulls (blanks) are excluded from the Index, No when nulls are included in the index.

Notice that by default all the properties for the LastName index you created are set to No.

You can use the Indexes popup window to create an index on another field or delete an existing index by deleting its row. To add a new index using this window, simply type the index name, select the field name, and specify sort order.

5. Close the Indexes window and close the Employees table. Select Yes if Access prompts you to save the changes to the Design View.
6. Close the ETD database.

As with the relationships, you can create, modify, and delete the index by using the Data Definition Query window. Unfortunately, we do not have room in this chapter to go into details on using this method. If you are interested just google the topic "Create Index SQL Access" or follow the link to the Microsoft documentation:

https://support.microsoft.com/en-us/office/create-index-statement-2aa192ea-bde6-4f2a-ab3e-4ed690b75eb2

SUMMARY

You have reached the end of this chapter and you should be familiar with the concepts of relating your tables and protecting your data with referential integrity. You also have the skills necessary to create a simple index. The topics covered in this chapter are the staples of database design. If something still does not click, it will soon, as you start working with the data. In future chapters, you will see how the relationships help you get information out from your tables, and how they protect the database from the bad data you don't want.

In the next chapter, it will get busier, as there is lots of data that needs to go into those tables. And there are many methods of bringing in the data. Take a break and come back when you're ready for more learning and doing.

5

POPULATING ACCESS TABLES WITH DATA

E mpty tables are pretty much useless. Before we can display and do any operations on data, we need to get the data into the database. This chapter deals with several ways of filling in Access tables. Here you learn how to import data from spreadsheets, text and XML files, and other databases.

IMPORTING DATA INTO AN ACCESS TABLE

When it comes to entering new information into your database, Access offers many built-in features to make this process quicker and less painful than the tedious and time-consuming manual data entry. Often the information you want to store in an Access database already exists somewhere else as an electronic file and can be moved into an appropriate Access table without reentering it. If you have data in a spreadsheet, a SharePoint list, another database, or a file format like text, XML, or HTML, you can import that data into an Access database with just a few steps. To understand what kind of data you can import into Access, open your database, and go to the External Data tab (Figure 5.1). In the Import & Link group you can see different kind of options available for data import. The New Data Source button is a drop-down list that organizes import options into four categories for easy access. The From File category allows you to import data from Excel spreadsheet, HTML document, XML file or a text file. These are the most used import options.

While you may feel familiar with the Excel spreadsheet format, the other three formats may need some introduction for most of the users who have never worked with databases.

- The *HyperText Markup Language*, or HTML is the standard markup language for Web pages and is used to create websites. In this language, special keywords known as HTML tags are used to markup text. These keywords are surrounded by angle brackets like `<title>` and often come in pairs `<title></title>` where the first tag in a pair is the opening or start tag and the next one is the closing or end tag. There are different tags for different parts of a document. For example, the beginning of a paragraph is indicated by the `<p>` tag and the end with the `</p>` tag. The next line is indicated by the `<br/>` tag. If you'd like to learn the basics of HTML markup, head on to the W3Schools (*https://www.w3schools.com/html/default.asp)* where you can get an overview of the different tags and use the provided playground to test your skills. Please note that learning HTML is not necessary to complete this chapter or this book, but it will come in handy if you ever need to deal with the HTML file imports.

- The *Extensible Markup Language* (XML) defines a set of rules for encoding documents in a format that is easy to read both by humans and machines. XML files are formatted much like HTML documents but use custom tags to define different objects and the data within each object. Many programs can open XML files and output its data to this format. This is a very common format for cataloging information about any set of related items. You can open the XML files in any text editor or using a Web browser. There are many XML editors available on the market that provide helpful syntax checking, editing and validation tools for working with XML files. To find more information about this file format, head to *https://www.w3schools.com/XML/xml_whatis.asp*. Again, this is an optional activity not required to complete this chapter. An example of the XML import will be given in one of this chapter's Hands-On.

- A text file is a file containing text, with no images and other non-text characters. These files can be easily recognized by the .txt extension although they can have other extensions such as .csv or .prn. Text files are easily open by the built-in Notepad editor in Windows or other dedicated text editors that you can download for free or purchase. Text files can be also open by most Web browsers and mobile devices. A text file is a common file format used in data imports and exports. There are two types of text files. One is called *fixed width* and the other is called *delimited*.

In fixed width files fields are aligned in column with spaces between each field. The delimited files, also called *Flat Files* are files where characters such as a comma, tab, pipe, or some other character separate each field. The most common types of delimited text files are:

- comma-separated values (CSV)

    These files use commas to separate fields. The end of each row is indicated with a newline character. They are given the file extension .csv. In these files, text that includes commas is enclosed in double quotes.

- tab-separated values (TSV)

    These files are like .csv files but instead of commas, they use tab characters to separate fields.

- pipe-delimited files

    These files use the pipe character "|" to delimit fields. Because pipe symbol is a rarely used character in text, it is often used to separate fields when the text contains characters that would otherwise be interpreted as delimiters. There is no special extension for pipe delimited text files. They have the standard .txt extension.

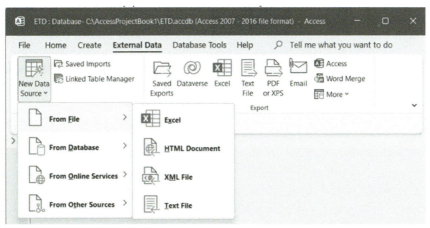

FIGURE 5.1. The External Data tab provides options for importing, linking, and exporting data from and into various file formats.

If you don't have a file to import but have access to a database from which data can be imported directly, the From Database category will allow you to bring data from another Access database, an SQL Server database, and Azure database or from a dBASE file which is a file format for a legacy dBASE database.

If the data you need is stored in a SharePoint list or can be accessed via a Web Service, the third category—From Online Services, offers options that will walk you through the process of retrieving such data.

If none of the above options applies to your situation, you can see if the fourth category—From Other Sources can give you access to your specific data. Here you can find options to connect to an ODBC database or an Outlook folder. The ODBC, which stands for *Open Database Connectivity*, is a standard *application programming interface* (API) for accessing database systems (DBMS). By using an ODBC driver, data requests can be submitted to a specific data source and results can be returned to your application. A data source can be a file, a particular database (i.e., SQL, Oracle, MySQL, Microsoft Visual Fox Pro, IBM DB2) or even a live data feed. The data can be located on the same computer as your Access database, or on another computer somewhere on a network. If an ODBC driver is available for a particular data source, you can easily bring its data to Access. In summary, ODBC, which was developed in 1992, makes it possible to access any data from any application; different types of database programs can talk to each other and understand the information being exchanged.

IMPORTING VERSUS LINKING

If, in addition to bringing data to Access, you would like to connect to another database and dynamically use its data, Access also offers a way to link to external data. Before we go further with our database tasks, it's important to understand the difference between importing and linking data.

When you import data, you simply copy the data you have in the chosen data source (a spreadsheet, text file, or another database) and store it in an Access table. If the external data source changes, that is new data is added, or existing data is modified, or deleted from the source, none of these changes will be reflected in your Access table. Also, once your imported data undergoes any modifications in Access, none of such changes will be reflected in the external source from which your data originated. Importing works very well when you want to populate empty Access tables with initial data and perhaps keep it updated from the external sources on a scheduled basis. Assume you work with one or more subcontractors or vendors who are required to provide you with the data they collected in a specific timeframe. The data comes in every week in a spreadsheet or text file format. You can use the New Data Source from File (Excel or Text) to add this data to your Access table. Every time you receive a new file you will simply add (append) the new data. If for any reason you want to share your full dataset with your vendor, you can create a data dump from your Access table by using the options that are available in the Export group of the External Data tab. Ask your vendor which data format they prefer, and simply output your data in this format. Each import or export feature in Access is driven by a built-in wizard that will walk you through the process step by step to get the desired output format.

Linking is different. Instead of filling in the local Access table with the external data, you simply store a link to that data source. The link will be listed in the Navigation pane of your database. When you click the link, Access will query the external source for its current data. So, for example, if your vendor wants to provide you with access to a specific table in their SQL database instead of sending you weekly data feeds, you can directly link to their table and always have the vendor data available in Access. You will not have to maintain this data. All the data additions, modifications and deletions will be handled outside of the Access database, in the source where the data resides. Your Access database will always have the most current data with no work on your part once you've established the link. You can also link to tables in another Access database. In Chapter 12, when we split the ETD database into front-end and back-end files, you will see the table linking processes in action. For now, our task is to quickly get going with populating the existing local Access tables with some initial data so we can build forms and reports and perform various database operations.

The following Hands-On exercises will walk you through various data importing tasks. The Companion files have many files in different formats that we will be perusing in this chapter. Let's get started.

IMPORTING DATA FROM A TEXT FILE

In Chapter 4, you worked hard with table relationships linking various tables in the ETD database with the primary and foreign keys. Except for the Employees table that already had some initial data entered manually in an earlier chapter, all the tables are currently empty and need to be populated (filled in) with data. Recall that we could not enforce the referential integrity rules between the Employees and Departments table because we did not have any data in the Departments table. Let's start then by bringing data to this table so we can modify this relationship.

NOTE	*Files for the Hands-On project may be found in the Companion files.*

Hands-On 5.1   Importing Departments Data From a Pipe Delimited Text File

1. Open the **Departments.txt** file located in the Companion files and review its contents depicted in Figure 5.2.

    Notice that this is a Pipe Delimited text file with two fields: DepartmentID and DepartmentName. These fields are separated by a special character, in this case pipe (|), known as a delimiter. All text fields containing text data are enclosed in quotation marks.

    We will load this data into the Departments table in the ETD database. It is a good practice to always review the data prior to importing, so you understand what type of data you are dealing with.

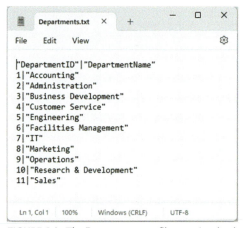

FIGURE 5.2. The Departments.txt file contains the data we want to import to the Departments table.

2. Close the **Departments.txt** file.
3. In the ETD database, click the **New Data Source** dropdown in the External Data tab and choose **From File | Text File**.

    Access displays the screen where it asks you to specify the source of the data.
4. Click the **Browse** button and locate the **Departments.txt** file and click **Open**. Notice that Access filters the folder data to only display the text files. The selected file name should now appear in the File name box (Figure 5.3). Access provides three options for importing the data. You can import the data into a new table in the current database or you can append the copy of the records to an existing table, or you can create a link to the text file. Each type of import provides an easy-to-understand description so you can make the right decision.

5. Select the **Append** option and chose the **Departments** table from the dropdown list and click **OK** (Figure 5.3).

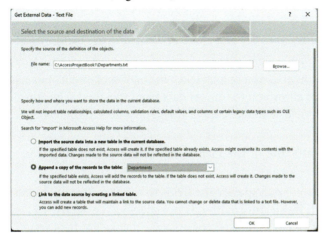

FIGURE 5.3. The Get External Data – Text File window allows you to specify the source of data and the type of import.

Access displays the next screen of the Import Text Wizard and attempts to recognize the format that describes your data. Unfortunately, the guess is incorrect. It's not a fixed width file but a delimited file. Let's correct that.

6. Click the **Delimited** option button (Figure 5.4).

FIGURE 5.4. The Import Text Wizard screen loads the selected text file and attempts to recognize the format of the data.

When dealing with delimited files you need to specify the Delimiter used.

7. Click the **Advanced** button to fill in the details of the Import specification.

8. In the **Departments Import Specification** (Figure 5.5) type do the following:

    a. Type the pipe character (|) in the Field Delimiter box.

    b. In the text qualifier select double quote (").

    c. Check the Skip box next to the DepartmentID field in the Field Information section.

    Recall that DepartmentID is a primary key in the Departments table, therefore Access will not allow you to import data from this field. The AutoNumber format on this field will take care of the department numbering scheme in your table.

    d. Enter **DepartmentName** in the FieldName column. This step is very important.

    The field information must specify the fields in the text file which you want to skip and import. If this information is not specified correctly, you will get the dreaded *Subscript out of range* error message that might take you hours if not days to troubleshoot.

    e. Click OK.

NOTE	*Access allows you to save the import specification using the Save As button so you can use the same settings next time you need to bring in more data. In this exercise, you don't need to save the import specification.*

FIGURE 5.5. The Departments Import Specification window allows you to specify the Field Delimiter and text qualifier used in the text file, as well as options for formatting date and time fields, decimal symbols, and names of fields in the text file that should be imported or skipped during import.

9. Back in the Import Text Wizard screen, click the **Next** button.
   Access now displays the delimiter and the text qualifier you selected.

10. Make sure that you click the box to tell Access that the First Row Contains Field Names (Figure 5.6).

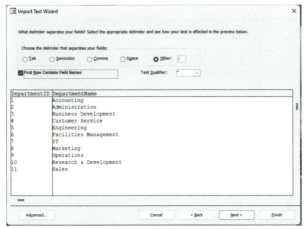

FIGURE 5.6. In the Import Text Wizard ensure that you have selected the correct delimiter and text qualifier for the type of text file you are importing, and you specified whether the text file contains the headings in its first row.

11. Click the **Next** button. This is all the Wizard needs to import your data. Just make sure you have selected the correct table, or you will run into problems (Figure 5.7).

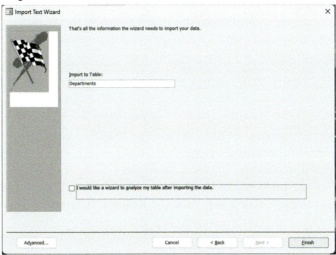

FIGURE 5.7. The last screen in the Import Text Wizard.

12. Click the **Finish** button.

Access imports the data and allows you to save the import steps.

13. Click the **Close** button.

14. Open the **Departments** table to check that the data was correctly imported (see Figure 5.8).

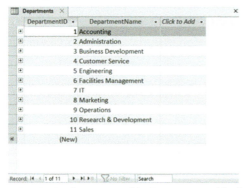

FIGURE 5.8. The contents of the Departments table after successful import from a pipe delimited text file.

15. Close the **Departments** table.

Now let's add the Department on the existing Employees table records. Until the Employees table have valid department IDs, we won't be able to enforce the referential integrity rules between these two tables.

16. Open the **Employees** table.

17. Enter **2** in the Department column for the Jessica Roberts record.

18. Enter **4** in the Department column for the David Lebovitz record.

19. Enter **5** in the Department column for the George Khan record.

FIGURE 5.9. Modifying the Employees table records with valid departments.

20. Close the **Employees** table saving the changes you made.

Now let's fix the Relationship diagram.

21. Choose **Relationships** from the Database Tools tab.

22. Double-click the join line between the Departments and Employees table.

23. In the Edit Relationships dialog box click the **Enforce Referential Integrity** and click **OK**.

Access creates the one-to-many relationship between these two tables indicating that each department can belong to many employee records (Figure 5.10).

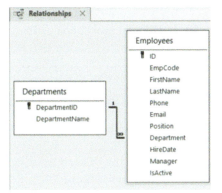

FIGURE 5.10. After modifying the Employees table with existing department IDs, we were able to enforce the referential integrity rules in the Relationships diagram.

24. Save and close the Relationships tab.

IMPORTING DATA FROM EXCEL WORKSHEETS

Access works very well with Excel. You can import an entire worksheet or a named range of cells to a new or existing table. You may want to create a named range in the worksheet if you are not planning to import a whole worksheet. During the data import each worksheet column becomes a field in an Access table. Like in a text import, if you want to use the first row of the worksheet for field names, you must check the First Row Contains Column Headings check box during the import process. All other rows from your worksheet will then become records in your Access table. Prior to import from Excel, it is recommended that you review your worksheet for data completeness and consistency. To avoid errors during the import process, each worksheet column should have entries in the same data type (numbers, text, dates, and so on).

You can make it easier for Access to correctly detect data types by ensuring that the first ten rows of your worksheet contain data.

- If there are any blank rows at the top, or in between the rows of data, remove them.
- If there are any internal titles, remove them as well.
- If the column headings are too long, shorten them so you don't run into the field name size issues during the import.
- When importing into an existing Access table, make sure that the number and order of worksheet columns matches the number and order of Access table fields.

The next step in our ETD database project calls for more data in the Employees table. In the Companion files, you will find an Excel workbook with several employee records that you can import. Let's find out how to use Excel as the data source for our import.

(◉) Hands-On 5.2   Importing Employee Data From an Excel Worksheet

1. Open the **AllEmployees.xlsx** Excel workbook file located in the Companion files.

   Notice that the first row in the worksheet contains the column headings and all the rows that follow list data for various employees (Figure 5.11). It looks like there are no gaps between the worksheet rows, no mixed data types within worksheet columns, but there is no data in the Manager column. The lack of data should not pose any issues during the import.

2. Open the **Employees** table in the ETD database and review its fields and data.

   It looks like all the field names in the Excel worksheet match those in the Access table. In the real-life scenario, this is rarely the case. Most often you will get the worksheet with non-matching field names, and you will need to make modifications in the source file to facilitate the import. Each data import can present you with several issues that can be difficult to resolve. Some data imports are very straightforward and easy, others are more complex and may require many passes at your data to get the results you need.

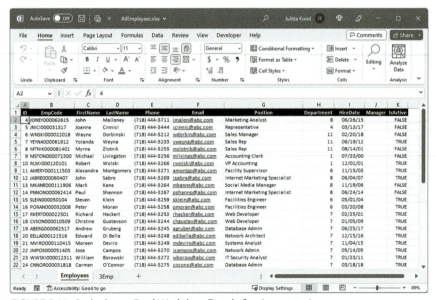

FIGURE 5.11. Reviewing an Excel Worksheet Data before Import to Access.

3. Close the **AllEmployees.xlsx** file and the **Employees** table before proceeding with the import process.

    To avoid any issues with the Import operation, each time prior to importing excel worksheets into Access, close and exit Access, then restart your database.

4. Click the **New Data Source** dropdown in the External Data tab and choose **From File | Excel**.

5. In the Get External Data – Excel Spreadsheet, click the **Browse** button and locate and open the **AllEmployees.xlsx** file.

    Access fills in the File Name box with the file you selected (Figure 5.12).

6. Click the second option button—**Append a copy of the records to the table** and select **Employees** from the drop-down box (Figure 5.12).

7. Click **OK** to proceed.

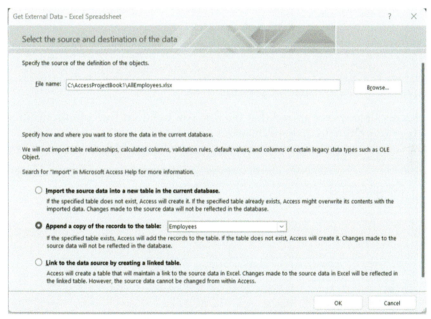

FIGURE 5.12. Completing the first screen of the Get External Data – Excel Spreadsheet import process.

Access displays the second screen of the Import Spreadsheet Wizard with a sample layout of the data as shown in Figure 5.13. Because the AllEmployees.xlsx workbook has multiple sheets, Access asks you to select the sheet or named range of cells containing data you want to import.

8. Make sure the **Employees** is selected and click **Next**.

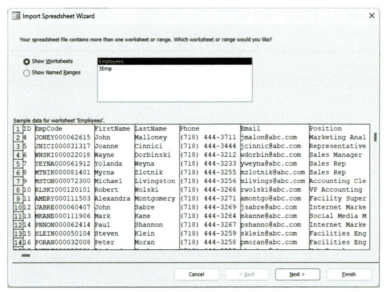

FIGURE 5.13. When there are multiple worksheets in the Excel workbook, Access allows you to specify which sheet, or a named range has data to import.

Access already recognized that the first row contains the column headings, so there is nothing to do here (Figure 5.14).

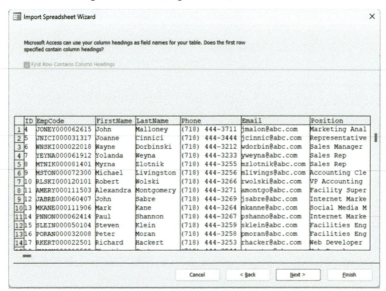

FIGURE 5.14. In this screen of the Import Spreadsheet Wizard, Access detects whether the first row of the spreadsheet data contains column headings.

9. Click the **Next** button to continue.

Access now notifies you that it gathered all the information it needs to import your data (Figure 5.15). It also lists the table name to which the data will be imported.

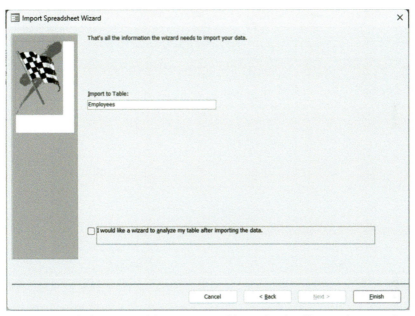

FIGURE 5.15. The last screen of the Import Spreadsheet Wizard notifies you that Access is ready to perform the import process.

10. Click the **Finish** button.

Access finalizes the import from the AllEmployees.xlsx to the Employees table and allows you to save import steps so that next time you can repeat the import operation without using the wizard (Figure 5.16).

NOTE	*If Access cannot perform the import operation for one reason or another, it will display an error message. At that time, you will need to close the Wizard and return to your Excel work-sheet and try to pinpoint the cause of the failure. If you see no problems with Excel data, close your database and exit entirely from Access. In many cases this should clear any problems that may have confused Access. Try the import operation again and it may succeed without any changes to the data.*

It is recommended that you always make a backup copy of the table to which you are planning to import data, so that you don't lose any existing data in an unsuccessful import operation. While import may seem successful, it is possible that the data you selected is not what you wanted to import.

11. In the Save Import Steps window, click **Close**.

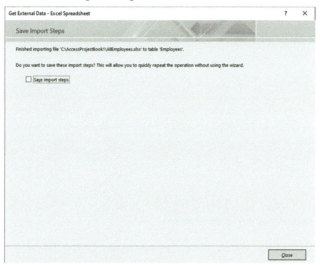

FIGURE 5.16. After completing the import process Access allows you to save your import steps for quicker use in the future imports.

12. Open the Employees table and verify that all the data from the Employees worksheet were correctly imported (Figure 5.17).

EmpID	EmpCode	FirstName	LastName	Phone	Email	Position	Department	HireDate	Manager	IsActive	Click to Add
1		Jessica	Roberts	(718) 444-3442	jroberts@abc.com	Secretary	2	4/10/2008		☑	
2		David	Lebovitz	(718) 444-3211	dlebovt@abc.com	Representative	4	12/11/2011		☑	
3		George	Khan	(718) 444-3121	gkhan0@abc.com	VP Engineering	5	6/20/1998		☑	
4	JONEY0000626:	John	Malloney	(718) 444-3711	jmalon@abc.com	Marketing Analy	8	6/26/2015		☐	
5	JNICI00003131:	Joanne	Cinnici	(718) 444-3444	jcinnic@abc.com	Representative	4	3/13/2017		☐	
6	WNSKI0000220	Wayne	Dorbinski	(718) 444-3212	wdorbin@abc.con	Sales Manager	11	2/20/2018		☐	
7	YEYNA0000619	Yolanda	Weyna	(718) 444-3233	yweyna@abc.com	Sales Rep	11	6/19/2012		☑	
8	MTNIK0000814	Myrna	Zlotnik	(718) 444-3255	mzlotnik@abc.con	Sales Rep	11	8/14/2001		☐	
9	MSTON000072:	Michael	Livingston	(718) 444-3256	mlivings@abc.com	Accounting Cler	1	7/23/2000		☐	
10	RLSKI00012010	Robert	Wolski	(718) 444-3266	rwolski@abc.com	VP Accounting	1	12/1/2001		☑	
11	AMERY0001115	Alexandra	Montgomery	(718) 444-3271	amontgo@abc.cor	Facility Supervis	6	11/15/2003		☑	
12	JABRE0000604C	John	Sabre	(718) 444-3269	jsabre@abc.com	Internet Market	8	6/4/2007		☑	
13	MKANE0001115	Mark	Kane	(718) 444-3264	mkanne@abc.com	Social Media M.	8	11/19/2006		☐	
14	PNNON000062	Paul	Shannon	(718) 444-3267	pshanno@abc.con	Internet Market	8	6/24/2014		☐	
15	SLEIN00005010	Steven	Klein	(718) 444-3259	sklein@abc.com	Facilities Engine	6	5/1/2004		☑	
16	PORAN0000320	Peter	Moran	(718) 444-3258	pmoran@abc.com	Facilities Engine	6	3/20/2008		☑	
17	RKERT0000225(	Richard	Hackert	(718) 444-3253	rhacker@abc.com	Web Developer	7	2/25/2001		☑	
18	CVSON0000105	Chrstine	Gustavson	(718) 444-3244	chgustav@abc.cor	Web Developer	7	1/5/2009		☑	

Record: 1 of 48 No Filter Search

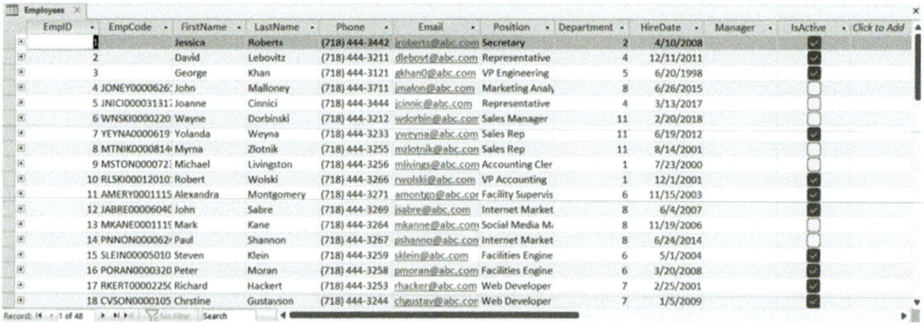

FIGURE 5.17. The Employees table after the Import Operation.

Notice that the original three records in the Employees table do not have the EmpCode. You will learn how to update these records in the chapter devoted to queries.

13. Close the **Employees** table.

Want to practice more? Proceed to Action Item 5.1 to import Excel data to the table Instructors.

Action Item 5.1

In the Navigation pane of the ETD database, right click the table Instructors and choose Copy. Right click anywhere in the empty area of the Navigation pane and choose Paste. Access will display the Paste Table as a dialog box as shown in Figure 5.18.

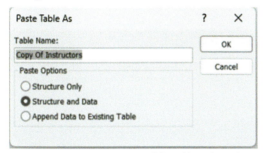

FIGURE 5.18. Creating a copy of the table with its data.

Click OK to proceed with the copy/paste operation. Access will add the newly created Copy of Instructors table to the Navigation pane of your database. Now, review the Instructors.xlsx file included in the Companion files before you begin its import. Make sure that the field names and their order in the spreadsheet matches the design view of the table Instructors. If you find any issues with the spreadsheet columns correct them and save and close the modified file. Next, using the steps outlined in the previous Hands-On, perform the import process by importing the Instructors.xlsx Excel workbook into the table Instructors.

Congratulations, if your import succeeded on the first try. If you reached the last screen of the Import Spreadsheet Wizard and got the message shown in Figure 5.19, you need to exit and go back to the Instructors.xlsx spreadsheet to do more troubleshooting. Do the field names match those in the Access table? Are there any misspellings? Correct them and try your import again. As you eliminate errors in your worksheet, Access may give you more user-friendly error messages in subsequent import attempts that will help you to successfully complete your import.

Figure 5.20 depicts the data that was loaded into the table Instructors.

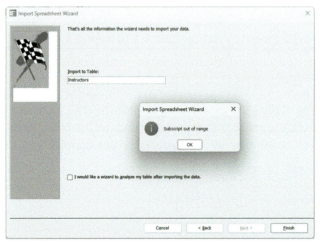

FIGURE 5.19. Import Spreadsheet Wizard found errors in the import file and displays a rather cryptic error message.

ID	Company	Last Name	First Name	Address	City	State/Province	ZIP/Postal Code	Home Phone	HireDate	HourlyFee	Inactive
1	INSASMITH	Smith	Adam	911 Beacon Stre Boston	MA		02109	6178354866	12/12/2017	$55.00	
2	INSVRAMIR	Ramirez	Victor	15 Cornell Stree Boston	MA		02101	6172416001	1/19/2018	$50.00	
3	INSAKENNE	Kennedy	Amy	550 Penn Lane Yonkers	NY		10470	9143762311	1/21/2018	$45.00	
4	INSMDUGLA	Douglas	Monique	201 Park Avenu New York	NY		10154	2128014435	6/6/2018	$65.00	
5	INSDPATEL	Patel	Deepak	699 Sunset Driv Garden City	NY		11530	5164092854	10/18/2017	$50.00	
(New)										$0.00	

FIGURE 5.20. The Instructors table after the Import.

Now, if you are wondering why the second column in Figure 5.20 is named Company instead of InstRefID, this has nothing to do with the import. This name comes from the `Caption` property, which Access uses to allow you to display a different label for your Access field in the Datasheet View or on a form or report. You can specify the text that should be used for your field captions in the Table Design View. Under Field Properties, on the General tab, click Caption and enter the new caption for the filed, and press Ctrl+S to save your change.

IMPORTING DATA FROM XML FILES

When importing data into Access it pays to be familiar with more than one file format. When one format can sometimes present many challenges in the import operation, another format may be more suited for a particular task. Data conversion issues can be better resolved in one format than another. For many years now XML format has been successfully used for exchanging information between various programs. This format can work well both with desktop and

Web data. You can easily export Access tables into XML files, and you can just as easily output Excel data into XML. The same goes for a multitude of other programs that are currently being used in various business environments. In this section, you will use the Companion XML files to populate the table Training-CourseLocations. In an XML file, special tags are used to describe the structure of the elements in a document. Look at Figure 5.21 that contains the XML data we are going to import.

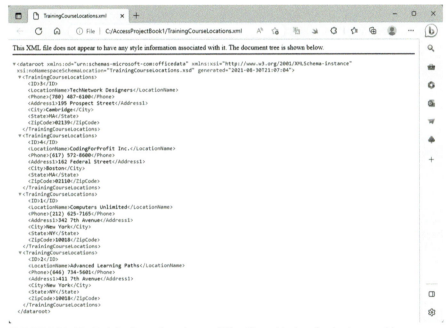

FIGURE 5.21. The TrainingCourseLocations.xml file will provide data for the Access table – TrainingCourseLocations.

When double-clicked in the Windows File Explorer, the XML document opens in your default Internet browser. The data is displayed as a collapsible document tree. When you open the same file in Windows Notepad, you will find in the first line of the file a processing instruction:

```
<?xml version="1.0" encoding="UTF-8"?>
```

Processing instructions begin with <? and end with ?>. The processing instruction contains an XML declaration. The version attribute tells the XML processor that the document conforms to version 1.0 of the XML specification. The encoding attribute indicates the type of character set used in the document.

By default, XML documents use the UTF-8 encoding of Unicode. The second line in the XML document is a *dataroot* element. This tag defines the *namespaces*. In XML document namespaces are used to ensure that element names do not conflict with one another and are unique within a particular set of names (a namespace). The attribute xmlns is an XML keyword for a namespace declaration. Because different XML documents can use the same tags that may have a different meaning and content, namespaces are used to ensure that if two documents with the same tags are merged there is no element name conflict. If you're interested in the details of XML documents, there is a lot of information available on the Web and in printed form on the structure of the XML documents. The good news is that you don't need to know anything about the XML declaration and namespaces to import an XML document into an Access table. What you need to focus on are the lines that follow. Notice that for each row (record) in a table you have a start tag <TrainingCourseLocations> and an end tag </TrainingCourseLocations>. It looks like the table has four different records. Within each row, there is a separate element for each column (field) in the table. So, your first record looks like this:

```
<TrainingCourseLocations>
<ID>3</ID>
<LocationName>TechNetwork Designers</LocationName>
<Phone>(780) 487-6100</Phone>
<Address1>195 Prospect Street</Address1>
<City>Cambridge</City>
<State>MA</State>
<ZipCode>02139</ZipCode>
</TrainingCourseLocations>
```

In Figure 5.21, notice how the dataroot element encloses all the elements in the XML file. Each element in the tree structure is called a *node*. The dataroot node contains child nodes for each row in the table TrainingCourseLocations.

As you can see, the Instructors.xml file stores only the data for the TrainingCourseLocations table. The table structure itself is defined in an accompanying schema stored in the TrainingCourseLocations.xsd file also included in the Companion files. Look again at the Figure 5.21 and notice that the name of the schema file is listed in the dataroot element.

In short, *schema files* describe XML data using the *XML Schema Definition* (XSD) Language and allow the XML parser to validate XML documents. The XML schema file contains information about the elements that are allowed in the XML document, their data types, number of allowed occurrences of the element, attributes that can be associated with a given element, default values for attributes, child elements and their sequence. Schema files are generated automatically by various applications when you choose to export data to the XML file format. Make sure that the schema file is in the same folder as the corresponding XML file. If Access cannot find the schema file, it will notify you and suggest that you update or remove the file reference and try again to import.

With that said, let's proceed to the next Hands-On exercise and see how Access can consume data from the XML document.

⊙ Hands-On 5.3   Importing TrainingCourseLocations Data From an XML Document

1. Make sure that the **TrainingCourseLocations.xml** file is closed.
2. In the Navigation pane of the ETD database, create a copy of the TrainingCourseLocatons table so you can restore the original table if anything goes wrong during the import.
3. Click the **New Data Source** dropdown in the External Data tab and choose **From File | XML File**.
4. In the Get External Data – XML File, click the **Browse** button and locate and open the **TrainingCourseLocations,xml** file.

    Access fills in the File Name box with the file you selected (Figure 5.22). While Access informs you that the source data will be imported into a new table in the current database, this is not exactly true. You will also be given an option to import data into an existing table.
5. Click **OK** to proceed.

    Access now displays the Import XML dialog box where it shows you the name and the structure of the table it found in the XML file (Figure 5.23). Three options are given for the import: Structure Only, Structure, and Data and Append Data to Existing Table(s).
6. Select the third option button to **Append Data to Existing Table(s)** and click **OK**.

    Access successfully executes the import steps and gives you an opportunity to save import for future use.
7. Click **Close** to exit.
8. Open the **TrainingCourseLocations** table to verify that all data was correctly imported (Figure 5.24).
9. Close the **TrainingCourseLocations** table.

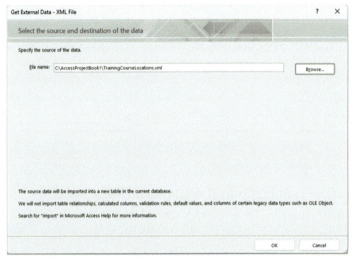

FIGURE 5.22. Specifying an XML file for Import.

FIGURE 5.23. Specifying the type of Import.

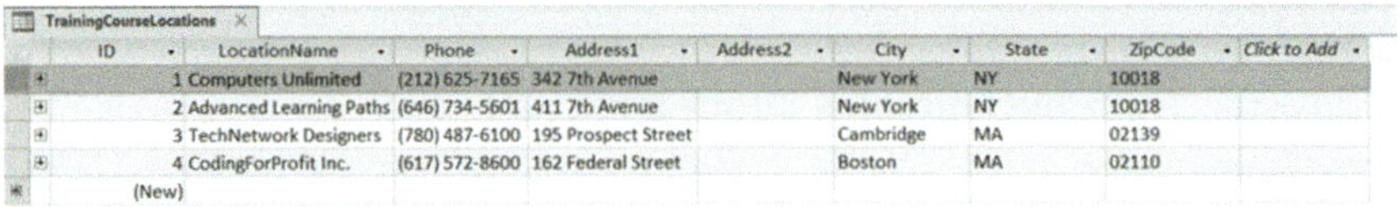

ID	LocationName	Phone	Address1	Address2	City	State	ZipCode	Click to Add
1	Computers Unlimited	(212) 625-7165	342 7th Avenue		New York	NY	10018	
2	Advanced Learning Paths	(646) 734-5601	411 7th Avenue		New York	NY	10018	
3	TechNetwork Designers	(780) 487-6100	195 Prospect Street		Cambridge	MA	02139	
4	CodingForProfit Inc.	(617) 572-8600	162 Federal Street		Boston	MA	02110	
(New)								

FIGURE 5.24. The TrainingCourseLocations table populated with data from an XML file.

The TrainingCourseLocatons table we just filled in with the data from an XML file is related to two other tables: Rooms and Training Session. Let's fill in the Rooms table next. Earlier you learned that there are different types of text files. The next section will introduce you to the *tab-delimited* text files.

IMPORTING DATA FROM A TAB-DELIMITED TEXT FILE

In the beginning of this chapter, you imported data from a *pipe-delimited* text file where pipe characters were used as field separators. Because text files can be formatted differently, it is important to open them and examine their structure before importing into Access. Figure 5.25 shows the Room data that we need to import into the Room table. Notice that this is a text file where tabs are used to separate each field, and text is enclosed in double-quotes. The first row contains headings, and each data row is shown on a separate line.

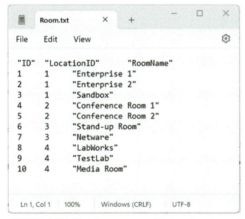

FIGURE 5.25. The Room.txt text file has data in a tab-delimited format.

NOTE	*While some programs save delimited text files with the .tab or a .csv extension, most text files have a .txt extension. Hence, it's important to open them to find out what delimited format they are in.* *Now that you know how your source data is formatted, the import process should go smoothly.*

⊙ **Hands-On 5.4   Importing Room Data From a Tab-Delimited Text File**

1. Make sure the **Room.txt** file is closed.
2. In the ETD database window, click the **New Data Source** dropdown in the External Data tab and choose **From File | Text File**.
3. In the Get External Data – Text File, click the **Browse** button and locate and open the **Room.txt** file.
4. Click the **Append a copy of the records to the table** option button and choose **Room** from the drop-down box. Click **OK** to continue.

   Access shows the content of the selected file and recognizes it as having delimited format (Figure 5.26).

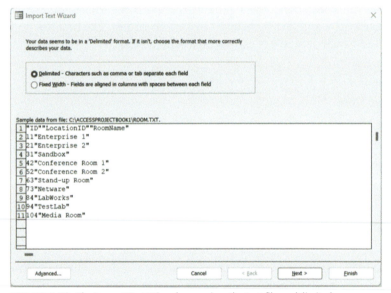

FIGURE 5.26. The Import Text Wizard recognizes the text file as delimited.

5. Click the **Advanced** button to tell the Wizard the type of delimiters being used.
6. Make sure that {**tab**} is selected in the Field Delimiter box and text qualifier is set to a double quote ("). In the Field Information section where all the fields are listed, click the **Skip** box next to the ID. As the ID is a primary key field in the Room table, you don't need to import it. When your selections match Figure 5.27, click the **OK** button.

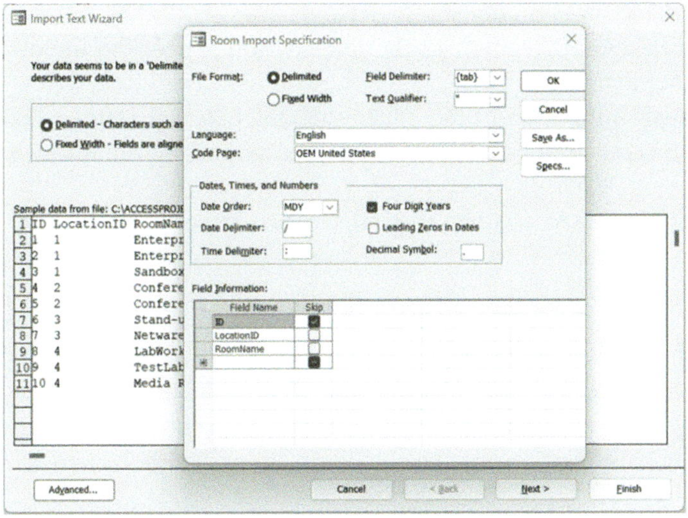

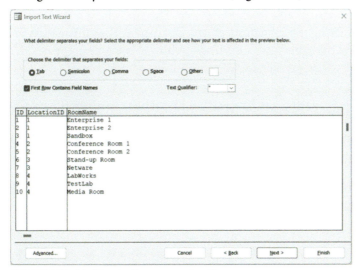

FIGURE 5.27. Filling in the Room Import specification.

7. Back in the Import Text Wizard screen, click the **Next** button.

   Access shows you the selections you have made so far and gives you a chance to make corrections to delimiters and a text qualifier and includes a check box so you can mark the first row as headings.

8. Click the check box **First Row Contains Field Names**. Notice that the grid changes when you make this selection (Figure 5.28).

FIGURE 5.28. Marking the first row as a heading row.

9. Click the **Next** button.

   Access notifies you that that's all the information it needs to import your data to the Room table.

10. Click the **Finish** button, and then Close the Get External Data – Text File screen when Access notifies you that it finished importing the Room.txt file to table Room.

11. Open the Room table to confirm that all the data from the text file appears correctly.

You've done a lot of work in this chapter and are becoming an expert in data imports. But, before we continue with other imports, let's look at some of the data you just imported. How can you see what Rooms belong to in what locations without having to open both the TrainingCourseLocations and Room table? To answer this question, you need to learn about datasheets and subdatasheets.

ABOUT DATASHEETS AND SUBDATASHEETS

When you open a table, Access displays its content in the Datasheet View, even if the table is empty. A *datasheet* is an Excel like representation of your data. Without any fancy formatting you can look at your data in rows and columns. If you have two tables that are in relationship with one another, you can embed the datasheet from one table in another table. The embedded datasheet is called a *subdatasheet*. Using the subdatasheet, you can display the information in more than one table at the same time. Let's find out how this works in the next Hands-On.

⦿ Hands-On 5.5   Using the Embedded Datasheet to View Related Data

1. In the Navigation plane, double-click the **TrainingCourseLocations** table.

   The table opens in the Datasheet View. Notice a little plus sign on the left-hand side of each record.

2. Click on the plus sign in the first row, and in the Insert Subdatasheet dialog box (Figure 5.29), click **Room**.

FIGURE 5.29. Inserting a Room Subdatasheet into the parent table (TrainingCourseLocations).

Behind the scenes Access checks the relationship between the open table and the table you selected and fills in the names of the two related fields. One is in the parent table, and the other in the subdatasheet. In other words, the Location ID field in the Room table is linked to the ID field in the Training-CourseLocations table. When you start writing queries you can filter the data displayed in the subdatasheet using the criteria defined in your query.

3. Make your selections as shown in Figure 5.29 and click **OK**.

Access embeds the Room datasheet in the TrainingCourseLocations table, and you can see that the Computer Unlimited location has three training Rooms: Enterprise 1, Enterprise 2, and Sandbox (Figure 5.30).

FIGURE 5.30. Looking at data from two tables at the same time is possible with the subdatasheet feature.

The More button in the Records group of the Home tab of the Ribbon lists different options related to using subdatasheets (Figure 5.31).

FIGURE 5.31. The embedded Subdatasheet features can be accessed from the More button on the Ribbon.

4. Review the Rooms available for each location by choosing the **Expand All** option.

5. Remove the Room Subdatasheet by choosing the **Remove** option.

6. Close the **TrainingCourseLocations** table. If asked to save changes in the layout of the table, click **No**.

Now that you know how you can look at the data in more than one table at once, take a break, and when you come back, we will continue with the remaining imports.

Action Item 5.2

Import all the records from the TrainingSchedule.xlsx file included in the Companion files to the table TrainingSchedule. The content of the workbook is shown in Figure 5.32.

Hint: To avoid the *"Subscript Out of Range"* error be sure to restart Access prior to import.

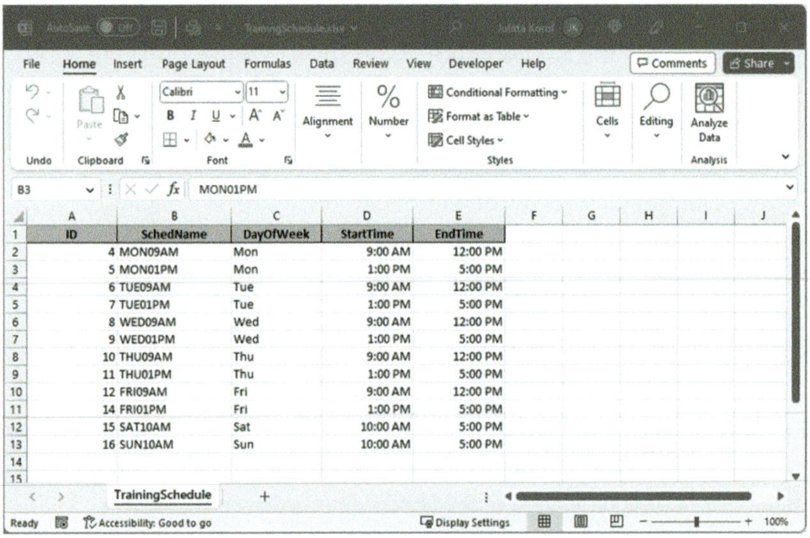

FIGURE 5.32. The Excel workbook with the data for the table TrainingSchedule.

Action Item 5.3

Import all the records from the **CourseCategories.csv** file included in the Companion files to the table CourseCategories. The content of this comma delimited text file is shown in Figure 5.33.

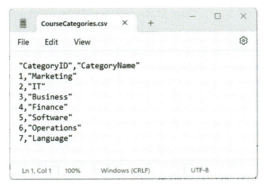

FIGURE 5.33. The text file in the .csv (comma-separated values) format contains data for the table TrainingCourse.

Notice that in the .csv file format the fields are separated with the comma delimiter and text is qualified with double quotes, and first row of data contains column headings. Be sure to make these selections when going through the Text Import Wizard.

Now that you know how to handle imports from Excel workbooks, text files, and XML documents, let's learn how to get data from another Access database.

IMPORTING DATA FROM ANOTHER ACCESS DATABASE

When the data you need is already in another Access database, you should decide whether you want to import it or link to it. When you link data, you tell Access that the data should stay where it is (in the external data source) and Access should get the data each time it is needed. In our scenario, we want to continue with the imports to ensure that we always have the data we need locally without having to maintain a connection to another database.

Access allows you to easily import any of its tables, queries, forms, and reports, as well as more advanced objects such as macros and modules, into another Access database. When importing a table, you can import only the table definition which is the structure you see in the Design View, or you can import both the definition and the data. The next Hands-On walks you through the process of acquiring data for the TrainingCourse table.

⊙ Hands-On 5.6 Importing Data From Another Access Database

1. Create a copy of the **TrainingCourse** table with the default name **Copy of TrainingCourse** just in case anything goes wrong with the import you are about to perform.

2. In the ETD database window, click the **New Data Source** dropdown in the External Data tab and choose **From Database | Access**.

3. In the Get External Data – Access Database, click the **Browse** button and locate and open the **TestData.accdb** database from your Companion files.

Access places the selected database name in the File name box (Figure 5.34). Notice that the first option button is selected.

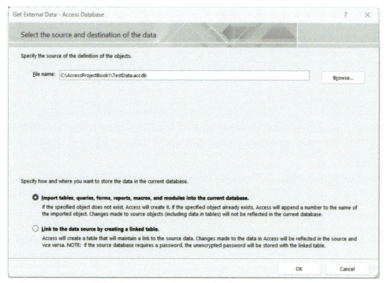

FIGURE 5.34. Specifying the source of data in the first screen of the Get External Data – Access Database.

4. Click **OK** to continue.

Access displays the Import Objects dialog box where you can select the type and name of the object you want to import.

> **NOTE**   *If Access displays the message notifying you that the active content in the file is blocked, click OK to continue.*

5. In the Import Objects dialog box, in the Tables tab, highlight **TrainingCourse** and click **OK** (Figure 5.35).

FIGURE 5.35. Specifying an Access object to import.

6. After Access notifies you that the object was imported successfully, click the check box Save Import Steps.

   Access expands the screen and asks for more information.

7. Fill in the data as shown in Figure 3.36 and click the **Save Import** button.

FIGURE 5.36. Saving Import Steps.

Notice that Navigation pane now contains a new table called **TrainingCourse1**. When you import an Access object, Access imports the object into an active database. It does not append the data from that object into an existing table.

If the active database already has an object with the same name, Access will append a number to the end of the name, hence you can see TrainingCourse1 after this import. So now what? How can we get this data into the existing table? We could write a query to append the data we need but we are not yet versed in this task. Let's stick to the method we already know and use often in cases like this. How about all mighty Copy & Paste technique? Yes, you can easily copy data from one table to another if their structure is the same.

8. In the Navigation pane double-click the table **TrainingCourse1**.

   The table should open in the Datasheet View.

9. Press **Ctrl+A** to select all the rows in the table and press **Ctrl+C** to copy the selected records to the clipboard.

   You can also highlight all the records by clicking in the gray box to the left of the ID field, and copy records using the Copy button on the Ribbon's Home tab.

10. In the Navigation Pane, double-click the **TrainingCourse** table and once it opens in the Datasheet View, press **Ctrl+A** and then **Ctrl+V** to paste the records.

    Access should notify you that you are about to paste 27 records (see Figure 5.37).

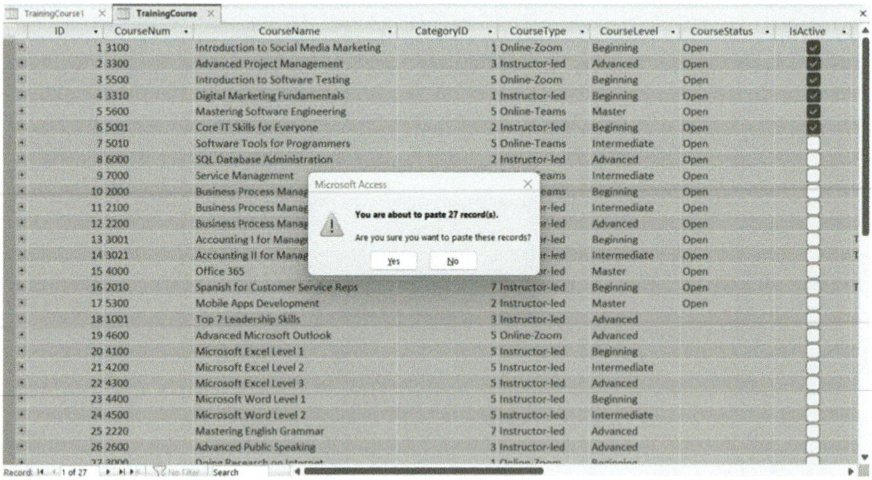

FIGURE 5.37. Data in the TrainingCourse table was pasted from another Access table that was imported from another Access database.

11. Click **Yes** to paste the records.

    All the records from the TrainingCourse1 that came from the TestData. accdb database should now appear in the TrainingCourse table.

12. Close both open tables (TrainingCourse1 and TrainingCourse).

13. In the Navigation pane select the **TrainingCourse1** table and press **Delete** on your keyboard to delete this table. Click **Yes**, to confirm the deletion.

REUSING SAVED IMPORTS

If for any reason you want to keep the TrainingCourse1 in your database, you can easily bring it back thanks to the import steps that you saved in the previous Hands-On. In the Import & Link group of the Ribbon's External Data tab you will find the Saved Imports button. When clicked, this button opens the Manage Data Tasks window with two tabs for Saved Imports and Saved Exports. The Saved Imports tab lists your saved import specification (Figure 5.38). If you'd like to change the name and / or description of your import, click the text you want to edit and enter new text.

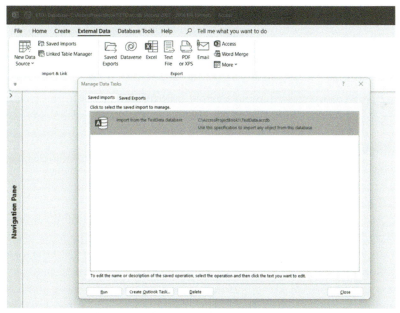

FIGURE 5.38. Saved imports and exports can be accessed and run again without a Wizard from the Manage Data Task window.

To repeat the saved import, click the Run button. Access will notify you that all objects were imported successfully and after you click OK to confirm this message, click Close to exit the Manage Data Tasks window.

If you followed exactly the steps mentioned in this section, the Training-Course1 table should appear again in the Navigation pane of the ETD database.

Let's keep it there for a while as it may come useful when you start working with queries in a later chapter.

HOW TO DEAL WITH UNSUCCESSFUL IMPORTS

Data imports can be very tricky. Many things can go wrong starting with the data source. If it is not formatted in the way Access expects it, you can expect the unexpected. You can be frustrated with the error messages that point you to nowhere as to how resolve your import failures. But, if you go back to the source of data and review the spellings of the fields used, their data types, and fix the issues that may have confused Access, your next attempt at import may produce a more user-friendly message of how to get the import working. You may be lucky with the full or partial import. The latter is when Access manages to import data for only some fields. The records for the fields that cannot be imported are then output to an error table which will appear in the Navigation pane. The error table will have a column with the type of error encountered and the field and row where the error occurred. One of the common errors is a type conversion failure which often occurs with .csv text files. Whenever field types don't match Access will be having trouble putting the data into the fields. For example, if you have a Number or Date field and the data in these fields contain text such as "N/A," "Unknown," and so on, Access recognizes that these are not valid numbers or dates, so it produces the "type conversion" error. Many times, when asked for the field types, change the field type of the problem field to Text and try to import. If the import succeeds you can always change your field type back to the way it was by going to Design View.

The Access Import Wizard offers different screens depending on whether you selected to create a new table or append data to an existing table and what kind of import you are trying to perform (text, Excel, XML/HTML file, or a database). Some of the screens allow you to change the data types of fields, others don't. If you click the Advanced button, you may be able to fix some of the issues by changing the default encoding. Again, this is a trial-and-error approach. If you try enough times, you may find a fix or workaround for your issue. If the import in one format seems to always fail, try to get this data into another format, or change the text file extension from .csv to .txt. This may work better for you, or it may give you a friendlier message of what's wrong. You can also try to import the data to a new table and then copy the data from it to your desired table. It is a good practice to always make a backup copy of your table prior to import and do import to this table first to see if it succeeds.

When your table is related to other tables it will take more steps to fix the damage that may have been created by a partial import of data. If you decide to delete the corrupted table and replace it with the backup, Access will require that you first remove the table from a relationship. Once you fix the issue you are having, you can recreate the broken relationship. As you can see, there is no one solution to getting the import process work at first try. Most often your source data will come from other people who are not aware that the special characters or format applied to their data output will affect your import. Always check your source data file first, and good luck with your imports.

IMPORTING WORKSHEET RANGES

The next step in our data importing marathon is populating the TrainingSession table. If you review the relationship diagram that you created in Chapter 4, you will see that this table has four foreign key fields (CourseID, ScheduleID, InstructorID, and LocationID) that link to the data in the following four tables: Traini ngCourse, TrainingSchedule, Instructors, and TrainingCourseLocatons. Because there is a many-to-many relationship between the Instructors and the Training-Session tables, we have used a junction table SessionInstructor that contains foreign keys that relate back to the primary keys of these two tables. Figure 5.39 depicts data in the Excel worksheet that serves as a source for your next import process. Notice that the worksheet contains the internal title in the first row.

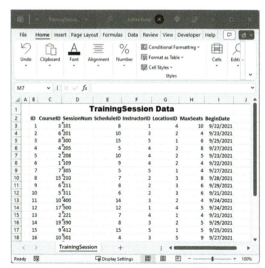

FIGURE 5.39. The TrainingSession.xlsx worksheet provides data for the TrainingSession table.

The simple Import Access Wizard that you have so far worked with will find this setup too confusing to work with. After analyzing the data, Access will display this message:

"The first row contains some data that can't be used for valid Access field names. In these cases, the Wizard will automatically assign valid field names."

When you click OK, to confirm this message, Access adds new column headings, and it looks quite messy. Your original headings are now listed as a data row (see Figure 5.40). There is no option here to tell Access to disregard the first row of the worksheet and treat the second row as the field headings. When you click the Finish button, Access displays a message:

"Field 'TrainingSession Data' doesn't exist in destination table 'TrainingSession'".

When you click OK in confirmation to this message, another message is displayed:

"An error occurred trying to import file 'C:\AccessProjectBook1\TrainingSession.xlsx'. The file was not imported."

You must then abandon the import, and do what?

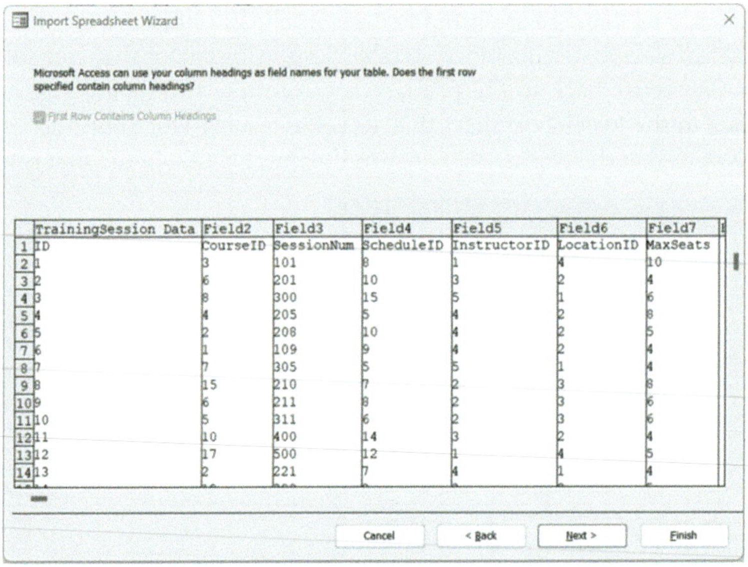

FIGURE 5.40. The Access Spreadsheet Wizard is having trouble correctly recognizing field headings in some spreadsheets.

Yes, you could easily delete the first row from the worksheet to allow the Access Spreadsheet Wizard to handle the import without any issues, but what if this not a viable solution? What if the training session data comes in daily and the import process needs to be fully automated?

If you're proficient in Excel you could define $B$2:$I$26 as the range to import using the Formulas | Define Name option in the Defined Names group of the Formulas tab. You would then select that defined name in the Access Spreadsheet Wizard. However, because we are in the process of learning Access, let's find out how to deal with this scenario.

The good news is that Access offers the `TransferSpreadsheet` method of the `DoCmd` object. With the `TransferSpreadsheet` method you can specify a range of cells you want to import. You can do this in a macro or from a Visual Basic editor screen. At this point in your Access learning, we will go with the Visual Basic, as it requires fewer setup steps.

As mentioned earlier in this book, Visual Basic for Applications (VBA) is a programming language that allows you to add new functionality to your application or automate many repetitive tasks. For example, instead of performing operations using a mouse, keyboard, or dialog box, you can write VBA code. Access, like other Microsoft 365 applications, has a built-in Visual Basic editor where you can write simple or complex code. In the next Hands-On you will learn how to use Visual Basic editor's scratchpad, known as *Immediate Window*, to write and execute the `TransferSpreadsheet` method, so that the data from the TrainingCourse.xlsx file is successfully inserted into the equivalent Access table without the need of editing the Excel source file.

Let's begin by examining the syntax of the `TransferSpreadsheet` method.

A syntax is a set of rules you must follow to create a valid programming statement. `DoCmd` object in Access has many methods that allow you to perform tasks such as opening windows, forms, reports, setting values of various controls, or performing various database operations. To import your data, you will begin with the following command:

```
DoCmd.TransferSpreadsheet
```

Most of the methods of the `DoCmd` object have *parameters*. Parameters, also referred to as *arguments*, are values that are needed for a method to do something. Some parameters are required, while others are optional. If you omit optional parameters, the parameters assume the default values for the method. The parameters for the `TransferSpreadsheet` method are listed in Table 5.1.

TABLE 5.1 Parameters of the TransferSpreadsheet Method

Name	Required/Optional	Data Type	Description
TransferType	Optional	AcDataTransferType	The transfer type you want to make. The following transfer types are allowed: 1. acExport 2. acImport 3. acLink The default is acImport.
SpreadsheetType	Optional	AcSpreadsheetType	The type of spreadsheet to import from, export to, or link to. We will use the acSpreadsheetTypeExcel12Xml data type for importing data from Microsoft Excel 2010–2021 xlsx files.
TableName	Optional	Variant	The name of the Access table you want to import data into, export spreadsheet data from, or link spreadsheet data to.
FileName	Optional	Variant	The file name and the path of the spreadsheet that you want to import from, export to, or link to.
HasFieldNames	Optional	Variant	Use True (1) to use the first row of the spreadsheet as field names. Use False (0) to treat the first row of the spreadsheet as normal data. If this argument is omitted, the default (False) is assumed.
Range	Optional	Variant	A valid range of cells or the name of a range in the spreadsheet. This argument only applies to importing data.
UseOA	Optional	Variant	This argument is not supported.

Using Table 5.1 as a guide. The following statement will import the spreadsheet **C:\AccessProjectBook1\TrainingSession.xlsx** into a table named TrainingSession, importing only the range B2:I26, while treating the first row in the specified range as containing field names.

```
DoCmd.TransferSpreadsheet acImport, acSpreadsheetTypeEx-
cel12Xml, "Copy of TrainingSession", "C:\AccessProject-
Book1\TrainingSession.xlsx", True,"B2:I26"
```

Notice that parameters are separated by a comma and are provided in the order they are listed in Table 5.1 above. Let's proceed to Hands-On 5.7 to find out where to enter and how to run this statement.

Hands-On 5.7   Importing a Spreadsheet Range

1. Create a copy of the **TrainingSession** table with the default name **Copy of TrainingSession** just in case anything goes wrong with the import you are about to perform.
2. In the ETD database window, choose the Database Tools tab and select **Visual Basic** (Figure 5.41).

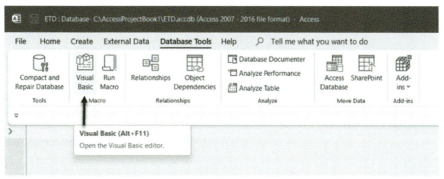

FIGURE 5.41. Activating Visual Basic Editor in Access.

Access loads its programming interface known as *VBE* (Visual Basic Editor) as shown in Figure 5.42. Notice that this is a separate window and while it is open you still have access to your ETD database. The VBE window can be made smaller or maximized to cover the entire screen. The Editor has its own menu and toolbars. It also has a project and properties window shown by default. The gray area on the right-hand side is a placeholder for loading modules where you can write programming code or load existing code as well as work with various supplemental windows. We will not go into details of using the programming environment in this chapter. All we need to do is perform our import task, so let's just focus on the very tool we need: the Immediate Window.

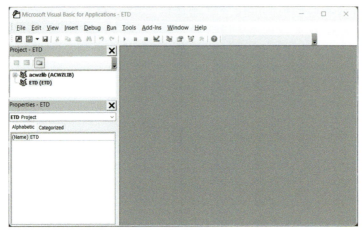

FIGURE 5.42. The VBE Screen on initial load.

3. From the VBE Editor menu, choose **View | Immediate Window**. Keep in mind that you can also use the keyboard shortcut: Ctrl+G (see Figure 5.43).

Access opens a window that looks like a little notepad. It has the word "Immediate" in its title bar. You can make this window bigger or smaller to suit your needs. You can move it anywhere in the VBE window, or you can dock it, so it always appears in the same area of the screen. The Docking setting can be turned on and off from the Docking tab in the Options dialog box (Tools | Options). Any Access command you type in this window is executed simply by pressing the Enter key. This window is a programmer's scratch pad where statements can be tested and executed before putting them permanently in your programming code.

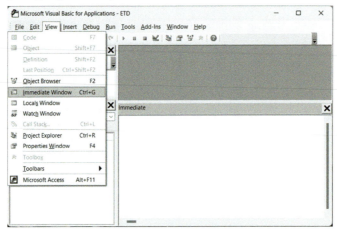

FIGURE 5.43. The Immediate window loaded into VBE screen.

> **NOTE**
>
> *Steps 4 through 12 guide you through the process of entering the* `TransferSpreadsheet` *instruction in the Immediate Window so that you can see how Access helps you with the syntax rules. Refrain from pressing the Enter key while typing your complete statement, until you are instructed to do so. Any time you press Enter you tell Access that the instruction on the line where the cursor is currently located should be executed. Remember that you don't want to execute anything until it is completed and checked for misspellings. To activate a specific line in the Immediate window without using an Enter key, simply click on that line.*

4. On the first line of the Immediate window type `DoCmd` followed by aperiod:

   `DoCmd.`

   As soon as you enter the period after the `DoCmd`, Access displays the drop-down listing the methods that the `DoCmd` object can accept. All methods are listed alphabetically.

5. While in the drop-down, type the letter T and notice that the list now shows the methods starting with this letter. Move to `TransferSpreadsheet` using the down key on your keyboard and press the Tab key.

   If you made a mistake and want to start over, simply delete everything starting from the period. Enter period again and you should see a list of options. When you perform this step correctly, Access should enter `DoCmd.Transfer-Spreadsheet` in the Immediate window. The next step will require entering some parameters.

6. Press the **Spacebar** and notice that Access displays the entire syntax of the `TransferSpreadsheet` method (Figure 5.44) giving you the names and possible values of parameters.

FIGURE 5.44. Built-in IntelliSense technology automatically provides you with syntax and programming assistance while you are entering VBA instructions.

7. Type the letter "a" and Access will list the possible values. Scroll down to `acImport` and press **Tab** and **enter a comma**.

   Access displays the drop-down with the types of spreadsheet format you can use.

8. Select the `acSpreadsheetTypeExcel12Xml` and press **Tab** and **enter a comma**.

   Notice that Access now highlights the `TableName` parameter in the syntax waiting for you to enter the name of the table.

9. Enter **"TrainingSession"** surrounding it by double quotes and follow it by the **comma**.

   Now Access expects the `FileName` parameter.

10. Ether the full path to the Excel file surrounded by double quotes: **"C:\ AccessProjectBook1\TrainingSession.xlsx"**

11. Enter a **comma** and type **True** to tell Access that the first row in the range has field names.

12. Enter a **comma** and type the range surrounded by double quotes: **"B2:I26"**.

    You have completed the statement that gives Access all the details it needs to proceed with the import. Double-check that there are no errors in the instruction you have entered (Figure 5.45).

FIGURE 5.45. The complete instruction to import data from an Excel range.

13. Make sure the cursor is on the same line as the instruction you typed and press the **Enter** key.

    Access goes to work and if it finds any issues with the import, you will see an error message, otherwise you can assume that the import was processed without any flaws.

    The type of error message you receive will depend on whether the error is with the command you entered, or the incompatible data found in the source file. If your entry was correct but there were some issues with the import data, you should get the error message shown in Figure 5.46. Access tells you that it was unable to append all the data to the table, and that it found five records with key violations. You can either proceed to import only the valid records or abandon this import and retry it later after you have located and fixed the records that violate referential integrity for a relationship defined between tables.

FIGURE 5.46. Access finds problems during the import process.

14. Click **No** to the message and click **OK** when Access displays the message that operation was canceled by user.

How do you find exactly what data has key violations? An easy way to find out is to open the Excel source file and put a filter on the key fields and verify each list against the primary keys used in the corresponding tables.

15. Open the **TrainingSession.xlsx** file from your Companion files. Select any field name in the heading row and press **Ctrl+Shift+L** to turn the filter on. For each table that participates in the relationship with the TrainingSession table check if the keys listed in the source spreadsheet dropdowns exist in the table that the key is pointing to. If the key does not exist, then you have found the key violation.

16. Open the **TrainingSession_badData.xlsx** file in the Companion files which shows the offending rows (Figure 5.47) that Access had trouble processing. Notice that they all have a bad key in the LocationID column. There is no Location ID equal to 5 in the TrainingCourseLocations table.

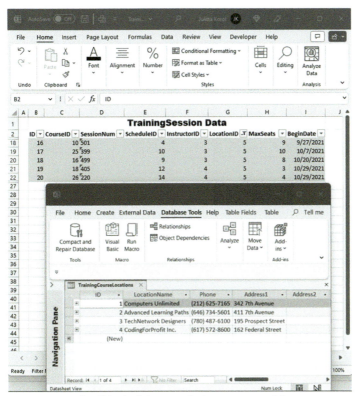

FIGURE 5.47. Identifying bad data rows in the source spreadsheet.

The TrainingSession_badDataFixed.xlsx file in the Companion files contains the correct data for the import. The invalid LocationID was replaced with valid references. Let's use this file as the new data source for the import.

17. Activate the Visual Basic Editor screen and change the source file name to in the command you typed earlier in the Immediate window.

NOTE	*If you closed the Visual Basic screen, please go back to the beginning of this Hands-On to repeat the import steps. Be sure to use the TrainingSession_badDataFixed.xlsx as the source of the import in any references that refer to the spreadsheet file.*

The revised command is shown below. Make sure to enter it on one line in the Immediate window.

```
DoCmd.TransferSpreadsheet acImport,acSpreadsheetTypeExcel12Xml,
"TrainingSession","C:\AccessProjectBook1\TrainingSession_bad-
DataFixed.xlsx", True, "B2:I26"
```

18. Position the cursor anywhere on the line with the revised command and press **Enter** to proceed with the import.

This time Access runs the command without any issues. You should see the blinking cursor on the second line in the Immediate window, indicating that all is well.

You can now close this window and exit the Visual Basic Editor screen.

19. In the Visual Basic Editor screen, choose **File | Close and Return to Microsoft Access**.

20. Double-check that all the data from the worksheet is now available in the **TrainingSession** table.

The last Hands-On was to demonstrate that no matter what import technique you use, some imports will present you with many challenges. Depending on your source data and the design of your database tables, you may have hard time identifying bad records. If this happens, do not despair. Take a break and have another look at the data later or ask a colleague to work with you on the issue. It's always easier to fix the bad data before it gets into the database. Each time you encounter a problem with a data import, make a note of its nature, and a fix that you applied to resolve the issue. After a while you will have a list of common issues to watch for and check before performing the import.

Action Item 5.4

Earlier in this chapter you learned about subdatasheets. Open the TrainingSession table and embed in in the following tables: TrainingCourseLocations and Room. The result is shown in Figure 5.48 below. Save your changes in the TrainingSession table and close it when you are finished.

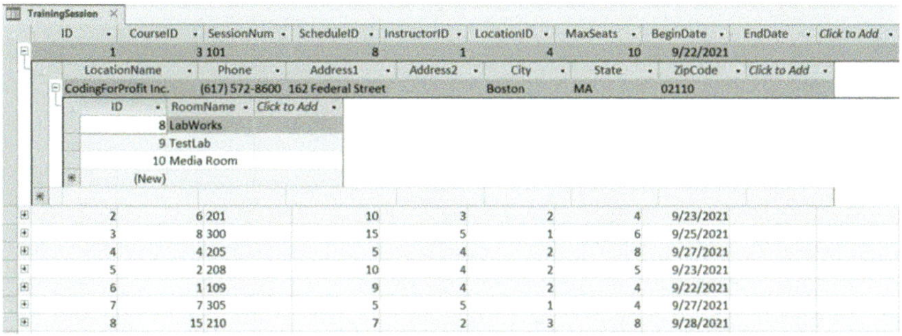

TrainingSession

ID	CourseID	SessionNum	ScheduleID	InstructorID	LocationID	MaxSeats	BeginDate	EndDate	Click to Add
1	3	101	8	1	4	10	9/22/2021		

LocationName	Phone	Address1	Address2	City	State	ZipCode	Click to Add
CodingForProfit Inc.	(617) 572-8600	162 Federal Street		Boston	MA	02110	

ID	RoomName	Click to Add
8	LabWorks	
9	TestLab	
10	Media Room	
(New)		

ID	CourseID	SessionNum	ScheduleID	InstructorID	LocationID	MaxSeats	BeginDate	EndDate	Click to Add
2	6	201	10	3	2	4	9/23/2021		
3	8	300	15	5	1	6	9/25/2021		
4	4	205	5	4	2	8	9/27/2021		
5	2	208	10	4	2	5	9/23/2021		
6	1	109	9	4	2	4	9/22/2021		
7	7	305	5	5	1	4	9/27/2021		
8	15	210	7	2	3	8	9/28/2021		

FIGURE 5.48. Embedding subdatasheets into the TrainingSession Datasheet.

Action Item 5.5

The Registration.xlsx workbook in the Companion files provides data for the Registration table. Use the Access Import Wizard to populate this table. Figure 5.49 displays the Registration table after the import.

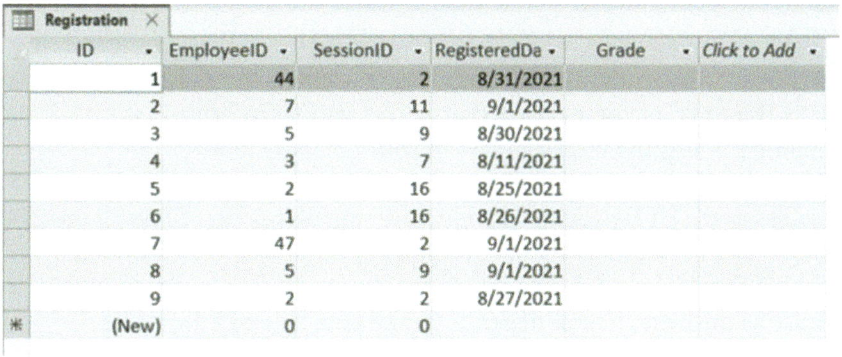

Registration

ID	EmployeeID	SessionID	RegisteredDa	Grade	Click to Add
1	44	2	8/31/2021		
2	7	11	9/1/2021		
3	5	9	8/30/2021		
4	3	7	8/11/2021		
5	2	16	8/25/2021		
6	1	16	8/26/2021		
7	47	2	9/1/2021		
8	5	9	9/1/2021		
9	2	2	8/27/2021		
(New)	0	0			

FIGURE 5.49. The Registration table populated with data.

Action Item 5.6

The **SessionInstructor.xml** file in the Companion files provides data for the SessionInstructor table. Use the Access Import Wizard to populate this table.

Figure 5.50 displays the ImportXML dialog box and the error you should receive upon clicking the OK button.

FIGURE 5.50. Importing XML data results in some import errors.

When you click OK to dismiss the message box, look for the ImportErrors table in the Navigation pane. While this table shows the type of error Access encountered during the data import, it does not tell you which record from the .xml file was not inserted (see Figure 5.51).

FIGURE 5.51. Access generates the ImportErrors table when it runs into issues during the import operation.

How do you find exactly which record is missing in the TrainingSession table? This is the topic of the next chapter where you learn how to work with data, including finding any discrepancies in your database tables.

If you completed all Action Items and Hands-On exercises in this chapter, all the tables in the ETD database should now have some data. Close all open tables and exit Access. If for any reason you skipped some sections in this chapter, this is a good time to go back and revisit the topic and its corresponding required exercise as the next chapter depends on the data being in the tables.

SUMMARY

In this chapter, you have become an Access Import wizard. You have learned many useful techniques of bringing data to your Access database from various external sources (text and XML files, Excel workbooks, and Access databases). You were also presented with common issues that could occur while importing data. While some import issues can be easily resolved by modifying a source file or simply restarting Access, others require more investigative skills which will be covered in the next chapter. Once you learn about queries and data joins, you'll be able to select and isolate records, find records that have no related records in another table, locate records with duplicate field values, and filter and sort your data according to your needs. As with data imports, there are multitude of query types that you can use to accomplish a specific task. We'll cover them all so get ready for a chapter full of database activities and new terminology.

Part **III**

CREATE AND WORK WITH QUERIES

P art III teaches you essential database operations skills such as finding, adding, updating, and deleting records. You learn how to use the Query Wizard, Query Design View as well as the Structured Query Language (SQL) to ask various questions of the data in your database. You will start by creating Select queries that search for information in the database tables based on the criteria you specify. You will find out how to use parameters to make your queries dynamic and learn how to use expressions and functions to analyze, calculate, group, and summarize data. Next, you will progress to another category of queries, known as Action queries, which are designed to manipulate data by inserting new data into a new table, deleting data from a table, or appending to data already in a table based on some criteria.

Chapter **6**

CREATING AND
WORKING WITH
SELECT QUERIES

N ow that you've brought initial data to your ETD database, it's time to learn how to work with the information you've stored in various tables. Next to tables, queries are the most important object in a database. To help you understand the concept of queries in Access, I have called upon the newest tool, the new AI-powered chat mode of Microsoft Bing. Here is the answer that AI (Artificial Intelligence) provided to the following topic:

EXPLAIN THE CONCEPT OF QUERIES AS USED
IN AN ACCESS DATABASE

"A query is a request for data results or action on the data from your database. You can use queries to find specific data by filtering on criteria, calculate or summarize data, automate data management tasks, or change data in your tables.

There are different types of queries depending on the task you want to perform. The most common type is a Select query, which retrieves data from one or more tables and displays it in a datasheet. You can also create action queries, which modify or delete data in your tables, such as update, append, delete, or make table queries."

I hope this helps you understand the concept of queries in Access.

With the AI-powered chat mode of Microsoft Bing you can now ask any question related to the topic you are learning if you know the key words. The previous response is just a partial answer, it goes on and on explaining how to use the specific tools like the Query Wizard or the Query Design View in Access, following with an example of how you can create a Select query to show the product names and prices from a Products table. While the example is not related to your database, it gives you an idea of how to achieve a specific task. If you need more details, you can ask any follow-up questions to continue learning about the specific topic. We will call upon the AI tool as we move through the rest of this book to guide us with the Access database and some maintenance tasks.

Action Item 6.1

You will need the Edge browser and an internet connection.

To activate the AI-powered chat mode in Windows 11, click the Bing logo next the Search bar. You can also open the Edge browser, click the Discover (Ctrl+Shift+.) Bing button at the top right corner of the window and enter your question in the New topic area. Figure 6.1 shows the AI generated answer to my inquiry.

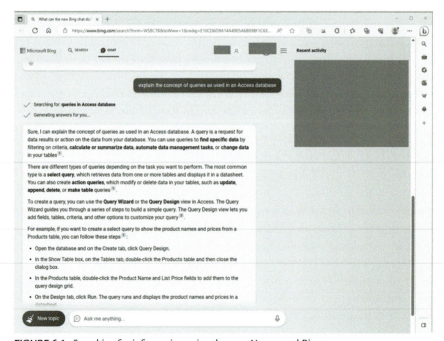

FIGURE 6.1. Searching for information using the new AI-powered Bing.

You can also use ChatGPT which just like Bing is an AI chatbot. You can try it at chat.openai.com. Bing and ChatGPT use a large language model known a s GPT, developed by OpenAI. Bing uses a more advanced version of GPT, called

GPT-4 which is more powerful and accurate than the older GPT-3.5 that Chat-GPT at the time of this writing uses. Both chatbots have different strengths and weakness, but both can help you in performing various tasks, such as writing code, finding up-to-date information or help you write in a specific style.

CREATING A QUERY

Instead of opening a specific table to view all the data, you can create a Select query that retrieves only the records that you need. Access provides a few methods of achieving this task. In this section you will work with the Queries group of the Access Ribbon's Create tab. There are two buttons available in the Queries group: Query Wizard and Query Design. We'll begin with the built-in Query Wizard that will guide you through creating your first query. Before you get started building your query it is a good idea to open the table or tables that contain the data you want to retrieve. In this first example, your manager requested that you give him a list of instructors that live in Boston. You only need to provide their first name, last name, and the home phone number. It is important to always get the exact query criteria before creating a query. This will save you lots of unnecessary revisions later. The table Instructors currently contains two persons that meet our query criteria. Let's get the Query Wizard to work on this task with us.

⊙ Hands-On 6.1   Retrieving Data With the Query Wizard

1. Open the **ETD** database.
2. Click the **Query Wizard** button in the Queries group of the **Create** tab. Access displays the New Query dialog box as shown in Figure 6.2. As you can see Access offers four types of queries you can create using the Wizard:

    - Simple Query Wizard creates a Select query from the fields you pick.
    - Crosstab Query Wizard creates a crosstab query that displays data in a compact, spreadsheet-like format.
    - Find Duplicate Query Wizard creates a query that finds records with duplicate field values in a single table or query.
    - Find Unmatched Query Wizard creates a query that finds records in one table that have no related records in another table.

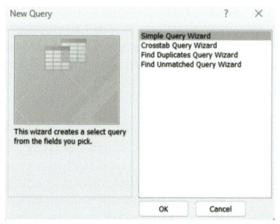

FIGURE 6.2. The New Query dialog box of the Query Wizard presents four types of queries you can create.

3. With the **Simple Query Wizard** selected, click **OK**.

   Access now prompts you to select the table or query that contains the source information and choose the fields you want to show in the query.

4. Choose the table **Instructors** from the Tables/Queries drop-down and select the fields as shown in Figure 6.3. Note that > moves the single field to the selected fields box, and >> moves all the fields. The < and << will reverse the previous actions. After moving a field to the Selected Fields box, the field no longer appears in the Available Fields box.

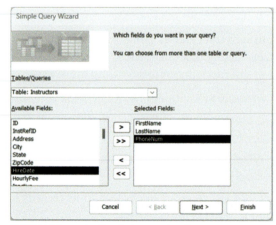

FIGURE 6.3. In the Simple Query Wizard screen you are prompted for the table name and the fields that should be included in your query.

5. Click the **Next** button to continue.

Now you are asked for the name of your query. Access suggests the name of the query based on the table name. You can revise the name to make it more specific and help to identify it easier as you create more queries using the same table. You can also change the name of the query in the Navigation pane after you've created your query.

6. Enter **Boston Instructors** for the name of your query (see Figure 6.4).

At this point Access has all the information the Wizards needs to create your query. However, you must decide for yourself if the information you supplied is enough for Access to create the outcome you need. As you recall, in this scenario, you need to get only the instructors that live in Boston. Access does not know this information therefore you will need to modify the query to get only the records you need.

7. Choose the **Modify the query design** option button and click **Finish**.

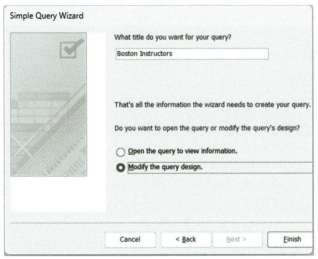

FIGURE 6.4. The last step in the Simple Query Wizard is assigning the name to your query and determining whether your query is finished or needs some modifications to meet the given criteria.

Access opens the Boston Instructors query in the Query Design View where the top portion of the screen displays the table Instructors, and the bottom area lists the columns (fields) you selected while working with the Query Wizard (see Figure 6.5). Notice that the Select button is currently highlighted in the Query Type group of the Query Design tab.

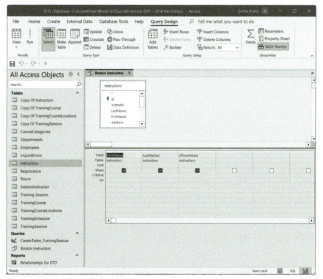

FIGURE 6.5. The Query Design View allows you to modify a query or create another query from scratch.

If you run this query as it was created by the Query Wizard, you should get a list of all Instructors.

NOTE	*You may have noticed that a table you added to a query contains an asterisk (∗) above the name of the first field. This asterisk is a wildcard character that matches zero or more characters. It can also be used to select all the fields from a table or specify a pattern for the criteria of a query. For example, if you drag the asterisk from the filed list to the design grid, you will select all the fields from that table.*

8. Click the Run button in the Results group of the Query Design tab to perform the actions specified in the query. Figure 6.6 shows the Instructors list generated by the query. Let's revise the query so it meets our criteria.

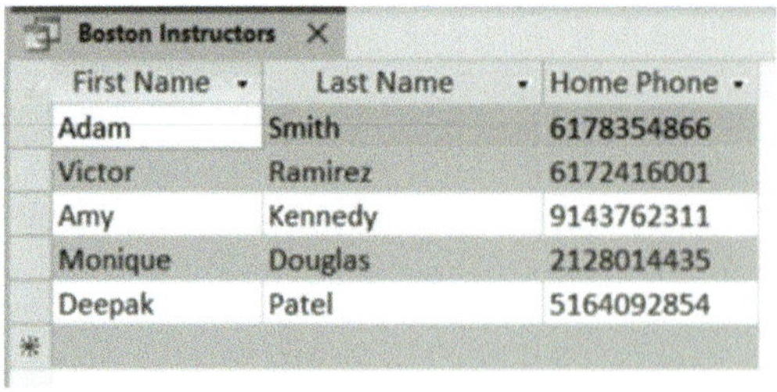

First Name •	Last Name •	Home Phone •
Adam	Smith	6178354866
Victor	Ramirez	6172416001
Amy	Kennedy	9143762311
Monique	Douglas	2128014435
Deepak	Patel	5164092854

FIGURE 6.6. The Datasheet view shows the results generated by the query.

9. Return to the Query Design View by clicking the **View** button on the Home tab.

   To meet the query criteria given by our manager, we will need to add another field to the query that will allow us to specify the instructor's city.

10. Click in the Field row of the first empty column in the Query Design View and choose **City** from the list of fields. You can also drag the City field from the fields listed in the table Instructors (shown in the top area of the Query Design) and drop it in the first empty column. Use the method you prefer. In the Criteria row of the City column, enter Boston. Access will add quotation marks to indicate that entry as a text string. Uncheck the checkbox in the Show row of the City column to ensure that it does not appear in the final list. See Figure 6.7 for the revised query.

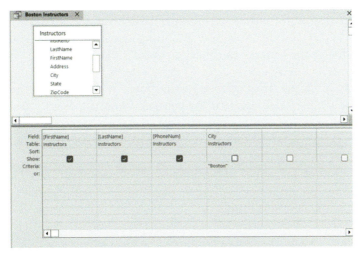

FIGURE 6.7. Revising the Select query to add the specified criteria.

11. Click the Run button to run the revised query.

   The Datasheet view should now list three columns of data for two instructors that live in Boston.

12. Close the Boston Instructors query. Access should detect that you have made changes to the query design. Click **Yes** to save your changes.

   The Boston Instructors query can now be run at any time by double-clicking its name in the Queries section of the Database Navigation pane. At any time, you can open the query in the Design View and modify it if you manager requests any changes.

Suppose your manager forgot to ask you to include the instructor's address. On your own, modify the Boston Instructors query to add the address field. You can do this by dragging and dropping the Address field on the top of the column City in the design grid. You should see a small icon with the plus sign when you are ready to drop the field. If you make a mistake, you can select the entire column by clicking in the white bar above the column and pressing Delete.

What if the manager decided to add to the existing list any instructors living in New York? Note that the lower grid of the Query Design View contains an "or" row. This is a place for an additional criterion. So, if you enter "New York" in the "or" row of the City column and run this query, you should get one extra record in your result set because we have one instructor living in New York.

13. If you tried the previous scenarios, return the query to the original state where we have three columns for instructors living only in Boston.

Note that when you modify the query by adding new specifications you may also need to change the name of the query to make it meaningful.

As you have seen in the previous Hands-On, the Query Wizard provides an easy start in creating simple Select queries. As you gain more experience working with queries, you may find out that it is quicker and more convenient to create your own queries from scratch. You can do this by using the Query Design button in the Queries group of the Create tab.

Let's create another query that will produce a list of employees sorted by the department name and employee last name. This time we will use the Query Design instead of the Query Wizard.

⊙ Hands-On 6.2　Retrieving Data Using Query Design

1. To start working with a new blank query, click the **Query Design** button in the Queries group of the **Create** tab.

Query Design will open with the Add Tables pane visible on the right-hand side. This pane has four tabs: Tables, Links, Queries, and All. The Queries tab displays all the queries available in the database. Currently you have a Boston Instructors query that you created in the previous Hands-On. Any new query you create can be based on existing queries or tables, or both, as well linked tables. A linked table is a table that is stored in another database or data source, such as Excel or SharePoint, but can be used in Access like a regular table. Linked tables are covered later in this book. Linked tables can help you avoid data duplication and keep your data consistent across different sources.

2. In the **Add Tables** pane, select the **Tables** tab. Access will display the names of all the tables in the database. Click the **Departments** table, and while holding the **Ctrl** key, click the Employees table. With both tables selected, click the **Add Selected Tables** button.

    The Employees and Department tables are now added to the top pane of the Query Design. To see all the fields available in the Employees table, drag down the bottom border of the box representing the Employees table. Notice that the Employees table is joined with the table Departments by the DepartmentID field. With the correct joins already in place, all you need to do now is add the required fields to your query.

3. Click and drag the following fields from the tables to the blank columns in the lower part of the Query Design View: **DepartmentName**, **EmpCode**, **FirstName** and **LastName**.

4. In the **Sort** row of the **DepartmentName** column in the Query Design grid, choose **Ascending** to apply a sorting scheme to query results. Also choose the **Ascending** order in the **Sort** row of the **LastName** column. The completed query is shown in Figure 6.8.

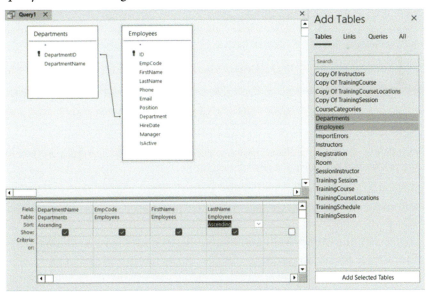

FIGURE 6.8. Creating a Select query from scratch using the Query Design View.

5. Run the completed query by clicking the Run button in the Results group of the Query Design tab.

    The query produces a list of employees by each Department sorted alphabetically in ascending order. Notice that some of the employees are missing an entry in the EmpCode field. This is something we can correct later in this chapter by using another type of query. Figure 6.9 shows the query results.

DepartmentName	EmpCode	FirstName	LastName
Accounting	JRROW000060614	James	Harrow
Accounting	MSTON000072300	Michael	Livingston
Accounting	LGUEZ000011109	Laura	Rodriguez
Accounting	RLSKI000120101	Robert	Wolski
Administration	OELLY000091202	Oscar	Donelly
Administration	KELLA000022712	Kathy	Matella
Administration	MLINA000091202	Margaret	Molina
Administration		Jessica	Roberts
Administration	JORTH000092316	John	Worth
Business Development	LDAMS000052301	Lillian	Adams
Business Development	RRADO000052301	Roberto	Dorado
Business Development	ATYKA000021906	Amanda	Partyka
Business Development	DNCER000040409	Douglas	Spencer
Customer Service	JDERA000060106	Julia	Bandera
Customer Service	ZRUCH000090914	Zenon	Baruch
Customer Service	JNICI000031317	Joanne	Cinnici
Customer Service		David	Lebovitz
Customer Service	MORRE000061507	Maria	Torre
Engineering		George	Khan
Engineering	PZMAN000081213	Peter	Rotzman
Engineering	SMITH000072314	Steven	Smith
Facilities Management	SLEIN000050104	Steven	Klein
Facilities Management	AMERY000111503	Alexandra	Montgomery
Facilities Management	PORAN000032008	Peter	Moran
IT	WWSKI000012311	William	Borowski
IT	JMPOS000051405	Jose	Campos

Record: 1 of 48   No Filter   Search

FIGURE 6.9. When you run a Select query you can often uncover some discrepancies in your data that may be fixed by creating and running other types of queries.

Bear in mind that when you create a query in the Query Design View Access automatically assigns a default name to your query such as Query1, Query2, and so on.

6. Right click the **Query1** tab and choose **Save**. In the Save As dialog box, enter **Employees by Department** as the new query name and click **OK**.

7. Close the Employees by Department Datasheet view.
   Notice that the name of your new query now appears in the Queries group of the Database Navigation pane.

You have now created two simple Select queries that retrieve data from the ETD database from one and more tables using the specified criteria and sorting the resulting data in a specified order. As stated earlier, you can modify your queries any time to fit your needs. You can include additional tables, fields, criteria, or change the sorting scheme. As Select queries simply display your data, you can run them at any time without doing any harm to your data. You can use your Select queries as a basis for forms and reports that we'll design in subsequent chapters.

Filtering a Query

At times you may want to apply a filter to a query to add extra criteria to search results in order to narrow down the results you need to focus on. The simplest way of filtering is to filter by Selection where you simply select any field returned by a query and filter the query results on that field. For example, in the Employees by Department query, you may want to only view the employees of the Customer Service department. To quickly produce the required view without modifying the query, click the down arrow in the DepartmentName column, deselect the (Select All) check box, check the Customer Service and click OK (see Figure 6.10).

FIGURE 6.10. Filtering a query using Filter by Selection.

After applying the filter, only the employees in the Customer Service department will be shown. When you no longer require a filtered view of your query, simply deselect the **Toggle Filter** button in the **Sort & Filter** group of the **Home** tab.

Another way of filtering your query results is **Filter by Form** option found in the **Advanced** command of the **Sort & Filter** group of the **Home** tab. When you use this option, each column of your data will be replaced by a combo box and each value in the combo box represents a unique value in the column of data as shown in Figure 6.11.

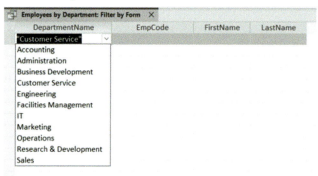

FIGURE 6.11. Filtering a query using Filter by Form.

To display specific data, select the unique option in the list and then click the Toggle Filter button in the Sort & Filter group of the Home tab. Using the Filter by Form you can easily filter your data from any column. Click the Toggle Filter button again to remove the filter.

There is also a third way of filtering your query results by using an Advanced Filter/Sort option in the Advanced command of the Sort & Filter group of the Home tab, as shown in Figure 6.12.

FIGURE 6.12. Selecting an Advanced Filter/Sort option.

Using the option selected in Figure 6.12, Access creates a copy of your query and displays it in the Query Design View. Here you can specify what criteria you want to use to filter with. Let's say, you want to find if there is any employee in the Customer Service department whose Last name begins with the letter "B" (see Figure 6.13 for the criteria used for this filter).

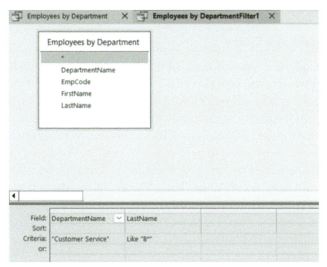

FIGURE 6.13. Filtering a query using an Advanced Filter/Sort option.

To create the filter, simply select the required field in the Field cell and enter the expression Like "B*" in the Criteria cell of the LastName column. Expressions are very helpful in building advanced filters and queries. Let's ask the Bing chatbot for some examples of expressions used in Access queries and filters. Here is the answer generated by the bot:

"Expressions are combinations of operators, constants, functions, and fields that evaluate to a single value. You can use expressions in Access queries and filters to calculate values, validate data, or set criteria. Here are some examples of expressions used in Access queries and filters:

- *To calculate the total price of an order, you can use an expression like this: =[Quantity]*[UnitPrice]*

- *To find records where the last name starts with "S", you can use an expression like this: Like "S*"*

- *To find records where the date of birth is before January 1, 1990, you can use an expression like this: <#1/1/1990#*

- *To find records where the region field is null (empty), you can use an expression like this: Is Null*

Remember, to apply the filter you must click the Toggle Filter button.

Now that we've covered creating simple Select queries and applying filters to the query results, let's look at some advanced query concepts that will be helpful in your data analysis.

Creating a Calculated Field in a Query

While creating Select queries you will most often choose existing fields from one or more tables. However, you can also add calculated fields to your query that will perform calculations based on the data that was extracted. To create a calculated field, you need to specify an expression that uses data from other columns to calculate a value for the new column. The expression can use arithmetic operators like +, -, *, / and parentheses to perform calculations. The data type of the calculated field is determined by applying the rules of data type precedence to the expressions specified in the formula. For example, let's assume that you want to see how much each instructor would earn per hour if we increased his hourly fee by 7 percent. To get the new rates, we need to access the table Instructors and multiply the instructor's hourlyFee by 1.07 and assign the result to the increasedFee column like this:

```
increasedFee = hourlyFee * 1.07
```

The increasedFee is the calculated column. We can assign any name we want to a calculated column if it is not a keyword or other reserved word. How do we go about creating this query in Access?

⊙ Hands-On 6.3   Creating a Calculated Field

1. In the ETD database, in the Create Tab, choose **Query Design**.
2. Use the Add Tables pane to add the table Instructors to your query.
   If the Add Tables is not available, click the Add Tables button in the Query Type group of the Query Design tab.
3. Add the LastName and HourlyFee fields to the Query grid. In the third column of the Query grid, in the Field row enter the following expression:
   HourlyFee * 1.07
4. Make sure to press Enter after typing the previous expression.
   Access will change your expression to: **Expr1: [HourlyFee]*1.07**
   Exp1, Expr2, and so on are the names that Access automatically assigns to each expression. The Expr1 will become the column header for the new data

that is calculated by the expression. Of course, we want a more meaningful name, so let's change it to something that makes more sense.

5. Replace **Expr1** with **increasedFee** leaving the colon and the rest of the expression intact. Figure 6.14 displays the completed query.

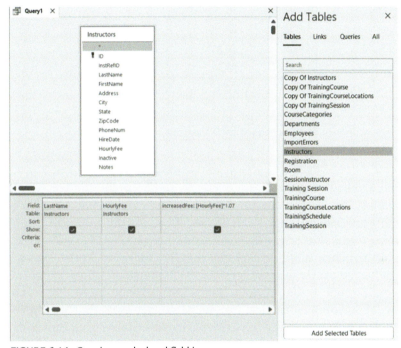

FIGURE 6.14. Creating a calculated field in a query.

6. Click the **Run** button to view the results.

The datasheet should list all the instructors and their current and the increased hourly fee. No changes are made to the actual data in the table. To make a permanent change, you would need to create an Action query, which will be covered in the next chapter. For now, let's modify the query to ensure that the first column contains the instructor's first and last name, and the entire result set is sorted in descending order by the HourlyFee column.

7. Return to the Query Design View by double-clicking the **View** button.

8. In the Sort row of the **HourlyFee** column select **Descending**.

9. Modify the Field cell of the first column of the Query grid using the following expression:

Instructor: [FirstName] + " " + [LastName]

    In the previous expression, we are telling Access to create a calculated field called Instructor by taking the value of the FirstName field and concatenating a space to it (" ") and then including the value from the LastName field.

10. Rerun the modified query. The query results are as follows:

Instructor	HourlyFee	increasedFee
Monique Douglas	$65.00	69.55
Adam Smith	$55.00	58.85
Deepak Patel	$50.00	53.5
Victor Ramirez	$50.00	53.5
Amy Kennedy	$45.00	48.15

11. Save this query as **Fee Increases by 7 Percent**.

Using the Expression Builder

    The ability to build expressions in queries is an important skill you should aim at mastering. To simplify the process of building expressions, Access provides you with a full-featured expression builder. To access this tool, open the Query Design View and either right click in a field where you want to enter an expression and then click Build or click the Builder command in the Query Setup group of the Query Design tab. Let's use the Expression Builder to improve the query you created in the previous Hands-On. It would be nice to format the increasedFee column entries as Currency.

    This can be done by using the **CCur** (Currency Conversion) function:

    increasedFee: CCur([HourlyFee]∗1.07)

◉ Hands-On 6.4   Working with the Expression Builder

1. Open in the Query Design View the **Fee Increases by 7 Percent** query you created in the previous Hands-On.

2. Right click in the **Field** cell of the **increasedFee** column and choose **Build**.

    Access displays the Expression Builder dialog where it displays an editable text box that lets you type the expression and the required operators by hand. The lower part of the dialog box shows three areas listing Expression Elements, Expression Categories, and Expression Values. Using these lists you can find the required functions, constants, and operators for your expressions. You can also access a list of common expressions like adding a current date, page number and so on. Let's look for the CCur function and apply it to our expression.

3. In the text box where you see your current expression, click in front of [HourlyFee] to position your cursor in the spot where we need to enter the function.

4. In the Expression Elements, click the plus (+) sign next to Functions and click Built-in Functions.

   In the Expression Categories list the **<All>** option is selected so the Expression Values list now displays all the built-in functions in the alphabetical order.

5. Click the **CCur** function in the **Expression Values** area.

   Notice that Access now displays the description and the format of the selected expression at the bottom of the dialog box. If you click on the CCur(expression) link you will be referred to an online help with many useful examples.

6. Double-click the **CCur** value in the **Expression Values** and notice that Access enters the selected expression in the upper edit box at the position of your cursor:

   increasedFee: «Expr» CCur(«expression») «Expr» [HourlyFee]*1.07

7. Edit your expression as follows (see Figure 6.15):

   increasedFee: CCur([HourlyFee]*1.07)

FIGURE 6.15. Creating expressions with Expression Builder.

8. Click **OK** to exit the Expression Builder.

    The updated expression is now shown in the Field cell of the increasedFee column.

9. Run your modified query and you should see the increasedFee column formatted as Currency.

10. Close your query and save the changes made in this Hands-On.

UNDERSTANDING QUERY TOTALS AND GROUPING

Now let's move to queries that will allow you to sum, count, average, find the minimum or maximum, or perform other aggregate functions on a column of data. To demonstrate this case, we will build a query that counts the number of sessions assigned to each instructor. The result of our query should look as follows:

Last Name	AssignedSessions
Douglas	7
Kennedy	6
Ramirez	5
Smith	2
Patel	2

This type of query requires that you add a Total row to the Query Design grid. Let's see how this is done.

Hands-On 6.4   Working with a Query Totals

1. Open the **Query Design** View.
2. Add the following three tables: **Instructors**, **SessionInstructor** and **TrainingSession**.
3. Drag the **LastName** from the table Instructors to the first column of the Query grid.
4. Drag the **SessionNum** from the table TrainingSession to the second column of the Query grid.
5. Click the **Totals** command button in the **Show/Hide** group of the Query Design tab.

    Notice that the Total rows appears in the Design grid and Group By appears in the row for each field in the query. If you run this query now, you should see the following output:

Last Name	SessionNum
Douglas	109
Douglas	205
Douglas	208
Douglas	220
Douglas	221
Douglas	405
Douglas	412
Kennedy	201
Kennedy	312
Kennedy	390
Kennedy	399
Kennedy	499
Kennedy	501

This is not exactly what we want. Let's revise the query to match our desired output.

6. Back in Design View, replace the Group By in the Total row of the SessionNum column with the Count function by selecting it from the drop-down.
7. In the **Sort** row of the **SessionNum** column choose **Descending**.
8. Run the modified query. This time your results should match the requirement we have set for this query.
9. Save the query as **Count Sessions by Instructor**.
Figure 6.16 shows the Query Design of this query.

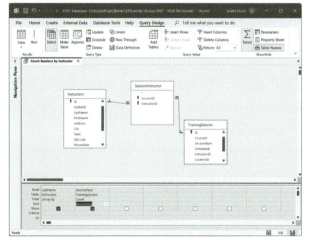

FIGURE 6.16. Creating a Query Totals.

CREATING A PARAMETER QUERY

To make your Select query more dynamic you can employ the concept of parameters. Access allows you to create a Parameter query so you can add specific search criteria every time you run a query. For example, let's say that you want to know which employees signed up for a particular course. With a Parameter Query you can prompt the user to enter a specific value before the query is run. Let's create this type of a query.

(◉) **Hands-On 6.5   Creating a Query With Parameters**

1. Choose **Create | Query Design**.
2. Add the following tables to the Query Design: **Employees**, **Registration**, **TrainingSession** and **TrainingCourse**.
3. Drag the following columns to the Query Design Grid: **FirstName**, **LastName**, and **CourseName**.
4. **Run** the Query.

    As you can see, the query you've build so far retrieves all employees who signed up for training courses. To transform this query into a parameter query you will need to add a new type of command to the Criteria row of a particular field.

5. Click View to return to Query Design.
6. In the Criteria row of the CourseName field, enter the following text (including the square brackets): **[Enter Course Name]**
7. **Run** the Query.

    You should see a popup dialog box that will prompt you to enter the course name (see Figure 6.17).

8. In the Enter Parameter dialog box, type **Core IT Skills for Everyone** and click **OK**.

    Access presents you with the list of employees that signed up for the specified training course.

FirstName	LastName	CourseName
Oscar	Donelly	Core IT Skills for Everyone
Joanne	Cinnici	Core IT Skills for Everyone
Marcus	Patel	Core IT Skills for Everyone
Joanne	Cinnici	Core IT Skills for Everyone
David	Lebovitz	Core IT Skills for Everyone

If you don't get any names, make sure you typed the name of the course exactly as it appears in the database. Notice that Joanne Cinnici name appears twice in the listing. This indicates that there is some sort of discrepancy here. You can pinpoint the problem with this record by adding more significant fields to this query and rerunning it. An employee should not be allowed to register twice for the same course / course session. We will need to return to this issue in a later chapter.

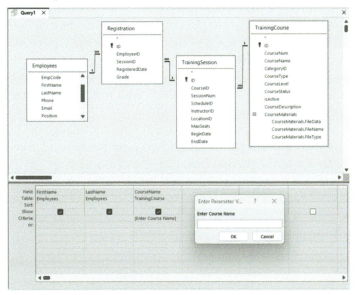

FIGURE 6.17. Creating a Parameter Query.

9. Click View to return to Query Design.

Access allows you to have multiple parameters inside a query. For example, we could add another parameter to find out if a particular employee registered for a specified course.

10. In the Criteria row of the **LastName** field, enter the following text: [**Enter Employee Last Name**]

11. **Run** the Query.

Access prompts you for the parameters in the order they appear in the layout of the fields in Design View.

12. Enter **Khan** in the first prompt and **Software Tools for Programmers** in the second prompt.

You should get one record matching the specified parameters.

Entering any values that are not in the database will not return any rows.

13. Click View to return to Query Design and remove the criteria in the **CourseName** by selecting it and pressing **Delete**.

14. Run the Query and enter **Weyna** for the employee's last name.

Access pulls out the record for Yolanda Weyna who signed up for Business Process Management Part 1.

15. Save the Query as: **qryPrmCoursesByEmployee**

As you have seen, creating a parameter query is quite simple. All you need is a prompt phrase enclosed in brackets in the criteria row of the desired field. But what if you don't know the exact name of the employee or the course name or another value you need to find quickly? If you try to type a wildcard character such as an asterisk (*) or question mark in the prompt box, you won't see any data. To enable wildcard characters in text fields, you need to insert the Like keyword before the prompt in your criteria.

For example, in the parameter query you created earlier, change the criteria for the LastName field to **Like [Enter Employee Last Name]** and when you run the query enter **K*** in the prompt box. Note that your prompt can include detailed instructions on using the prompt (see Figure 6.18). Prompts may not exceed 255 characters and can't include certain special characters like periods (.), exclamation points (!), accents (`), and brackets ([]); the latter can only be used to surround the prompt.

FIGURE 6.18. Creating a Parameter Query that allows wildcards.

You can also build your parameter query in such a way that the user does not need to enter the wildcard to look for data that starts with, contains, or ends with the characters entered. To do this, you need to use the ampersand (&) to add the asterisk to the criteria, such as:

Like "*" & [Enter Employee Last Name] & "*"

Parameters can also be set in other types of queries that will be covered in a later chapter.

Using Multiple Parameters

You've already seen in steps 9–10 of Hands-On 6.5, you aren't limited to using parameters in only one field. In addition, you can create multiple prompts for the same field. For example, let's find employees who registered for courses in specified date range.

Action Item 6.2

In the Database Navigation pane, right click the query qryPrmCoursesByEm-plyee and select Copy. Right click again in the Navigation pane and select Paste. In the Paste As dialog box, enter the new name: qryPrmCoursesRegisteredBy-DateRange. Right-click the newly created query and choose Design View. In the Query Grid, delete the criteria from the Criteria row of the LastName field. Drag the RegisteredDate to the first empty column in the grid. Enter the following in the criteria cell:

Between [Enter Beginning Date] and [Enter Ending Date]

Run the modified query by entering 8/10/2021 for the first date prompt, and 8/30/2021 for the second. Access should display a list of employees who registered for courses between the specified dates.

Save and close the modified query.

In Action Item 6.2, you learned how to use the between operator with parameters to let the user enter a date range for a particular field. You can add more criteria prompts to further limit the results. As stated earlier, the parameter query displays the prompts in the order they appear in the design grid. However, at times you may want to display the prompts in different order. That is why Access offers a special Query Parameter dialog where you can set the order in which they appear. In addition, the Query Parameter dialog lets you set the data type for each prompt. When you run the query, Access will then be able to validate the user entry to make sure it's the correct type. Now, let's see how we can use the Query Parameter dialog to improve our query.

(◉) Hands-On 6.6   Using the Parameter Dialog

1. Open in the Design View the query you created and modified in Action Item 6.2.
2. In the Show/Hide Group of the Query Design, click the Parameters button to define query parameters for your query.

    You should see an empty Query Parameters dialog with two columns: Parameter and Data Type. Access does not know which parameters are in your query so you will need to enter them manually. The easy way to do this is by copying the prompts from the criteria cells of your Query design grid and then selecting the data type from the drop-down in the data type column. To copy data from the query grid to the dialog box, use the shortcut keys: Copy (Ctrl+C) and Paste (Ctrl+V).

3. Fill the Query Parameters dialog as shown in Figure 6.19.

Notice that parameters are still enclosed in brackets and each parameter must be entered on a separate line. If there were more parameters in this query, you would need to enter them in the order in which you wish the user to be prompted.

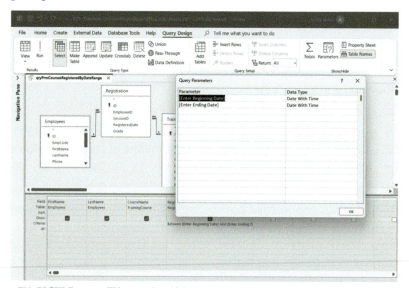

FIGURE 6.19. Specifying parameters and data types in the Parameter dialog box.

4. Click OK to close the Query Parameters and use the Run button in the Query Design to run the query. Enter 8/01/2021 in the first prompt, and 8/25/2021 in the second.

Access displays two employees who registered for the course during the specified period.

5. Run the query again this time providing some invalid data types. For example, enter any text in the beginning date prompt and notice that Access validates your entry informing you that the value you entered isn't valid for this field. When you click OK to the message you can correct your entry.

6. Save and close your modified query.

Parameter queries are great for creating quick dynamic queries however they may be awkward to users who certainly would prefer working with combo boxes that provide them with valid entries. You can meet this need by creating a customized prompt form which is covered in the chapter devoted to creating Access forms.

CREATING CROSSTAB QUERIES

Another special type of Select query is a crosstab query which is very helpful when you need to work with numbers and require various calculations. A crosstab query can calculate your data using a sum, average, count, and other type of total, and it can group the result showing it like a spreadsheet across the top and down the datasheet's left side. Access can guide you in creating crosstab using its built-in Crosstab Query Wizard. Crosstab queries can be built using the data in one or multiple tables, however, to include fields from more than one table, you must first create a Select query containing all the fields you need and then use this query to make the crosstab query.

As our ETD database does not contain data that can properly demonstrate the power of crosstabs, we will utilize the data from the Northwind sample database found in the Companion files.

(⊙) **Hands-On 6.7 Creating a ProductSalesByCountry Crosstab Query**

1. Copy the **Northwind 2007.accdb** database from the Companion files to your **AccessProjectBook1** working folder.
2. Open the database and click **OK** to the message that the active content has been disabled. Discard the security warning message after the database loads and close the startup screen.
3. Choose Create | Query Design.
4. Create a Select query as shown in Figure 6.20.
    Notice that this query uses selected fields from three tables: Products, Order Details, and Orders. Join the Products table with Order Details table by dropping the Products.ID field on the [Order Details].ProductID field. Join the Order Details table with the Orders table by dropping [Order Details].[Order ID] field on the Order.[Order ID] field. Fill the Query Design grid with the following fields: ID (Products), Product Name (Products), Order ID (Orders), Ship City (Orders), and Quantity (Order Details).
5. Run the query and save it as **qryProductOrders**. The partial output this query produces is shown in Figure 6.21.
6. Close the **qryProductOrders**.
    Now that you have extracted the data for your analysis, you can begin creating the crosstab.

7. Choose **Create | Query Wizard**, highlight the **Crosstab Query Wizard** in the New Query dialog and click **OK**.

8. In the first page of the wizard, click the **Queries** option button, highlight the **qryProductOrders** which contains the fields you want for the query results and click **Next**.

9. In the second page of the wizard, select **Product Name** in the Available Fields box and click > to move this field to the Selected Fields box. In the sample area in the Query Wizard, dialog Access uses the Product Name field as the first-row heading. You can select up to three fields as row headings.

10. Click Next to proceed.

11. In the third page of the wizard, select Ship City for your column heading. Access shows you in the sample area that the Ship City will appear in each column.

12. Click next to proceed.

13. In the fourth page of the wizard, select **Quantity** and in the Functions box, select **Sum** (see Figure 6.22). Here you have told Access to give you the total quantity of each product sold by city.

14. Click Next to proceed.

15. In the fifth (final page) of Query Wizard, type the name of your query, such as **qryProductSalesByCity_Crosstab**, and then click **Finish**.

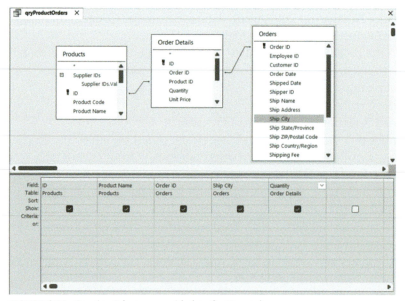

FIGURE 6.20. Creating Select query with data for Crosstab.

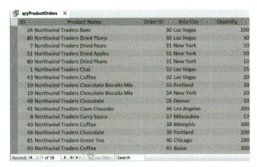

FIGURE 6.21. Partial data outputted by the Select Query.

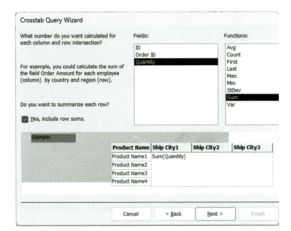

FIGURE 6.22. The fourth page of the Crosstab Query Wizard displays the structure of the crosstab query.

FIGURE 6.23. The fifth page of the Crosstab Query Wizard asks for the query name.

Access generates the crosstab query and displays the results as shown in Figure 6.24.

Product Name	Total Of Quantity	Boise	Chicago	Denver	Las Vegas	Los Angelas	Memphis	Miami	Milwaukee	New York	Portland	Salt Lake City	Seattle
Northwind Traders Almonds	20		20										
Northwind Traders Beer	487			87	100				300				
Northwind Traders Boysenberry Spread	100		10					90					
Northwind Traders Cajun Seasoning	40		40										
Northwind Traders Chai	40				15								25
Northwind Traders Chocolate	200			10					50		140		
Northwind Traders Chocolate Biscuits Mix	85		10							20	55		
Northwind Traders Clam Chowder	290					200	50	30				10	
Northwind Traders Coffee	650	300			20		305						25
Northwind Traders Crab Meat	120						50	30					40
Northwind Traders Curry Sauce	65					3		20	17		25		
Northwind Traders Dried Apples	40								30	10			
Northwind Traders Dried Pears	40								30	10			
Northwind Traders Dried Plums	75		15		30			20		10			
Northwind Traders Fruit Cocktail	40			40									
Northwind Traders Gnocchi	10					0				10			
Northwind Traders Green Tea	275		200			0		50					25
Northwind Traders Long Grain Rice	40									40			
Northwind Traders Marmalade	40									40			
Northwind Traders Mozzarella	90										40	50	
Northwind Traders Olive Oil	25							25					
Northwind Traders Ravioli	100											100	
Northwind Traders Scones	20		20										
Northwind Traders Syrup	50					50							

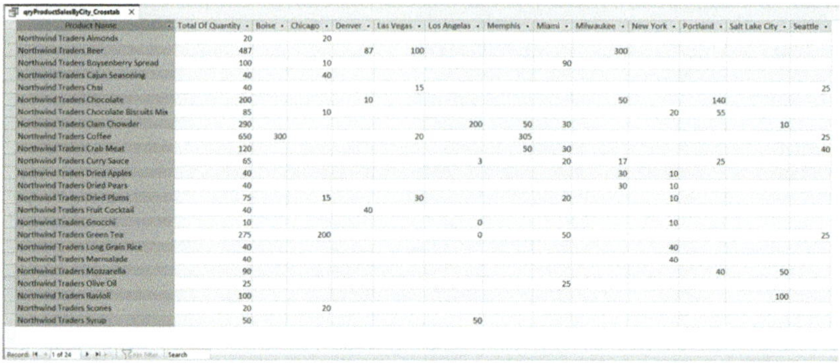

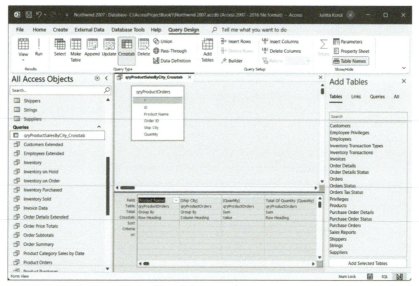

FIGURE 6.24. The Datasheet view of the crosstab query with the product names as rows and the cities as columns.

16. Click the **View** button to display the completed crosstab query in the Design View (see Figure 6.25).

FIGURE 6.25. The Query Design View of the crosstab query generated by the Crosstab Query Wizard. Notice that the Query type is displayed in the Query Design Ribbon.

If you look at the query design grid you will notice that the crosstab query adds the Crosstab and Total rows to the grid. The Crosstab row allows you to select where the field will appear in the query. For the field to appear on the left side, select Row Heading. You can have multiple Row Headings in a Crosstab query. For the field to appear as a column in a query, select Column Heading. You should select the Value to have the field appear in the query's data portion. You can only have one Column Heading and one Value.

If you don't want to see the field in the query, choose the (not shown) option from the Crosstab row drop-down list.

The Total row specifies how the field will be used. You should select Group By for each Row / Column Heading. Select one of the aggregate functions such as Sum, Avg. Count, Min, Max, etc. to perform a calculation on the Value field. If your query needs additional criteria, select Where from the Total drop-down. Where clauses will be discussed later in this chapter. Criteria fields often don't need to be displayed in the query results, so you may want to select (not shown) in the Crosstab cell for the Where clauses.

Notice that you can also sort the data in the crosstab query by selecting either Ascending or Descending in the Sort cell.

17. Save and close the **qryProductSalesByCity_**Crosstab query.

Now that you understand the elements of the crosstab query design, you should be able to create other crosstab queries either with the Crosstab Query Wizard or directly in the Design View by selecting the Crosstab Query type, selecting tables/queries for your crosstab and filling in the query grid with fields that will serve as Row and Column headings and specifying what calculation the query must perform. You can also use parameters in a crosstab query, but you must define them in the Query Parameters dialog as demonstrated earlier in this chapter.

DEVELOPING SQL SKILLS USING SELECT QUERIES

Inside every Select query you created in this chapter, as well as in other types of queries you'll be introduced to later, there is an SQL statement. SQL is the language used to retrieve, update, insert, and delete records in your database tables. Whether you use the Query Design View or Query Wizard to create your queries, you are building an SQL statement. This statement is a special instruction that consists of various identifiers, parameters, variables, names, data types and SQL reserved words. In simple words, the SQL statement tells Access what you want to do with the data. There are four basic SQL Statements that perform different operations:

SELECT—This statement selects data from database tables. This is the statement you will find in all the queries created in this chapter.

UPDATE—This statement updates existing data in database tables.

INSERT—This statement inserts new data into database tables.

DELETE—This statement deletes existing data from database tables.

The UPDATE, INSERT, and DELETE statements will be covered in Chapter 7.

SQL is used for data retrieval and updates, as well as modifications to the database structure, in many other relational database systems such as SQL Server, MySQL, and Oracle.

The SQL specification (known as ANSI SQL-89) was first published in 1989 by the American National Standards Institute (ANSI). The ANSI standard was revised in 1992; this version is referred to as ANSI SQL-92 or SQL-2. This revised specification is supported by the major database vendors, many of whom created their own extensions of the SQL language. Because of that some SQL statements you create using Access may not work in other products.

Access 2021 supports both SQL specifications and refers to them as ANSI SQL query modes. ANSI-89 is the default setting for a new Access database. Because the two ANSI SQL query modes are not compatible, you must decide which query mode you are going to use for the current database. In this chapter you will work with the default ANSI-89 SQL. In the future if you need to change the query mode to SQL Server compatible syntax (ANSI 92), choose File | Options and select Object Designers. In the Query Design section of the Access Options dialog, look for SQL Server Compatible Syntax (ANSI 92) and click the **This database** checkbox. When the **This database** checkbox is not selected, the query mode is assumed to be ANSI-89 SQL.

Now that you know what SQL is, let's take a closer look how you work with it.

(◉) Hands-On 6.8   Understanding the SQL View

1. In the ETD database Navigation pane double-click the **Boston Instructors** query that you created in Hands-On 6.1.

   The Datasheet view should display two records with the names and phone numbers of instructors residing in Boston.

2. In the Views group of the Ribbon's Home tab, click the down arrow in the **View** button and choose **SQL View**.

   Access opens the query in the Query Design SQL view as shown in Figure 6.26. The SQL view contains a gray area which is used to display and modify the SQL statement underlying the query. In the screen's status bar, you can see toggle buttons that allow you to switch between different views: Datasheet view, SQL View, and Design View. The Query Type group in the Query Design tab indicates that the Select query is currently displayed.

The SQL view shows the SQL Select statement that tells Access to display FirstName, LastName and PhoneNum from the Instructors table where the field City in the table Instructors equals Boston.

The SELECT keyword tells Access to retrieve data. This keyword is followed by a list of fields that need to be displayed. Notice that each field name is preceded by the name of the table it belongs to and a period. Including the name of the table with the field name is not necessary when all the fields belong to the same table, but Access follows its default pattern. You could rewrite the statement as shown here to make it look less cluttered:

```
SELECT FirstName, LastName, PhoneNum
FROM Instructors
WHERE (((City)="Boston"));
```

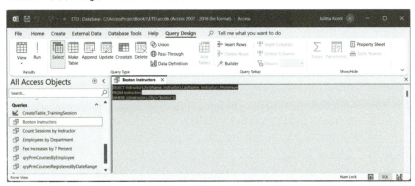

FIGURE 6.26. A Select query opened in the SQL View.

If you have a table or field names that contain spaces, you must enclose the field names and table names in brackets like this:

```
SELECT [First Name], [Last Name], [Phone Num]
FROM [Course Instructors]
WHERE (((City)="Boston"));
```

And, if you would rather display all the fields in this query, simply enter:

```
SELECT *
FROM Instructors
WHERE (((City)="Boston"));
```

The asterisk (*) tells Access to get all the fields.

The FROM keyword appears after the list of fields and designates the table or tables where the fields listed after the SELECT keyword are located. Next comes the WHERE clause that is used to specify the criteria for the query. When you enter a value in the criteria field in the Query Design View, Access puts the WHERE clause into the SELECT statement. This clause is followed by the name of the field used for the criteria and the value entered in the criteria cell. Notice that the WHERE clause includes multiple sets of parentheses which makes the statement harder to read but might be useful in understanding the SQL statement when multiple criteria are used. Again, you can simplify the statement as follows:

```
SELECT FirstName, LastName, PhoneNum
FROM Instructors
WHERE City="Boston";
```

The last part is the semicolon (;) which indicates the end of the SQL statement. Access does not require it so no worries if you forget it when writing your own statement. However, keep in mind that some SQL database systems allow you to write more than one SQL statement at a time and semicolon is required to separate these statements.

Notice that the previous SQL statement appears on multiple lines. You could write the entire statement on one line, but when you break it down into smaller sections on separate lines it makes the statement easier to read.

When creating queries, you can start in the Design View and later switch to SQL View to make other necessary adjustments if required. Let's modify the query to ensure that the resulting data is sorted in Descending order. Recall that in the Query Design View you sort the data by selecting Ascending or Descending from the Sort cell's drop-down list. To sort data in an SQL statement you will use the ORDER BY clause at the end of the SQL statement. After the ORDER BY simply type a field name. By Default, Access will sort data in Ascending Order. To specify Descending order, use the DESC keyword after the field name as shown in the next Step.

3. Enter the following statement in the SQL view overwriting the statement that Access generated:

```
SELECT FirstName, LastName, PhoneNum
FROM Instructors
WHERE City="Boston"
ORDER BY LastName DESC;
```

To sort by more than one field, which may be useful when the sort field contains duplicate data, enter the field names separated by commas in the order you want them sorted.

4. Use the tiny **Datasheet** button at the bottom right corner of the SQL view to see the sorted list.

Note that now the first row has data for Adam Smith, and the second row shows data for Victor Ramirez. You may also notice that the names of fields are different than those specified in the SQL statement. The reason for it is the `Caption` property in the table Instructors. This property specifies the label for the field when used on a view. If you open the table Instructors in the Design View and remove the entry in the `Caption` property, then the field name will be used as the label. When the `Caption` property is empty, Access will allow you to give a field a different name in the query. In the SQL statement, you can use the `AS` keyword to create an alias (a new name) for the columns like this:

```
SELECT FirstName AS First, LastName AS Last, PhoneNum AS Phone
FROM Instructors
WHERE City="Boston"
ORDER BY LastName DESC;
```

The previous assumes that there are no assigned Caption properties for fields in this table.

5. Save and close the modified **Boston Instructors** query.

You have now learned the basic syntax of the SQL Select statement. You must follow the rules as described to create valid statements. Writing a SELECT query is quite simple but mastering SQL statements, its various keywords, and rules, will require some practice. The good news is that Access helps you with the learning curve by writing the statements for you when you use its built-in Query Designer and Query Wizard.

Action Item 6.3

This action will expand your knowledge of the SQL language. Open each query you created in this chapter and view its underlying SQL statement. Write down the keywords you don't know and review the explanations.

Query: Employees by Department

```
SELECT Departments.DepartmentName, Employees.EmpCode,
Employees.FirstName, Employees.LastName
FROM Departments INNER JOIN Employees ON
Departments.DepartmentID = Employees.Department
ORDER BY Departments.DepartmentName, Employees.LastName;
```

The previous query uses two tables to retrieve employees by department name. Recall that when you create a Select query, you select the required fields from one or more tables. When you add two or more tables to a query, Access creates joins that are based on relationships that have been defined between the tables. If there are no relationships defined, you can manually create joins in queries. Like the query criteria, joins establish rules that the data must match to be included in the query operations. In addition, joins specify that each pair of rows that satisfy the join conditions will be combined to form a single row. Figure 6.27 shows the Employees by Department query in the Design View. The line between the tables represents the join. To review or change the type of join, double-click a join line. The Join Properties dialog shows which table is which in the join and which fields are used to join the tables. There are three option buttons, each one representing a different type of join. Option 1 represents an inner join. Notice that in the SQL statement Access uses the INNER JOIN keyword to join the tables when option 1 is selected. As you can see in this option's description, the result set will only include rows where the joined fields from both Departments and Employees tables are equal. In other words, if there are departments with no employees or employees not assigned to a department, you won't get those records. You can modify the join to select option 2 (called LEFT JOIN), or option 3 (called RIGHT JOIN) if you need to include all records either from Departments or Employees. To find out more details about various types of joins and the SQL syntax for them, click the question mark button in the Join Properties dialog.

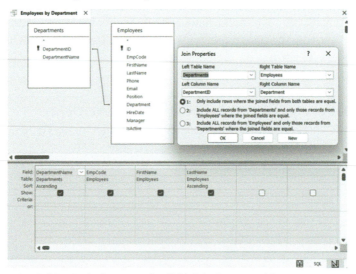

FIGURE 6.27. Reviewing types of available joins between tables.

The INNER JOIN syntax is as follows:

```
FROM table1 INNER JOIN table2 ON
table1.field1compopr table2.field2
```

In the previous syntax, `table1`, `table2` are the names of the tables from which records are combined. In our example query, we have Departments as `table1`, and Employees as `table2`.

Next comes the `ON` clause that specifies the join conditions, that is how the tables should be joined. `Field1`, `field2` are the names of the fields that are joined. If they are not numeric, these fields must be of the same data type. The `compopr` is a relational comparison operator:"=," "<," ">," "<=," ">=," or "<>."

Note that you can link several `ON` clauses in an INNER JOIN statement and you can also nest INNER JOIN statements as shown in our next query – Count Sessions by Instructor.

Query: Count Sessions by Instructor
```
SELECT Instructors.LastName,
Count(TrainingSession.SessionNum) AS CountOfSessionNum
FROM TrainingSession INNER JOIN (Instructors
INNER JOIN SessionInstructor ON
Instructors.ID = SessionInstructor.InstructorID) ON
TrainingSession.ID = SessionInstructor.SessionID
GROUP BY Instructors.LastName
ORDER BY Count(TrainingSession.SessionNum) DESC;
```

In addition to using several inner joins, the previous SQL statement uses GROUP BY statement. This statement is used with aggregate functions such as COUNT(), MAX(), MIN(), SUM(), AVG() to group the results by one or more columns. In the previous query, we are grouping the data by instructor's last name, and counting the number of sessions for each instructor using the COUNT() function by passing to it the SessionNum field. When working with aggregate functions it is customary to use an alias to rename the column. This is done with the AS keyword. If you don't specify an alias, Access will assign a generic name (e.g., Expr1, Expr2) to the filed.

Also note that aliases are only usable in the query output. You cannot use them in other parts of the query. So, to sort by the aggregate column, you must not enter its alias, but repeat the expression being aliased. Another thing to know is while you can't order by aliases, you can order by column index. Therefore, we could enter ORDER BY 2 DESC; and Access will not question your choice. However, if you add more columns to your query the indexes will change, and you might forget to modify the index number in the ORDER BY clause and get an unexpected sort order.

The next query, Fee Increases by 7 Percent, uses the CCur conversion function to calculate increased hourly fee. Notice how the plus (+) operator is used to concatenate (combine) two fields. You can also use the ampersand (&), like this:

```
SELECT [FirstName]& " " & [LastName] AS Instructor
```

Query: Fee Increases by 7 Percent
```
SELECT [FirstName]+" "+[LastName] AS Instructor,
    Instructors.HourlyFee, CCur([HourlyFee]*1.07) AS increasedFee
FROM Instructors
ORDER BY Instructors.HourlyFee DESC;
```

In the parameter query, qryPrmCoursesByEmployee, you can see another example of multiple inner joins that are also nested. The interesting part is the WHERE clause that is used to limit the query results by using criteria. The Like operator used in the WHERE clause searches for a specified pattern in the Last-Name column that will be supplied by the user when the query is run. The [Enter Employee Last Name] is a prompt for the parameter. Once supplied, the wildcard character (*) is appended to the parameter value to find a range of values instead of the exact value entered.

Query: qryPrmCoursesByEmployee
```
SELECT Employees.FirstName, Employees.LastName,
TrainingCourse.CourseName FROM
(TrainingCourse INNER JOIN TrainingSession ON
TrainingCourse.ID = TrainingSession.CourseID)
INNER JOIN (Employees INNER JOIN Registration ON
Employees.ID = Registration.EmployeeID) ON
TrainingSession.ID = Registration.SessionID
WHERE (((Employees.LastName)
Like "*" & [Enter Employee Last Name] & "*"));
```

Another parameter query we created in this chapter, qryPrmCoursesRegisteredByDateRange, uses two SQL statements in the SQL view. These statements are separated by semicolon (;). The first one declares the name and data type of each parameter in a parameter query by using the PARAMETERS declaration. The second statement is like the previous query, except that in the WHERE clause we are prompting the user for a date range. The Between...And operator determines whether the value of an expression falls within a specified range.

Query: qryPrmCoursesRegisterdByDateRange

```
PARAMETERS [Enter Beginning Date] DateTime,
[Enter Ending Date] DateTime;
SELECT Employees.FirstName, Employees.LastName,
TrainingCourse.CourseName, Registration.RegisteredDate
FROM (TrainingCourse INNER JOIN TrainingSession ON
TrainingCourse.ID = TrainingSession.CourseID)
INNER JOIN (Employees INNER JOIN Registration ON
Employees.ID = Registration.EmployeeID) ON
TrainingSession.ID = Registration.SessionID
WHERE (((Registration.RegisteredDate) Between
[Enter Beginning Date] And [Enter Ending Date]));
```

The last SQL statement we need to examine is the one we created in the North-wind 2007.accdb database. The first statement in this crosstab is TRANSFORM that is followed by an aggregate function SUM() that operates on the selected data. Next comes the SELECT statement that specifies the fields or expressions you want to use to create row headings in the query's result set. The GROUP BY clause specifies row grouping. Finally, the PIVOT statement specifies the column that will be used to categorize the aggregation that is performed in the TRANSFORM statement. This will create a column for each unique value in the table that exists in that column.

Query: in Northwind 2007.accdb – qryProductSalesByCity_Crosstab

```
TRANSFORM Sum(qryProductOrders.Quantity) AS SumOfQuantity
SELECT qryProductOrders.[Product Name],
Sum(qryProductOrders.Quantity) AS [Total Of Quantity]
FROM qryProductOrders
GROUP BY qryProductOrders.[Product Name]
PIVOT qryProductOrders.[Ship City];
```

You can look up the meaning and usage of any SQL keyword by clicking on it in the SQL view and pressing F1.

PREDICATES IN SQL STATEMENTS

Creating useful queries often boils down to limiting the number of records retrieved. The SELECT statement can contain various predicates that can limit a query's results. Let's look at some examples of scenarios where your ability to use predicates will come in handy.

Using the DISTINCT Predicate

You can use the DISTINCT predicate to omit records that contain duplicate data in the selected fields. Let's say you want to create a list of positions that the employees hold in your company.

⊙ Hands-On 6.9   Using the DISTINCT Predicate

1. In the ETD database, choose **Create | Query Design** and switch to the SQL View.

    The SQL window opens, and you should see the word SELECT followed by a semicolon.

    This is where you'll be entering your own SQL statements.

2. To retrieve all the positions from the table Employees, enter the following statement in the SQL View window:

```
SELECT Position from Employees;
```

3. Switch to the Datasheet view.

    Now you've got the positions but some of the positions appear more than once (see Figure 6.28).

4. Return to SQL View and modify this query to eliminate duplicate cities from the results:

```
SELECT DISTINCT Position from Employees;
```

FIGURE 6.28. Caption Please.

5. Switch to the **Datasheet** view and verify the duplicate positions only show once.

Because now you added the DISTINCT predicate, each position appears only once, even though it may exist on multiple records.

Note that when you use the DISTINCT predicate the output of the query is not updatable and does not reflect subsequent changes that were made by other users. What you get is really a read-only snapshot of the unique values retrieved from the specified column. The DISTINCT predicate will come in handy when you start creating controls for your forms. Combo boxes are often used on forms to provide users with consistent data entry. The combo box's Row Source property can be set to the SQL statement shown in this example to provide a drop-down list of unique positions.

6. Save the query as **qryEmployeePositions** and close it.

Using the DISTINCTROW Predicate

Another useful predicate is DISTINCTROW. Use this instead of DISTINCT when you're using multiple tables and want to eliminate duplicates from your query's results. In the ETD database the TrainingCourse table lists the available courses and does not have any duplicates. However, there are duplicates in the table TrainingSession because each course can have many sessions. So how do we get a list of training courses that have at least one session? We use the DISTINC-TROW predicate like this:

```
SELECT DISTINCTROW TrainingCourse.CourseName
FROM TrainingCourse INNER JOIN TrainingSession ON
TrainingCourse.ID = TrainingSession.CourseID
ORDER BY TrainingCourse.CourseName;
```

When you enter the previous statement in the SQL view and run your query by switching to the Datasheet view, you should see the unique list of courses with sessions. If you followed along, name this query qryCoursesWithSessions and close it.

Important thing to remember is that the DISTINCTROW omits data based on entire duplicate records, not just duplicate fields. The DISTINCTROW predicate is ignored if your query includes only one table, or if you output fields from all tables. If you omit DISTINCTROW, the previous query will produce multiple rows for each training course that has more than one session.

Using the TOP Predicate

At times you may need to retrieve only a certain number of records that fall at the top or the bottom of a specified range. Say you want to retrieve the top three instructors teach the most sessions. Earlier in this chapter we created a query Count Sessions by Instructors. Let's work with this query in the next Hands-On.

(◉) Hands-On 6.10   Using the TOP Predicate

1. Open the **Count Sessions by Instructors** query in the **Datasheet** view.
   Notice that the list contains the names of all instructors and number of sessions they teach.
2. Switch to the **SQL view** and copy (**Ctr+C**) the entire SQL statement. You can quickly select the statement by pressing **Ctr+A**.
3. Choose **Create | Query Design**, switch to the SQL View, and press **Ctrl+V** to paste the SQL statement you copied.
4. Modify the statement as follows:
```
SELECT TOP 3 Instructors.LastName,
Count(TrainingSession.SessionNum) AS CountOfSessionNum
FROM TrainingSession
INNER JOIN (Instructors INNER JOIN SessionInstructor ON
Instructors.ID = SessionInstructor.InstructorID) ON
TrainingSession.ID = SessionInstructor.SessionID
GROUP BY Instructors.LastName
ORDER BY Count(TrainingSession.SessionNum) DESC;
```

   Notice that we just added the TOP 3 after the SELECT statement, which will limit the result set to just three top records. When using the TOP predicate in a query, you must use an ORDER BY clause. To get the list of top values, make sure to sort the values in descending order by using the DESC keyword in the ORDER BY clause. If you want the bottom three, simply change the sort order to ascending (ASC).
5. Switch to the **Datasheet view** and examine the results.
6. Save this query as **qryTop3_Instructors**.
7. Close this query.

Note that if the number following the TOP predicate is larger than the number of records that exist in the results, you will get all the records. You can also use the PERCENT reserved word to return a percentage of records that fall at the top or the bottom of a range specified by the ORDER BY clause. For example, to get a list of instructors who are in the top 5 percent according to the number of sessions, use the following statement:

```
SELECT TOP 5 PERCENT Instructors.LastName,
Count(TrainingSession.SessionNum) AS CountOfSessionNum
FROM TrainingSession INNER JOIN (Instructors INNER JOIN
SessionInstructor ON
Instructors.ID = SessionInstructor.InstructorID) ON
TrainingSession.ID = SessionInstructor.SessionID
GROUP BY Instructors.LastName
ORDER BY Count(TrainingSession.SessionNum) DESC;
```

UNDERSTANDING AND USING SUBQUERIES

You already know from this chapter that by adding criteria to specific fields you can cut down the number of returned records. In Access, a query can be linked to another query, thus enabling values to be passed between queries. A Select statement that is nested inside another query is called a *subquery*. A subquery returns a set of records to which the rest of a query can apply further criteria. Because of this feature, subqueries allow you to create more complex and flexible queries. They are often used to perform the same operation that would otherwise require complex joins and unions between tables and queries.

There are two types of subqueries: correlated and non-correlated. A *correlated subquery* references another query or queries outside the subquery and is executed once for each record a referenced query returns. A *non-correlated subquery* contains no reference to outside queries, so it only executes once.

SQL Keywords used in Subqueries

Subqueries are linked to other queries using predicates, such as IN, EXISTS, ANY, SOME, NOT, and ALL, and /or comparison operators (+, <>, <, >, <=, and >=).

- IN: returns records in the main query for which some record in the subquery contains an equal value.
- NOT IN: returns records in the main query for which no record in the subquery contains an equal value.
- EXISTS: returns true or false depending on whether the subquery returns any records.
- ANY or SOME: returns records in the main query that satisfy the comparison with any records in the subquery.
- ALL: returns records in the main query that match all the records in the subquery.

Let's look at some examples using these keywords.

The IN and NOT Operators

You can use the IN operator to match conditions in a list of expressions. Let's look at the following simple Select statement:

```
SELECT *
FROM TrainingCourse
WHERE TrainingCourse.[CourseLevel] IN ("Beginning","Intermediate");
```

In the previous statement, we tell Access to retrieve from the TrainingCourse table only the records that have a value of "Beginning" or "Intermediate" in the CourseLevel field. Notice that the values are enclosed in parentheses and each value is enclosed in quotes. You may use single or double quotes. To exclude these values from the query results, simply add the NOT operator like this:

```
SELECT *
FROM TrainingCourse
WHERE TrainingCourse.[CourseLevel]
NOT IN ("Beginning","Intermediate");
```

When you run this query, only the records with the other course levels ("Advanced," "Master") will be returned.

Now, suppose you want to find employees registered for the beginning, intermediate, advanced, or master course level. You could write the following SQL statement that uses several inner joins to get to the relevant data:

```
SELECT Employees.FirstName, Employees.LastName,
TrainingCourse.CourseLevel
FROM (TrainingCourse INNER JOIN TrainingSession
ON TrainingCourse.ID = TrainingSession.CourseID)
INNER JOIN (Employees INNER JOIN Registration
ON Employees.ID = Registration.EmployeeID)
ON TrainingSession.ID = Registration.SessionID
WHERE (((TrainingCourse.CourseLevel)="Beginning"
OR (TrainingCourse.CourseLevel)="Intermediate"
OR (TrainingCourse.CourseLevel)="Advanced"
OR (TrainingCourse.CourseLevel)="Master"))
ORDER BY Employees.LastName;
```

In the previous SQL example, the OR keyword is used to specify different conditions for the CourseLevel field. Instead of using the OR, you can simplify the query syntax by using the IN operator, like this:

```
SELECT Employees.FirstName, Employees.LastName,
TrainingCourse.CourseLevel
```

```
FROM (TrainingCourse INNER JOIN TrainingSession
ON TrainingCourse.ID = TrainingSession.CourseID)
INNER JOIN (Employees INNER JOIN Registration
ON Employees.ID = Registration.EmployeeID)
ON TrainingSession.ID = Registration.SessionID
WHERE (((TrainingCourse.CourseLevel) IN
("Beginning","Intermediate", "Advanced", "Master")))
ORDER BY Employees.LastName;
```

The IN operator / predicate is also quite handy when using subqueries. The following SQL statement returns a list of employees who registered for session 2 and 16.

```
Select ID, FirstName, LastName from Employees WHERE
ID IN (Select EmployeeID from Registration
where SessionID = 2 or SessionID = 16);
```

In the previous example, the Select statement in the WHERE clause is a non-correlated subquery.

The IN predicate is used to compare the employee IDs in the Employees table to employee IDs in the Registration table. The WHERE clause in the subquery instructs Access to retrieve only the employee IDs from the Registration table that have the SessionID equal to 2 or 16.

To match any condition opposite the one defined, use the NOT operator as in the following:

```
Select ID, FirstName, LastName from Employees WHERE
ID NOT IN (Select EmployeeID from Registration where
SessionID = 2 or SessionID = 16);
```

Notice that a subquery linked by the IN predicate can only return one column and must be enclosed in parentheses. When you execute this query, Access processes the subquery first retrieving the employee IDs from the Registration table and then pulling the IDs and names of the employees matching the IDs retrieved by the subquery. The previous example query, can be rewritten using the INNER JOIN, like this:

```
SELECT Employees.ID, Employees.FirstName,
Employees.LastName, Registration.SessionID
FROM Employees INNER JOIN Registration ON
Employees.ID = Registration.EmployeeID
WHERE (((Registration.SessionID) In (2,16)));
```

The EXISTS Predicate

The EXISTS predicate is used to check for the existence of a value in the correlated subquery. Recall that correlated subqueries reference queries outside the subquery and are executed once for each record a referenced query returns. To demonstrate the use of the EXISTS predicate, let's build a query to retrieve BeginDate, CourseNum, CourseName, and InstructorID for training classes taught by Instructors that live in Boston.

```
SELECT BeginDate, CourseNum, CourseName, InstructorID
FROM TrainingSession INNER JOIN TrainingCourse ON
TrainingCourse.ID = TrainingSession.ID
WHERE EXISTS (SELECT ID FROM Instructors
INNER JOIN SessionInstructor ON
SessionInstructor.InstructorID= Instructors.ID
WHERE Instructors.ID = TrainingSession.InstructorID
AND Instructors.City = "Boston");
```

Remember that while learning about various SQL statements you can ask Microsoft Bing, powered by AI, to provide needed explanations. Following is what the AI engine wrote in response to this query:

> *"This query selects the begin date, course number, course name and instructor ID from the TrainingSession table and the TrainingCourse table, which are joined on the common field ID. It only returns the rows where there exists an instructor in the Instructors table and the SessionInstructor table, which are joined on the common field InstructorID, who has the same ID as the instructor in the TrainingSession table and who lives in Boston. In other words, it shows the information of the training sessions that are taught by instructors from Boston."*

This is a great explanation How about asking AI about the usage of EXISTS predicate in this query? Here is the answer it provided:

> *The EXISTS predicate is used to test whether a subquery returns any rows. It returns TRUE if the subquery returns at least one row, and FALSE otherwise. In this query, the EXISTS predicate is used to filter the rows from the TrainingSession and TrainingCourse tables based on the existence of a matching instructor in the Instructors and SessionInstructor tables. If there is no instructor who meets the criteria in the subquery, the row from the main query will not be returned.*

The results of the EXISTS subquery are shown in the following table:

BeginDate	CourseNum	CourseName	InstructorID
9/22/2021	3100	Introduction to Social Media Marketing	1
9/28/2021	6000	SQL Database Administration	2
9/29/2021	7000	Service Management	2
9/21/2021	2000	Business Process Management Part I	2
9/24/2021	2200	Business Process Management Part III	1
10/19/2021	4200	Microsoft Excel Level 2	2
10/20/2021	4400	Microsoft Word Level 1	2

When you switch to the Design View, Access shows the query grid as depicted in Figure 6.29.

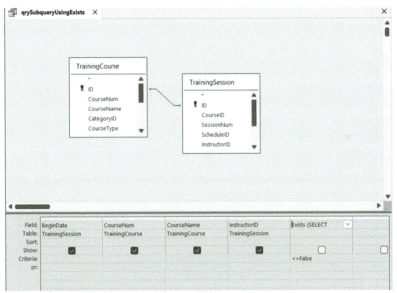

FIGURE 6.29. In the Design View, the Exists subquery is shown as one of the fields and the Criteria row of the field shows the expression < > False.

To retrieve courses taught by instructors who do not live in Boston, use the NOT operator with the EXISTS predicate like this:

```
SELECT BeginDate, CourseNum, CourseName, InstructorID
FROM TrainingSession INNER JOIN TrainingCourse ON
TrainingCourse.ID = TrainingSession.ID
WHERE NOT EXISTS (SELECT ID FROM Instructors
INNER JOIN SessionInstructor ON
```

```
SessionInstructor.InstructorID= Instructors.ID
WHERE Instructors.ID = TrainingSession.InstructorID
AND Instructors.City = "Boston");
```

The ANY, SOME, and ALL Predicates

The ANY and SOME predicates can be used interchangeably to retrieve records from the main query that match any records in the subquery. They are used with comparison operators (=, <>, <, >, <+, and >=).

Let's look at the following example that uses the ANY predicate:

```
SELECT BeginDate, CourseNum, CourseName, InstructorID
FROM TrainingSession INNER JOIN TrainingCourse ON
TrainingCourse.ID = TrainingSession.ID
WHERE InstructorID > ANY (SELECT ID
FROM Instructors Where HireDate = #1/23/2018#);
```

Again, when asked from Bing, the following explanation is provided:

> *"This query selects the begin date, course number, course name and instructor ID from the TrainingSession table and the TrainingCourse table, which are joined on the common field ID. It only returns the rows where the instructor ID is greater than any of the instructor IDs from the Instructors table who were hired on January 23, 2018. In other words, it shows the information of the training sessions that are taught by instructors who have higher IDs than those who were hired on that date."*

The output of this query is shown here:

BeginDate	CourseNum	CourseName	InstructorID
9/25/2021	5500	Introduction to Software Testing	5
9/27/2021	3310	Digital Marketing Fundamentals	4
9/23/2021	5600	Mastering Software Engineering	4
9/22/2021	5001	Core IT Skills for Everyone	4
9/27/2021	5010	Software Tools for Programmers	5
9/21/2021	3001	Accounting I for Managers	4
9/25/2021	4000	Office 365	5
10/29/2021	4600	Advanced Microsoft Outlook	4
10/29/2021	4100	Microsoft Excel Level 1	4
9/24/2021	4500	Microsoft Word Level 2	4

It is possible to use more conditions in the WHERE clause to limit the results. Consider the following query that limits the previous output to only include the courses that contain the word Software anywhere in the CourseName field:

```
SELECT BeginDate, CourseNum, CourseName, InstructorID
FROM TrainingSession INNER JOIN TrainingCourse ON
TrainingCourse.ID = TrainingSession.ID
WHERE CourseName Like "*Software*" AND
InstructorID > ANY (SELECT ID FROM Instructors
WHERE HireDate = #1/23/2018#);
```

The ALL predicate retrieves records from the main query that match all the records in the subquery. The following SQL statement can be used to find out the information on the training courses that are taught by instructors that have lower IDs than those that were hired on January 23, 2018:

```
SELECT BeginDate, CourseNum, CourseName, InstructorID
FROM TrainingSession INNER JOIN TrainingCourse ON
TrainingCourse.ID = TrainingSession.ID WHERE
InstructorID < ALL (SELECT ID FROM Instructors
Where HireDate = #1/23/2018#);
```

The comparison operator (<) combined with the ALL predicate tells Access to retrieve records from the main query that are less than all the records in the subquery. The output of this query is shown here:

BeginDate	CourseNum	CourseName	InstructorID
9/22/2021	3100	Introduction to Social Media Marketing	1
9/28/2021	6000	SQL Database Administration	2
9/29/2021	7000	Service Management	2
9/21/2021	2000	Business Process Management Part I	2
9/24/2021	2200	Business Process Management Part III	1
10/19/2021	4200	Microsoft Excel Level 2	2
10/20/2021	4400	Microsoft Word Level 1	2

UNDERSTANDING NULL VALUES IN DATA

In database parlance, Null refers to data that is either missing or unknown. It is possible that the data does not exist for a particular field in a record, or the data exists, but you don't know what it is at the very moment of the data entry.

You may leave the field blank (Null) and return to it when you gather the missing information. If you know for sure that the data does not exist you may want to enter NA in the field to let other users know that the data for the field is not available (NA) or you can simply enter a *zero-length string* (""), also known as an *empty string* to indicate that the entry has no characters.

Understanding how Access works with Null values is very important when you create queries, table relationships, use expressions and functions.

Null is not a value of zero (0), it does not equal zero, and it is not an empty string (""). Access sees a zero-length string as an entry, recognizing that something exists in the field and the length of it is zero (0). If the field value is missing or unknown, then it is interpreted as a Null value. The length of the Null value is Null as we cannot measure the length of something that is unknown. An important thing to understand is that a Null value does not equal to anything. You cannot compare Null to any value using the equals operator.

The IS NULL operator is used to determine if a field contains data. The following statement retrieves the records from the Employees table that have a Null value in the EmpCode field:

```
SELECT Employees.*
FROM Employees
WHERE Employees.EmpCode Is Null;
```

When you know that you have Null values in your data you can include or exclude them. To exclude the records with the blank EmpCode simply use the Is Not Null:

```
SELECT Employees.*
FROM Employees
WHERE Employees.EmpCode Is Not Null;
```

You cannot perform any math operations on Null values. Any expression you build, will return Null if it references at least one Null value. The exception are some aggregate functions, such as Sum, Avg, Max, Min, and so on. These functions ignore Null values and only return Null if every record contains a Null value.

When using the Count() function to count records you can avoid the Null value issue by using Count("*") instead of Count(FieldName). Another tidbit to remember is that you can't join two records on a Null value. Recall that while the primary key cannot contain a Null value, a foreign key can contain Null values. However, if there is no data in a foreign key then you won't be able to relate child records (foreign key records) with the parent (primary key).

Now that you know how Access interprets and responds to Null values, let's continue to the next section where you will find out how to determine if a field contains or does not contain data.

FINDING UNMATCHED DATA

When working with databases you can expect all kinds of issues with the data that either need to be corrected or analyzed. One of such issues is detecting unmatched data. If you need a list of records that don't have matching records in another table, you can run the Find Unmatched Query Wizard, or you can write the SQL statement yourself. In the following SQL we can use the IS NULL operator to get a list of employees that didn't register for any of the training courses.

```
SELECT Employees.FirstName, Employees.LastName
FROM Employees LEFT JOIN Registration ON
Employees.[ID] = Registration.[EmployeeID]
WHERE (((Registration.EmployeeID) Is Null));
```

Action Item 6.4

Use the Find Unmatched Query Wizard to create a query that shows employees without a matching registration. Follow the instructions and prompts in the Query Wizard windows. Employees table will contain records you want in your query results. The Registration table is the related table. The matching fields should be ID and EmployeeID. The query results should show two columns with employee FirstName and LastName. When you run the query created by the Query Wizard and look at its SQL statement, it should match the previous statement.

FINDING DUPLICATE DATA

In the process of analyzing data, it may be helpful to see a list of values that appear more than once in a field. The Find Duplicates Query Wizard can walk you through the steps required to check a field for duplicate data, or you can write the SQL statement yourself once you learn the SQL syntax. To write this type of SQL on your own, you need to be familiar how to use the GROUP BY and HAVING clauses to group and filter data. Earlier in this chapter we used GROUP BY when we counted sessions taught by an instructor. GROUP BY clause is used in queries that contain at least one aggregate function. The HAVING clause is used with GROUP BY clause to define conditions on groups of data calculated from aggregate functions.

Suppose you want to find which employee first names exist more than once in the Employees table. The following SQL can be written to provide the answer:

```
SELECT Employees.FirstName,
FROM Employees
GROUP BY Employees.FirstName
HAVING Count(*)>1
```

Notice that the HAVING clause must follow the GROUP BY clause.

When you run this query, you will find that you have more than one occurrence of the following names: John, Mark, Paul, Peter, Richard, and Steven. If you need to know how many times each name appears, modify the statement as follows:

```
SELECT Employees.FirstName, Count(*) As TotalCount
FROM Employees
GROUP BY Employees.FirstName
HAVING Count(*)>1
```

After running the previous query, we found out that in our ETD database, John is the most popular employee first name. Figure 6.30 shows the Design View for this query.

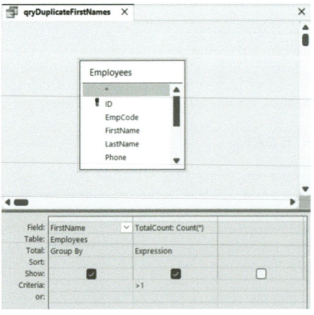

FIGURE 6.30. The Design View shows how Access interprets the SQL statement when the GROUP BY and HAVING clauses are used.

Many times, you will see the HAVING clause inside the WHERE clause. The WHERE clause will be used to filter rows before any data is grouped. The HAVING clause will filter the rows after data is grouped. Let's look at a query that uses both the HAVING and the WHERE clauses. Suppose you want to count the total number of positions that employees have in departments with the IDs greater than 5, and you wonder which department has at least 5 positions. Figure 6.31 shows the Design View for the following SQL statement,

```
SELECT Employees.Department,
Count(Employees.Position) AS CountOfPosition
FROM Employees
WHERE Department > 5
GROUP BY Department
Having Count(Employees.Position) >=5
```

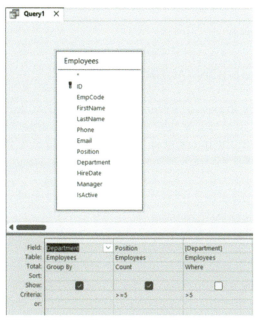

FIGURE 6.31. The Design View shows how Access interprets the SQL statement when the WHERE, GROUP BY, and HAVING clauses are used.

It is important to remember that when you use the GROUP BY clause with the WHERE clause the GROUP BY clause must appear after the WHERE clause.

Action Item 6.5

Use the Find Duplicates Query Wizard to find out if Registration table contains any employees who signed up for more than one course. Look for duplicates in the Employee ID field.

The Query Wizard should produce the following SQL statement and the output:

```
SELECT First(Registration.[EmployeeID]) AS [EmployeeID Field],
Count(Registration.[EmployeeID]) AS NumberOfDups
FROM Registration
GROUP BY Registration.[EmployeeID]
HAVING (((Count(Registration.[EmployeeID]))>1));
```

EmployeeID Field	NumberOfDups
2	2
5	2

CREATING AND USING A UNION QUERY

Access has a special type of query, known as *Union* that is used to combine the results of two or more SELECT statements or tables into a single result set. This type of query cannot be created in the query grid; you must use the SQL view. The syntax for the union query is:

```
SELECT column1, column2, …
FROM table1
UNION [ALL]
Select column2, column2, …
FROM table2
```

The UNION keyword combines the results of two SELECT statements; the first selects records from the first table and the second selects records from the second table. The ALL keyword specified that all rows should be returned, including duplicates. If the ALL keyword is not specified, duplicate rows are removed from the result set.

Action Item 6.6

Suppose you just received an Excel spreadsheet with new training locations, and you need to create a list of all training locations. After you import the external data to Access, you can create two Select statements; one will retrieve the data from the TrainingCourseLocations table and the other from the NewTraining-gLocations table that you create from the Excel spreadsheet. Both statements should be joined by the UNION keyword. The Excel spreadsheet is included in the Companion files—see the file named **NewTrainingLocations.xlsx**. Figure 6.32 displays the contents of the spreadsheet.

	A	B	C	D	E	F
1	LocationName	Phone	Address1	City	State	ZipCode
2	Computer Labs	(516) 294-9090	50 Hilldale Road	Albertson	NY	11507
3	Express Training Center	(516) 235-6512	114 Manhasset Road	New Hyde Park	NY	11040
4	WebWorks	(617) 736-1649	59 Beacon Street	Boston	MA	02108

FIGURE 6.32. An Excel spreadsheet contains the data to be used in the UNION query.

Follow these steps to prepare the SELECT statements:

1. Import the Excel spreadsheet to an Access table named **NewTrainingLocations**.
2. Use the Query Design window to create the first Select query that will retrieve **Location Name**, **Address1**, **City**, and **State** from the **NewTrainingLocations** table.
3. Create another Select query that will retrieve the same fields from the **TrainingCourseLocations** table.

Follow these steps to create the UNION query:

1. Choose **Create | Query Design** and click the **Union** button in the Query Type group of the Query Design tab.

   You should see that Access opens a new Query window in the SQL view. This is where you put together your Union query. To avoid typing, you can copy the SQL statements from the two queries you created earlier.
2. Switch to the SQL view of the query you created in Step 2 and copy the entire statement by selecting it and pressing Ctrl+C, or right click the selected statement and choose Copy.
3. Switch to the SQL view of the Union query window, and press Ctrl+V to paste the statement you just copied. Delete the semicolon that appears at the end of the statement.
4. Press Enter and type UNION and press Enter.
5. Switch to the SQL view of the query you created in Step 3 and copy the entire statement.
6. Switch to the SQL view of the Union query window and press Ctrl+V to paste the statement you just copied.

   The entire SQL statement for the Union query you just created is shown in Figure 6.33. Figure 6.34 displays the results after you run this query.

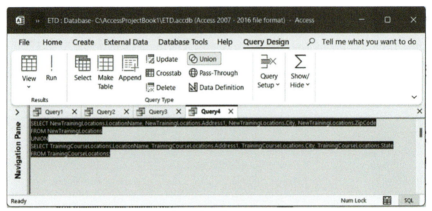

FIGURE 6.33. The UNION query combines data from two SELECT statements.

LocationName	Address1	City	ZipCode
Advanced Learning Paths	411 7th Avenue	New York	NY
CodingForProfit Inc.	162 Federal Street	Boston	MA
Computer Labs	50 Hilldale Road	Albertson	11507
Computers Unlimited	342 7th Avenue	New York	NY
Express Training Center	114 Manhasset Road	New Hyde Park	11040
TechNetwork Designers	195 Prospect Street	Cambridge	MA
WebWorks	59 Beacon Street	Boston	02108

Record: ◄ ◄ 1 of 7 ► ►I ► No Filter Search

FIGURE 6.34. The UNION query result set shows combined data from two SELECT statements.

7. Save the Union query as **qryUnion_TraningLocations**.
8. Close all the query windows. There is no need to save the other two queries.

SPEEDING UP YOUR SELECT QUERIES

In Chapter 4, you learned that an index on specific fields in a database table can help Access find and sort records faster. An index stores the location of records based on the field or fields that you choose to index. Many Select queries that you create will require joining several tables to extract rows and columns, and perhaps sorting the results in a specified order. As your tables become larger, the data retrieval operations will become more time consuming, and you may need to add extra indexes to speed up your queries. The fields you index depend on the data and the queries that you use. However, keep in mind some general guidelines:

- You should index fields that you search frequently, sort, or join to other tables in multiple table queries.

- You should index fields that have many different values and can filter out many rows. If many of the values in the field are the same, the index may not significantly speed up queries.

- You should index fields that have data types that are compatible with indexing, such as Short Text, Long Text, Number, Date/Time, AutoNumber, Currency, Yes/No, or Hyperlink. You cannot index fields whose data type is OLE Object, Calculated, or Attachment.

- You should avoid indexing fields that are frequently updated or inserted, as this can slow down the performance of these operations.

- You should consider creating multiple-field indexes for queries that use more than one field in the WHERE clause or the join condition. The order of the columns in the index is important as it can affect how well the index matches the query. The columns that you use in the WHERE clause or the join condition should be placed first in the index, followed by the columns that are used for sorting or grouping. This way, the index can reduce the number of rows that need to be accessed and sorted.

To create an index in Access, you can use the Create Index dialog box in Design View (see Chapter 4), or you can use a Data-Definition query in SQL view, as shown in the last section of Chapter 7.

SUMMARY

In this chapter, you learned various methods of creating basic Select queries that retrieve data from one or more tables with or without criteria, sorted in ascending or descending order. You also learned how to use various expressions, aliases, and aggregate functions. You practiced creating more advanced Select queries that can use parameters to set a query's criteria at runtime and cross-tab queries that summarize data in a familiar row/column format. You spent quite a bit of time in this chapter learning the SQL language behind queries. Now, instead of relying on the Access Query Designer or Query Wizard, you can create queries from scratch by typing statements directly in the SQL view. You saw how by using predicates (DISTINCT, DISTINCTROW, TOP) and the

IN operator you can limit a query's results. You were introduced to the concept of Null values and empty strings. Finally, you learned how to find unmatched and duplicate records in your database tables by using the Find Duplicates and Find Unmatched Query Wizard and saw equivalent SQL keywords (GROUP BY, HAVING) used to build these types of queries. You have also learned how you can combine the results of two or more independent queries or tables into a single result set using the UNION query. Throughout this chapter we have called upon Bing, powered by AI, to provide answers to some Access related questions.

In the next chapter, you will work with queries that can perform specific actions in the database.

Chapter 7

Performing Database Operations With Action Queries

In the previous chapter, we focused on creating and working with Select queries that retrieved records based on criteria that were entered. With these skills mastered, you can now move to more advanced queries that are specifically designed to insert new data into a table, delete old data from a table, or append to data already in a database based on criteria. As these queries perform some operation on database tables, they are commonly referred to as *action queries*. There are four types of action queries in Access:

Make Table query	This type of query creates a new table from data returned by a select query. You can use this query to create summary tables, archive data, or copy data to another database. Recall that in Chapter 3 we used this type of query to create the TrainingCourseLocations table in the ETD database.
Append query	This type of query adds new records to an existing table from another table or query. This query is often used to combine data from multiple sources, or to import data from another database.
Update query	This type of query changes the values of fields in existing records based on certain criteria. This query is often used to correct errors, apply changes, or calculate new values for your data.
Delete query	This type of query deletes records from a table that match certain criteria. This query is often used to remove unwanted data from your database.

Action queries are very powerful but can be very dangerous when executed unintentionally. Because action queries can affect your data in ways that you did not anticipate or want, it is important to:

- Always make a backup of your data prior to running an action query.

  Do this in case something goes wrong, for example, you update fields with incorrect values or accidentally delete records that match certain criteria. The backup will allow you to restore the data to the state as if was before the change.

- Always view the action query in Datasheet view before executing it.

  The Datasheet view will show you what data will be affected by the query; you can return to the Design View of your action query to correct any problems you find.

- Turn on the confirmation messages that Access displays when you run your action queries.

  Access allows you to turn these messages off, but it is important to keep them on, so you are always prompted to verify that you want to make the changes. Remember that it's better to be safe than sorry. By clicking No in the confirmation message, you can save yourself from hours of aggravation and additional work rectifying unwanted changes. As some changes cannot be easily undone, it pays to be extra cautious when dealing with action queries.

USING MAKE TABLE QUERIES

The least dangerous of all four action queries is a Make Table query. As its name suggests, this query creates tables; it does not make any changes to the data. At times when you return some records from the select query, you may want to copy the output to a stand-alone table to analyze it or modify it later. A Make Table Query will allow you to do just that. Suppose your manager needs all the fields and data from the Employees the Registration tables presented as one table. Before you can create this table, you need to return the requested data by using the select query. Let's work on it in Hands-On 7.1.

Hands-On 7.1   Creating a Make Table Query

1. In the ETD database, choose **Create | Query Design**.
2. Add the Employees and Registration tables.

3. To add all the fields from the Employees table, drag and drop the asterisk (*) onto the first column in the Query design grid. Do the same for the Registration table dropping the asterisk onto the second column.

4. Switch to the Datasheet view to see if the query returns the data your manager requested.

It looks like your query returns all the fields from both tables, but only employees with a matching registration record are shown. Let's fix this to display all the employees regardless of their course registration. You will need to change the type of join between the two tables.

5. Return to the Datasheet view and double click on the join line to view the Join Properties dialog. Select option **2** in the dialog box to tell Access to use Outer Join and click **OK**.

Notice that Access represents the new type of join by the arrow pointing to the Registration table.

6. Switch to the SQL view to see the SQL statement that Access has prepared:

```
SELECT Employees.*, Registration.*
FROM Employees LEFT JOIN Registration ON
Employees.ID = Registration.EmployeeID;
```

This statement uses the LEFT JOIN keywords in the FROM clause to instruct Access to display all the records in the table Employees even if they don't have a record in the Registration table.

7. Now switch to the Datasheet view. A partial output of the data is shown in Figure 7.1

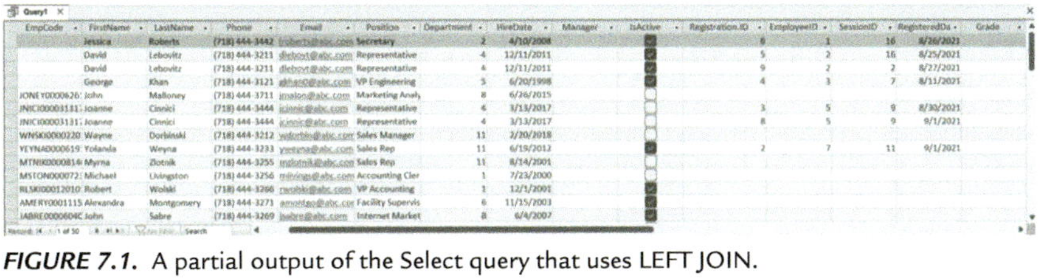

FIGURE 7.1. A partial output of the Select query that uses LEFT JOIN.

Every time your Select query returns results, they are stored in a temporary table in your computer's memory. Now that you've got the results your manager wants, let's turn them into a table.

8. Switch to the Design view and click the Make Table button located in the Query Type section of the Query Design View (see Figure 7.2).

The Make Table dialog box will appear.

9. Enter **EmployeesAndRegistrations** as the Table Name and click **OK** to create this table in the current database.

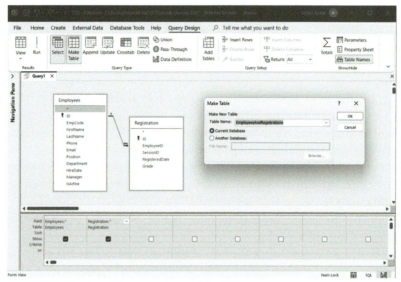

FIGURE 7.2. Turning a Select query into a Make Table query.

It looks like Access returns to the Design view and does not create a table. All we've done so far is tell Access how to name the table. Now we need to run the Make Table query to create the table.

10. With the Query1 in the Design view, click the Run button.

Access displays the message shown in Figure 7.3.

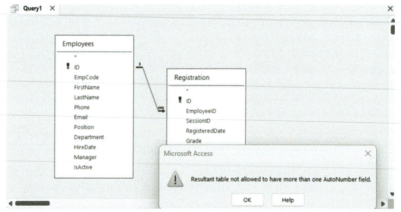

FIGURE 7.3. Access will inform you why it cannot create the requested table when you run the Make Table query while in Design View.

It looks like there is some problem with the fields we selected, and we must resolve that before Access can create the resultant table. Many times, the issue you encounter when creating tables has to do with the primary key.

11. Click **OK** to the message. Delete the Registration.* from the second column in the Query Design view. Select and drag EmployeeID, SessionID, RegisteredDate and Grade fields from the Registration table to the Query grid, then click the **Run** button.

Access displays the message informing you that you are about to paste 50 rows into a new table (see Figure 7.4).

FIGURE 7.4. Access warns you that you cannot undo the requested operation and reverse the changes that are about to be made in the database.

12. Click **Yes** to create a new table with the selected records.

Access creates the EmployeesAndRegistration table and updates the Database Navigation pane so you can see the new table in the list of all the tables in the database. The Query1 is still open. You can close the query window if you don't plan to rerun the query, or you can save your query for future use. Just in case your manager requests some changes after viewing the table, let's preserve our work.

13. Right-click the Query1 tab and select **Save**. Enter **CreateTable_Employ-eesAndRegistrations** as the name of your query and click **OK**.

The new query appears in the Queries category of the Database Navigation view. Notice a special icon image that appears in front of the query name (Figure 7.5).

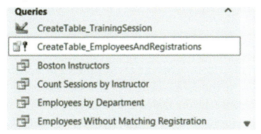

FIGURE 7.5. Access helps you to identify different objects in the Database Navigation pane by assigning it a unique icon image.

14. Close the Query Design view.

Action Item 7.1

To get more practice with the Make Table query, save the results of the query qryEmployeesWithNoCourses in a stand-alone table. Check the table you created and then delete it from the Navigation pane.

Tables you create with Make Table query can be safely deleted if you or other database users no longer need them. When you try to close the qryEmployeesWithNoCourses query, Access will ask you if you want to save changes to the design of this query. You must be careful here because if you select Yes, Access will update the query type, replacing your selected query with a Make Table query. The good news is that you can always turn back the Make Table query into a select query by opening it in Design view, clicking the Select button in the Query Type section of the Query Design tab and closing the query. Access will save the query as the Select type when you choose Yes to its message. When closing queries pay attention to what is going to avoid unintentionally creating objects in your database.

USING APPEND QUERIES

In the previous section, you learned about Make Table queries that were suitable for permanently saving sets of records in stand-alone tables. This section will introduce you to another type of database operation as well as another type of action query, known as an Append query. A frequent database operation is addition of new records to database tables. The Append query is designed exactly for this task. Let's assume that you have the NewRegistrations table that contains the information about several employees who also signed up for training courses, but their records do not appear in the Registration table. You need to quickly append the new records to the existing table without affecting the records that already exist. Let's create an Append query to perform this task.

(◉) **Hands-On 7.2   Creating an Append Query**

1. Import **NewRegistrations** table from **the ETD_Supplement.accdb** file located in the Companion files to the ETD database. On the **External Data** tab, click **New Data Source**, choose **From Database | Access**. Browse to the **CompanionFiles**, select the specified database, and click **Open**. Click **OK** in the dialog box. In the Import Object dialog, select **NewRegistrations** table and click **OK**.

2. Open the imported **NewRegistrations** table (see Figure 7.6) and note that it contains registration information for five employees and has several fields with the same data types as in the Employees and Registration tables.

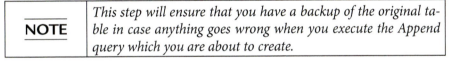

ID	EmpCode	FirstName	LastName	Phone	EmployeeID	SessionID	RegisteredDate
4	MVICH000042603	Mark	Antonovich	(718) 444-3293	34	5	4/25/2023
3	JRROW000060614	James	Harrow	(718) 444-3299	30	7	4/19/2023
5	DNCER000040409	Douglas	Spencer	(718) 444-3252	40	12	4/4/2023
2	HANAK000040516	Helen	Romanak	(718) 444-3281	25	17	4/25/2023
1	CVSON000010509	Chrstine	Gustavson	(718) 444-3244	18	21	4/28/2023
(New)							

FIGURE 7.6. New registration data to be appended to the Registration table.

3. Close the **NewRegistrations** table.
4. In the Navigation pane, right lick the **Registration** table and choose **Copy**. Click anywhere in the Navigation pane and choose **Paste**. Click **OK** to have Access create a new table named **Copy of Registration** with the same structure and data as the Registration table.

NOTE	*This step will ensure that you have a backup of the original table in case anything goes wrong when you execute the Append query which you are about to create.*

5. Choose **Create | Query Design**.
6. In the **Query Design** tab, add the **NewRegistrations** table, and drag the following fields to the query grid: **EmployeeID**, **SessionID**, and **RegisteredDate**.
7. Click the **Append** button.

8. In the Append dialog box (Figure 7.7), choose **Registration** from the **Table Name** drop-down and click **OK**.

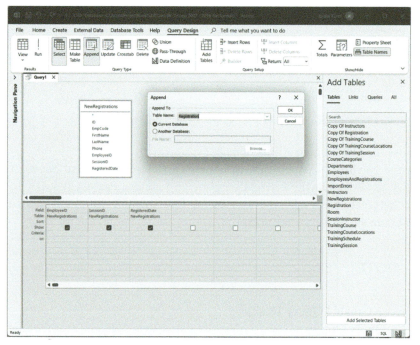

FIGURE 7.7. Creating an Append query.

Notice that the Show row in the Design grid is now replaced with the Append To row, stating which field the query will add the information to (see Figure 7.8).

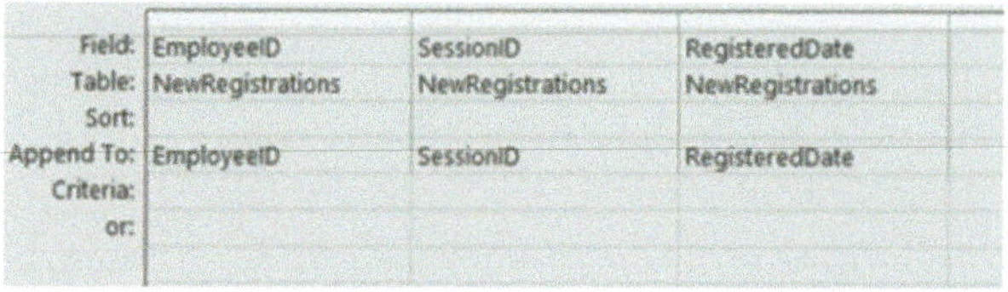

Field:	EmployeeID	SessionID	RegisteredDate
Table:	NewRegistrations	NewRegistrations	NewRegistrations
Sort:			
Append To:	EmployeeID	SessionID	RegisteredDate
Criteria:			
or:			

FIGURE 7.8. Access replaces the Show rows with the Append To row when you create an Append Query.

9. Click the **Run** button to execute this query, and then click **Yes** when prompted to confirm that you are about to append five rows to a table.

10. Open the **Registration** table in Datasheet view to see the new entries (see Figure 7.9).

    Notice that new rows appended to a table with an AutoNumber primary key are automatically assigned a new unique value.

ID	EmployeeID	SessionID	RegisteredDa	Grade	Click to Add
1	44	2	8/31/2021		
2	7	11	9/1/2021		
3	5	9	8/30/2021		
4	3	7	8/11/2021		
5	2	16	8/25/2021		
6	1	16	8/26/2021		
7	47	2	9/1/2021		
8	5	9	9/1/2021		
9	2	2	8/27/2021		
10	18	21	4/28/2023		
11	25	17	4/25/2023		
12	30	7	4/19/2023		
13	34	5	4/25/2023		
14	40	12	4/4/2023		
(New)	0	0			

FIGURE 7.9. Registration table with the records appended from the NewRegistrations table.

11. Close the Registration table and return to the **Query1** tab that displays your Append query.

    Note that if you run this query again, Access will add the same records to the Registration table with new unique keys, creating duplicate records. See the next section in this chapter to find out how this issue can be prevented.

    Let's look at the SQL statement behind this query.

12. Switch to SQL view.

    Access shows the following SQL statement:

```
INSERT INTO Registration (EmployeeID, SessionID, RegisteredDate)
SELECT NewRegistrations.EmployeeID, NewRegistrations.SessionID,
NewRegistrations.RegisteredDate
FROM NewRegistrations;
```

Append queries are also called Insert queries since they use **INSERT INTO** command as their SQL syntax. These keywords are used to specify the table name and the column names to insert values into. The values in this case are obtained from the fields listed by the Select statement. The **FROM** clause specifies the table to select from.

Note that it is also possible to create a new record in the Registration table by specifying the field values like this:

```
INSERT INTO [Registration]
(EmployeeID, SessionID, RegisteredDate)
SELECT 28 AS EmployeeID, 9 AS SessionID,
#5/11/2023# AS RegisteredDate;
```

Hardcoding specific values in the Select statement is handy when you need to make a quick insert of data that may not be saved in any file or table.

13. Return to the **Design** view and save the query that was used to append records to the Registration table as **qryAppend_NewRegistrationRecords**, then close it.

Using Criteria With Append Queries

In the previous section's Hands-On, you took records from one table and inserted them into another. Instead of appending all the records from a table, you can use some criteria to refine your selection of records to append. For example, you might want to only append records of employees who hold a position in a specific department. Because the NewRegistrations table does not have information about the department, you would need to add the Employees table to your query design and then specify the conditions your query needs to meet. You should try to do this on your own when you get a chance. If you get stuck, ask the Bing powered AI for help. You may need to formulate your question more than once to get a working solution.

In this section, we will focus on preventing Append query from inserting duplicate rows. As mentioned earlier, if you run the qryAppend_NewRegistrationRecords query more than once, Access will create duplicate rows in the destination table because it always does exactly what you tell it to do. Right now, there is no WHERE clause in our query that limits the inserted records in one way or another.

In Access, there are at least four ways you can use to filter out the records that already exist in the destination table:

- Use the NOT EXISTS keywords.
- Use the NOT IN keywords.
- Use the LEFT JOIN with IS NULL operator.
- Use the DELETE query.

Let's start with the NOT EXISTS approach. Recall that these keywords were introduced in Chapter 6.

Hands-On 7.3   Modifying an Append Query to prevent Duplication of Records.

1. In the Navigation pane, right-click the **qryAppend_NewRegistrationRecords**, choose **Design** view.
2. In the SQL view, modify the existing SQL statement as follows:

```
INSERT INTO Registration (EmployeeID, SessionID, RegisteredDate)
SELECT NewRegistrations.EmployeeID, NewRegistrations.SessionID,
NewRegistrations.RegisteredDate
FROM NewRegistrations WHERE
NOT EXISTS (Select SessionID from Registration
WHERE Registration.SessionID = NewRegistrations.SessionID AND
Registration.RegisteredDate = NewRegistrations.RegisteredDate);
```

To better understand every component of any complex SQL statement, you can ask the AI-powered copilot for the web for the explanation. Figure 7.10 shows the answer that the AI gave me, when I provided it with the previous query.

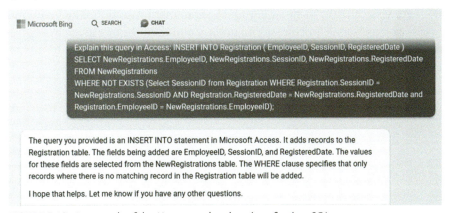

FIGURE 7.10. An example of the AI-generated explanation of a given SQL query.

The more questions you ask about a specific topic, the more detailed answer will be provided based on the conversation context. For example, here is the explanation of the same query which I received after I have been chatting with the bot for a while:

"This query is an append query that copies records from one table to another. It has the following components:

- INSERT INTO Registration (EmployeeID, SessionID, RegisteredDate): *This specifies the destination table and the fields that will receive the data.*

- SELECT NewRegistrations.EmployeeID, NewRegistrations.SessionID, NewRegistrations.RegisteredDate FROM NewRegistrations: *This selects the data from the source table and the fields that will provide the data.*

- WHERE NOT EXISTS (Select SessionID from Registration WHERE Registration.SessionID = NewRegistrations.SessionID AND Registration.RegisteredDate = NewRegistrations.RegisteredDate and Registration.EmployeeID = NewRegistrations.EmployeeID): *This filters out the records that already exist in the destination table based on the SessionID, RegisteredDate, and EmployeeID fields. It uses a subquery to check if there is a matching record in the Registration table for each record in the NewRegistrations table. If there is no match, the record is appended. If there is a match, the record is skipped.*

The purpose of this query is to add new registrations to the Registration table without creating duplicate records."

As you can see, by breaking up the statement into individual components, this explanation is much easier to understand than the one given in Figure 7.10.

3. Execute the modified query by clicking the Run button in the Results section of the Query Design tab.

Access displays a confirmation message as shown in Figure 7.11.

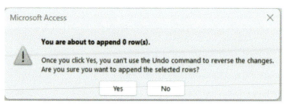

FIGURE 7.11. Even if there are no rows to append Access still displays a confirmation message.

4. As there are no new records in the **NewRegistrations** table, click **No**.

Clicking Yes will have no effect on the data, as there are 0 new rows.

5. Save the modified query and close it.

6. Open the **Registration** table to check that indeed it does not contain duplicate records.

Action Item 7.2

In the SQL view, create a new Append query named **qryAppend_with_NOT_ IN** that will insert to the Registration2 table (which is the copy of the Copy of Registration table created in Hands-On 7.2, Step 4), only the records from the **NewRegistrations** table that are not already present in the **Registration2** table. Rewrite the query we modified in Hands-On 7.3 so that it uses in the WHERE clause the **NOT IN** condition to filter out the records. The subquery should select the EmployeeIDs from the Registration2 table where the RegisteredDate and SessionID match those in the NewRegistrations table. When completed, run the query twice and check the records in the Registration2 table after each run to ensure that the query works as intended, and no duplicate records are added in the second run.

The SQL statement can be found in the Companion files - **Solution_Append_with_NOT_IN.txt**.

Action Item 7.3

In the SQL view, create a new Append query named **qryAppend_with_LEFT_ JOIN** that will insert to the Registration3 table (which is the copy of the Copy of Registration table created in Hands-On 7.2, Step 4), only the records from **NewRegistrations** that do not have a matching record in the **Registration3** table. Rewrite the query we modified in Hands-On 7.3, so that it uses the **LEFT JOIN /IS NULL** condition to filter out the records. When completed, run the query twice and check the records in the Registration3 table after each run to ensure that the query works as intended, and no duplicate records are added in the second run.

The SQL statement can be found in the Companion files - **Solution_Append_with_LEFT_JOIN.txt**.

The fourth approach of dealing with duplicate records that might be created by the Append query is using the SQL DELETE statement. With this statement, you can remove the duplicate rows from the source table before appending them to the destination table. We will handle this scenario when we cover Delete queries later in this chapter.

USING UPDATE QUERIES

An update query in Access is a type of action query that can make changes to several records at the same time. For example, you can raise course instructors' hourly fees by a certain percentage without having to create a new column of calculated data. The update query can perform calculations directly on the table data. We will walk through this example in the next Hands-On. Update queries are also used to correct or modify existing data in tables based on different criteria.

Hands-On 7.4   Creating an Update Query to Perform Calculations

1. Choose **Create | Query Design** and add the table **Instructors** to the query.
2. In the first column of the query grid, in the field row, select **HourlyFee**.
3. Run the Select query to view the current fees.

   Let's give our instructors a 10 percent increase if the fee is less than $60.00. Based on these conditions, 4 out of 5 instructors will be given this raise.

4. Return to the Design View and in the Query Type group of the Query Design tab, click the **Update** button to convert the select query to an Update query.

   Notice an Update To row appears in the design grid.

5. In the HourlyFee field's Update to row, write the following expression:
   [HourlyFee] *1.10

6. In the **Criteria** row for the **HourlyRate** field, enter the following expression:
   <60

   Figure 7.12 shows the completed Update query.

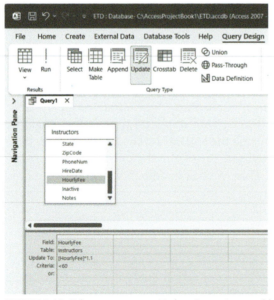

FIGURE 7.12. When you create an Update Query Access adds the Update To row to the query grid.

7. Click the Run button to execute the query.

   Access will warn you that you are about to update four rows and you can't use the Undo command to undo the changes.

8. Click **Yes** to make these changes and then open the table Instructors to see the new fees.

9. Return to the Query Design view and save the query as **qryUpdate_HourlyFees_By_10Percent.**

10. Switch to the SQL view to examine the SQL statement behind this query.

    To make the requested update, Access has created the following SQL statement:

```
UPDATE Instructors
SET Instructors.HourlyFee = [HourlyFee]*1.1
WHERE (((Instructors.HourlyFee)<60));
```

The SQL UPDATE statement is used to update records in a table.

The UPDATE keyword is used to specify the table to update. The SET keyword is used to specify the column to update and the value to insert into the column. The value can be specified as an expression. You can update more than one column by using the following syntax:

```
SET field1 = expression1, field2 = expression2 (and so on)
```

The Update query we created in this Hands-On will update the HourlyFee column of the Instructors table by multiplying the current HourlyFee value by 1.1, which is equivalent to adding 10 percent to the current value. The WHERE keyword is used to set conditions on retrieved data, in this case only records where the HourlyFee value is less than 60 will be updated.

11. Close the **qryUpdate_HourlyFees_By_10Percent** query.

Action Item 7.4

As mentioned earlier, an update query can be used to correct issues with the data. Using the SQL view, write and run the update query that will fix the misspelling in the first name of the employee with the ID equal to 18.

The SQL statement can be found in the Companion files - **Solution_Update_FirstName.txt**.

Action Item 7.5

Write an Update statement that will update the EmpCode column for every employee where the EmpCode field is blank.

The missing codes are provided in the Companion files (see the **3Emp** sheet in the **AllEmployees.xlsx** Excel workbook).

Perform the following tasks:

- Import the **3Emp** sheet to Access (Choose **External Data | From Excel**. Follow the steps in the Get External Data – Excel Spreadsheet wizard. Make sure to choose **ID** as your own primary key.
- Create a Select query that joins the **Employees** table with the **3Emp** table.

```
SELECT Employees.EmpCode, Employees.FirstName, Employees.LastName
FROM Employees
INNER JOIN 3Emp ON Employees.ID = [3Emp].ID;
```

- **Run** the Select query to ensure you get three records with the blank **Emp-Code**.
- Change the query type to the **Update** query and switch to the **SQL view**.
- Write the SQL statement that will update the **EmpCode** column in the **Employees** table with the **EmpCode** from the **3Emp** table.

The SQL statement can be found in the Companion files – **Solution_Update_EmpCode.txt**.

USING DELETE QUERIES

A Delete query is another type of an action query that is available in Access. Delete queries are used to quickly remove information that you no longer need in your database tables. These may be the old records that are useless or obsolete, or to remove duplicates that were inadvertently created by Append queries. By removing useless data from your tables, you can decrease the size of your database, improve its performance, and make it easier to maintain.

If you want to know which records will be deleted by a Delete query, first examine the results of a Select query that uses the same criteria, and then, if all is good, run the Delete query. Be sure to always maintain backup copies of your data. Like with other action queries, the Delete operation cannot be undone.

Note that Delete queries are never used to delete data from fields in database tables; they can only delete entire records. To remove data from a field, use the Update query.

Earlier when we discussed the Append queries you learned that you could use the Delete query to remove duplicate rows from the source table before appending them to the destination table. Let's see how this is accomplished in the next Hands-On.

Hands-On 7.5   Creating a Delete Query

1. In the ETD database, create a copy of the **NewRegistrations** table. Save the backup as **Copy of NewRegistrations**.
   Recall that you created the **NewRegistrations** table in Hands-On 7.2.
   Because we will be deleting records, it is recommended that you first make a backup of the data.
2. Open the NewRegistration table in the Datasheet view and manually add the following record:

EmpCode	FirstName	LastName	Phone	EmployeeID	SessionID	RegisteredDate
VDURA0001103	Vincent	Candura	(781) 444-3282	26	17	4/25/2023

3. Save the **NewRegistrations** table and close it.
   The table now contains 6 records; 5 of them were already appended to the Registration table when we created and run the Append query in Hands-On 7.2. The following steps will delete from the NewRegistrations table the 5 records that already exist in the Registration table.
4. Choose **Create | Query Design** and switch to the **SQL** view.
5. Enter the following SQL Select statement:

```
SELECT NewRegistrations.EmployeeID, NewRegistrations.SessionID,
NewRegistrations.RegisteredDate FROM NewRegistrations
WHERE (((NewRegistrations.[EmployeeID]) IN
(Select EmployeeID from Registration WHERE
Registration.RegisteredDate = NewRegistrations.RegisteredDate
And Registration.SessionID = NewRegistrations.SessionID)));
```

Note that this query selects three fields from the NewRegistrations table where the EmployeeID is in the list of EmployeeIDs returned by the subquery. The subquery's WHERE clause specifies the selection criteria.

6. Click **Run** to execute the previous SQL statement.
   The returned 5 records are the records that already exist in the Registration table; therefore, they can be safely deleted from the NewRegistrations table. As mentioned earlier, always select first the records you intend to delete to ensure that the criteria used in your select query works as intended.

7. Switch to the Design view and click the **Delete** button in the Query Type group of the Query Design tab.

Access adds the Delete row to the query grid when you create a Delete query (see Figure 7.13). The drop-down in the Delete row contains two options, Where and From. The Where clause instructs Access to delete the data based on the criteria you enter. The criterion for the deletion is provided by the sub-query. The From clause is used when you create a Delete query based on the information from two or more tables.

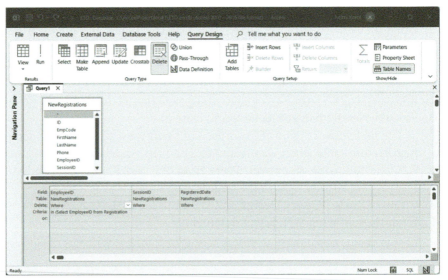

FIGURE 7.13. When you create a Delete Query, Access adds the Delete row to the query grid.

8. Switch to the SQL view to examine the SQL statement behind this Delete query:

```
DELETE NewRegistrations.EmployeeID, NewRegistrations.SessionID,
NewRegistrations.RegisteredDate FROM NewRegistrations
WHERE (((NewRegistrations.EmployeeID) IN
(Select EmployeeID from Registration WHERE
Registration.RegisteredDate = NewRegistrations.RegisteredDate
And Registration.SessionID = NewRegistrations.SessionID)));
```

Notice that the only difference between this statement and the statement we wrote in Step 5, is the use of a different keyword. To turn your Select query into a Delete query simply use the DELETE keyword in place of SELECT.

9. Click the **Run** button to execute this query. Click **Yes**, to confirm the deletion.
10. Open the **NewRegistrations** table and notice that it has only one record. This record does not exist in the Registration table; therefore, it was not deleted by the Delete query.
11. Return to your Delete query and save it as **qryDelete_Matching_NewRegistrations** and then close it.
12. In the Navigation pane, double click the **qryAppend_NewRegistrationRecords** to run the query. Click **Yes** to the warning message.
13. Check the **Registration** table to see that the new record was successfully added.

You can delete all the records from any table by using the following syntax (but please do not try this on your production database):

```
DELETE FROM [tableName];
```

Now that we are done with appending records from the NewRegistrations table, use the following syntax to delete all records from it:

```
DELETE FROM NewRegistrations;
```

NOTE	*Sometimes the Delete query or another action query you write in the SQL view may not execute even though there is nothing wrong with the syntax used. I have found that compacting and repairing the database will resolve many database problems. You will find the Compact & Repair Database button when you choose File	Info.*

OTHER TYPES OF QUERIES IN ACCESS

There are two other types of queries that you may find useful when you begin working with Access at a more advanced level. These queries are: Pass-Through and Data Definition. These queries are not considered action queries, but like the Union query, they can only be created in the SQL view. They are often referred to as SQL Specific. Due to the limited scope of this Access Project book, the Pass-Through and Data Definition queries will not be covered, but here's a short description of each of them:

- In Microsoft Access, a Pass-Through query allows you to send commands directly to an external database server. This query is executed on the server and the results are returned to Access. You would use this type of query when you need to execute an SQL statement that is not supported by Access or when you want to execute an SQL statement that is more efficient when executed on the server. To create a pass-through query in Access, you need to select Pass-Through from the Query Type group of the Create tab. You can then enter your SQL statement in the SQL view of the query designer. The SQL statement could include a function like OPENROWSET that specifies the provider and data source, and the SELECT statement specifying the data to retrieve from a specific sheet in an Excel workbook, like this:

```
SELECT *
FROM OPENROWSET('Microsoft.ACE.OLEDB.12.0',
'Excel 12.0;Database=C:\Data\ExcelData.xlsx;HDR=YES',
'SELECT * FROM [Sheet1$]')
```

- In Microsoft Access, a Data Definition query is used to create or modify tables, indexes, and relationships. You can use these queries to create new tables, add fields to existing tables, and modify the structure of existing tables.

  - To add an additional column called Notes to the Employees table, you can use the ALTER TABLE SQL statement with the ADD COLUMN statement, in the SQL view, after selecting the Data-Definition query type:

    ```
    ALTER TABLE Employees ADD COLUMN Notes Text(255);
    ```

    To create an index on the Employees table that will order results by the LastName field, and in case there are duplicate last names, the results will be ordered by FirstName, use the following SQL:

```
CREATE INDEX idx_FullName ON Employees (LastName, FirstName);
```

The CREATE INDEX statement is followed by the name of the index, the ON keyword, the name of the table, and the list of fields you want to index, separated by a colon, and enclosed in parentheses.

When listing the indexed fields, you can specify the sort order ASC or DESC. For example, the following SQL will create an index where the results will be ordered first in DESC order by LastName and ascending order by FirstName:

```
CREATE INDEX idx_FullName ON Employees (LastName DESC, FirstName ASC);
```

As the ascending sort is the default order, you can omit the ASC keyword.

For a step-by-step introduction to Data Definition queries and learning how to program Microsoft Access using its programming language – Visual Basic for Applications (VBA), see my book titled *"Access 2021 / Microsoft 365 Programming by Example"* (ISBN: 9781683938416) by Mercury Learning and Information.

SUMMARY

This chapter has introduced you to action queries that allow you to find and modify data in your database tables instead of merely searching for the data. You have learned the functionality of each type of action query starting from making a new table, appending new records to an existing table, modifying values in specific fields in a table, and deleting data from a table. Action queries are very powerful but can cause many unwanted problems in your database if executed without careful thought. You learned that by making backups of your data prior to running action queries, paying close attention to Access warning messages, and creating and checking Select statements with the same criteria as an action query, you can protect your database from unintended data loss.

In the next chapter, we will move to an entirely new topic of making your database easier to use by creating forms for editing data.

CREATE AND WORK WITH FORMS

Part IV focuses on creating and working with Access forms. You learn about designing various types of forms that can be used for data input and viewing.

Chapter 8

DESIGNING AND USING FORMS

With the basic database tasks mastered, you are now ready to delve into creating an attractive and intuitive user interface for your database application. With Access, you can easily create good looking forms that allow users to quickly scroll through datasheets, see various views of the data, perform data entry operations and updates. Access forms development is a huge subject that certainly cannot be fully covered within the pages of this book. This chapter will focus on showing you several ways of creating various types of forms in Access, explaining how you can use them to control access to data for different users and how you can add command buttons and other form controls to enhance the user interface.

ABOUT ACCESS FORMS

Forms in Access are database objects that are used to create a user interface for your database application. Forms allow you to display, enter, or edit data from a data source which can be a table, query, or SQL statement. They can be customized and designed to suit the specific needs of database users depending on the type of the database.

Forms can be *bound* or *unbound*. A bound form is a form that is directly connected to a data source. You will work with bound forms in this chapter. An unbound form is a form that is not connected to any data source, such as a table or query. This means that the form does not display or edit any exiting data but is used to collect or display information that is not stored in the database. You can create unbound forms by using the Blank Form tool on the Create tab, or by creating any bound form and removing the record source from the form and the controls. We will not cover unbound forms in this chapter as these forms require using Visual Basic for applications (VBA) code or macros to manipulate the data and the controls and rely on writing custom code to handle errors and exceptions that may occur when working with data.

DESIGNING FORMS

You can use different tools to create a form based on a table or query. For example, the Form tool, the Split Form tool, the Multiple Items tool, Datasheet, Modal Dialog, the Form Wizard, Navigation, or the Blank Form tool. Access provides these various tools of forms creation in the Forms group of the Create tab as shown in Figure 8.1.

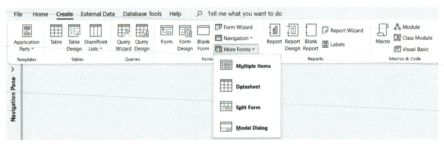

FIGURE 8.1. The Create tab of the Ribbon shows various tools for creating forms.

The Form Tool

The quickest way to create a form in Access is to select a table or query in the Navigation pane and click the Form tool on the Create tab. When you select your data source and use the Form tool Access creates a form with all the fields from the data source and adds a Subform when there is a one-to-many relationship. Figure 8.2 shows the Employees form created in this manner.

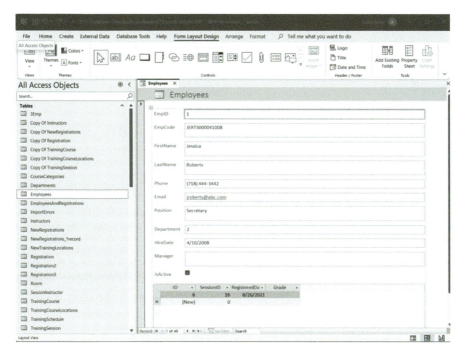

FIGURE 8.2. When you use the Form tool, Access creates a form with all the fields from the data source.

Once created, you can modify the layout or appearance of the form, removing the fields you don't need and arranging them in the way that suits your needs. Keep in mind that well designed forms should provide the right information to specific people and hide data you don't want them to view. A form created with the Form tool lays your data out on a single screen and allows you to focus on one record at a time. When you switch this form to Design View you can easily remove the layout applied to the controls on the form by selecting the cross tool and choosing Remove Layout button in the Table section of the Arrange tab (see Figure 8.3).

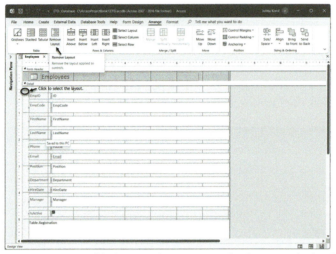

FIGURE 8.3. To modify the size and arrangement of various controls placed on the form display form in the Design View and use the Remove the Layout button on the Arrange tab of the Ribbon.

The Form Wizard

If you need an attractive form based on the answers you provide, use the Form Wizard. When you use this tool, you can select the fields, layout, style, and title of the form. Using the Form Wizard takes more steps to create a form but at least you get the form based on your choices. You may still require some adjustments in Layout view or Design View to customize the form to your liking. Figure 8.4 shows using the Form Wizard to create a form based on the table Instructors. Notice that you can select only the fields you need.

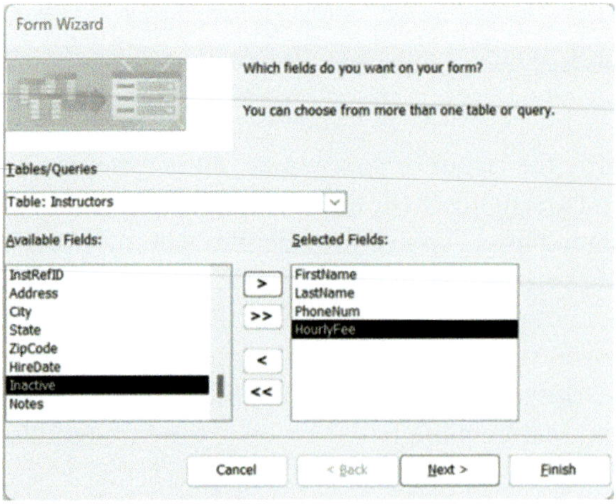

FIGURE 8.4. Using the Form Wizard to create a form.

The next screen of the Wizard allows you to specify the layout for your form: Columnar, Tabular, Datasheet, or Justified. You can click on the option button to see the visual representation of the layout before you decide.

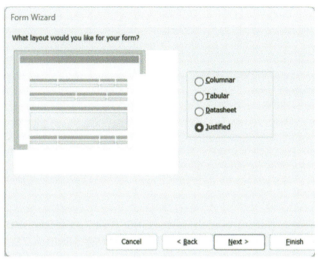

FIGURE 8.5. Using the Form Wizard you can specify the layout of the form.

- The Columnar layout shows the form in a classic, one record per-page format.
- The Tabular layout is multiple records per -page form. This layout is great for tables with few fields. When there are too many fields, you will need to scroll back and forth when you select this layout.
- The Datasheet layout is a spreadsheet-like format. This is like an Access Datasheet view embedded in a form.
- The Justified layout shows one record of data laid out across who entire form over multiple rows. This is a layout often used when you must present memo fields.

In the last screen of the Form Wizard, you can enter the title you want for your form and tell Access to open the form in the Form or Design View (see Figure 8.6).

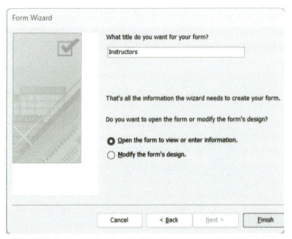

FIGURE 8.6. Using the Form Wizard you can specify the title for your form and how the form should be opened when it is completed.

Once you click the Finish button you should see the resulting form with the fields, layout, and title you specified in the Form Wizard (see Figure 8.7).

FIGURE 8.7. The Instructors table created by the Form Wizard shows only specified fields and displays the form controls in the Justified layout.

To further customize the form, you can open it in Design or Layout view, adjust control sizes and apply different colors and fonts, or select the desired theme from the Themes dropdown in the Form Design tab. Figure 8.8 displays the Wizard created customized form where the title band was enhanced using an Office Theme from the Themes drop-down and the look of the form field labels was modified by using the Back Color and Fore Color properties in the Property sheet after selecting the corresponding label from the drop-down box at the top of the Property sheet. Form and control properties are discussed in detail further in this chapter.

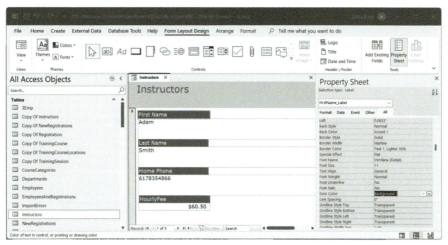

FIGURE 8.8. The Instructors table created by the Form Wizard is now enhanced with the colors, fonts, and themes available via the Form Layout Design and the Properties sheet.

The Form Design and a Blank Form

The third way of creating an Access form is by using the Form Design and Blank Form buttons. Both these tools allow you to start with a blank form and build from the ground up by adding any fields and controls you want. This takes more time but gives you full control over the design of the form. When you use this method to create your form, you need to know how to work with different properties available in the Property Sheet. The first step is specifying an existing data source for your form using the Record Source property of the Form or building your record source by clicking on the ellipsis button next to the Record Source property (see Figure 8.9). Access will then display a query builder for your form where you can add the tables or queries, or both, that will provide data for your form (see Figure 8.10).

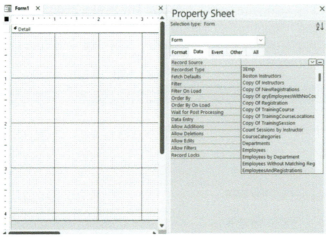

FIGURE 8.9. When you create a form from scratch you need to specify the Record Source for the form from the sources that already exist in your database or by creating a new data source.

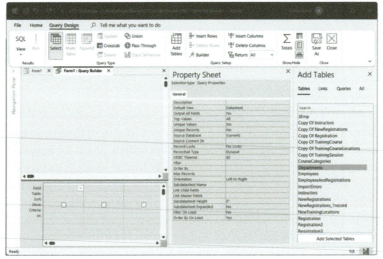

FIGURE 8.10. When you click the ellipsis button next to the Record Source property of the form, Access displays the Query Builder that allows you to choose the tables and fields that will serve as the data source for your form.

By dragging the required tables or queries to the query view and selecting the appropriate fields in the query grid you can specify the data source for your form (see Figure 8.11).

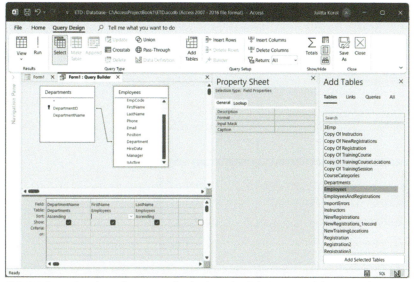

FIGURE 8.11. Creating a data source for the form that is being created from scratch.

You don't even need to save it as standalone query. Simply right click the Form1: Query Builder tab and choose Save. Upon doing this Access will close the Query Builder tab and fill the Record Source property with the SQL statement (which is behind the query you created). Figure 8.12 displays the Record Source property. To see the Zoom window, click the Record Source property and press Shift+F2.

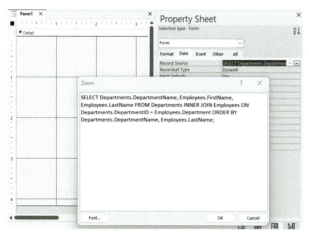

FIGURE 8.12. An SQL statement created using the Query Builder can serve as the Record Source for your new form.

With the Record Source specified for your form, you may begin placing the required fields on your form. This is done via the Add Existing Fields button in the Tools section of the Form Design tab (see Figure 8.13).

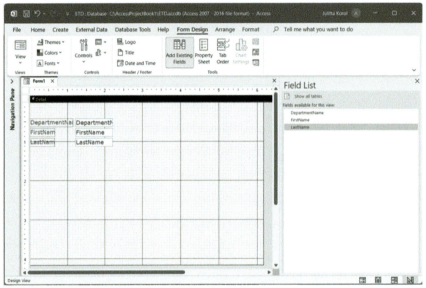

FIGURE 8.13. The Field List pane provides the fields from your Record Source that can be placed on your form. To get access to fields in other tables, click the Show all tables hyperlink.

As you can see creating forms from scratch takes longer and requires many form and control design skills that can only be acquired by lots of practice and patience. By using the Form Wizard and other Form tools you can save lots of time. When you have Access do most of the difficult stuff you can focus on adding the finishing touches that will make your forms stand out.

Access forms can easily display data from multiple related tables.

The Multiple Items Forms

Use the Multiple Items form to create a form with records from the data source shown in a datasheet-like format. Multiple Items form allows you to see all records at a glance, and it recommended with tables that contain only a small number of fields (see Figure 8.14).

FIGURE 8.14. Creating a Multiple Items form.

The Split Form

An interesting type of a form you can create in Access is a Split form. Split forms display one record at the top half of the form and all records at the bottom half. This type of a form format allows you to easily browse records in the bottom portion of the form (the Datasheet view) and view and edit each record's detail in the upper portion of the form (the Form view) as shown in Figure 8.15. To quickly create the form depicted in this figure, select TrainingCourse table in the Navigation view as the data source, and choose Create | More Forms | Split Form. The Split Form tool creates a form that shows a Form view and a Datasheet view of the same data source.

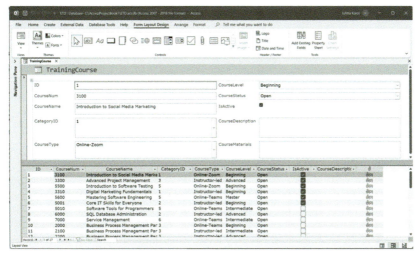

FIGURE 8.15. Creating a Split form.

The Modal Dialog Forms

The More Forms drop-down offers yet another type of form you can generate in Access. A Modal dialog form is often used to display important information or requesting user input that requires immediate attention. When you choose Modal dialog, Access opens a form in a Design View and adds two command button controls (OK, Cancel) as shown in Figure 8.16. Each command button comes with an automatically defined on Click event that determines what happens when the user clicks the button. By default, Access creates embedded macros for its different events. By clicking the ellipsis button next to the OnClick property of the command button in the Property Sheet, you can check out the macro Access has created to understand the action it performs. Figure 8.17 displays the macro assigned to the Command1 button (currently labelled OK on the form). This macro tells Access to close the window when the OK button is clicked. Macros are covered in Chapter 12 of this book.

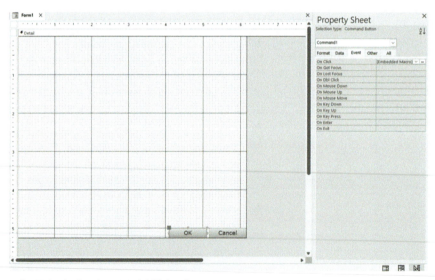

FIGURE 8.16. Creating a Modal Dialog form.

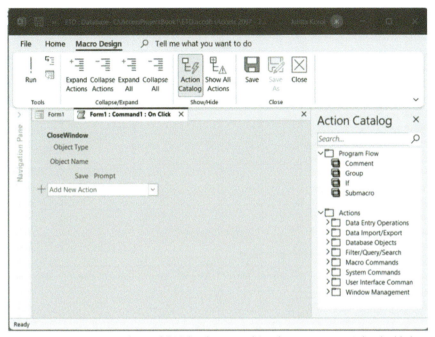

FIGURE 8.17. Buttons on the Modal Dialog forms are driven by Access generated embedded macros which you can enhance to suit your needs.

When you open a Modal Dialog form in a Form view it will open as a modal window, which means you must close it before you can move the focus to another object in your database. You can turn any existing form into a Modal Dialog form by setting the Modal property to Yes in the Property sheet of the form. You can also set the PopUp property to Yes to ensure that the form stays on top of other windows. When you use the popup modal forms you should set the BorderStyle property to Dialog to give the form a dialog-style border and title bar (see Figure 8.18). Setting the Record Selectors and Navigation Buttons to No will give the Modal Dialog form a clean look. You can add any controls you want to the Modal Dialog form, such as text boxes, labels, and command buttons. You will work extensively with various form controls in the next chapter.

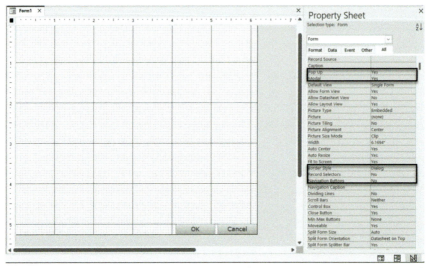

FIGURE 8.18. The Property Sheet of the Modal Dialog form shows important settings that need to be turned on or off.

Modal Forms versus Popup Forms

The following table explains the difference between a Modal form and a Popup form.

Modal Form	This form stays on top of other forms, and you cannot click on anything behind it until you close the modal form. The purpose of it is that the user does not change something that the form relies on.
Popup Form	This form stays on top of other forms, but you are allowed to click on forms behind it. You can move the popup anywhere you want on the database screen even outside of it.

The Navigation Forms

To switch between different forms and reports in your database, you may want to create a user-friendly navigation form that contains a Navigation control. Use the Forms group of the Create tab to access the Navigation tool as shown in Figure 8.19. Access will present you with various styles of navigation forms. You can choose from Horizontal or vertical tabs, or a combination of both. When you make your selection, Access will create a form with a navigation control and a subform and will open it in the Layout view. At this point all you need to do is drag and drop the forms or reports you want to access from the Navigation pane to the Add New tab. A navigation button will be added for each form or report, and upon clicking the button the form or report will be displayed in the view area of the navigation form.

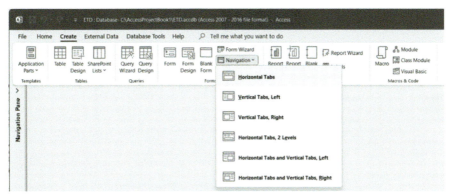

FIGURE 8.19. Creating a Navigation Form in Access.

In Figure 8.20, two forms were placed in the left Vertical tab navigation control. You can easily change the label at the top of the navigation form by double-clicking on it and entering a new text. Also, each caption of the navigation button can be changed by right clicking on it and selecting Form Properties from the shortcut menu. On the Property Sheet, simply type a new caption in the Caption field. Remember that you can switch between different forms in the navigation form by clicking its navigation buttons. To view the navigation form in the Form view, click View on the Home tab.

Once created a navigation form can be set up as the default display form for your database, so it opens automatically when you open a database. To enable this setup, choose File | Options | Current Database. Under Application Options, in the Display Form drop-down, select the name of your navigation form and click OK. Access will warn you that you must close and reopen the current database for the specified option to take effect. Click OK to the message. Save your work and close the database, then reopen it. Your navigation form should open automatically.

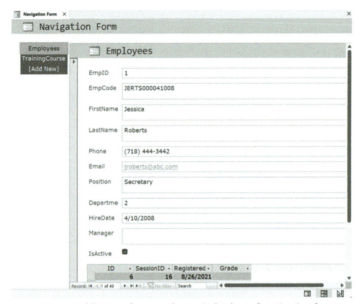

FIGURE 8.20. Adding two forms to the Vertical Tabs, Left navigation form.

Navigation Forms vs Switchboard Forms

Navigation forms allow users to create more visually appealing navigation forms than it was possible using Switchboard forms that were popular in Access prior to version 2010. The Switchboard feature is still available in the current version of Access, but you need to use the Switchboard Manager tool which is not available on the Ribbon by default. You can add the Switchboard Manager command to the Quick Access toolbar in the following way:

- Click the down arrow on the Quick Access Toolbar which appears to the left of the title bar of your database window and click More Commands.

- In the Choose commands from combo box, select All Commands.

- Select Switchboard Manager and then click Add.

- Click OK to save your changes. Access will warn you that you must close and reopen the current database. Click OK to the message, then close and reopen the database.

- Once the database reloads, on the Quick Access toolbar, to the right of the Save button, you should see the Switchboard Manager button (see Figure 8.21). Click this button to open the tool.

- Access will look for a valid switchboard in the current database and if it cannot find it, you will be able to click Yes in the message box to create one.

- Access creates a Main Switchboard (Figure 8.22). You can either add all your switchboard commands to the Main Switchboard or create secondary switchboards, by clicking New.

- Figure 8.23 shows the types of commands you can add to the Main Switchboard.

To add items to a Switchboard, use the following guidelines:

- In the Edit Switchboard page, click New.

- In the Edit Switchboard Item Dialog box, type a name of the switchboard item in the Text box. This name will appear on the switchboard button.

- In the command list, select the action you want the button to perform. For example, you can open a form, run a macro, or exit the application. To open the form Employees, enter the Edit Employees in the Text box. Choose Open Form in Edit mode from the Command drop-down, and specify the Employees form in the Form dropdown, then click OK. You should see the Edit Employees entry added to the items area in the Edit Switchboard page. Continue adding more items to your switchboard. You can have up to eight items on each switchboard page. When you are done, click Close the Edit Switchboard Page dialog box.

To display your completed switchboard form, double-click the Switchboard entry in the Forms group of the database Navigation pane. Figure 8.24 displays the switchboard with the Edit Employees button that was added using the Edit Switchboard page. When you click on this button, the form Employees will open in another tab.

FIGURE 8.21. Switchboard Manager command button added to the Quick Access Toolbar allows to create the legacy style navigation forms.

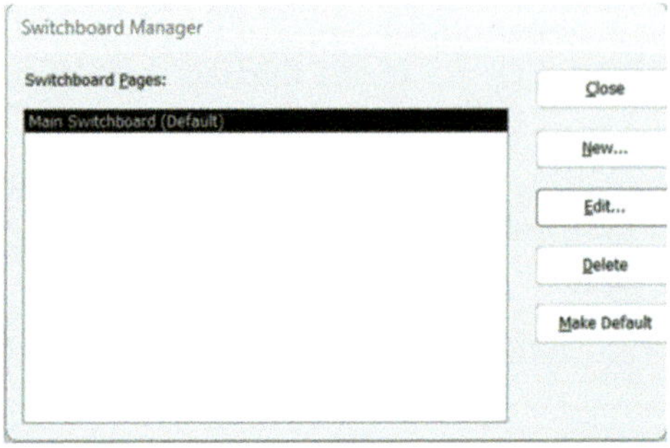

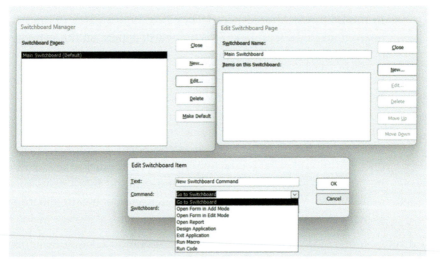

FIGURE 8.22. Access automatically creates a Main Switchboard page for your navigation needs.

FIGURE 8.23. Use the Edit Switchboard button to add various commands to your switchboard.

FIGURE 8.24. The Main Switchboard with a button that navigates to the form Employees.

Like the newer navigation forms, switchboard forms can be set to automatically open when you open the database. Use the same steps to set up this feature as explained in the discussion of the navigation forms.

When you begin programming in Access, you will conclude that you can design the most useful and attractive navigation forms by creating custom menu forms.

UNDERSTANDING FORM VIEWS

Access forms can be displayed in several ways depending on how you intend to use them. Forms can be designed or modified in Layout or Design View. These views are great for fine-tuning the appearance and functionality of forms. In the Layout view, you can modify the layout and appearance of various form controls while viewing data the form displays, and in the Design View you can make detailed adjustments in the structure and properties of the form. When you are finished designing the form you will want to see it in the Form view. This view displays the data that is connected to the form and is a view typically displayed to the database users. No design changes are allowed in the Form view. To switch between different views, use the view buttons on the right side of the status bar (see the bottom area in Figure 8.20 earlier).

UNDERSTANDING FORM PROPERTIES

Access form object has multitude of properties that are listed on the Property Sheet (see Figure 8.25). They are grouped into four main categories: Format, Data, Event, and Other. The All tab lists properties in all categories. Most of the properties have default values so you don't need to set them unless you need to change the form look or behavior.

FIGURE 8.25. The Form Properties dialog box.

Format Properties

Using the properties listed in the Format tab, you can control the look and feel of your forms.

The Default View property tells Access how to open the form. A Single Form setting (the default) displays one record at a time. The other choices are: Continuous Form, which displays multiple records, Datasheet, which displays data in rows and columns like a worksheet. Another setting is a Split Form.

Once you determine how you'd like the form to open, you can specify what views of the form are allowed. For each available view (Form, Datasheet, Layout) you can determine if users will have them available while working with the form.

Forms can be enhanced by adding pictures so there are several property settings in the Format tab, that will allow you to manage this aspect of your forms: Picture Type, Picture, Picture Tiling, Picture Alignment, and Picture Size Mode. The best way to learn about these properties is by creating a simple form, adding a picture to it and setting its various picture properties.

Depending on the number of fields shown in a form, the size of the form should be made be bigger or smaller by typing the new value in the Width property. When the form is displayed, you can also specify if it should be auto centered (Auto Center), auto resized, or fit to screen, and what type of border it should have. The choices are: Sizable, Thin, Dialog, or None. When the Border Style is set to Sizable the form users will be allowed to resize the form at runtime. The control box that appears on the form will have Minimize and Maximize buttons enabled. When the Border Style is set to Dialog, the Minimize and the Maximize buttons are disabled. As mentioned earlier this setting is used for pop-up forms. The Thin border will fix the size of the forms at runtime and the Minimize and the Maximize buttons will be enabled. You can also choose None as the Border Style setting to specify that no border should be present. This setting is often used for splash forms, that display briefly when the database application starts or performs a long-running operation.

Some forms will not require scrollbars, so you can use the Scroll Bars property to disable the vertical and horizontal scrollbars on your form. You can also turn on or off the record selectors. Most forms have navigation buttons that Access uses to handle record navigation. But if you want to program your own navigation controls, you can turn off the Navigation Buttons.

Forms have Minimize, Maximize, and Close buttons. You can control the display of these buttons via the Control Box property. When the Min Max buttons are enabled, users will be able to minimize or maximize forms on their desktops. The Close Button property set to close will allow users to use the control menu to close the form. If this property is set to False, you will have to provide them with other ways of closing the form. It pays to remember, that you can always close the form with a shortcut combination: Ctrl+F4 or Alt+F4.

There are several formatting settings helpful for working with split forms and subdatasheets. A subdatasheet is a datasheet that is nested within another datasheet and contains data related or joined to the first datasheet. Recall that Access automatically creates a subdatasheet when you create a table that is in one-to-one or one-to-many relationship with another table.

Each of the settings in the property sheet can be looked up online by clicking the setting and pressing the F1 key.

Data Properties

Data properties (see Figure 8.26) are used to tell Access how a form should present and work with the data. Access forms can be bound to tables, queries, SQL statements, or they can be unbound.

The Record Source property is where you determine the source of data for your form. This property can be determined when you design the form or when you run the form. The latter requires some programming knowledge.

The Recordset Type property lets you specify what kind of recordset is available to a form. A Dynaset is a default setting which allows you to edit bound controls based on a single table or tables with one-to-one relationship. For controls bound to fields based on tables with a one-to-many relationship, you can't edit data from the join field on the "one" side of the relationship unless cascade update is enabled between tables. The other two available settings are: Snapshot (no tables or the controls bound to their fields can be edited) and Dynaset (inconsistent updates) where all tables and controls bound to their fields can be edited.

Property Sheet		✕
Selection type: Form		ᴬᶻ↓
Form	⌄	
Format Data Event Other All		
Record Source	Employees	
Recordset Type	Dynaset	
Fetch Defaults	Yes	
Filter		
Filter On Load	No	
Order By		
Order By On Load	Yes	
Wait for Post Processing	No	⌄
Data Entry	No	
Allow Additions	Yes	
Allow Deletions	Yes	
Allow Edits	Yes	
Allow Filters	Yes	
Record Locks	No Locks	

FIGURE 8.26. The form Data Properties.

The Fetch Defaults property indicates whether Access shows default values for new rows on the specified form before the row is saved.

The Filter On Load property determines whether the Filter property is applied when the form is loaded.

The Order By On Load property determines whether the sorting specified by the Order By property is applied when the form is loaded.

The Wait For Post Processing property specifies that the form waits until processing of any operations (running a macro, or VBA code) triggered by a user change to form data is complete before proceeding with the next operation.

The Data Entry property set to Yes will restrict a user from seeing existing data. The user will be able to only enter new data.

A bunch of data settings (Allow Additions, Allow Deletions, Allow Edits, Allow Filters) specify what users can do with the data. Users may or may be allowed to edit the data, delete existing data, filter records, or add new data. To make your form read-only, set the Allow Edits property to No.

The Record Lock property is useful when you need to determine how records are locked and what happens when two users try to edit the same record at the same time. When a user edits a record, Access can automatically lock that record to prevent other users from changing it before the first user is finished. For forms, this property specifies how records in underlying table or query are locked when data in a multiuser database is updated. When there are no locks, two or more users can edit the same record simultaneously. This is called "optimistic" locking. If two users attempt to save changes to the same record, Access displays a message to the user who tries to save the record second. This user can then discard the record, copy the record to the clipboard, or replace the changes made by the other user. When the All Records setting is selected in the Record Lock property, all records in the underlying table or query are locked while the form is open in Form or Datasheet view. Users can read records, but no one can add, edit, or delete any records until the form is closed. The Edited Record setting activates so called "pessimistic locking." In this case, a record can be edited by only one user at a time. The record stays locked until the user moves to another record.

Event Properties

Access forms interact with users and many of these interactions are controlled via the code behind the form. This can be the VBA programming code, Expression builder, or embedded macros. There are numerous operations (events) that occur when a user works with an Access form. These events are listed in the Event Properties of the Access form. You can use the event properties to modify the default behavior of forms. For example, you can specify what happens when the form opens, closes, or is activated or deactivated, or what occurs when a user makes any modifications to the current record. If you don't specify any events, Access will handle the form in its default way. Earlier in this chapter, in Figure 8.16, you saw an embedded macro assigned to the On Click event of a command button of a form. You'll find other examples of Form events as you proceed to the Hands-On section of this and the next chapter.

Here are some of the concepts that a beginner user should know about events in Access forms:

- To view or select the available event for a form, click the Event tab and then click the drop-down arrow next to the event property you want to modify and choose a macro or an event procedure that should run when the event occurs.

- To create or edit event procedure using the Visual Basic Editor, click on the Build button (...) next to an event property and choose Code Builder. This will open the Visual Basic Editor where you can write or modify the code for the even procedure. You can also access the Visual Basic Editor by pressing Alt+F11 from any Access window.

- Form and control events occur in a specific order depending on the user action or the data change that triggers them. Knowing when and how events occur can help you avoid errors and unexpected results in your macros or event procedures. For example, to validate data entered by the user before saving it to a table, use the BeforeUpdate event.

- When writing event procedures, you should know how to use variables, constants, functions, and expressions. These concepts are the subject of more advanced Access books that prepare you for a programming work. However, further in this chapter, as a demonstration, we will put together a complex expression using the programming code.

- When writing custom event procedures, you must know how to test and debug them. You can use various tools and techniques to fix errors in your code. Again, these tools and techniques are beyond the scope of this book.

Other Properties

The form properties categorized as Other Properties (see Figure 8.27) help the form designers to control many important aspects of the form's behavior and appearance. Here you can specify whether a form is a Pop Up. Pop up forms appear as child forms of the Access window. They sit on top of all other forms and can be placed anywhere on the Access desktop.

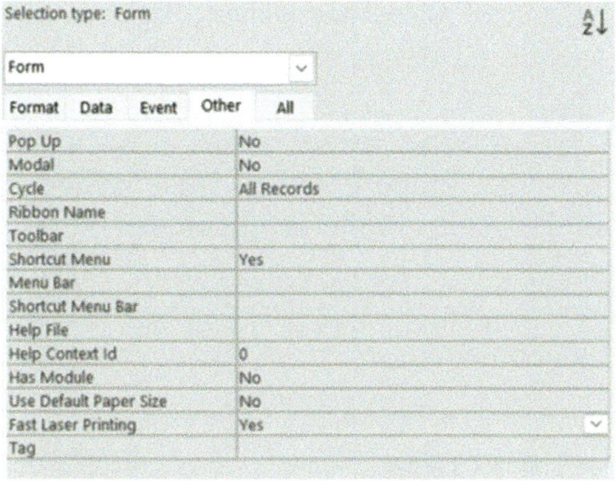

FIGURE 8.27. The form Other Properties.

The Modal setting set to True will prevent any other form from receiving the focus until the modal form is closed.

The Cycle property specifies what happens when you press the Tab key. The All Records choice will ensure that when you press the Tab key from the last control on the form, the focus will move to the first control in the tab order in the next record. The Current Record choice will ensure that pressing the Tab key from the last control on a record moves the focus to the first control in the tab order in the same record. Finally, the Current Page choice specifies that pressing the Tab key from the last control on a page moves focus back to the first control in the tab order on the page.

The Ribbon name property allows you to set the name of the custom ribbon that should be displayed when the form is loaded. Designing custom ribbons is covered in my book *Access 2021 / Microsoft 365 Programming by Example* (Mercury Learning and Information, 2022).

If your form needs to be loaded with a custom toolbar this should be specified using the Toolbar property. To allow users to access shortcut menus when they right click the form, set the Shortcut Menu property to Yes. To display a custom menu for a form, set the Menu Bar property to the name of that menu bar. If you have a help file that explains to the user how the form works, you can specify it in the Help File property. The Help Context ID property specifies the context ID of a topic in the custom Help File property setting.

The Has Module property indicates whether a form contains programming code. When set to No, Access will remove all code written behind the form, and the form will be loaded very quickly. Writing code behind the form in an advanced topic. If you are interested in this subject, refer to the aforementioned book that will introduce you to Access programming.

When printing a form, you can specify in the Use Default Paper Size property whether the default paper size of the current printer is used. To make printing faster, set the Fast Laser Printing to Yes.

The Tag property is a string that you can use to store extra information about a form without affecting any of the other properties. This value will be saved with the form. This is a very useful property when programming Access. To see how this property can be used in Access without programming, see the file AI_Forms_TagProperty.pdf in the Companion files. The example was generated by the Microsoft AI Bing Chat engine.

CREATING AND MODIFYING A FORM

Now that you've learned about different types of Access forms and their properties, the remaining sections of this chapter will focus on Hands-On exercises that will enforce your understanding and use of the built-in form tools. In addition, you will learn how to format your forms to make them more appealing and useful to the database users.

Before you create a form, you must ask yourself some questions: What is the purpose of this form? How will this form be used? What type of form should it be? What fields will it contain? Which Access tool is most suitable for the form I'm about to create?

Suppose you need to create a form that will allow you to add a new employee to the table Employees. Obviously, the purpose of the form is data entry. The form should contain all the required fields from the table Employees. It should be a stand-alone form that only allows to enter new data; does not display any existing employee records. This form should not have any scrollbars or record selectors. Recall that Form tool in Access allows you to create a form that allows you to enter information for one record at a time. This type of form can give you a quick start in creating the data entry form. We'll walk through the steps required to create this type of form with the requirements mentioned in Hands-On 8.1.

⊙ Hands-On 8.1   Creating a Data Entry Form

(Part I—Laying Out the Form)

1. In the database Navigation pane select the table Employees and choose Create | Form.
2. When Access creates the form, switch to Design View.

3. Click the Table.Registration subform control to select it. When the control is selected you will notice an orange border around it (see Figure 8.28). Press the Delete key to remove the subform from the form.

4. Resize the form to eliminate the empty area at the bottom. One way to do it is click in the empty form area to select the Form Details section and then point the mouse just above the Form Footer until you see the black line crossed with a black double-sided arrow. Hold and drag the cursor up to about 5.5 inches on the vertical ruler.

5. To resize the controls on the form, click on any control on the form (do not click on the control label). Point the mouse to the selection handle in the right edge of the selected control until you see the horizontal double arrow, hold, and drag it to the left to a position of 5 inches on the horizontal ruler. All the controls should be resized by performing this action. If you release the mouse and nothing happens, you need to repeat these steps to ensure that the correct cursor appears before you begin the dragging operation.

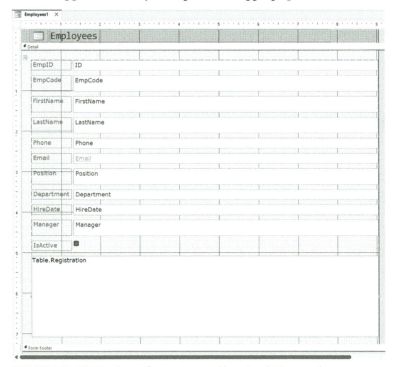

FIGURE 8.28. The Employees form was created by using the Form tool.

6. Resize the EmpCode and Phone control to a width of 3.5 inches on the horizontal ruler.

To move and resize controls independently without affecting other controls you must remove the layout that Access applied to the form controls.

7. Click the EmpCode control and choose Arrange | Select Layout (you can also click the layout selector box at the upper-left corner of the layout. This box appears to the left of the EmplID label in Figure 8.28).

8. Once all the controls are selected, click Remove Layout on the Arrange tab. When the layout is removed you will no longer see the selection box on the form. At this point, you can individually resize the required controls by selecting them and dragging the right edge of the selection border to the left to the desired location. If the control moves, press Undo (Ctrl+Z) to cancel the operation and try again.

9. Resize the ID control so its width ends at 2.5 inches on the ruler.

10. Click the label control in the Form Header and type New Employee Data Entry as the new form header.

11. Resize the New Employee Data Entry label to 5 inches on the ruler.

12. Reduce the width of the form to 7 inches on the horizontal ruler by clicking anywhere in the empty area of the form and dragging the right edge of the form to the left and dropping it at the specified position.

After completing all 12 steps, your form should match Figure 8.29.

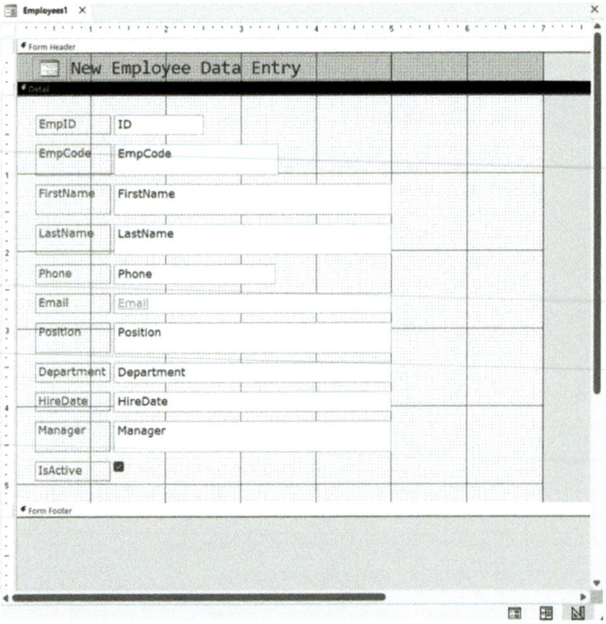

FIGURE 8.29. The modified Employees form in the Design View.

13. Switch to the Form view.

   You will notice that the form displays the first record from the table Employees and the record selector at the bottom of the form allows to move to other employee records or to search for a specific record. As specified in the form requirements earlier, we need to take the necessary steps to turn this form into a data entry form. To do this we will work with the Form Property sheet.

14. Return to the Design View and in the Form Design tab, click the Property Sheet.

15. Click the box to the left of the horizontal ruler. This action selects the form. The Form entry should be selected in the drop-down box at the top of the Property Sheet. Consider that if you click in different areas of the form, the Property Sheet selection drop-down entry will change accordingly.

16. With the form selected, click the All tab in the Property sheet and make the following adjustments to the form properties:

Property Name	Property Setting
Pop Up	Yes
Record Selectors	No
Navigation Buttons	No
Scroll Bars	Neither
Data Entry	Yes

17. Switch to the Form view to view your changes. Your form should match Figure 8.30.

   Notice that the form is now a Pop Up form, and you don't see other employee records. This form can be easily moved anywhere on your desktop by left-clicking the title bar and dragging it anywhere you like. Because this is not a Modal form, you have full access to any other Access feature. All you can do in this form is enter a new employee record. But before making any data entry, let's make other necessary adjustments to this form. When entering data, you will not need to enter the EmpID number as this is an AutoNumber field and Access populates it automatically every time you add a new record. Therefore, it makes no sense to have a user stop at this field during the data entry. Let's make this field read-only.

18. Switch back to the Design View and click the ID text box next to the EmpID label. The Property Sheet should display ID in its drop down. Find and set the Enabled property of the ID control to No.

19. Switch to the Form view and notice that the EmpID label now appears in dim font and the ID control is shaded in gray indicating that it is not enabled. The selection pointer appears in the EmpCode text box control. Since this is a data entry form, we won't want the user to manually create the EmpCode as it is prone to data entry errors. Let's remove this control entirely from the form and have Access create EmpCode upon adding the new record to the table.

20. Switch back to Design View. Click the EmpCode label, hold down Ctrl key and click EmpCode text box, then press Delete to remove both controls from the form.

21. Move all the controls that appeared below the EmpCode up so there is no gap between them and the EmpID field. You can select all the controls by dragging a rectangle around them and releasing the mouse button to select them. Once they are selected move them up as a group by click and drag.

22. Right click the Form tab to save the changes you made in the Form design. For now, save the form as Employees1.

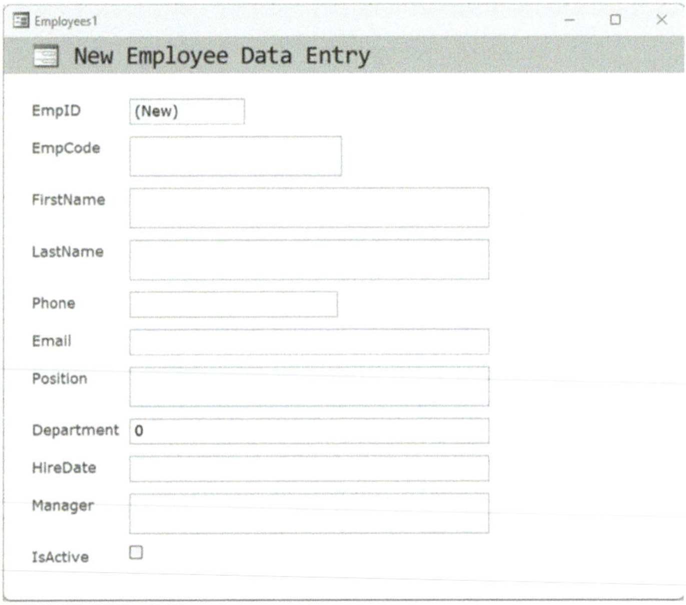

FIGURE 8.30. The modified Employees form after making changes in the Form properties.

You can make other changes to enhance the form appearance when you get a chance. But for now, let's tackle the data entry aspect of this form. How do we tell Access to enter a new record, assign the EmpCode, and display a new blank form so the user can continue entering more records? And how do we dismiss the data entry screen when it is no longer needed?

This brings us to another topic related to the forms.

Understanding Form Controls

As forms perform various actions on the database, they include various controls that allow users to interact with data on the form or in the database. You can access them via the Controls group of the Form Design or Form Layout Design tab when you are working with a form in Design or Layout view (see Figure 8.31). Some controls are hidden from the view and to reveal them you must click the down arrow in the lower-right corner of the Controls group.

FIGURE 8.31. Access features a wide range of controls that can be used in a form.

By pointing to a control in the Controls group, Access displays the tooltip with the name of the control. The following is the description of various controls.

Control Name	Image	Description
Select		Selects different objects on the form.
Text Box	ab	A text box can hold any type of data except graphical. Click this control and then click and drag an area in the Form design to add the text box.
Label	Aa	Most controls have an associated label that tells what the control is called. You use it by clicking this control in the Controls group and dragging an area in the form.
Button		Buttons are used to perform some action. For example, a button can be used to save or cancel the form. To add a button to a form, click the button control and click and drag the size of the button you want.
Tab Control		This control has a series of tabs. Each of these tabs can have its own options which is very useful when you have many controls in your form and you need to organize them by a different category.
Link		This control will create a link to another file, a different location in the same document, a Web page, or a resource that is external to the database.
Edge Browser		Use this control to specify a URL and show web pages on a form. You can also browse files and folders by specifying a file URL. This control is available only for users of Access for Microsoft 365.

(Contd.)

Control Name	Image	Description
Navigation Control		This is a special Access control that contains buttons that make it easy to switch between various forms and reports in the database.
Option Group		This control is used for grouping various radio buttons. To group option buttons, select the Option Group control, and click and drag a box around them.
Insert Page Break		Used to create a cut-off point when printing a document. A new page will print when a page break is encountered.
Combo Box		Used to add a box with a list of options that users can select when they click the pull-down arrow.
Line		Click and drag to draw a line in the form. Often used to divide form into different areas so they are easier to read.
Toggle Button		A toggle button's command will stay in effect when clicked and will remain so until it is clicked again.
List Box		A box that works like a combo box but shows an expanded list of options to pick from.
Rectangle		Used to draw a rectangle in the form. Useful for creating visual groups of related form components.
Check Box		A small box that can be checked or unchecked. When checked, the condition bound to the check box is true or active, and when unchecked it is false or inactive.
Unbound Object Frame		Used for creating a frame inside the form to display a spreadsheet, PDF document, or another external resource.
Attachment		When you attach files and graphics to the records in your database, you can use the Attachment control to view your attachments.
Option Button		Also known as a radio button, this control is used to select a certain option and often appears in groups of two or more.
Subform/Subreport		This control allows you to create a form inside a form or a report inside a report.
Bound Object Frame		If you store pictures in Microsoft Access tables, you can display them on a form or report using the Bound Object Frame. A bound object frame is bound to a filed in an underlying table.

Control Name	Image	Description
Image		Use this control to place a picture in your form.
Web Browser Control		You can use this control to specify a URL and show web pages on form. To access this control, you must expand the Controls group by clicking its drop down.
Chart		Use this control to embed a chart that displays Microsoft Access data from a form or report. To access this control, you must expand the Controls group by clicking its drop down.

When you expand the Controls drop-down, you will find additional options as shown in Figure 8.32.

FIGURE 8.32. The Expanded Controls group.

- Set Control Defaults

  If you modified some properties of a control, you could use this command to revert a control's properties back to the default setting.

- Use Control Wizards

  Toggle this command to have Access automatically start a Wizard to help you with the creation of different commands (Option Buttons, Combo Boxes, List Boxes, Command Buttons, Subforms, and Subreports) in the form.

  Turn the Control Wizard off to design the control on your own when you need more control over the control's behavior.

- ActiveX Controls

  These are special types of controls that can be used on Access forms to further enhance the functionality of a form. For example, you could use the Microsoft TreeView Control to display a hierarchical list of items, like the way files and folders are displayed in the left pane of the Windows Explorer feature.

Selecting and Deselecting Controls

After you add a control to a form, you can resize it, move it, or copy it. To select a control on a form, the Select command which looks like an arrow in the Controls group must be chosen. To select a control, click anywhere on the control. The selected control will show from four to eight handles. These are small squares around the control, located at the corners and midway along the sides. To move the control, click the move handle which is in the upper-left corner—it is the largest handle. Use the other handles to resize the control.

When you select a single control that has an attached label, you will also see the move handle for the label.

You can select multiple controls by clicking each control while holding down the Shift key. You can also drag the pointer around the controls you want to select, or simply click and drag in the ruler to select a range of adjacent controls. When selecting multiple controls, you will notice a rectangle as you drag the mouse. Be sure not to touch controls or labels you don't intend to select.

To deselect a control, click anywhere in the unused portion of the form.

Resizing a Control

To make a control bigger or smaller, you can use any of the smaller handles in the upper, lower, and right edges of the control. To increase or decrease both width and height of the control at the same time, use the sizing handles in the control corners. Use the handles in the middle of the control sides to size the control in one direction, left or right. When you move the mouse pointer to the corner sizing handle, the pointer becomes a diagonal double arrow (see Figure 8.33). At this point you can begin dragging the sizing handle until the control is the desired size. If the mouse pointer touches a side handle of the selected control, the pointer will change into a horizontal or vertical double-headed arrow. Access can automatically size the control to best fit the text contained in the control. To do this, simply double-click on any of the sizing handles. You can cancel the sizing operation by pressing Ctrl+Z or clicking the Undo button in the Access Quick Toolbar.

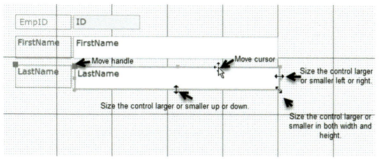

FIGURE 8.33. Sizing and moving a control.

The Size/Space drop-down in the Sizing and Ordering group of the Arrange tab, offers many options for controlling the arrangement of controls (see Figure 8.34).

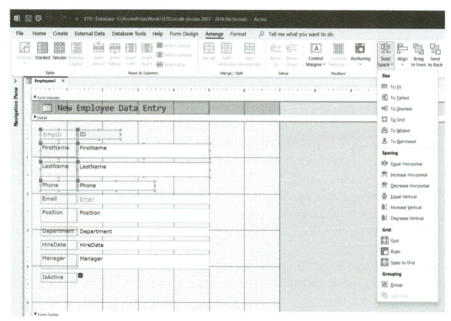

FIGURE 8.34. Form controls can be sized and arranged using various options of the Size/Space command.

You can also access the Size/Space commands from the shortcut menu by right clicking the selected controls.

Moving and Aligning Controls

There are several ways to move a control after you select it:

- Click the control and hold down the mouse button. When the mouse pointer changes into a four-directional arrow, drag the mouse to move the control to a desired location.

- Click the control to select it and move the pointer to any of the highlighted edges of the control. When the mouse pointer changes to a four-directional arrow, drag the mouse to move the control to a desired location.

- Click the control to select it and use the arrow keys on the keyboard to move the control to the desired location.

- Click the control to select it and press Ctrl+X on the keyboard to cut the control then click anywhere else in the form and press Ctrl+V to paste the control. By default, the control will appear in the upper left corner of the form. At this point you can move it to the desired location.

When multiple controls are selected, you can move the selected controls together.

To cancel the moving operation, press Esc key before you release the mouse button. After the move operation is complete, use the Undo button on the Quick Access toolbar to undo the changes.

If you need to align the controls on the form, select the controls and use the options provided in the Align command in the Sizing and Ordering group of the Arrange tab. Controls can be aligned to the Grid when that the top-left corners of the selected controls are aligned to the nearest gid point. Access displays a small grid of dots across the entire form in Design View which assists you in aligning controls. Use the Snap to Grid command in the Size/Space command to align controls to the grid as you place them on the form. When Snap to Grid is off, Access ignores the grid and allows you to place the control anywhere you want.

You can also align the left edge of the selected control with the leftmost, rightmost, topmost, and bottommost selected control using the Left, Right, Top, and Bottom options.

Adjusting Spacing Between Controls

The spacing commands in the Size/Space command (see Figure 8.34 earlier) allow you to adjust the distance between controls based on the space between the first two selected controls. Choose the Equal Horizontal command to make the horizontal space between selected controls equal. This command will only work when three or more controls are selected. The Increase Horizontal command increases the horizontal space between selected controls by one grid unit. Use the Decrease Horizontal to decrease the horizontal space. The same options are available for adjustment of the Vertical spacing: Equal Vertical, Increase Vertical, and Decrease Vertical.

Copying Controls

If you need several of the same type of controls on the form, create the control you need on the form, then select it and press Ctl+C to copy it. Click anywhere on the form, and press Ctrl+V to paste the copy of the control. The copy will be placed at the top of the form most likely on top of another control. Simply use the moving handle to move it to a new location. Be sure to also move the control's label. Copying of controls can greatly speed up the form creation process especially when the form must contain multiple controls of the same type.

Action Item 8.1

Working with form controls requires lots of patience and practice. Use Access form tools described earlier to have Access create a couple of forms in the ETD database and play with the form controls by selecting them, moving, copying, and resizing them. Adjust the spacing and alignment of controls, until you feel comfortable and productive.

Working With Controls and Their Properties

Having learned how to add controls to an Access form and how to manipulate them, it's time to put these skills to practical use. In Part II of the Data Entry Form that we started in Hands-On 8.1, we will add two buttons to the form, place them in the desired location on the form. We will format them to look appealing to the eye and program them to execute the required actions. The first button will submit the form, set the EmpCode, and ensure that a new blank form is displayed. The second will dismiss the form. During this exercise, you will gain some working knowledge of using the Code Builder and VBA Editor. You will learn how to write VBA code and use various functions. You will also learn how to validate the form.

Hands-On 8.1   Creating a Data Entry Form

(Part II—Adding Command Buttons)

1. Open the **Employees1** form in Design View and make sure that the Property Sheet is visible to the right of the form. You can turn the Property Sheet on and off by clicking the Property Sheet button in the Tools group of the Form Design View.

2. In the Controls group of the Form Design tab, click the **Button** control. When the button control is selected there will be a border around it in the Controls group and the Property Sheet will indicate that the Selection type is Default Command Button. With the Button selected, begin drawing a rectangle to the right of the FirstName text box. If Access displays the Command Button Wizard, click the Cancel button, because you will not be using the standard actions provided by the Wizard but will program the button yourself.

    Access creates a button on the form and assigns it a default name and caption, Command, followed by a number.

3. While the command button is selected, in the Format tab of the Property sheet change the **Caption** property to **&Save and New** and press Enter. The button should now show the new label. Notice that the ampersand (&) that you typed in front of the letter "S" is used to assign a shortcut key to the button. In the Form view, instead of clicking the button, the user will be able to use keyboard combination Alt+S to activate this button.

4. While the button is still selected, click the Other tab in the Property Sheet and change the **Name** property of the command button to **cmdSave**.

5. In the form, resize the button so the entire text is visible. You can do this quickly by double-clicking the sizing handle in right border of the selected button.

6. In the same way, add a second button to the form positioning it below the first button. Set its **Caption** property to **&Cancel**, and the **Name** property to **cmdCancel**. Resize the button to the size of the first button.

7. In the Controls group of the Form Design, click the Rectangle control and draw a rectangle around both buttons (see Figure 8.35). In the Format tab of the Property sheet of the rectangle, set the **Border Width** property to **2 pt**.

8. Press **Ctrl+S** to save all the changes you made to the form.

FIGURE 8.35. The Employees1 form is shown here with two command buttons and a rectangle surrounding the buttons.

After adding the main components to your form, it is always a good idea to see the form in the Form view.

9. Change the form to the Form view. Use the **Tab** key to move between the form fields to ensure that the data entry happens in the logical way. The user should be able to efficiently move from field to field without having to jump around. If the order of fields is incorrect, you can adjust it by returning to the Design View and clicking the Tab Order button which is in the Tools group of the Form Design tab (see Figure 8.36).

10. While the form is displayed, press Alt+C and notice that the Cancel button is selected. Press Alt+S to select the Save and New button. At this point, none of these buttons perform any actions. In Part III of the Data Entry form (Hands-On 8.1), we will begin to implement the form logic.

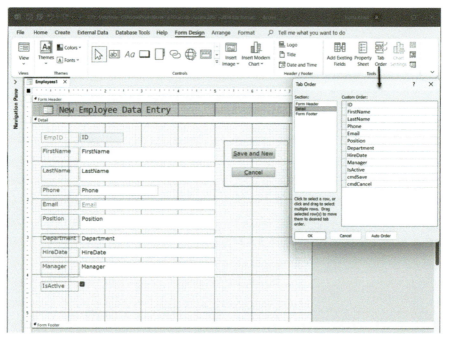

FIGURE 8.36. The Tab Order window displays the list of all the controls on the form. Click on any control and drag it up or down to set its tab order.

Hands-On 8.1   Creating a Data Entry Form

(Part III—Programming Command Buttons)

1. In the Form Design View of the Employees1 form, click the **Cancel** button to select it.

   Now, let's tell Access to close the form when this button is clicked.

2. In the Property Sheet, select the Event tab that lists all the events that are available for command buttons. When the user clicks the button, Access triggers the OnClick event. This is where you need to write code to handle the click event.

3. In the dropdown next to the On Click event, select [Event Procedure] and click the ellipses next to it. This will display the VBA (Visual Basic Editor) screen. Access creates the cmdCancel_Click procedure template for you. All you need to do now is write a statement that will close the form.

4. In the empty line above the End Sub keywords (see Figure 8.37) that denote the end of the VBA subprocedure code, enter the statement shown here:

```
DoCmd.RunCommand acCmdClose
```

DoCmd is a property of the Access Application object. You can use various methods of the DoCmd object to run Microsoft Access actions from your Visual Basic programming code. These actions can perform tasks such as closing windows, opening and closing forms, and setting the values of controls.

The RunCommand method, runs a built-in Access command. Each menu and toolbar command in Microsoft Access has an associated constant that you can use with the RunCommand method to run the command from Visual Basic. The command constants which begin with the acCmd prefix, can be looked up online:

https://learn.microsoft.com/en-us/office/vba/api/access.accommand

The acCmdClose is the constant you need to use to close the Access form. Notice that the constant is preceded by a space after the DoCmd.RunCommand statement.

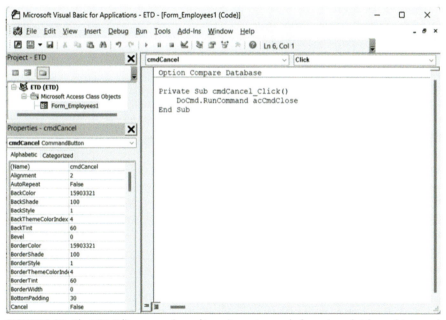

FIGURE 8.37. The VBA Editor screen is used to write custom code for various database objects such as your form or form controls.

The top of the Visual Basic code window displays two drop-down boxes. The one on the left displays various form controls and form sections for which you could write an event that you select from the Event box (which is the drop down box at the right hand-side).

5. Save the changes in the VBA Editor screen by clicking the Save icon on the toolbar or press **Ctrl+S**.

6. Close the Visual Basic window. You can do it by using the Control box or choosing **File | Close and Return to Microsoft Access**. Or simply, press **Alt+Q**.

   Now you should be back in Form Design View. Let's test the button we just programmed.

7. Switch to the Form view and click the **Cancel** button.

   The form disappears from the view. This is what was our objective. Now let's program the other button.

8. Open the **Employees1** Form in Design View and click the **Save and New** button to select it.

9. Right click on the **Save and New** button and choose **Build Event** from the shortcut menu.

   Access displays the Choose Builder dialog box where you can specify which builder to use.

10. Select the **Code Builder** and click **OK**.

    Access opens the Visual Basic Editor screen and adds another procedure below the one you wrote for the Cancel button.

11. In the empty line above the End Sub keywords (see Figure 8.38), enter the statements shown here:

```
DoCmd.RunCommand acCmdSaveRecord
[EmpCode] = UCase(Left([FirstName], 1)) & _
UCase(Right([LastName], 4)) & "0000" & _
IIf(Month([HireDate]) < 10, "0" & _
Month([HireDate]), Month(HireDate)) & _
IIf(Day([HireDate]) < 10, "0" & _
Day([HireDate]), Day(HireDate)) & _
Right(Year([HireDate]), 2)
DoCmd.GoToRecord , , acNewRec
```

The first statement in the previous code tells Access to save the current record. It is assumed that user entered data in the form fields before clicking the Save and New button. You will add code to validate user's data later in this exercise. For now, let's focus on the second statement, which is displayed on fine lines. Its purpose is to create an employee code for the EmpCode field.

This code is a combination of the following criteria:

● Get the first letter of the FirstName field; it should be displayed in uppercase.

   To extract characters from a beginning of a text string, use the Left function, provide the name of the field where the data is located, and the number of characters you want to extract. To ensure that the extracted characters appear in uppercase, use the UCase function.

So, the first part of the expression we are creating in the second statement is:

```
UCase(Left([FirstName], 1))
```

This expression is assigned to the EmpCode field, like this:

```
[EmpCode] = UCase(Left([FirstName], 1))
```

If the FirstName field contains Henry, we will get the letter H in the EmpCode.

The expression we entered in Step 11 is quite complex. It could be written on one line, but we broke it into several segments to make it easier to understand. To connect different parts of a complex expression we use the ampersand (&). This is called a concatenation operator. To create a line break in the statement we follow the ampersand (&) by a space and an underscore (_) and a space. This last space is not visible, but it must be there or Visual Basic will complain and will turn the entire statement in red font, indicating an error. Let's look at the second part of our expression.

- Get the last four characters from the LastName field and display them in uppercase and add four zeros (0000) to the string.

To extract characters from the end of a text string, use the Right function, provide the name of the field where the data is located, and the number of characters to extract, then display them in uppercase using the UCase function. So, there you go, the second part of our expression for the Emp-Code is:

```
UCase(Right([LastName], 4)) & "0000"
```

This code will extract last four letters from the LastName field, and change them to the uppercase characters, and will append four zeros at the end of this string. For example, if the last name is Kennedy, the returned string would be: NEDY000

Now we get into a more complicated syntax.

- Get the month number from the HireDate field and if it is less than 10, add a leading zero (0) in front of the month number, otherwise return the month number.

You use the Month function to return an integer specifying a whole number between 1 and 12 inclusive, representing the month of the year. For example, if the HireDate is 1/5/2023, we should return 01. If the HireDate is 11/5/2023 we should get 11.

Use the IIF function to evaluate expressions. The syntax of this function is:

IIF (expression, truepart, falsepart)

The expression is: Month([HireDate]) < 10

The *truepart* is the value you want to return if expression is True. So, for any month that is less than 10, the *truepart* should add the leading zero to the returned month. The *falsepart*, should just return the month number.

- Get the day number from the HireDate and if it is less than 10, add a leading zero (0) in front of the day number, otherwise return the day number.

  Note that this criteria only slightly differs from the previous one. Instead of getting the Month, we are working with the Day by using the Day function, which returns the whole number between 1 and 31 inclusive, representing the day of the month.

- Get the last two digits from the year.

  Use the Year function to return an Integer containing a whole number representing the year.

  After extracting the year with the Year function, use the Right function to get the last 2 digits from the returned year.

The completed expression should assign HNEDY0000010523 to the EmpCode for Henry Kennedy who was hired on 1/5/2023.

The last statement in the click event, tells Access to go to a new blank record on the form. It uses the GoToRecord method of the DoCmd object to make the specified record the current record in the open form. The two commas after the method are the placeholders for the ObjectType and ObjectName arguments that were left blank because they are not required here, as the active object is assumed. The acNewRec constant tells Access to make a new record current.

To find out more details about the use of specific methods, objects, and constants, click its name in the Visual Basic editor screen and press F1.

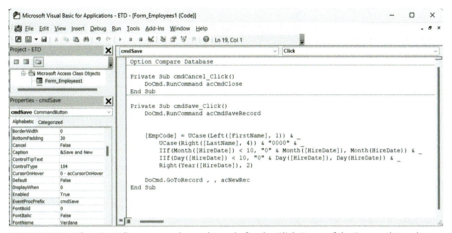

FIGURE 8.38. The VBA Editor screen shows the code for the Click Event of the Save and New button.

12. Press **Ctrl+S** to save the work you've done in the VBA screen and return to your form. Switch to the Form view to test your form.
13. Enter the data shown in Figure 8.39 and press the Save and New button when done.

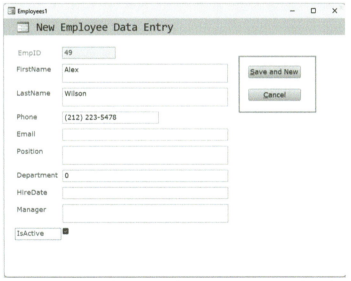

FIGURE 8.39. Entering the data in the form and testing the Save and New button.

Data entry forms that you set up may display various error messages as Access attempts to create a new record. At this point, our data entry form does not indicate to the user which fields are required. As some forms will not require all the fields to be filled in, it will be helpful to format the form, so the user knows immediately what data is expected.

If you check the Employees table where the data is to be inserted, you will notice that it does not have any fields with the Required property set to Yes. So why is Access complaining about the Department field (see Figure 8.40)? As you recall from an earlier chapter, the Departments table is in a relationship with the Employees table. We must supply a valid department code before Access can create a new record in the Employees table.

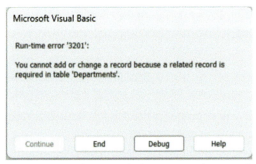

FIGURE 8.40. When you submit a new record, Access checks various table relationships behind the scenes and notifies you when it encounters a problem with a related record.

14. Click **End** in the message box to return to the data entry form.
15. While the form stays open, use the Database Navigation pane to open the **Departments** table to recall the types of available department codes.
16. Enter **11** in the **Department** field on the data entry form as shown in Figure 8.41.

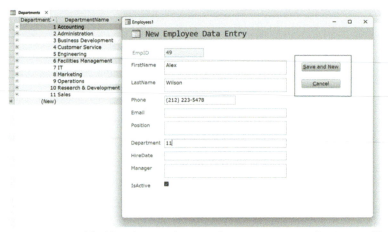

FIGURE 8.41. While debugging your data entry forms you can open other Access tables to double check their values or properties.

Debugging is a term often used by programmers to refer to the process of finding errors and mistakes in their programming code.

17. With the Department field filled in, click the **Save** and **New** button.

Access now notifies you that it found Invalid use of Null (see Figure 8.42).

Microsoft Visual Basic

Run-time error '94':

Invalid use of Null

| Continue | End | Debug | Help |

FIGURE 8.42. If there is an error in the Visual Basic code, you can click the Debug button in the. message box to find the erroneous location in your code.

18. Click the **Debug** button.

Access bring up the Visual Basic Editor screen and highlights the statement it has trouble executing (see Figure 8.43).

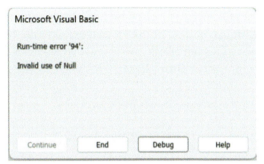

```
Option Compare Database

Private Sub cmdCancel_Click()
    DoCmd.RunCommand acCmdClose
End Sub

Private Sub cmdSave_Click()
    DoCmd.RunCommand acCmdSaveRecord

    [EmpCode] = UCase(Left([FirstName], 1)) & _
        UCase(Right([LastName], 4)) & "0000" & _
        IIf(Month([HireDate]) < 10, "0" & Month([HireDate]), Month(HireDate)) & _
        IIf(Day([HireDate]) < 10, "0" & Day([HireDate]), Day(HireDate)) & _
        Right(Year([HireDate]), 2)

    DoCmd.GoToRecord , , acNewRec
End Sub
```

FIGURE 8.43. Visual Basic code window is displayed here in break mode. A yellow arrow appears in the margin to the left of the statement where the procedure was suspended due to an error. The entire statement is also highlighted in yellow.

Break mode is used often to step through the procedure code line by line while testing the code or troubleshooting it due to an error. Let's try to understand what Access complains about. The statement in yellow is the expression we built earlier to create the employee code (EmpCode). This expression references various fields on the form. To return a result from any expression, you need to ensure that the referenced fields contain valid values. What we are missing here is now obvious. The HireDate field was left blank, therefore Access complains about a Null value, as it cannot evaluate the expression. While there are many ways to fix this issue, we will revise the code by introducing the IsNull function that will check for existence of data in the HireDate field and display a message to the user when the field is left blank.

19. In the Visual Basic Editor screen, choose **Run | Reset**. This will exit the Break Mode.

20. Modify the cmdSave_Click() procedure as shown in Figure 8.44.

```
cmdSave                                            ▼   Click
    Option Compare Database

    Private Sub cmdCancel_Click()
        DoCmd.RunCommand acCmdClose
    End Sub

    Private Sub cmdSave_Click()
        DoCmd.RunCommand acCmdSaveRecord

        If IsNull([HireDate]) Then
            MsgBox "You must fill in the Hire Date field."
            Exit Sub
        Else
        [EmpCode] = UCase(Left([FirstName], 1)) & _
            UCase(Right([LastName], 4)) & "0000" & _
            IIf(Month([HireDate]) < 10, "0" & Month([HireDate]), Month(HireDate)) & _
            IIf(Day([HireDate]) < 10, "0" & Day([HireDate]), Day(HireDate)) & _
            Right(Year([HireDate]), 2)
        End If

        DoCmd.GoToRecord , , acNewRec
    End Sub
```

FIGURE 8.44. When using expressions in your VBA procedures, always check if they have the required values to work on.

The If … Then … Else statement helps us to choose an action depending on a condition. The syntax of this statement is as follows:

```
If condition Then
  statement1
Else
statement 2
End If
```

Our condition here is the test for the value of the HireDate field. The Visual Basic function IsNull will check if the specified field is left blank:

```
IsNull([HireDate])
```

If the IsNull function is true (HireDate is blank) then we will display a message to the user using the built-in MsgBox function:

```
MsgBox "You must fill in the Hire Date field."
```

Message boxes in Access can contain one or more buttons. Here we have not specified any, so Access will display only the OK button when the message appears.

    The next line of the code will tell Access to exit the procedure so that the user can continue filling in the missing data when the message box is dismissed.

```
Exit Sub
```

More statements can be placed between the If and Else depending on your needs.

    In the Else clause, we tell Access what to do if the condition we specified evaluated to False. So, if there is data in the HireDate field, Access should be able to evaluate the EmpCode expression. Of course, we assume here that FirstName and LastName fields contain data. You can add more conditions to the If ... Then ... Else statement by using the AND and OR logical operators. The Companion file includes code for creating a separate function that tests the FirstName, LastName, and HireDate field for data and shows how to call that function from the cmdSave_Click event. See the document titled "DataEntry_ValidationFunction.txt."

    It is important to remember to always include the End If statement at the end of the conditional block of statements unless the entire statement is written on one line of code.

21. Save the changes you made in the Visual Basic code and return to the Access window with the New Employee Data entry form. Fill in the HireDate field by entering 5/9/2023. You can either type the date or use the calendar control that appears to the right of the HireDate field when the field is selected (see Figure 8.45).

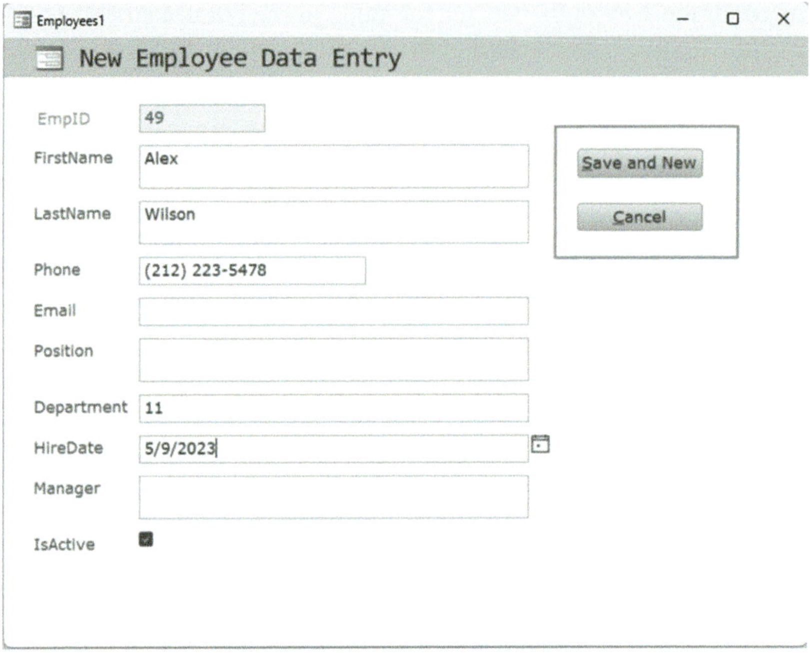

FIGURE 8.45. Modifying the data entry form with the HireDate data.

22. Click the **Save and New** button.

    Access goes to work, creates a new record in the Employees table, and displays a blank form ready for your next entry.

23. Click **Cancel** to exit the form.
24. Open the Employees table to check for the new data for Alex Wilson (see Figure 8.46).

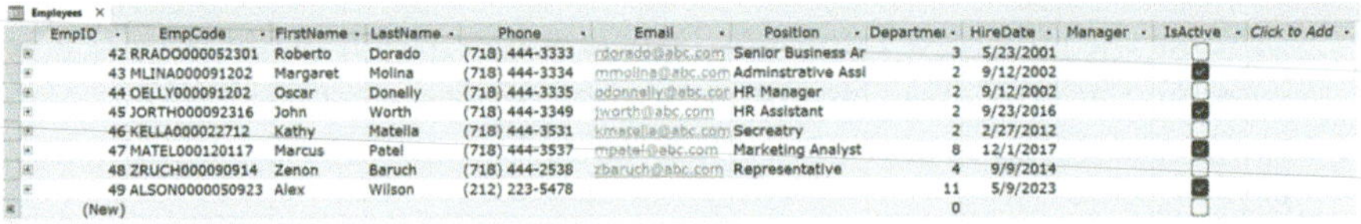

Employees

EmpID	EmpCode	FirstName	LastName	Phone	Email	Position	Departme	HireDate	Manager	IsActive	Click to Add
42	RRADO000052301	Roberto	Dorado	(718) 444-3333	rdorado@abc.com	Senior Business Ar	3	5/23/2001		☐	
43	MLINA000091202	Margaret	Molina	(718) 444-3334	mmolina@abc.com	Adminstrative Assi	2	9/12/2002		☑	
44	OELLY000091202	Oscar	Donelly	(718) 444-3335	odonnelly@abc.cor	HR Manager	2	9/12/2002		☐	
45	JORTH000092316	John	Worth	(718) 444-3349	jworth@abc.com	HR Assistant	2	9/23/2016		☑	
46	KELLA000022712	Kathy	Matella	(718) 444-3531	kmatella@abc.com	Secreatry	2	2/27/2012		☐	
47	MATEL000120117	Marcus	Patel	(718) 444-3537	mpatel@abc.com	Marketing Analyst	8	12/1/2017		☑	
48	ZRUCH000090914	Zenon	Baruch	(718) 444-2538	zbaruch@abc.com	Representative	4	9/9/2014		☐	
49	ALSON000050923	Alex	Wilson	(212) 223-5478			11	5/9/2023		☑	
(New)							0			☐	

FIGURE 8.46. When testing data entry forms, always check if data appears as intended in the underlying table.

25. Close the Employees table and Employees1 form.
26. In the Navigation pane rename the **Employees1** form to **EmployeeDataEntry**.

Action Item 8.2

In the EmployeeDataEntry form, after Access displays the message when the HireDate is blank, you want the mouse pointer to move to the HireDate field. To implement this feature, add the following code in the cmdSave_Click event procedure by entering it on a line just above the Exit Sub keywords:

```
Me.HireDate.SetFocus
```

In VBA, the Me keyword provides a way to refer to the form where the code is executing. Therefore, Me.HireDate references the HireDate control on the current form and the SetFocus method tells Access to set the focus to the specified control on a form. The comma in the code is not an operator, but a separator. It is used to separate the arguments of a procedure call or a function. In this case, the procedure is SetFocus. The arguments are Me and HireDate, which refer to the current form and the control named HireDate, respectively. The comma indicates that the SetFocus takes two arguments: the form and the control.

Save the change you made to the procedure code and test the form. Enter any first and last name and the department code and press the Save and New button. When you dismiss the message box, the focus should be set on the HireDate field. Save and close the form. You will continue customizing it further in the next chapter.

SUMMARY

In this chapter, you learned about different options for creating various form types. By providing form wizards and other form tools to create common forms, Access forms can be created quickly even by the novice users. We discussed different form views: Form, Design, and Layout view, and various Form properties that can be accessed via the Property Sheet. While creating a data entry form, you were also introduced to various form controls that allow users to interact with data on the form or in the database. You learned how to select and deselect controls, resize them, move and align them, align spacing between them, and copy them. You saw how the Tab Order window can show you the list of all the controls on your form and how you can set the order of controls by clicking on any control and dragging it up or down. The Hands-On focus in this chapter was creating a data entry form with two command buttons that utilized VBA programming code. You were introduced to working in the Visual Basic Editor window, entering, and modifying code for the Click event procedures. You learned how to use various built-in functions to create a complex expression that creates an employee code based on the entries in three form fields. You also learned how to add field validation and test your form.

In the next chapter, which includes mostly Hands-On activities, we will focus on the form customization while working with form controls such as combo and list boxes as well as check boxes.

Chapter 9   FORM CUSTOMIZATION

In the previous chapter, we began the process of building a data entry form. Thanks to the built-in form tools, getting started with a custom form was quite easy as Access helped us to quickly lay out all the fields for our form. Once the fields were selected for the form, the real work began. To design a custom data entry form you needed to set many form properties and learn how to work with form controls, including writing code for the onClick event of command buttons.

Oftentimes the individual controls need to be moved around, sized, and aligned. Like forms, controls come with many properties that you can set to change their data source, look and behavior. In this chapter, we will focus on form customization and get hands-on experience working with various form controls. Among many other things, you will learn how to apply special effects to selected controls and how to change one control type to another to improve the process of entering data for your form end-user.

APPLYING SPECIAL EFFECTS TO FORM CONTROLS

Access controls have a Special Effect property that can be found under the For-mat tab in the Property Sheet as shown in Figure 9.1. This property is used to specify whether special formatting will apply to the specified control. The fol-lowing are the choices you can select to modify the look of your control:

Property Setting	Visual Basic Setting	Description
Flat	0	The control appears flat and has the system's default colors or custom colors that were set in Design View.
Raised	1	The control has a highlight on the top and left and a shadow on the bottom and right.
Sunken	2	The control has a shadow on the top and left and a highlight on the bottom and right.
Etched	3	The control is surrounded by a sunken line.
Shadowed	4	The control has a shadow below and to the right.
Chiseled	5	There is a sunken line below the control.

FIGURE 9.1. A Special Effect Property for a text box control.

Let's apply special formatting to the EmployeeDataEntry form as created in Chapter 8, to visually indicate to the form user which fields need to be filled in.

⊙ Hands-On 9.1   Applying Special Formatting to Form Controls

1. Open the EmployeeDataEntry form in Design View and make sure that the Property Sheet is visible.
2. Click on the following fields on the form to select them: FirstName, LastName, Department, and HireDate.

    At the top of the Property Sheet, you should see Multiple selection as selection type.
3. With the four controls selected, click the Format tab in the Property Sheet and set the following properties as follows:

Property Name	Property Setting
Border Color	Green, Accent 5
Special Effect	Shadowed
Fore Color	Green, Accent 5

4. Press **Ctrl+S** to save changes in the form and close the form.
5. In the Navigation view, find the modified form and open it.

    The form should look as depicted in Figure 9.2.

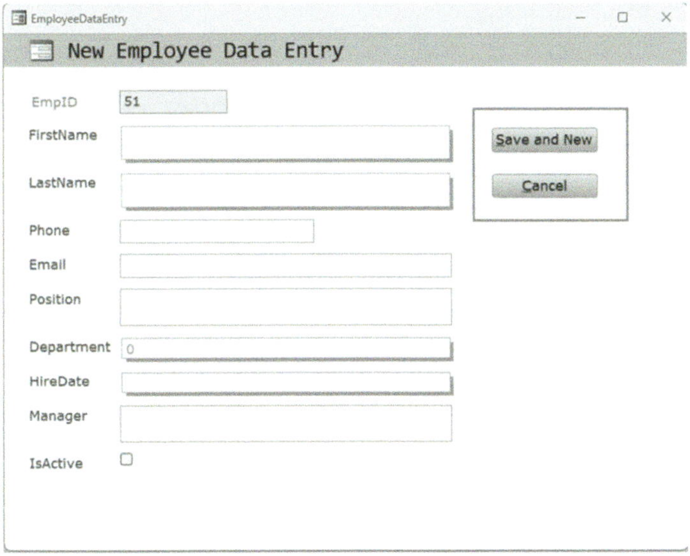

FIGURE 9.2. The overall look of the form was changed by applying different formatting settings to four text box controls.

Let's add a label control to the form to inform the user that all fields in green are required.

6. In the Form Design View, select the **Label** control in the controls group of the Form Design tab and draw a rectangle at the bottom of the screen as shown in Figure 9.3. Enter the text as shown and change the **Fore Color** property of this label control to **Accent 5**. Access might display a warning to the right of the label control which you can ignore as this label does not need an associated control.

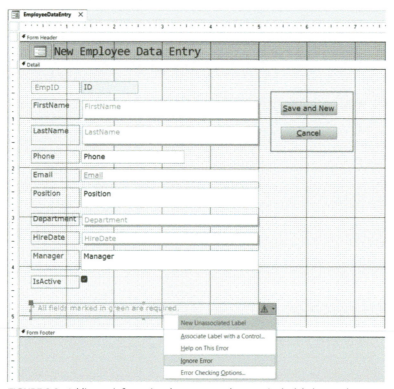

FIGURE 9.3. Adding an informational message to the user via the label control.

7. Be sure to save your changes before checking out the form in the Form view.

CHANGING A CONTROL TYPE

When Access creates a form, it uses text box controls for displaying data. Sometimes it makes more sense to show the data using another control type. For example, in our EmployeeDataEntry form, the Department field is a text box, and it will be extremely difficult for the end-user to fill in the correct department without the knowledge of the department codes. The good news is that you can easily change the Department text box control to a combo box so that it will allow a user to select a department name from the drop-down list. Let's work on this in Hands-on 9.2.

Hands-On 9.2   Replacing a Text Box With a Combo Box

1. Open the **EmployeeDataEntry** form in the Design View.
2. Right click on the **Department** text box control
3. From the popup menu, click Change **To**.
4. Under Change To, click the **Combo Box** as shown in Figure 9.4.

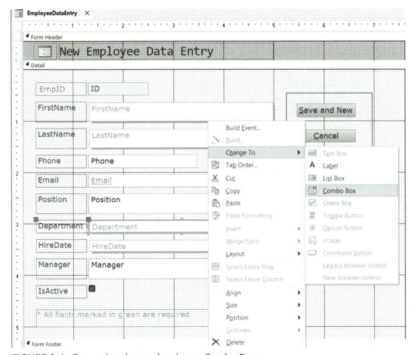

FIGURE 9.4. Converting the text box into a Combo Box.

Access changes the text box to a combo box, and you should notice the drop down to the right of the Department control. Before we can work with this combo box, we need to set the Row Source for this combo box so you can get the department names list from the Departments table.

5. Press **Ctrl+S** to save your changes to the form or click the Save button in the Quick Access toolbar.

NOTE	*It is always a good idea to save the form after a major design change, as Access can occasionally crash under the heavy load of unsaved changes. This can be quite frightening especially when you've spent lots of time on your form modifications. Forms can easily get corrupted so make backups of your form often.*

6. Click the Department combo box control and in the Property Sheet window, under Data tab click on the **Row Source Type** and select **Table/Query** from the drop-down list.

7. Click in the Row Source property to activate it and then click the ellipsis button (…) next to the Rows Source field as shown in Figure 9.5.

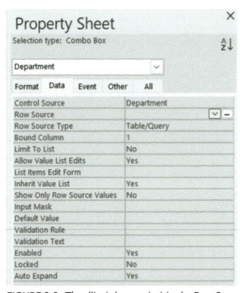

FIGURE 9.5. The ellipsis button (…) in the Row Source property brings up the Query Builder where you can tell Microsoft Access how to provide data for your combo box.

8. When Access opens the Query Builder, in the Add Tables pane, double click on the Departments table to add it to the Query Builder. Select both DepartmentID and DepartmentName fields in the table and drag them to the Query Grid as shown in Figure 9.6.

9. Close the Query Builder and click Yes when prompted to save your changes.

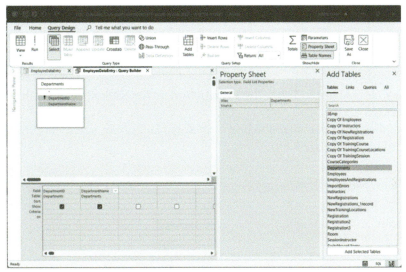

FIGURE 9.6. Use the Query Builder to specify the Row Source for the combo box.

In the Property Sheet, the Row Source property is now filled with the Select query that you created using the Query Builder (see Figure 9.7).

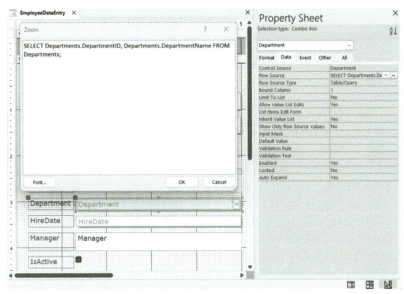

FIGURE 9.7. The Row Source property displays the SQL Select statement that selects DepartmentID and DepartmentName fields from the Department table.

NOTE	*While in this example we have used the Query Builder to create the SQL statement for the combo box Row Source, you can type your statement manually using the Zoom box. To activate Zoom box, click in the Row Source property, and press Shift+F2.*

10. Save your changes and click the View button on the Ribbon's Home tab to view the form.
11. Click the Department combo box drop down and notice that Department IDs are listed (see Figure 9.8).

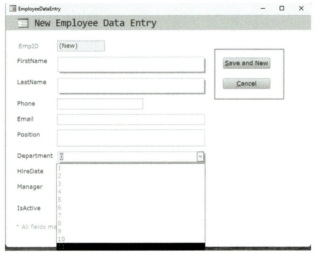

FIGURE 9.8. By Default the Combo Box control displays the values from the first field in the underlying Table/Query.

Let's get back to Design View and modify some properties so we can select the department names not their IDs.

12. In Design View, click the **Department** combo box to select it.
13. In the Property Sheet under Format tab change the value of **Column Count** field from 1 to **2**.
    This will tell Access to include both columns from the query that we created earlier. The first column, DepartmentID will be stored in the table when we save the record, and the second field, the DepartmentName will be displayed in the combo drop down list.
14. Click next to the **Column Width** property and type: **0;2**
    This will tell Access to set the width of the first column to 0 (since we do not want to see it), and set the second column width to 2 inches, so we can see the

full department name (see Figure 9.9). Notice that the semicolon (;) separates the width measurements. Access adds double quotes automatically.

FIGURE 9.9. After setting the Row Source property for the Combo Box, modify the Column Count and Column Widths properties to ensure that the combo box displays the desired data.

15. Save the form and click the **View** button to view it.
16. Click the **Department** drop down.
    You should see the list of department names (see Figure 9.10).

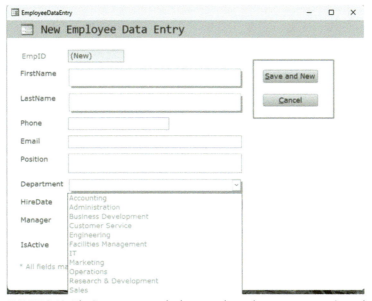

FIGURE 9.10. The Department combo box now shows department names instead of their IDs.

17. Save and close the form.

Action Item 9.1

Test the EmployeeDataEntry form to ensure that the Department field changes from the text box to the combo box control works as intended by adding data for a new employee, and then check the newly added record in the Employees table.

COMBO BOX AND LIST BOX: SYNCHRONIZATION

In this section, you will learn how to use a combo box and two list box controls in the same form and how to synchronize them so the value you select in the combo box will update the first list box, and the record selected in the first list box updates the display of records in the second list box. Figure 9.11 displays the Courses by Category form which is the focus of the next Hands-On exercise.

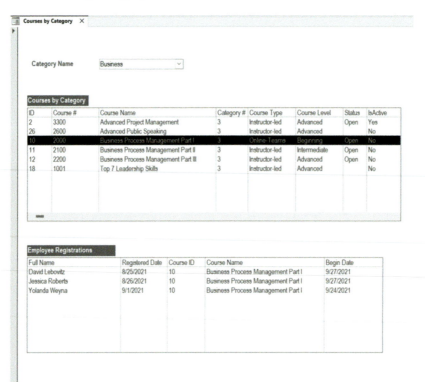

FIGURE 9.11. This form will demonstrate synchronizing combo box with a list box, and a list box with another list box.

Hands-On 9.3 Creating the Courses by Category Form

(Part I—Adding and Formatting a Combo Box Control)

1. In the Forms group of the **Create** tab, click **Form Design**.
   Access creates a blank form named Form1.
2. Right click the form name and choose Save. Enter **Courses by Category** as the form new name and click **OK**.
3. In the Property Sheet choose **Form** from the drop-down and in the Format tab, enter **8.2083**" for the **Width** property.
4. Expand the form height to 7 inches on the vertical ruler by dragging down the form's bottom edge.
5. In the Controls group of Form Design, select the **Combo Box** control and click in the upper area of the form at about 2 inches on the horizontal ruler and 0.5 inch on the vertical ruler.
   This action should invoke the Combo Box Wizard as shown in Figure 9.12.

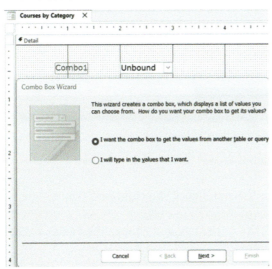

FIGURE 9.12. Using the Combo Box Wizard.

6. With the first option button already selected, click the **Next** button.
7. Select the **CourseCategories** table and click **Next**.
8. Move both fields, **CategoryID** and **CategoryName**, from Available Fields to **Selected Fields** box and click Next.
9. Select **CategoryName** from the first drop down to indicate that you want to sort in ascending order by this field and click **Next**.
   The wizard now asks about the width of the columns in your combo box. You can adjust the size of the column by dragging its right edge.

10. Click the **Next** button.
11. Enter **Category Name** for the combo box label and click **Finish**.
    The Category Name combo box appears on the screen. It consists of a label and an Unbound drop down.
12. Select both the label and the drop down by dragging a mouse around it. The top area of the Property sheet should indicate **Multiple selection**.
13. In the Format Tab on the Property Sheet change the **Font Name** property value to **Arial Narrow**.
14. Deselect the combo box control by clicking outside it.
15. Select only the label part of the combo box and in the Property Sheet (Format tab) set the **Font Weight** property value to **Bold**.
16. Activate the **Form view** and test the combo box control. You should see the list of course categories as shown in Figure 9.13.

FIGURE 9.13. Testing the Combo Box control.

17. Return to the Form Design View and click the Unbound combo box control to select it.
18. In the Property Sheet, click the Other tab, and change the value of the **Name** property to **cboCourseCategory**.

It is very important to name the control if you are planning to synchronize it with another form control or refer to it in a VBA programming code or a macro.

NOTE	*When you create a combo box using the Combo Box Wizard, Access automatically sets the Row Source property as well as the Column Count and Column Width properties of the combo box.*

Let's continue to Part II of Hands-On 9.3, where you build a query that will serve as a Row Source for the Courses by Category list box control.

⊙ Hands-On 9.3 Creating the Courses by Category Form

(Part II—Creating a Query for the Row Source of a List Box Control)

1. In the Queries group of the Create tab, click the Query Design.
2. In the Add Tables pane, select **CourseCategories** and **TrainingCourse** table and add them to the Query Design. Note that these tables are joined on the CategoryID field.
3. Add the following fields to the Query grid: **ID**, **CourseNum**, **CourseName**, **CategoryID**, **CourseType**, **CourseLevel**, **CourseStatus** and **IsActive**. Change the names of these fields by creating aliases as shown in Figure 9.14. For example, to rename CourseNum to Course #, enter Course #: in front of the CourseNum field name in the first row of the Query grid.

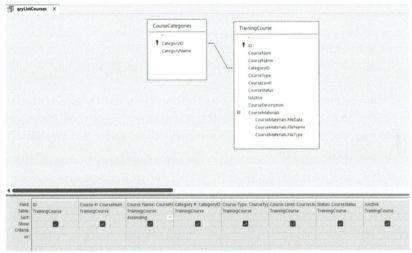

FIGURE 9.14. Creating a Select query for the list box control.

4. Set the ascending sort order in the Course Name column.
5. Save this query as **qryListCourses** and close it.

Let's continue to Part III of Hands-On 9.3, where you add the Courses by Category list box control and format it.

Hands-On 9.3   Creating the Courses by Category Form

(Part III—Creating and Formatting a List Box Control)

1. In the Form Design View, in the Controls group, select the **List Box** control and click approximately 1 inch below the combo box control.
   This action should invoke the List Box Wizard that shows the same option buttons as the Combo Box Wizard screen shown in Figure 9. 12.
2. Click the **Next** button, change the view to Queries by clicking the **Queries** option button and select **qryListCourses**, then click **Next**.
3. Select the following fields: **ID, Course #, Course Name, Category #, Course Type, Course Level, Status, and IsActive**, and click **Next**.
4. Choose **Course Name** to sort by and click **Next**.
5. Adjust the column widths as instructed by the List Box Wizard, then click **Next**.
6. Choose **ID** as the field that uniquely identifies the row and click **Next**.
7. Enter **Courses by Category** as the label for your list box and click **Finish**.
   The completed list box should now appear in Design View, and we will need to format its properties to fit our needs.
8. With the List Box control selected in Design View, use the Property Sheet to change the Name of the List Box to **lboxCourses**. Change the **Column Heads** property to **Yes**. Set the **Border Color** to **Blue, Accent 1**. Set the **Font Name** property to **Arial Narrow**.

9. Move the Label control (Courses by Category) so that appears above the list box as shown earlier in Figure 9.11.
10. Click on the Label above the list box to select it and format it as follows: set **Font Name** to **Arial Narrow**, **Font Weight** to **Bold**, **Back Color** to **Blue, Accent 1**, and check that the **Fore Color** is set to **Background 1** which should give you white letter on the blue background.
11. Resize the List Box control by changing its **Width** property to **7.9167"** and its **Height** property to **2.3333"**.
12. Click the **View** button to view the form in the Form view.
   You should see the list box populated with all the courses as shown in Figure 9.15. However, we want to only see the courses for the course category we select from the combo box. We must inform Access about our criteria.

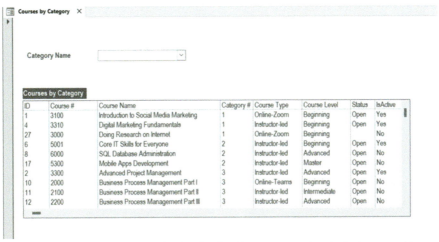

FIGURE 9.15. List Box control populated with a list of courses. Note that the list box control is not yet synchronized with the Combo Box Control.

13. Return to the Form Design View and select the List Box control on the form. The Property Sheet should say at the top of the pane that List Box is the selection type.

14. Click the Data Tab and click within the Select statement that appears to the right of the Row Source Property and then click the ellipsis button (…).

Access opens the Query Builder screen. Here we need to enter the criteria that connects the combo box control with the list box control.

15. In the Query Design grid at the bottom in the Criteria row for the Category # field enter the following expression: **[Forms]![Courses by Category]![cboCourseCategory]**

This expression (see Figure 9.16) tells Access to use the value of the combo box as the filter for the query.

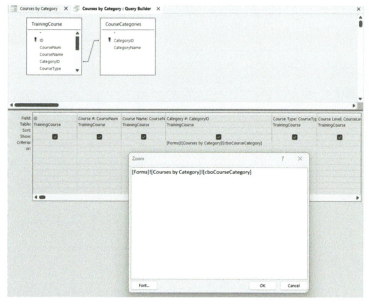

FIGURE 9.16. Setting the criteria to refer to the Combo Box control.

16. Save and close the modified query. If prompted to update the SQL property, click Yes.

17. Switch to the Form view and notice that now the list box is empty. Select an entry from the combo box and notice that nothing happens; no entries appear in the list box no matter what you select in the combo box. We still need to tell Access to refresh the list box as we make different selections in the combo box.

18. Return to the Design view and select the combo box.

19. In the Property Sheet for the cboCourseCategory, on the Event tab, click the On Change property, and then click the Build (ellipsis) button.

This opens the Choose builder dialog box.

20. Select Code Builder and click OK.

This opens the Visual Basic Editor with a new subroutine for the combo box Change event.

21. In the subroutine, type: **Me.lboxCourses.Requery**

This tells Access to refresh the list box whenever the combo box value changes.

The completed subprocedure should look as follows:

```
Private Sub cboCourseCategory_Change()
Me.lboxCourses.Requery
End Sub
```

22. Save changes in the Visual Basic editor by clicking the Save icon on the toolbar, and then close the Editor window.
23. Activate the Form view and test the combo box. You should see that the list box shows only the records that match the combo box selection.

Action Item 9.2

Now that our Courses by Category form has a combo box and a list box that are synchronized with one another, it's time to create the second list box that displays a list of Employee registrations based on a course selected in the first list box. The process is like the one we just went through so I will leave it to you to create the second list box on your own. Set the same properties and use the same values as in the first list box, except for the Name property that should be set to lboxRegistrations and the Row Source property that should have the following SQL statement (see also Figure 9.17):

```
SELECT qfrmRegisteredForCourse.[Full Name],
qfrmRegisteredForCourse.[Registered Date],
qfrmRegisteredForCourse.[Course ID],
qfrmRegisteredForCourse.[Course Name],
qfrmRegisteredForCourse.[Begin Date]
FROM qfrmRegisteredForCourse
WHERE (((qfrmRegisteredForCourse.[Course
ID])=[Forms]![Courses by Category]![lboxCourses]))
ORDER BY qfrmRegisteredForCourse.[Full Name];
```

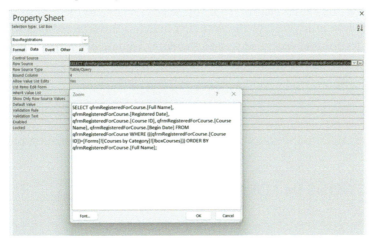

FIGURE 9.17. Select statement in the Row Source property of the second list box.

Note that the criteria that connects the first list box with the second one is stated in the SQL WHERE clause. The qfrmRegisteredForCourse is the query you will need to create for the Row Source of this list box. The Design View of this query is shown in Figure 9.18.

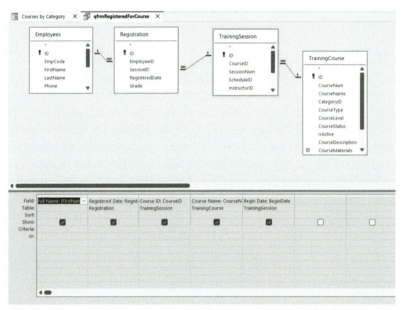

FIGURE 9.18. This query will supply the data for the second list box – lboxRegistrations.

One more thing to do is to make sure that the second list box is updated whenever the first list box values change, so if you select a course in the first list box, the second list box only displays the data that matches the selected row in the first list box. To do this, you need to add the After Update event procedure to the first list box. The code of this procedure is as follows:

```
Private Sub lboxCourses_AfterUpdate()
Me.lboxRegistrations.Requery
End Sub
```

If you get stuck, refer to the completed ETD database in the Companion files.

USING FUNCTIONS IN FORM CONTROLS

In the previous chapter, you saw how easy it is to create a Split form in Access using the Split Form tool on the Create tab. This tool automatically created a Split form based on a table or query that you select from the Navigation pane or have open in the Datasheet view. Recall that a Split form is a type of form that gives you two views of your data at the same time: a Form view and a Datasheet view. The two views are connected to the same data source and are synchronized with each other. Once created the Split form can be customized depending on your needs and preferences.

This section's Hands-On will teach you how you can add additional fields to the Form view of the Split form to show information that is not in the record source of your form but can be obtained from another table. All this is possible thanks to the domain aggregate functions which perform calculations on a set of records that match a specified criteria. These functions can be used in queries, forms, reports, and macros. They are easily recognized as they start with the letter D. The following table shows some examples of the domain aggregate functions.

TABLE 9.1 Examples of Domain Aggregate Functions in Access

Function Name	Description
DLookup	Returns a single value from a field in a table or query. For example, =DLookup("ProductName," "Products," "ProductID=5") returns the name of the product with the ID 5 from the Products table.
DFirst, DLast	Return the first or last value from a set of records. For example, =DFirst("OrderDate," "Orders") returns the earliest order date from the Orders table.
DMin, DMax	Return the minimum or maximum value from a set of records. For example, =DMax("Price," "Products," "Category='Books'") returns the highest price of the products in the Books category from the Products table.
DStDev, DStDevP	Return the standard deviation of a set of records based on a sample or a population. For example, =DStDev("Quantity," "Order Details") returns the sample standard deviation of the quantity ordered from the Order Details table.
DSum	Returns the sum of a set of records. For example, =DSum("Amount," "Payments," "CustomerID=1") returns the total amount paid by the customer with ID 1 from the Payments table.
DCount	Returns the number of records from a table or query that meets a certain criteria. For example, =DCount("[SessionID]," "Registration," "[Registered] = True") returns the count of the SessionID field from the Registration table where the Registered field is True (checked).

You will use the DLookup() and DCount() functions that appear in this list when you navigate Hands-On 9.4.

Hands-On 9.4   Customizing a Split Form Using Controls With Functions

1. In the Navigation pane highlight the **Employees** table and choose **Create | More Forms | Split Form**.

   Access creates the form, assigns it a default name (Employees1) and displays it in the Layout View as shown in Figure 9.19.

2. Right click the form tab and click **Save**. Enter **frmViewEmployees** as the form name and press **OK**.

3. Switch to Design View and select all the controls in the details section, then click **Arrange | Remove Layout**.

4. Click outside the selection and make changes to this form as depicted in Figure 9.20.

   Notice that the EmpID, CodeCode, Department, and HireDate text boxes were made smaller and the IsActive field was moved just below the Phone field. Also, the form has been made a bit bigger.

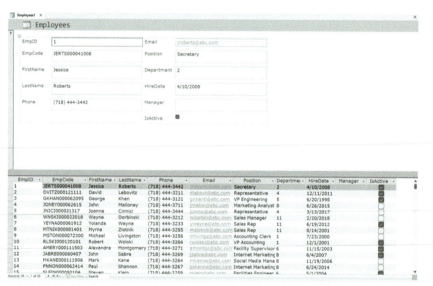

FIGURE 9.19. The Split form created by Access displays all employees in the Datasheet view at the bottom and shows the selected employee record in the Form part at the top.

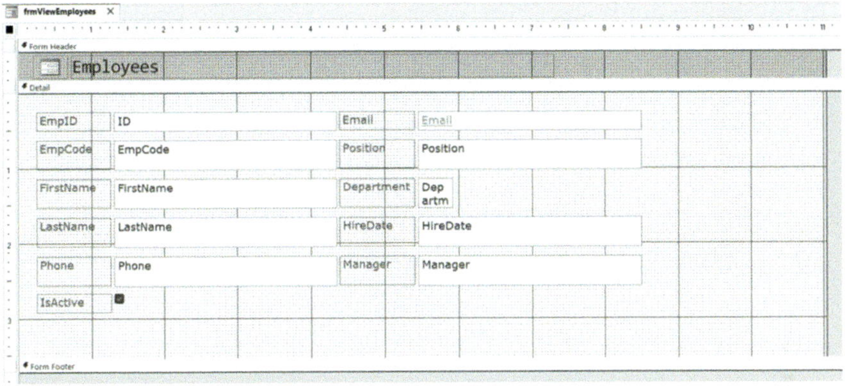

FIGURE 9.20. The modified Split form.

5. Add a new text box control to the right of the Department text box. The right edge of this text box should align with the right edge of the Position text box in Figure 20.

6. In the Property Sheet on the Other tab, change the Name property of the selected text box to **txtDeptName.**

7. Click the label control that was created with this text box and press Delete on the keyboard. The updated Design View is shown in Figure 9.21.

FIGURE 9.21. The Split form now includes the Unbound text box control without its label.

We will use this Unbound text box to display the Department name from the Departments table by using the DLookup function.

To use DLookup you need to specify three arguments: the field name, the table or query name, and the criteria. The criteria argument is where you can filter the records based on the value of a control on your form.

8. While the txtDeptName text box is selected (the Unbound control), on the Data Tab of the Property Sheet click in the Control Source field and click the Builder (the ellipsis) button.

9. In the ExpressionBuilder that appears, enter the following expression, and click **OK** when done (see Figure 9.22).

```
=DLookUp("DepartmentName","Departments","DepartmentID = " &
    [Forms]![frmViewEmployees]![Department])
```

FIGURE 9.22. The Expression Builder activated from the Control Source property of a text box control is used to write an expression that looks up the name of the Department in the Departments table based on the value of the Department text box on the form.

10. Activate the Form view so you can check if the expression works as intended. In the text box next to the Department code you should now see the name of the department (see Figure 9.23). Also, note that a field named txtDeptName now appears in the Datasheet view.

FIGURE 9.23. The vorm now shows the Department name data retrieved from the Departments table thanks to the Expression you wrote earlier. The Datasheet automatically shows a new column named txtDeptName.

11. Save the form and return to Design View. Add a check box control with the label IsRegistered and a text box control with the label # of Sessions (see Figure 9.24).

FIGURE 9.24. Adding additional controls to the form: a check box and a text box.

As we scroll through the employees in the Datasheet view of the Split form, we want to know if the employee is registered for a course, and if so, how many sessions they have signed up for. As you know the Employees table that provides the Row Source for this form does not contain any information about employee registrations and number of sessions. Like with the Department Name field, we can get the required data using the DLookup and DCount functions.

12. Click the check box control next to the IsRegistered label and, in the Property Sheet on the Other tab and change the name property to **IsRegistered**. We need to reference this name in the expression that we build next.

13. Click in the **Control Sou**rce property on the Data tab and click the **Build** (ellipsis) button to invoke the Expression Builder.

14. Enter the following Expression (see Figure 9.25) and click **OK** when done.

```
=Nz(DLookUp("RegisteredDate","Registration","EmployeeID = " &
[Forms]![frmViewEmployees]![ID]),False)
```

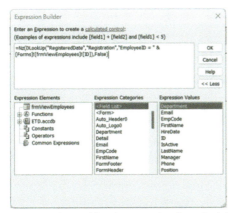

FIGURE 9.25. Writing the expression for a check box on a form.

The DLookup function shown in the previous expression, will look up the RegisteredDate field from the Registration table where the EmployeeID matches the value of the ID control on the frmViewEmployees form. However, when using the DLookup in a checkbox there might be an issue when the DLookup function returns a Null value which means that there is no record that matches the criteria, or the table is empty. In this situation, the checkbox will show an error message instead of being empty. To avoid this issue, we used the Nz function to convert Null values to False. The Nz function has the following syntax:

```
Nz (Value, ValueIfNull)
```

In the Value argument, we put the DLookup function and in the ValueIfNull argument we specified to return False if the DLookup function returns Null.

15. Click OK to close the Expression Builder and switch to the Form Design View to check if the IsRegistered checkbox behaves correctly (see Figure 9.26).

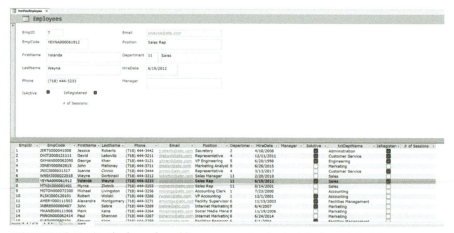

FIGURE 9.26. Testing the form after adding an expression for the IsRegistered check box.

It looks like Access is retrieving correct information about the employee registrations.

Now, let's create another expression that will get us the number of sessions for the registered employee.

16. Return to the Form Design View and click the Unbound text box next to the # of Sessions label.

17. In the Property Sheet on the Data tab, click in the Control Source property and click the Build (ellipsis) button to invoke the Expression Builder.

18. Enter the following expression (see Figure 9.27) and click OK when done.

```
=DCount("[SessionID]","Registration","Forms!frmViewEmployees!
    [IsRegistered]=True and EmployeeID =" & [Forms]!
    [frmViewEmployees]![ID])
```

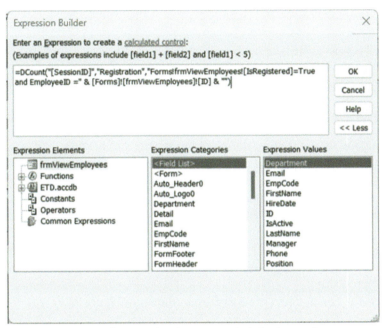

FIGURE 9.27. Writing the expression that returns calculation in a text box.

To display the count of sessions based on the Registered check box, we can use the DCount function. This function returns the number of records from a table or query that meets a certain criteria. Because we want to use the DCount based on the selected EmployeeID, we added a criteria argument to the DCount function that will filter the records based on the EmployeeID value on the form. Note that you can also write the criteria by enclosing them in single or double quotes. For example:

```
=DCount("[SessionID]", "Registration", "[Registered] = True
And [EmployeeID] = '" & Forms!Registration!ID & "'")
```

19. Check the output of the expression you wrote by switching to the Form view. The form should now display the number of sessions if the IsRegistered check box is checked (Figure 9.28).

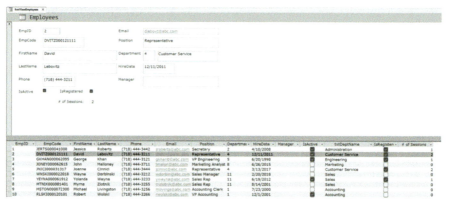

FIGURE 9.28. Testing the form after adding an expression for the # of Sessions text box.

All looks good except that we don't need to see the # of Session field when the employee has not registered. Let's fix it by making the control not visible based on our condition.

20. Switch to Design View and at the top of the Property Sheet, choose **Form** from the drop-down. Click the **Event** tab and click in the **On Current** property and choose [Event Procedure] from the drop-down, then click the Build (ellipsis) button.

    This activates the Visual Basic Editor screen with the stub of the Form_Current event procedure.

21. Complete the Form_Current procedure as shown in Figure 9.29.

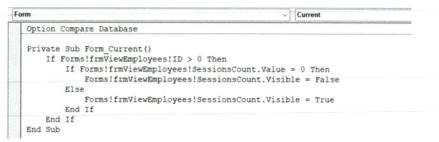

```
Form                                              Current

    Option Compare Database

    Private Sub Form_Current()
        If Forms!frmViewEmployees!ID > 0 Then
            If Forms!frmViewEmployees!SessionsCount.Value = 0 Then
                Forms!frmViewEmployees!SessionsCount.Visible = False
            Else
                Forms!frmViewEmployees!SessionsCount.Visible = True
            End If
        End If
    End Sub
```

FIGURE 9.29. Writing VBA code to hide the control if the DCount is False (returns 0).

22. Save and close the Visual Basic Editor window.

23. Switch to the Form view and select the employee that has not registered.

    The # of Sessions text box should no longer be visible (see Figure 9.30).

    Now, if you scroll down to the bottom of the Datasheet you will notice that there is a blank new row that can be used for adding new records to the Datasheet portion of the Split form. Let's completely remove this row.

24. Return to the Design View and in the Property Sheet, make sure that the **Form** is selected in the drop-down at the top.

25. On the Data tab, in the **Allow Additions** drop-down list, select **No**.

   This will prevent users from adding new records to the Datasheet portion of the Split form.

26. Activate the Form view and notice that the new record row is no longer available at the bottom of the Datasheet (see Figure 9.30).

FIGURE 9.30. The Form portion of the Split form no longer displays information about session if the employee has not registered for any courses. The Datasheet portion of the Split form no longer allows the addition of new employee records.

NOTE	*You can also prevent users from editing or deleting data in the Datasheet portion of the Split form, by selecting Form from the drop-down list at the top of the Property Sheet and on the All tab of the Property Sheet, in the Split Form Datasheet property, choosing Read Only.*

27. Save and close the form.

SUMMARY

In this chapter, you learned how you can customize a form by adding advanced controls such as a combo box and a list box, and you became aware of how these controls can interact with each other. You've worked extensively with various control properties that gave our form a more polished look. You also saw how the control events can be used to ensure that a control refreshes whenever the value in another control changes. You learned how you can easily convert a text box into a combo box to simplify data entry. We walked through different screens of the Combo Box and List Box Wizards and saw how these tools can streamline the task of creating these controls.

You were also taught how you can use domain aggregate functions in your form controls, specifically DLookup() and DCount(), to display data from other tables based on given criteria. In this chapter you've spent quite a bit of time on form design. As you learn new tricks, your custom forms will require less development time. There is a lot to learn about form design. Microsoft provides many Access database templates which you can download and learn from.

In the next chapter, we will move our focus to designing and formatting reports.

CREATE AND WORK WITH REPORTS

Part V guides you in the report creation process. You learn how to provide your data for presentation and printing.

Chapter 10 DESIGNING AND USING REPORTS

Like an Access form, a report is a database object that can display data from tables or queries, but it has a different purpose and futures than a form. Table 10.1 shows the differences and similarities between Access forms and reports.

TABLE 10.1 Access Forms versus Access Reports

Access Form	Access Report
Mainly used to view, add, or update data in tables. It can be displayed on the screen or printed as a hard copy.	Mainly used to analyze or print data using a specific layout. It can contain calculations, charts, graphs, and other visual elements to help you summarize and present the data. It can only be previewed on the screen or printed; it can't be edited.
A form can have multiple views: Form view, Layout view, Design View, and Datasheet view.	A report also offers multiple views: Report view, Design View, Layout view, and Print Preview.
Can be made interactive; can respond to user input, such as filtering, sorting, searching, or editing data.	A report is static; it does not allow user interaction.
A form can be bound to a single table or a query, or it can be unbound and not linked to any data source.	A report must be bound to a table or query that provides the data for the report.
A form can be used as a subform within another form to display related data from another table or query.	A report can be used as subreport within another report to display related data from another table or query.

Reports are an integral part of database applications and Microsoft Access offers users powerful reporting features for viewing and printing summarized information contained in the database. You can display information at the level of detail you desire, and you can print it in a variety of formats. You can lay out your reports automatically with the help of the built-in report tools, or you can design them from scratch by adding all the data and formatting elements yourself in Report Design View or Layout View. You can also use the VBA programming code to create your reports. Reports are often requested and reviewed by people who never use databases daily, like your company Management team, but who make important decisions based on the data they contain. Well-designed reports are therefore vital in ensuring that the data presented in them is correctly interpreted.

DESIGNING REPORTS

You can use different tools to create a report based on a table or query. For example, the Report tool, Report Design, Blank Report, Report and Labels Wizards. Access provides these various tools for report creation in the Reports group of the Create tab a shown in Figure 10.1.

FIGURE 10.1. The Create tab of the Ribbon shows built-in tools for creating reports.

The Report Tool

The quickest way to create a report in Access is to select a table or query in the Navigation pane and click the Report tool on the Create tab. For example, Figure 10.2 shows the reports instantly generated by Access after selecting the TrainingCourseLocations table in the database Navigation pane.

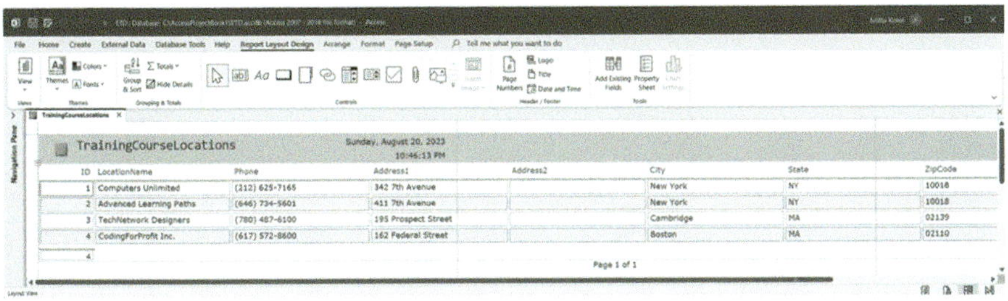

FIGURE 10.2. When you use the Report tool, Access creates a report with all the fields from the selected data source.

Depending on the number of fields in the data source, the generated report may have columns spread across multiple pages which is indicated by the existence of the vertical page breaks. It is up to the user to clean up the report so that it displays correctly on the screen and in print. Notice that the report appears in the Report Layout view, and for a better fit, you can size its columns manually in the same way did while working with various form controls. To adjust the column, click the column heading and then use the two-headed arrow that appears when the mouse is over the column's right edge and move the edge to the left to make the column header narrower. Double-clicking the right edge of the column heading will automatically resize the column to the width of its text which can be a quick way of sizing the columns containing shorter text entries, like ID, State, and ZipCode fields. You may want to switch to the Design View to narrow the width of the report and make other adjustments, like deleting the fields you don't want, perhaps shortening the column names, and moving the controls in the Page Footer area to the left. Figure 10.3 shows the same report in Design and Layout View after adjusting the width of the report and its controls and removing the Address2 column.

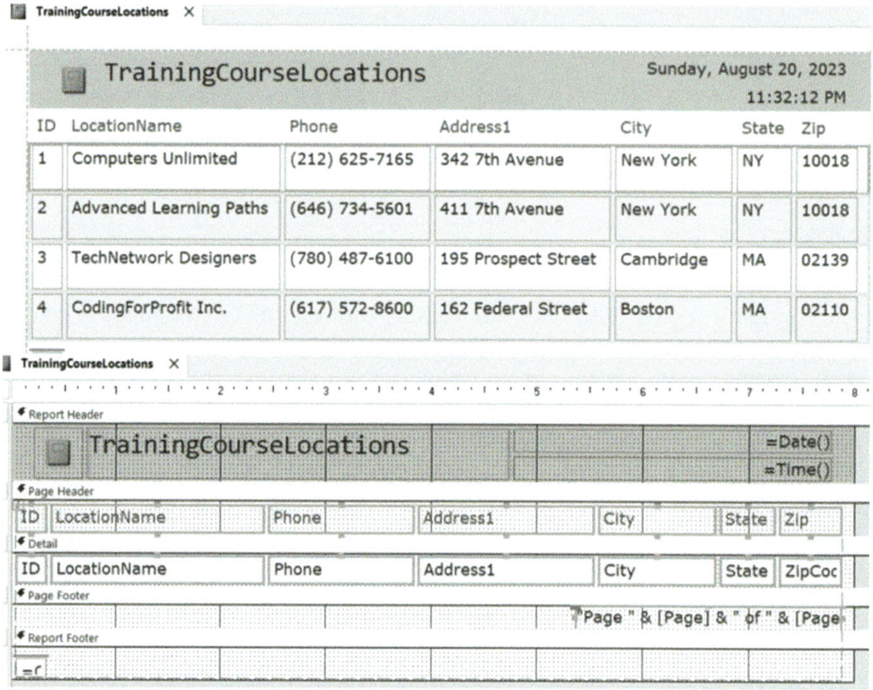

FIGURE 10.3. The Report generated by the Report tool after it has been modified by the user.

When the report is open, Access displays several new tabs that contain tools and controls that allow users to work with the report layout (Report Layout Design tab), arrangement (Arrange tab), formatting (Format tab) and page setup (Page Setup tab) (see Figure 10.4).

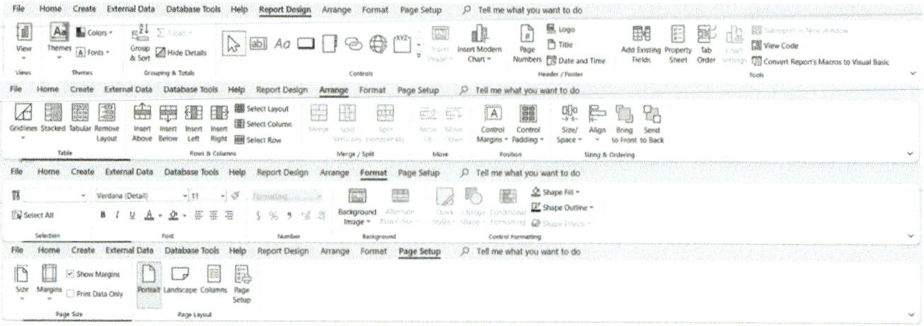

FIGURE 10.4. There are various tabs available for working with reports.

If you don't like the current report layout, you can experiment with different layout settings using the Arrange tab. For example, to change the layout from tabular to Stacked, click the Stacked button in the Tables group. Note that you must select the controls on the report prior to changing the layout. Figure 10.5 shows the same report with the Stacked layout applied. As you can see this type of layout displays labels to the left of each field. To return to the previous layout, simply undo your selection by clicking the Undo button on the Quick Access toolbar.

FIGURE 10.5. The Report Tabular layout was replaced with the Stacked Layout.

The Report Design and a Blank Report

The Report Design and Blank Report are other two options for creating a report in Access. They have different advantages and disadvantages depending on your needs and preferences.

The Report Design option allows you to create a report from scratch in Design View (see Figure 10.6), where you can customize the layout, appearance, and data sources of your report. You can add fields, controls, labels, graphics, and code to your report using the Report Design tools. This option gives you more flexibility and control over the design of your report, but it also requires more time and effort to create a report that meets your specifications.

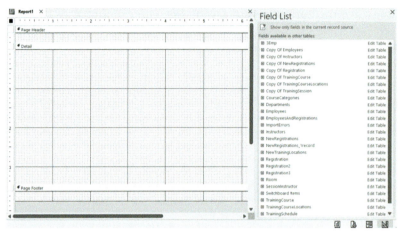

FIGURE 10.6. The Report Design screen.

The Blank Report option creates a blank report in Layout View (see Figure 10.7), where you can add fields from the Field List pane to your report. You can also use the Layout tools to adjust the size, position, and formatting of your fields. This option is faster and easier than the Report Design option, but it also offers less customization and functionality. You can switch to Design View later if you want to make more advanced changes to your report.

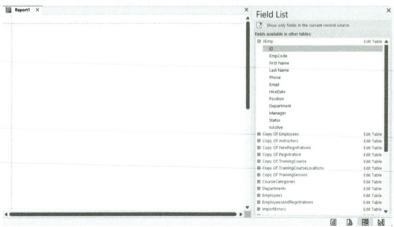

FIGURE 10.7. The Blank Report screen.

The Report Wizard

To design a more complex report you can launch the Report Wizard that will take you through several dialog boxes in which you can configure your report.

The Report Wizard can be very helpful when designing reports that must include fields from more than one table or query and require grouping levels. For example, in Hands-On 10.1 you will create a report that displays the employees in each department and groups them by their position.

(◉) **Hands-On 10.1   Creating a Report Using the Report Wizard**

1. In the database Navigation pane, select the Employees table and choose **Create | Report Wizard**.

    Access displays the first screen of the Report Wizard where it asks you for the fields you want on your report. The Tables/Queries drop-down shows Employees, as this table was selected when you started the Report Wizard. Note that one you select fields from one table or query, this screen allow you to choose another table or query to select additional fields.

2. From the fields available in the Employees table, select **FirstName, LastName, Phone**, and **Position** and then choose the **Departments** table in the Tables/ Queries drop-down and add the **DepartmentName** to the list of **Selected Field** (see Figure 10.8).

FIGURE 10.8. The Report Wizard (first screen) asks you for field names for your report. You may select fields from different tables/queries.

3. Click the **Next** button.

    Access shows the next screen, where it asks you how you want to view your data.

4. Click **By Departments** as shown in Figure 10.9.

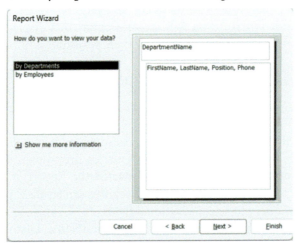

FIGURE 10.9. The Report Wizard (second screen) asks you by how to view your data and shows visual representation of your selection.

5. Click the **Next** button.

Now Access asks you if you need to add any grouping levels and displays the list of fields you can group by. Within each Department we have employees working in different positions, so let's group by the Position field.

6. Choose **Position** in the list of fields and click the ">" button. Access should update the report representation image to show you the layout of your report with the added grouping (see Figure 10.10).

FIGURE 10.10. The Report Wizard (third screen) asks you if you need to add any grouping levels.

NOTE	*The Grouping Options button in the Report Wizard screen will display the dialog box that will allow you to specify whether to group by the entire field value or just by the first few letters. This comes in handy for example when you need to create an alphabetical listing of employees. To group by some other portion of the field, you can create a calculated column in your query and then choose the calculated field to group by.*

7. Click the **Next** button.

Now Access asks you to specify how you would like to sort data in the Reports detail section. If you need to also sort groups, you can adjust that in the Layout or Design View once the report has been created.

8. Select **LastName** in the first drop-down and **FirstName** in the second drop-down (see Figure 10.11) and click **Next**.

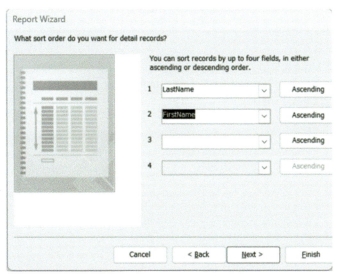

FIGURE 10.11. The Report Wizard (fourth screen) asks you how to sort the detail records.

Access now asks you about the layout of your report (see Figure 10.12) and offers three predefined layouts to choose from. You can select each of these options and the image will change to show how that layout is defined. You can also switch the page orientation to a landscape view and also ensure that all fields fit within one page width.

FIGURE 10.12. The Report Wizard (fifth screen) asks you the layout of the reports and its orientation.

9. Choose **Stepped** Layout and **Landscape** Orientation and click **Next**.

10. Enter the **Employees by Department Name** as the name for your report (see Figure 10.13) and click **Finish**.

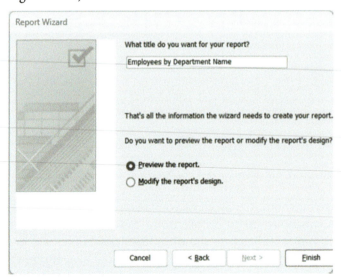

FIGURE 10.13. The Report Wizard (6th Screen) asks you for the name you want for your report and whether to open it in the Preview or Design View.

Access displays the preview of the completed report (see Figure 10.14). It looks like this report needs a few improvements. First, it appears that Access totally ignored the Phone number field that we specified to include. Some of the columns were not sized correctly and the applied shading is not what we want. We'll work on the improvements in the next Hands-On, but first we'll look at another Wizard included in the Reports group of the Create tab.

FIGURE 10.14. The Report Wizard generated report often requires additional work on the part of the user.

11. Save and close the **Employees by Department Name** report.

The Labels Wizard

Access has a handy Label Wizard built right in that allows you to quickly generate labels for the selected data source. Suppose you want to send correspondence by the postal service to your course instructors. Simply select the table Instructors in the database Navigation pane and click Create | Label. Access will open the Label Wizard (see Figure 10.15) which displays the available label stock that you can filter by manufacturer. The product number, its dimensions, and number of labels that will be printed across the page, can be easily selected from the filtered list of label stock.

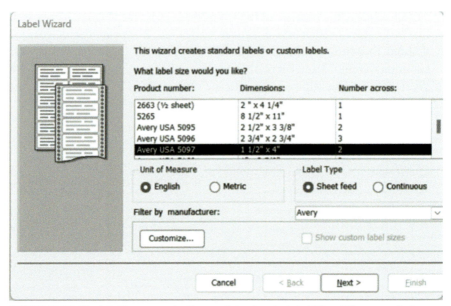

FIGURE 10.15. The Label button on the Create tab invokes the Label Wizard (first screen) where you can specify the type of label you want to use.

If you don't find the label size you need, you can click the Customize button to define a new label template (see Figure 10.16). In the New Label Size dialog that appears, click the New button. Access will display the New Label dialog, where you can specify the name for your custom label and its dimensions, unit of measure, the label type, and its orientation. There are nine measurements that you need to enter in the text boxes in the image at the bottom of the New Label dialog. Use inches for the English Unit of Measure and the centimeters for the Metric system. The Dimensions field will be filled automatically as you supply the measurements. When you're done, click OK and the custom label will be listed in the New Label Size dialog. Close this dialog to return to the wizard. Any custom labels you define will appear in the first dialog of the Label Wizard when you click the Show custom label sizes check box. This check box is disabled in Figure 10.15 as there are no custom labels defined.

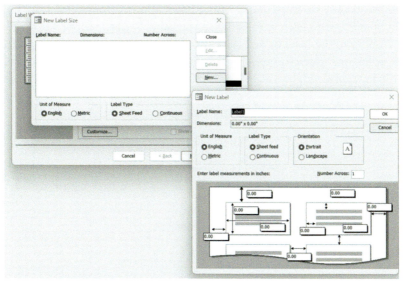

FIGURE 10.16. Defining a new label template.

After selecting the label stock (for example, Avery US 5097), click Next, and you'll see the second dialog box of the Label Wizard (see Figure 10.17) that is used to define the text appearance of your labels. Let's use the default values and click Next.

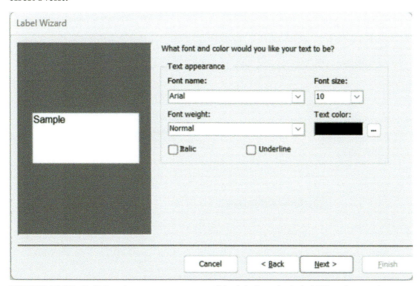

FIGURE 10.17. Defining the text appearance of the label on the Label Wizard second screen.

Now Access shows the third dialog of the Label Wizard where you must specify what text should go on each line. Note that the Label Wizard supports up to 8 lines of text. You build the label by selecting the fields on the left and clicking the ">" button. Access will place the selected field in the Prototype label box and enclose it in curly braces (see Figure 10.18). If you need a space or a comma you can press a spacebar and type the required character using your keyboard. Press Enter to move to the next line until you are finished creating your label structure.

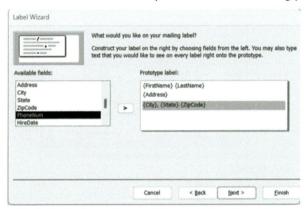

FIGURE 10.18. The third screen of the Label Wizard is used to construct your label.

With the Prototype label defined, click Next. In the fourth dialog screen, you need to specify the sort order (see Figure 10.19).

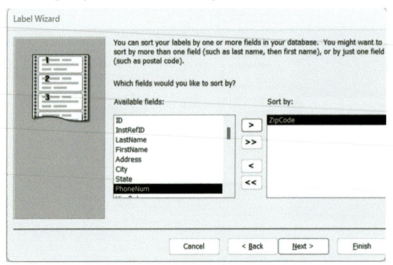

FIGURE 10.19. The fourth screen of the Label Wizard is used to specify sort order.

Click Next, and Access displays the final dialog of the Label Wizard (see Figure 10.20) where you specify the name for your label report and determine whether the report should be opened in Print Preview or in Design View.

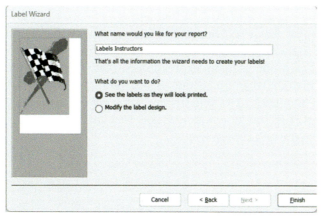

FIGURE 10.20. The fifth and final screen of the Label Wizard.

When you click Finish, the Labels Instructors report is displayed in the Print Preview screen (see Figure 20.21).

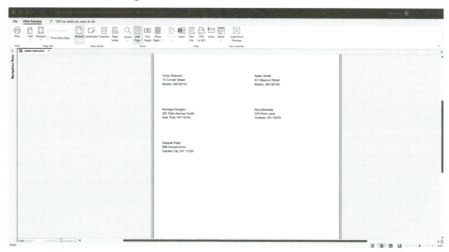

FIGURE 10.21. The completed Instructors Labels report is shown in Print Preview.

Note that the Print Preview window has numerous buttons that allow you to print the report, select the paper size, adjust the margins, and page layout, zoom in and out, display one or more pages, and save the report to other formats such as Excel, Text File, PDF, or XPS, or email it. The More button offers additional options like saving to Word, XML, and HTML files, and when installed, other database formats.

When you close the Print Preview, the label report is shown in the Design View (see Figure 10.22).

As you can see, to construct a label, three text boxes were placed in the Details section of the report. Each text box is the line you entered in the Label Prototype while working with the Label Wizard. The Control Source property defines the content of each line using an expression consisting of the names of fields, any static text surrounded in double quotes and the ampersand (&) which is a concatenation operator used in joining strings. Some expressions were used as an argument of the Trim function which makes sure that any leading and trailing spaces found in the text are removed.

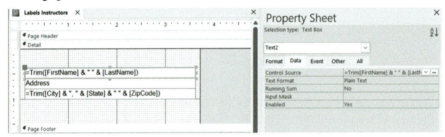

FIGURE 10.22. The completed Instructors Labels report is shown in Design View.

THE MAIN PARTS OF A REPORT

If you open the report you created in Hands-On 10.1 in the Design View (see Figure 10.23), you will notice that it consists of different parts or sections, each with a specific purpose and appearance. Table 10.2 explains the purpose of each part of an Access report.

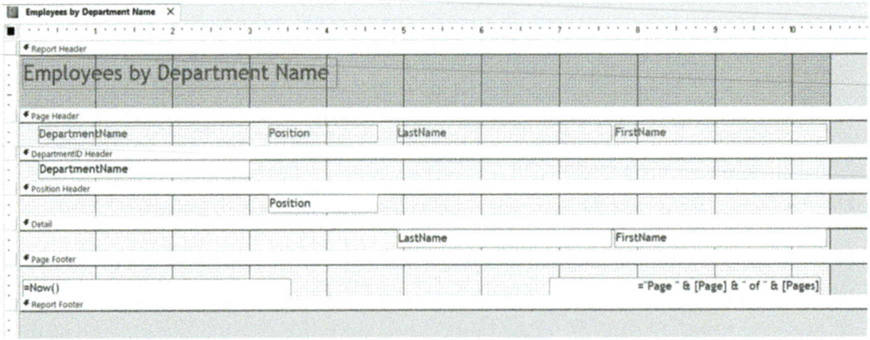

FIGURE 10.23. The Employees by Department Name report shown in the Design View.

TABLE. 10.2 The Main Parts of an Access Report

Report Section	Description
Report Header	This section appears at the top of the report before the other sections and is used to display information that apply to the entire report, such as a report title, a logo, a date, or some text describing the purpose of the report. The report header is printed only once per report.
Page Header	This section appears at the top of every page in the report. You should place here the information that you want to repeat on each page, such as report title, page number, company name, and column headings.
Group Header **(Can have multiple group headers)**	Groups are used to combine data that is logically related. The Group Header section appears at the beginning of each new group of records in the report. Use this section to display information that identifies the current group, such as the group name or a summary of the group data. In the Employees by Department Name report we have a Group Header called DepartmentID that groups employee records by Department Name. You can have multiple group headers in a report, depending on how many levels of grouping you have applied. In our example report, we have also the Position Header that groups employee records by their position in the company.
Detail	This section contains the main body of the report. Here you display the individual records from your record source. You can use this section to show any fields or calculated value that you want to include in the report.
Group Footer **(Can have multiple group footers)**	This section will appear at the end of each group of records in the report. You can use Group Footer to display information that summarizes the group data, such as totals, averages, or counts. You can have multiple group headers in a report depending on how many levels of grouping you have applied.
Page Footer	This section appears at the bottom of every page in the report. You can use it to display information that you want to repeat on each page, such as the date, the time, page number, or a disclaimer.
Report Footer	This section appears at the very end of the report, after all sections. You can use it to display information that is relevant to the entire report, such as grand totals, overall summaries, and recommendations. The report footer is printed once per report.

MODIFYING THE REPORT

As mentioned earlier there are a few issues with the Employees by Department Name report that was created by the Report Wizard in Hands-On 10.1. Let's start by adjusting the report layout so we can squeeze in the missing Phone field.

⊙ **Hands-On 10.2   Modifying the Report**

1. Open the **Employees by Department Name** report in the **Design View**.

   Access displays the report as shown in Figure 10.24. Notice that there is a small green triangle in the upper left corner of the Report Design View. This is how Access notifies you that your report width is greater than the page width which can cause extra blank pages to be printed. When you click on the triangle, you'll get the yellow exclamation mark icon that has a dropdown where you can see more details about the error and possible solutions. To fix this error, you will need to decrease the size of the report controls and adjust the width of the report.

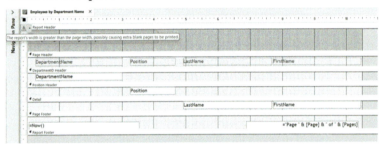

FIGURE 10.24. Access alerts you to possible problems with printing of the report by displaying special icons in the Design View.

2. Adjust the names of controls to include a space between the words, so DepartmentName appears as **Department Name**, **LastName** as **Last Name** and **FirstName** as **First Name**. You can do this by clicking the control select it and then clicking again to edit it, or you can make these changes in the Property Sheet by modifying the Caption property of the selected control.

3. In the Page Header section, select all the label controls (**DepartmentName, Position, LastName** and **FirstName**) by dragging the mouse around them. You can also click on the **DepartmentName**, hold down the Shift key and click on each of the remaining controls.

4. With the controls selected, move the mouse to the right edge of the First Name control, and when you get a double arrow, double-click the edge. This will narrow all the selected controls to the width of the text they contain.

5. Adjust the placement of the Position control so that its left border begins at 2.4167" on the horizontal ruler. The easiest way to do this, is by entering this value in the Left property of the selected Position_label in the Property Sheet. If the Property Sheet is not visible, turn it on by pressing F4. When working with the properties, always ensure that the correct control is selected from the drop-down list at the top of the Property Sheet.

6. Position the First Name label control at 7.2083".
7. In the Position Header section, move the Position text box to the left so that it's left edge aligns with the Position label control in the Page Header. Use the Property Sheet to change the Width property of the Position text box to 2.75".
8. In the Detail section, select the LastName text box and in the Property Sheet, change the Width property to 2.25".
9. In the Detail section, select the FirstName text box and in the Property Sheet, change the Width property to 1.625" and the Left property to 7.2083".
10. In the Page Footer section, click the text box containing the expression that displays the page number information and in the Property box, set the left property to 6.5".

	About Calculated Controls
	Some reports generated by the Report Wizard have in the Page Footer section text box controls with date and page numbers. They are a type of calculated controls; they contain a formula in the Control Source property.
	To retrieve the current date, use the Now() function in the Control Source property of a text box. You must precede the function name with the equals sign (=). The equal sign indicates that the expression is a calculated value.
	To show information about the number of pages in your report,
NOTE	*use the following formula:*
	`="Page " & [Page] & " of " & [Pages]`
	The double quotation marks (") enclose the text that will be displayed as it is, such as "Page " and " of". The ampersand (&) is a concatenation operator that joins the text and the values together. The square bracket ([]) enclose the names of the properties that return the current page number ([Page]) and the total number of pages ([Pages]) in the report. These are built-in properties that can be used in any report.
	You can add page numbers in any section of the report you like.

11. In the Property Sheet on the Format tab, select Report from the dropdown, and change the report's Width property to 10.4".

    The error message exclamation icon and the green triangle should now disappear from the Report view. Now let's add the missing Phone field.
12. In the Tools group of the Report Design tab, click the Add Existing Fields.

    Access displays a Fields List pane to the right of the Report Design View, as shown in Figure 10.25.

13. Drag the Phone field from the Field List to the right of the FirstName text box in the Detail section. Set the Left property of the Phone text box to 8.9167".

14. Click the Phone label control to select it. We must move it now to the Page Header section. To do this, press Ctrl+X to cut the label control then click the Page Header section and press Ctrl+V. The label control should appear partially on the top of the Department Name label. Press F4 to show the Property Sheet and set the Left property of this label to 8.9167".

The modified Design View of this report is shown in Figure 10.25.

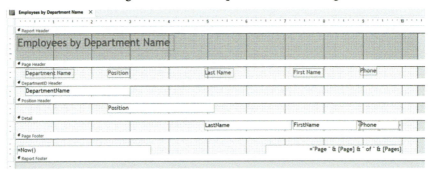

FIGURE 10.25. The appearance of the report after adjusting report and its controls in the Design View and in the Property Sheet.

Let's examine the Report view to see what else needs to be adjusted.

15. Switch to the Report view.

Access displays the modified report as shown in Figure 10.26.

Department Name	Position	Last Name	First Name	Phone
Accounting				
	Accounting Clerk			
		Livingston	Michael	(718) 444-3256
	Controller			
		Harrow	James	(718) 444-3299
	Financial Analyst			
		Rodriguez	Laura	(718) 444-3245
	VP Accounting			
		Wolski	Robert	(718) 444-3266
Administration				
	Adminstrative Assistant			
		Molina	Margaret	(718) 444-3334
	HR Assistant			
		Worth	John	(718) 444-3349
	HR Manager			
		Donelly	Oscar	(718) 444-3335
	Secretary			
		Matella	Kathy	(718) 444-3531
		Roberts	Jessica	(718) 444-3442

Employees by Department Name

FIGURE 10.26. The Report View displays the report after initial user modifications.

Notice that the Phone label needs to be moved a bit down to align with the remaining labels in the Page Header section. The Phone text boxes have borders around them; it does not look very professional. We need to remove them. Also, some lines use confusing shading. We only want to shade the lines that indicate a different department name.

16. Switch to the Layout view as it will be easier to work in this view to make the aforementioned adjustments.

17. Click the Phone label and, in the Property Sheet, set the Top property to 0.0417". You should immediately see this change in the report.

18. Click the text box that displayed phone number. Notice that Access highlights all the text boxes on the report. In the Property Sheet, set the Border Style to Transparent. Now the border is removed in the report.

19. Click the first shaded line and in the Property Sheet notice that the GroupHeader1 is selected. This is the PositionHeader that you saw in the Design View. In the Property Sheet, in the Alternate Back Color property, choose No Color from the drop-down list. The shaded lines should disappear only for the selected section.

20. Now click the remaining shaded line (Roberts Jessica) and notice that this line is part of the Detail section. In the Property Sheet, in the Alternate Back Color property, choose No Color from the drop-down list. Now the selected line is no longer shaded.

21. Click the Accounting under the Department Name label. All the department names should now be selected. Click to the left of the Accounting to select the entire line. All the department names lines should be selected. The Property Sheet should show that GroupHeader0 is our selection type. Change the Back Color to Access Theme 4 by selecting it from the Back Color drop-down. Set the Alternate Back Color to No Color.

NOTE	*Access automatically assigns the names to the group header and footer sections. To change the default name into something more meaningful, select the GroupHeader0 in the Property Sheet and change the Name property to DepartmentID_GroupHeader, Do the same for the Position header by changing its name from GroupHeader1 to Position_GroupHeader.*

22. Click again the Accounting and notice the Department Name is selected in the Property Sheet. Change the Back Color property to Access Theme 4. Figure 10.27 displays the reformatted report.

Depending on your reporting requirements, you can spend many hours formatting the report to your liking. This report is by no means finished. You can make other changes to it like using different font size and font style, adding a logo, and inserting other images, changing colors, or applying different themes. Consider also using lines, rectangles, and other special effects such as shadows. If your report contains groupings, you can also use the Hide Details button in the Grouping & Totals group of the Report Layout Design tab to hide the records at the next lower level of grouping as shown in Figure 10.28.

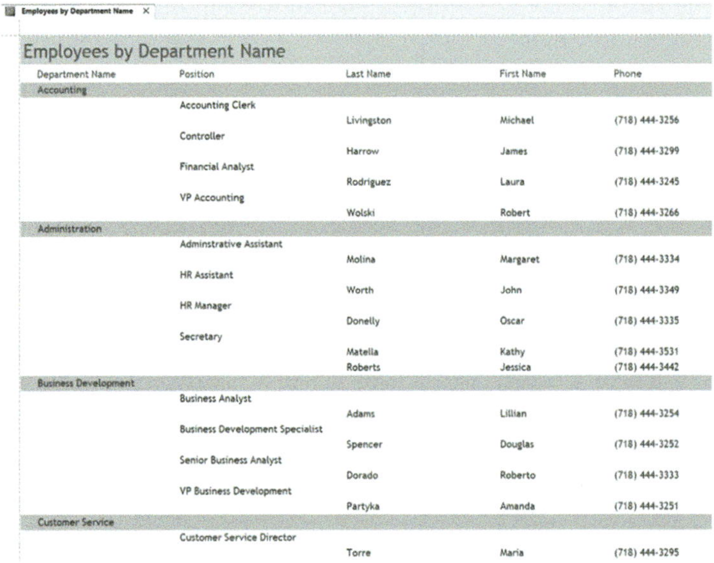

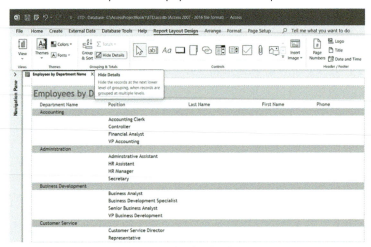

FIGURE 10.27. The Layout View displays the reformatted report.

FIGURE 10.28. The Layout View with hidden detail rows.

23. Save and close the report.

Action Item 10.1

To get more hands-on experience with formatting report controls and report sections, use various properties of these controls and other available special effects to improve the appearance of the TrainingCourseLocations report (shown in Figure 10.3) and save it under a different name.

Adding Page Breaks

When Access generates a report, it fills the first page with as many records that can fit on that page and then starts another page. Once the report is created, you can control where the new pages should start. You can insert forced breaks based on groups or within sections, except for the Page Header and Page Footer sections.

Suppose in the Employees by Department Name report you would like to have a separate page for each department, as shown in Figure 10.29.

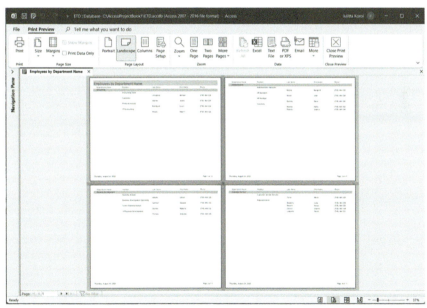

FIGURE 10.29. A report with a forced page break before the DepartmentID_GroupHeader.

To force page breaks every time the group value changes, set the Force New Page property of the group section (DepartmentID_GroupHeader) to Before Section.

There are four Force Page property settings:

- **None:** Default setting which indicates no forced page break.
- **Before Section:** Prints the current section at the top of a new page every time there is a new group.
- **After Section:** Prints the next section at the top of a new page every time there is a new group.
- **Before & After:** Uses both the Before and After Section setting.

To force a page break that is not based on a grouping, use the Page Break control from the Controls group of the Report Design tab. Simply drop the control on the report where you want a page break to occur each time the page prints.

Using Expressions in the Group Header

At times you may want to add additional data to the controls placed in the Group Header. For example, in the Employees by Department Name report shown in Figure 10.30, the DepartmentName header has been replaced by an expression so now each department name is followed by the count of employees.

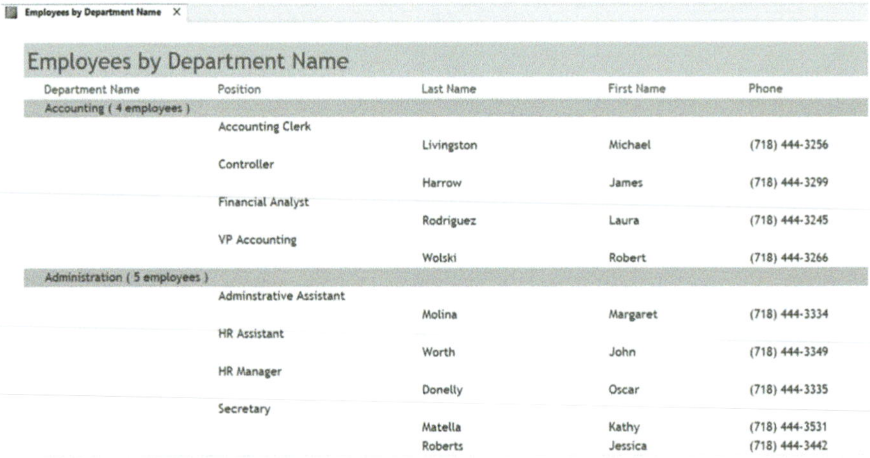

FIGURE 10.30. The report created earlier is shown here with the modified Group Header.

Recall that when you used the Report Wizard and specified that you wanted to group the employees by department name, Access created a text box control that was bound to a field named DepartmentName. To display the count of employees in the group header text box, you need to replace the Control Source property of the DepartmentName text box with the following expression that will count the number of employees in each department and display it along with the text "employees":

```
=[DepartmentName] & " ( " & Count([LastName]) & " employees )"
```

Make sure to include all the spaces as shown.

Use the Expression Builder dialog box from the Control Source property, to enter the previous expression (see Figure 10.31).

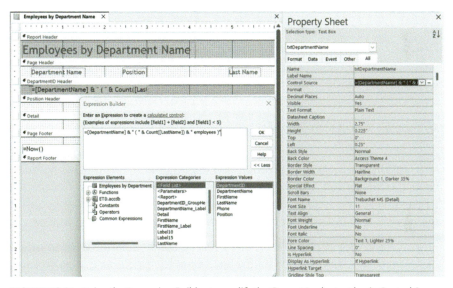

FIGURE 10.31. Using the Expression Builder to modify the Group Header text box's Control Source.

Another change you must make is the value of the Name property of this text box control. The Report Wizard has used the name of the field (Department-Name) as the default control name. Let's change it to something else, like txtDe-partmentName in Figure 10.31. If you omit this step and return to the Design View after entering the expression in the Control Source, Access will complain that the control has a circular reference (see Figure 10.32).

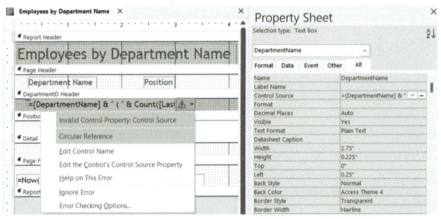

FIGURE 10.32. When the name of the control conflicts with the name of the field referenced in the Control Source expression, Access displays a Circular Reference error.

Understanding Circular References

A circular reference error occurs when a formula or expression refers to itself or to another formula or expression that depends on it, creating a loop that prevents the calculation from being completed. This can happen in Access reports when you use expressions to calculate values based on other fields or controls in the report. To avoid circular reference errors, you can follow these steps:

- Check your expressions for any references to themselves or to other expressions that refer to them. For example, if you have a control named `Total` that has the expression `=Sum([Price]*[Quantity])+[Total]`, this will cause a circular reference error because the control is using its own value in the calculation.

- Use fully qualified field names in your expressions to avoid ambiguity. A fully qualified field name consists of the table name (or table alias) and the field name, separated by a dot. For example, if you have a table named `Departments` and a field named `DepartmentName`, you can use `Departments.DepartmentName` to refer to that field in your expressions. This will help you avoid confusion with other fields or controls that have the same name. In Figure 10.31 we renamed the control to txtDepartmentName to avoid the circular reference error. If you'd rather not rename the control, you should change the Control Source expressions to the following:

```
=[Departments.DepartmentName] & " ( " & Count([LastName]) &
" employees )"
```

SUMMARY

In this chapter, you learned about different options for creating reports. By providing two wizard interfaces, Report Wizard and Labels, as well as other report tools (Report, Report Design, and a Blank Report) to create common reports, Access reports can be created quickly even by the novice users. Like forms, reports have different views that help you with Report Design and printing and have various properties that can be accessed via the Property Sheet.

In this chapter, you've learned how to create labels report based on the table Instructors. You also generated a report with the Report Wizard. This report showed a list of employees in each department grouped by the Position field. You used many report and report control properties to make the report more visually appealing. You learned about reports being divided into many sections and used various properties to reformat them. You worked with page breaks and expressions and learned about circular references. By further experimenting with various report features you can create any report you want.

In the next chapter, which is mostly Hands-On, we will focus on the report customization while creating more advanced reports.

Chapter 11 REPORT CUSTOMIZATION

A s you have discovered in the previous chapter, creating basic reports in Access is quite straightforward thanks to the built-in reporting tools, such as the Report Wizard that can quickly create your report structure, adding the required sections and placing the appropriate controls on your report. However, without the application of special formatting techniques, your report may not be as useful and presentable as you would like it to be. As a matter of fact, to create a report that perfectly suits your needs, a lot of formatting skills and effort will be required on your part. Working on a report that uses data from multiple tables can be very challenging. The skills you need to succeed in your report writing endeavor can be obtained by practice only. In this chapter, we will focus on report customization that will allow you to create more complex reports.

In the first Hands-On project you will create the Course Registrations Report (see Figure 11.1) that uses a multitable Record Source, with employee groupings by course name and course section; add sorting, calculations, and create expressions that help you draw attention to important records in the report; include page and section headers and footers that can be hidden depending on whether a specific field in the data source contains data or is blank. While you could use the Report Wizard to help you create the structure of this report with the required groupings, the laying out of the controls would require many tedious and time-consuming adjustments, therefore we will create this report entirely from scratch. This Hands-On will introduce you to using the Group, Sort, and Totals pane; writing complex expressions with the Intermediate IF Function (IIF); using On Format event in report sections, as well as customizing the properties of various report controls to get the look that matches Figure 11.1.

In the second Hands-On project, you will create a handy user interface for previewing and printing reports as depicted in Figure 11.2. Here you will utilize many of the skills you acquired in the chapters that focused on Access forms and you will enhance your knowledge by learning how to use the Command Button Wizard to generate embedded macros for your buttons that perform specific actions, and then learn how to convert them into Visual Basic code for further modification.

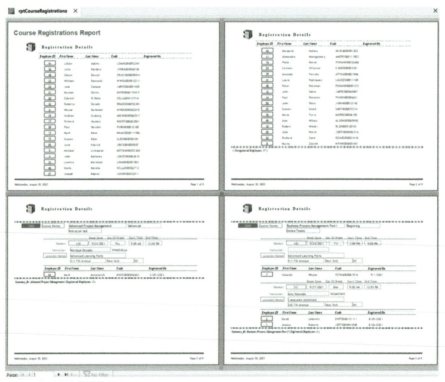

FIGURE 11.1. This complex report is created in Hands-On 11.1.

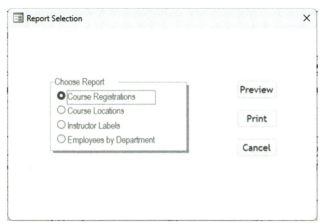

FIGURE 11.2. This pop-up form provides a user interface for previewing and printing reports (see Hands-On 11.2).

CREATING A RECORD SOURCE FOR THE REPORT

The first step in designing a custom report from scratch is creating a Record Source that will provide all the necessary fields and records for your report. This can be done by creating a standalone query or an SQL statement which you then bind to the report's Record Source property. However, unless you are planning to reuse the same query for other forms or reports, or as a source for another query, there is no need to create and save extra queries in your database. In Part I of Hands-On 11.1, you will use the Query Builder to create an SQL statement for your Course Registration Report Record Source.

(⊙) **Hands-On 11.1   Creating a Course Registrations Report**

(Part I—Defining the Source of Data)
1. In the ETD database, choose **Create | Report Design**.
    Access creates a blank report using the Design view. By default, this report has three sections: Page Header, Detail, and Page Footer, and it assigned a default name: Report1.
2. Right click the Report1 tab and choose **Save**. Enter **rptCourseRegistrations** for the name of this report and click **OK**.
3. In the Property Sheet make sure that the selection type is **Report**.
    If the Property Sheet is not visible, activate it using the **Property Sheet** button in the Tools section of the Report Design tab or press **F4**.

4. In the Property Sheet on the **Data** tab, select the **Record Source** property and click the ellipsis (…) button to start the Query Builder.
5. Use the **Add Tables** pane to add the following tables to the Query Builder: **Employees**, **Registration**, **TrainingSession**, **TrainingSchedule**, **TrainingCourseLocations**, **TrainingCourse**, **SessionInstructor**, and **Instructors** (see Figure 11.3).
6. Reposition the tables to match Figure 11.3.
    This step will help you take a closer look at the table joins that Access automatically created. When creating a complex report, oftentimes you may need to change the type of join between tables.
7. Double click on the line joining the **Employees** and **Registration** tables.

    Access displays the Join Properties dialog where the first option (1) is selected. As you may recall from the chapter on queries this option indicates an INNER JOIN type between the two tables. If we leave it as is, our report will only display records for the registered employees. However, in this report we want to display all the records from the Employees table, even if they do not have a matching record in the right table (Registration). To indicate which employees have registered for a course, and which ones have not, we need to tell Access to create a LEFT JOIN (Option 2).
8. Change the Join type as shown in Figure 11.4 and click **OK**.

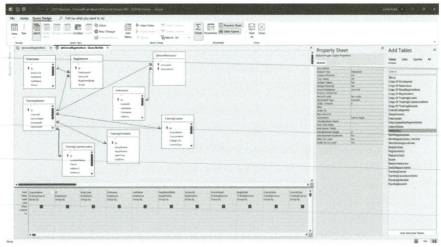

FIGURE 11.3. Using the Query Builder to create the Record Source for the report.

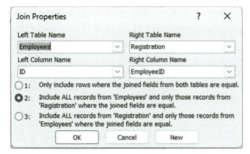

FIGURE 11.4. Modifying the Join Type between the tables.

9. Edit all the remaining join types to ensure that the relationships between tables visually match Figure 11.3. The following table specifies the joins you should implement:

TABLE 11.1 Modifying the Join Type Between Tables

Left Table Name	Right Table Name	JOIN Option
Employees	Registration	2
TrainingSession	Registration	3
TrainingSession	SessionInstructor	2
Instructors	SessionInstructor	3
TrainingCourse	TrainingSession	3
TrainingSchedule	TrainingSession	3
TrainingLocations	TrainingSession	3

10. Drag the following fields from the tables to the Query Design grid: TrainingCourse.CourseName, Employees.ID, Employees.EmpCode, Employees.FirstName, Employees.LastName, Registration.RegisteredDate, Registration.SessionID, TrainingSession.SessionNum, TrainingSession.BeginDate, TrainingCourse.CourseNum, TrainingCourse.CourseType, TrainingCourse.CourseLevel, TrainingCourseLocations.LocationName, TrainingCourseLocations.Address1, TrainingCourseLocations.City, TrainingCourseLocations.State, TrainingCourseLocations.ZipCode, TrainingSchedule.DayOfWeek, TrainingSchedule.StartTime, TrainingSchedule.EndTime, Instructors.InstRefID, Instructors.FirstName, Instructors.LastName

11. In the **Show/Hide** group of the Query Design tab, click the **Totals** button to show the Total row in the Query Design grid.

    The Total row should be set to **Group By** in all the columns as shown in Figure 11.3.

    Now, let's see the results of this query.

12. Click the **Run** button on the Ribbon.

    Access displays all the employee records starting with the employees that did not register for any course. These employees don't have matching records in the Registration table, therefore the corresponding fields in the query result are blank (null) (see Figure 11.5).

13. Click the drop arrow in the View button and select SQL view. You can also right click the rptCourseRegistrations: Query Builder tab and choose **SQL** view.

    Access displays a quite complex SQL statement (see Figure 11.6).

    It is a good idea to copy the entire statement to a Windows Notepad and save the file so you can get back to business quickly in case your report ever gets corrupted or messed up. It is always a pain to recreate a complex query, and having the SQL statement handy can save your day.

NOTE	*The SQL_rptCourseRegistrations.txt file in the Companion files provides the SQL statement for this query.*

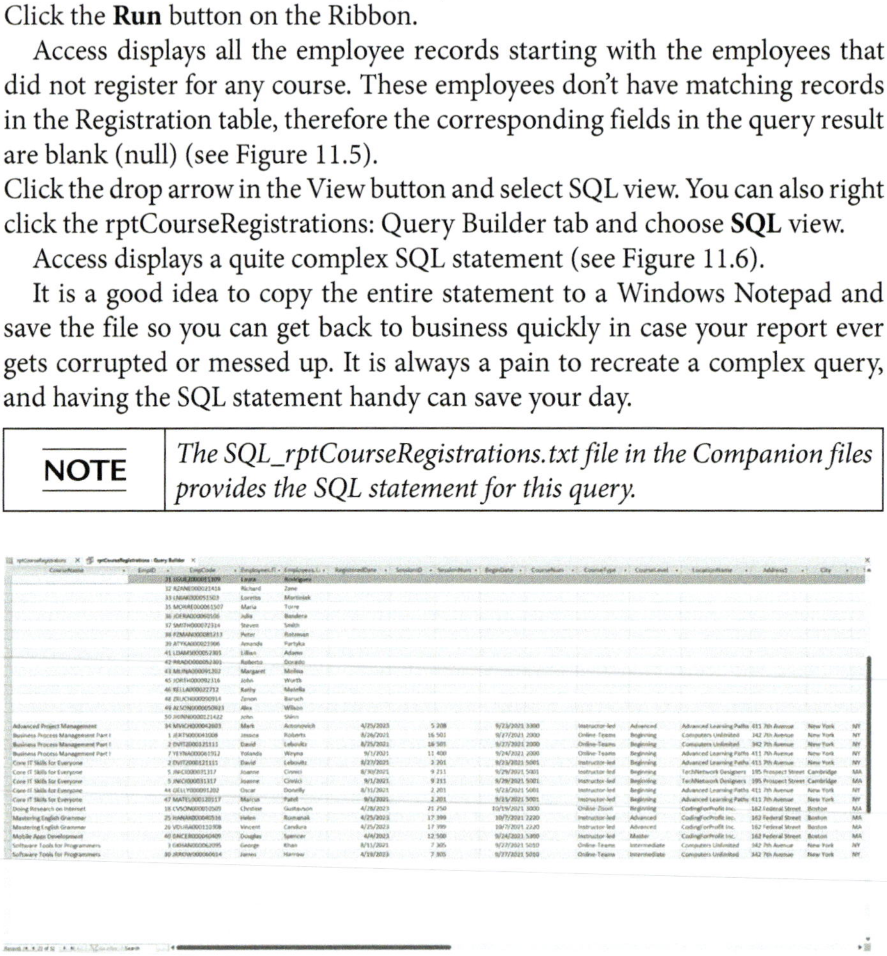

FIGURE 11.5. A partial output from running the query to verify that we get the desired records for the report.

FIGURE 11.6. The SQL view of the Query Builder shows the SQL statement that Access created based on the tables, joins and fields that you specified.

14. **Save** and close the **rptCourseRegistrations:QueryBuilder.**

Notice that the SQL statement now appears in the Record Source property of the report (Figure 11.7).

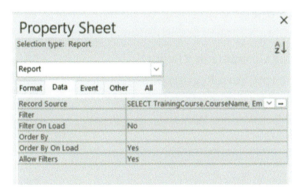

FIGURE 11.7. The Record Source property specifies the source of data for a report.

NOTE	*If you need to add additional tables, fields, or criteria to your report you can modify the RecordSource property. Also, if you need to create a report with similar design, you can copy the report in the Navigation view, then open it in the Design view and change the RecordSource property to display data from a different table, query, or SQL statement.*

15. Save the report by pressing **Ctrl+S**.

Congratulations! You have completed Part I of your report. Now that the data source has been defined, it's time to assign the grouping structure to your report.

DEFINING THE GROUPING STRUCTURE IN A REPORT

When you create a report with the Report Wizard, the group sections are created automatically based on the fields you specify. When you create a report from scratch, you must rely on your own knowledge of grouping. By assigning grouping to a report, you tell Access to divide the records in the report into categories based on the value of one or more fields. Grouping helps you to organize and summarize the information in your report and present it in a more readable and eye-appealing layout. Groups can be formatted with colors, fonts, and borders so it is easy to distinguish one group from another. In the rptCourseRegistrations report, we will add two groupings: by CourseName and by SectionID. You can add or modify grouping and sorting options in a report by using the Group, Sort, and Total pane in Layout View or Design View. This pane can be opened by clicking the Group & Sort button in the Grouping & Totals group on the Report Design tab.

⊙ **Hands-On 11.1   Creating a Course Registrations Report**

(Part II—Implementing Grouping in a Report)

1. In the Design view of the **rptCourseRegistrations** report, click the **Group & Sort** button on the Ribbon.

   Access displays the Group, Sort, and Total pane at the bottom of the Design view, as shown in Figure 11.8.

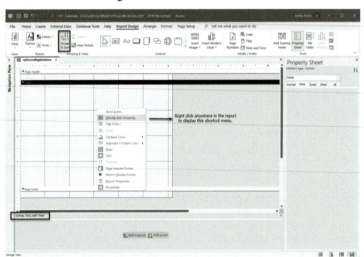

FIGURE 11.8. There are two ways of activating the Group, Sort, and Total pane. Use the button on the Ribbon or the shortcut menu option.

2. Click the **Add a group** button and select the **CourseName** field for this grouping (see Figure 11.9).

FIGURE 11.9. Adding a grouping to a report.

Access adds the Group on CourseName line to the Group, Sort, and Total pane and the CourseName Header section appears in the Report Design view (see Figure 11.10).

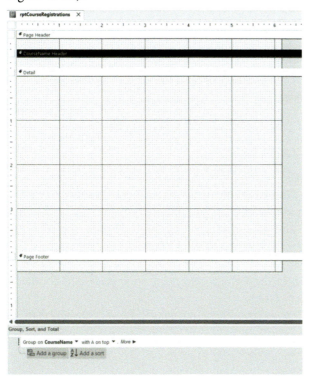

FIGURE 11.10. The Group, Sort, and Total pane lists current groupings in the report.

Notice that the CourseName field is set to ascending sort order (with A on top), which means that all the courses will display alphabetically starting with names beginning with A and ending with Z. You can easily change the sort to descending order by selecting Z on top from the drop-down menu.

The More button in the Group, Sort, and Total pane will expand to show more options for the group as shown in Figure 11.11 in the next step. These options are a list of different phrases. By clicking on a phrase link, you can choose other available options. The group configuration line in the Group, Sort, and Total pane contains the following phrases:

TABLE 11.2 Description of Options Available for a Report Grouping

Group Option Name	Description
Group on <field name>	Used to select a field to group on.
with A on top	Used to select the type of sort order: ascending (with A on top) or descending (with Z on top).
by entire value	Used to indicate how the records are grouped. You can group by the entire field value (default) or specify to group by the first one or two characters or a specified number of characters.
with no totals	Used to select the type of summary that should be applied to the group. For example, records can be counted. The selections shown depend on the type of field that is selected for the group.
with title click to Add	Allows you to add a title for the group.
with a header section	Used to add or remove a header section.
with a footer section	Used to add or remove a footer section.
do not keep group together on one page	Determines how page breaks are used within a group. For example, you can specify to keep whole group together on one page or keep the header and first record together on one page.

Take notice that you can delete the grouping from the report by selecting the Group on <field name> and clicking the Delete button in the right corner of the selection. The up and down buttons that appear before the Delete button allow you to change the positioning of the group in your report when you have multiple groups.

3. Click the **More** button in the Group, Sort, and Total pane and choose **with a footer section (Figure 11.11)**.

   The CourseName Footer should now appear in Report Design view.

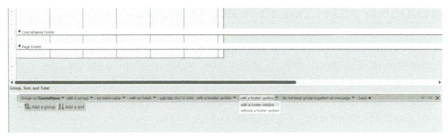

FIGURE 11.11 Displaying and setting the additional group options.

4. Click the **Less** button to hide the additional options.

5. Click the **Add a group** button and select **SessionID** to add a new group.

Notice that Access adds SessionID Header section to the report. We will not add a footer for this section.

6. Close the Group pane by clicking the Group & Sort button on the Ribbon.

We have finished specifying groupings for our report. The next thing is adding the Report Header and Footer.

7. Right click anywhere in the report and select **Report Header | Footer** from the shortcut menu (see Figure 11.12).

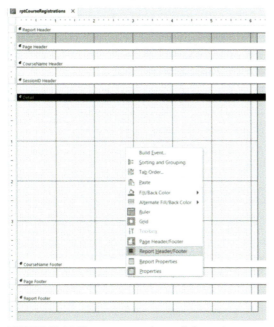

FIGURE 11.12 The report now shows all the sections we need.

8. Press **Ctrl+S** to save the report.

WORKING WITH THE REPORT HEADER

The Report Header section appears only once at the top of the first page of the report. This section can contain controls that display report title, logo, current date, and anything else you'd like to include for your specific report. The Report Header section is optional. Recall that you had to specifically tell Access to include it in your report. Let's add a title to our report and apply some formatting to it.

⊙ Hands-On 11.1   Creating a Course Registrations Report

(Part III—Report Header—Adding and Formatting the Report and Report Title)

1. Resize the **Report Header** by selecting it and in the Property Sheet, change its **Height** Property to **0.625"**.
2. To add a title to the Report Header section, select the **Label** control in the Controls group of the Report Design tab and then click inside the Report Header and type **Course Registrations Report**. Click outside of the label when you finish typing.
3. Click on the label to select it and in the Property Sheet, on the Format tab, set the following properties to the shown values:

Property Name	Property Value
Width	5.5417"
Height	0.4167"
Top	0.0833"
Left	0"
Font Name	Arial
Font Size	24
Font Weight	Bold
Fore Color	#3B8194

4. At the top of the Property Sheet select ReportHeader from the selection drop-down list and set the **Back Color** property of the ReportHeader to **Background 1**. This can be done by clicking the ellipsis (…) button and choosing the white color from the Theme Colors as shown in Figure 11.13.

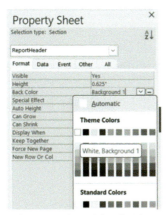

FIGURE 11.13 Applying the Theme Colors.

Now let's resize the report canvas so that we can fit all the controls we need when working with the remaining sections.

5. At the top of the Property Sheet select **Report** from the drop-down list, and in the Format tab, set the **Width** property to **10.375**".

When you make this change, Access displays at the top of the report a green triangle indicating that there is a problem with the page width. Let's correct this.

6. Click the **Page Setup** in the Ribbon and select **Landscape**.

If you are still getting a green triangle in the report, you must increase the left and right margins due to the difference in the printer drivers.

7. Click the **Page Setup** button in the Page Layout group of the Page Setup tab and set the left and right margins to **0.3** as shown in Figure 11.14 and click **OK**.

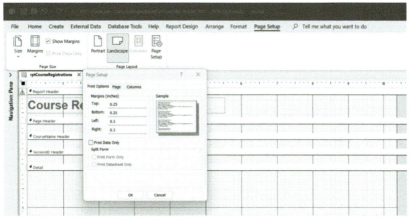

FIGURE 11.14 Changing the margins of the printout.

Access should remove the error triangle from the report. If not, return to the Page Setup and increase a bit more the left and right margins.

8. In the Property Sheet ensure that the **Report** is still selected and set its **Caption** property to **rptCourseRegistrations** and its **Default View** property to **Print Preview**.

9. Save the changes you made in the report by right clicking the report tab or pressing **Ctrl+S**.

We have finished formatting the report and its header, and we are ready to work with the Page Header section.

PREPARING THE PAGE HEADER

The Page Header Section appears at the top of each page of the report. You can use this section to display a report title or subtitle, add an image to make your report pages more attractive, and add other information that should appear on each page of your report. In our Course Registration Report, the Page Header will include the following elements: an image displaying a bunch of bound reports; a label control with the page subtitle captioned Registration Details, the column headings that will appear over the detailed records of unregistered employees, and horizontal lines above and below the headings. Recall that in this report data source we requested the course registration data for all employees whether they registered or not. Let's go ahead and work on this section.

(⊙) **Hands-On 11.1   Creating a Course Registrations Report**

(Part IV—Page Header—Formatting the Page Header Section and Its Controls)

1. In the Report Design View, click the **Page Header** section name to select it and in the Property Sheet, set the **Height** property of the PageHeaderSection to **1.0417"** and **Display When** property to **Print Only**.

2. In the Controls group of the Report Design tab, click **Insert Image** button and in the Image Gallery that appears, choose **Browse**. In the Insert Picture dialog, select the image named **reports.png** from the Companion files, and click **OK**.

You should see an image icon attached to the mouse pointer. Click in the Page Header blank area to insert the image.

3. With the image selected, use the Property Sheet to change the following properties to resize the image control:

Property Name	Property Value
Width	0.625"
Height	0.625"
Top	0.0833"
Left	0.5833"

Notice that when you inserted the image Access has increased the width of the Page Header section to accommodate its size. Now that we have made this image smaller, go ahead and reset the section width to the size we set in Step 1.

4. In the Report Design tab's Controls group, select the label control, click to the right of the image control in the Page Header section, type **Registration Details**, and click outside the label control.

5. Click the **Registration Details** label to select it and, in the Property Sheet, set the following properties to the shown values:

Property Name	Property Value
Width	2.6667"
Height	0.2667"
Top	0.25"
Left	1.4583"
Font Name	Times New Roman
Font Size	14
Font Weight	Heavy
Text Align	Distribute
Fore Color	Text 2

6. If Access displays a green triangle in the left corner of the Registration label, click the triangle, open the exclamation mark drop-down menu, and choose **Ignore Error** as shown in Figure 11.15.

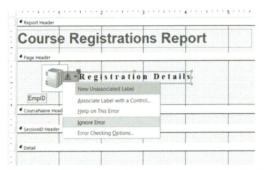

FIGURE 11.15 Access displays an error message when it finds a label that is not associated with a control.

Now let's bring the fields and their labels to our report. We will work with the Detail and Page Header sections.

7. In the Tools group of the Report Design tab, click the **Add Existing Fields** button.

    Access displays the field list pane, that lists all the fields we have selected for this report in our query.

8. In the Field List pane click the **ID** field, hold down the **Shift** key, and click the **RegisteredDate** field. This will highlight all the fields we need (**ID, EmpCode, Employees.FirstName, Employees.LastName**, and **RegisteredDate**).

9. Click and drag the highlighted fields to the Report Design, dropping them in the **Detail** section as shown in Figure 11.16.

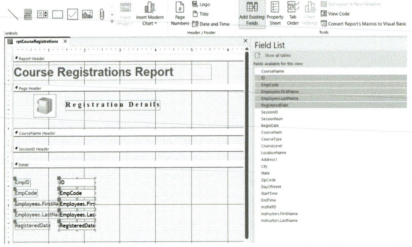

FIGURE 11.16 To place fields on the report canvas, drag them from the Field List pane to the desired location.

When you drag fields from the Field List, Access automatically creates a Label control with the field name attached to the Text Box control to which the field is bound. Notice the labels that you drag from the Controls group on the Ribbon aren't associated with any text boxes or any other control on the report.

Notice that Access has placed the controls in the Detail section using a stacked layout that resembles a form that you fill out. The fields are stacked on top of each other. Let's change this arrangement of controls to tabular layout which better suits our needs. A tabular layout is like a spreadsheet. Labels are positioned across the top and the data is aligned in columns below labels.

10. With the controls still selected as shown in Figure 11.16, click the **Tabular** button in the Table group of the **Arrange** tab.

    Access moves the labels to the Page Header section and leaves the text box controls in the detail section (see Figure 11.17).

11. With the layout still selected as shown in Figure 11.17, click the Property Sheet button on the Ribbon to display the Property Sheet, and set the **Top** property of the **Multiple selection** to **0.7"** and the **Left** property to **1.5"**.

    This will move the selection down, and a bit to the right so that the label controls appear at the bottom of the Page Header section below the Registration Details label control (see Figure 11.18). Remember that while working in the Report Design view, if you miss a step or want to return to the previous arrangement of controls or their settings, you can press the Undo button on the Quick Access toolbar.

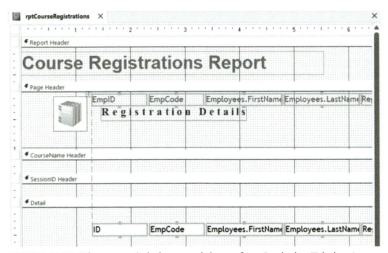

FIGURE 11.17 When you switch the controls layout from Stacked to Tabular, Access moves the label controls to the Page Header section.

12. With the controls group still select as shown in Figure 11.18, click the **Remove Layout** button on the **Arrange** tab.

    This action removes the layout applied to controls so we can move them freely within the sections.

13. Click anywhere in the blank area of the Page Header section, and then click the **ID** label and, in the Property Sheet, change the **Caption** property to **Employee ID**.

14. Change the Caption properties for the remaining labels as follows: EmpCode to **Code**, Employees.FirstName to **First Name**, Employees.LastName to **Last Name**, RegisteredDate to **Registered On.**

15. Reposition the labels so they appear in the following order: **Employee ID**, **First Name**, **Last Name**, **Code**, and **Registered On.**

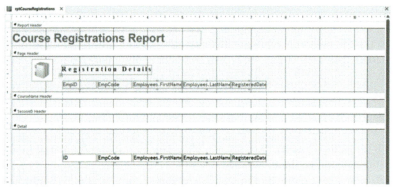

FIGURE 11.18 The entire controls group was repositioned using Top property setting in the Property Sheet.

16. Select all the labels and in the Property Sheet, set the following properties as follows:

Property Name	Property Value
Font Name	Times New Roman
Font Size	11
Font Weight	Bold
Font Italic	Yes
Text Align	Right
Fore Color	#000080

17. In the Report Design tab's Controls group, select the **Line** control and click above the **Employee ID** label control. Access will draw a short line. Use the Property Sheet to set the following properties:

Property Name	Property Value
Width	8"
Height	0"
Border Style	Dash Dot Dash
Border Color	#008080
Border Width	1 pt

18. Click outside the selected line to see the formatting changes.

19. Copy and paste this line positioning it at the bottom of the labels. To copy, right click the line and choose **Copy**, then right click anywhere in the Page Header section, and choose **Paste**. Access will position the copied line at the top of the Page Header section. Drag it down so it appears at the bottom of the labels. The completed Page Header section is shown in Figure 11.19.

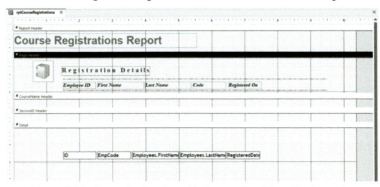

FIGURE 11.19 The Report Design view with the completed Page Header section.

20. Save all the changes you've made so far in this report.

This is a good time to take a break before moving to the next section where we begin placing controls in the first report group which is the CourseName Header.

PREPARING THE COURSENAME HEADER

The CourseName Header's function is to group the employee registration records by CourseName field. This section should display course information from the following fields: CourseNum, CourseName, CourseLevel, and CourseType. The completed CourseName Header section is shown in Figure 11.20. Notice that at the top of the section we have a custom formatted horizontal line and underneath the line we display information about the courses. There is only one label in this section, and it is associated with the CourseName text box control.

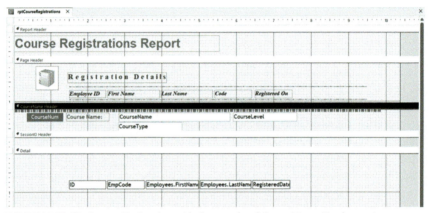

FIGURE 11.20 The Report Design view with the completed CourseName Header section.

⊙ Hands-On 11.1   Creating a Course Registrations Report

(Part V—CourseName Header—Formatting the CourseName Header Section and Its Controls)

1. Use the **Line** control from the Ribbon's Controls group to place a horizontal line at the top of the CourseName Header section. Use the following settings for the specified line properties:

Property Name	Property Value
Width	9.8333"
Height	0.0417"
Top	0"
Left	0"
Border Style	Dash Dot
Border Color	#3B8194
Border Width	3 pt

2. Click the **Add Existing Field**s button on the Report Design tab and drag to the CourseName Header section the following fields: **CourseNum**, **CourseName**, **CourseLevel**, and **CourseType**.

Access places the selected fields in the report using the Stacked layout. Notice that two fields (CourseType, CourseLevel) are formatted as combo box controls instead of a text box (see Figure 11.21).

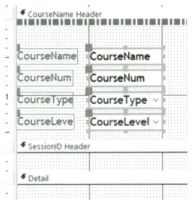

FIGURE 11.21 Access may assign a different type of control than you need when you drag the field from the Field List pane to your report.

3. Right click on the **CourseType** combo box control and select **Change To | Text Box**. Do the same for the **CourseLevel** combo box.
4. Select the labels for **CourseNum**, **CourseType**, and **CourseLevel** and press the **Delete** key to remove them.
5. In the Property Sheet, change the **Caption** property for the remaining label to **Course Name:**.
6. Reposition the remaining controls and make them bigger as shown in Figure 11.20.
7. Change the **Back Color** property of the **CourseNum** text box to **#3B8194** and the **Fore Color** property by selecting it and clicking the ellipsis (…) button and choosing **white** box in the Theme Colors.
8. Save all the changes you made in the report.

We will return to this section later when we discuss the report section events.

NOTE	*While working on your report, you should often preview it in the Report View, Layout View, and Print Preview to find out how the layout is displayed and what other formatting changes you need to make to get the results you want.*

PREPARING THE SESSIONID HEADER

In the ETD database, the training courses can be given in one or more sessions. The SessionID Header's function is to group the employee registration records by the session they registered for. This section should display session information from the following fields: SessionNum, BeginDate, DayOfWeek, StartTime, EndTime. In addition, we should include the instructor's first and last name, and their referenceID. Finally, we must know the location of the session: LocationName, Address1, City, and State. Keep in mind that we will not be showing the Room information as we did not include it in the design of the TrainingSession table.

⊚ Hands-On 11.1   Creating a Course Registrations Report

(Part VI—SessionID Header—Formatting the SessionID Header Section and Its Controls)

1. Click the **Add Existing Field**s button on the Report Design tab and drag to the SessionID Header section the following fields: **SessionNum**, **BeginDate**, **DayOfWeek**, **StartTime**, and **EndTime**.
   Access places the selected fields in the designated location in the report.
2. Change the Caption property of **SessionNum** label to **Session:**.
3. Change the Captions for the remaining labels as follows: **Begin Date**, **Day of Week**, **Start Time**, and **End Time**. You can do this quickly by clicking inside each label and adding required spaces.
4. Select all controls except for SessionNum and its label, and in the **Arrange** tab, click **Tabular**.
   Access repositions the controls leaving text boxes in the SessionID Header section and moving their labels to the PageHeader section. We need these labels in the same section as the text boxes. Let's relocate them then.
5. Click in an empty spot outside the selection, and then reselect just the labels that were moved to the top of the Page Header section. Right click the selected labels and choose **Cut**. Then right click in the SessionID Header section and choose **Paste**.
6. Reposition all the labels and fields as shown in Figure 11.22 adding a horizontal line below the labels.

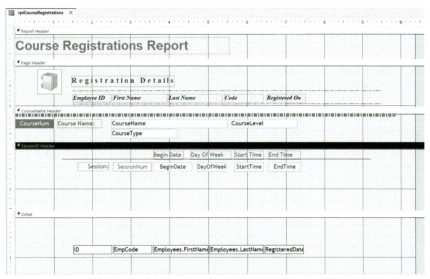

FIGURE 11.22 The SessionID Header section with the Session information.

7. Change the **Width** property of the Line control to **8"**, the **Border Width** to **1 pt**, and the **Border Color** to **#008080**.

8. Select all the text boxes in this section and set the **Text Align** property of the multiple selection to **Center**.

9. Click the **SessionNum** text box and set its **Border Width** to **Hairline, Border Style** to **Solid, Border Color** to **#3B8194,** and **Fore Color** to **#3B8194**.

   Now let's add the fields for the instructor data.

10. Click the **Add Existing Field**s button on the Report Design tab and drag to the SessionID Header section the following fields:**Instructors.FirstName** and **InstRefID**.

    Note we are not adding the instructor's last name as we will show the full name in one text box control.

11. Click the **First Name** label control and rename it **Instructor:**.

12. Click the label associated with the **InstRefID** text box and delete it.

13. Reposition the instructor related controls as shown in Figure 11.23.

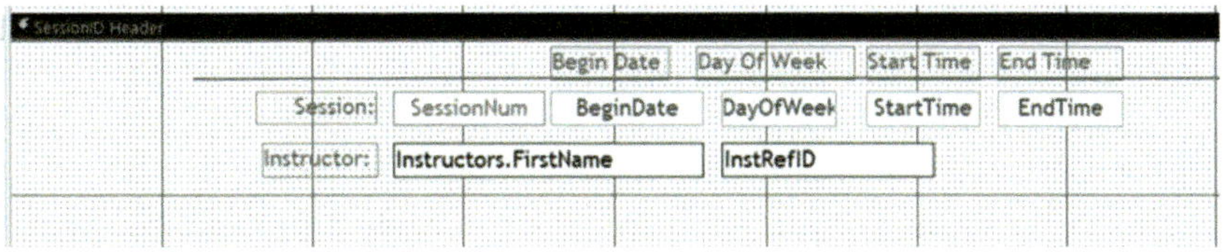

	Begin Date	Day Of Week	Start Time	End Time
Session: SessionNum	BeginDate	DayOfWeek	StartTime	EndTime
Instructor: Instructors.FirstName	InstRefID			

FIGURE 11.23 The SessionID Header section with the instructor's data fields.

Now, let's make other changes to ensure that we show the full name of the session's instructor.

14. Click the **Instructors.FirstName** text box control and, in the Property Sheet, change the **Name** property **FullName.**, then click the **Control Source** property and the **ellipsis** (…) button.

15. In the Expression Builder dialog, enter the expression as shown in Figure 11.24.

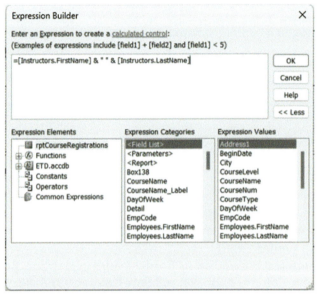

FIGURE 11.24 The Expression Builder is used to create a calculated control. Here we simply concatenate instructor's first and last name.

16. Click **OK** to close the Expression Builder.

Now, the last part for the SessionID Header section is adding the location information.

17. Click the **Add Existing Field**s button on the Report Design tab and drag to the SessionID Header section the following fields: **LocationName**, **Address1**, **City**, and **State**.

18. Change the **Caption** of the **LocationName** label to **Location Name:**.

19. Select the **Address1**, **City** and **State** label controls and delete them.

20. Position all the location related controls as shown in Figure 11.25.

In the SessionID Header section, we will need headings for the employee records. We can copy them from the Page Header section.

21. In the Page Header section select the label controls (**EmployeeID, First Name Last Name, Code, Registered On**) and the two horizontal lines, then right click the selection and choose **Copy**.

22. Right click in the **SessionID** Header section and choose **Paste**.
23. Drag the pasted controls to position it at the bottom of the SessionID Header section as shown in Figure 11.25. Be careful not to reposition the other controls. Press **Ctrl+Z** to undo the operation if you are having a difficulty and try again.

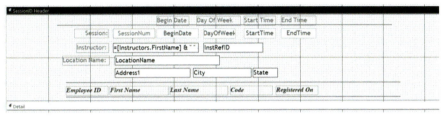

FIGURE 11.25 The SessionID Header section now contains all the data and formatting we need.

24. If Access displays a green triangle error in each label control, fix it by choosing **Ignore Error** from the exclamation mark drop-down menu.
25. Select both horizontal lines and set their **Border Style** to **Solid**.
26. Save the changes in your report.

Now, it's time to format the Details section.

PREPARING THE DETAIL SECTION

The Detail section is present in every report. This section repeats once for each record in the table or query that the report is based on. In an earlier part of this project, we placed the required fields in this section and now we just need to add some formatting to make the report look more attractive. We will also include a Unbound text control box that we will use for drawing attention to errors that may exist in employee records.

Hands-On 11.1   Creating a Course Registrations Report

(Part VII—Detail Section—Formatting the Detail Section and Its Controls)

1. In the Detail section reposition the text boxes so they appear in the order of the labels in the SessionID Header section.
2. Select all the text boxes and move the selection to the top of the Detail section aligning the ID text box with the Employee ID label in the SessionID Header section.

3. Click on the **ID** text box and format it as follows:

Property Name	Property Value
Width	0.5833"
Border Style	Solid
Border Color	#000080
Border Width	Hairline
Fore Color	#000080
Text Align	Center

4. Select the remaining text boxes and set their **Border Style** to **Transparent**.
5. Click on the Detail section heading and, in the Property Sheet, set the **Height** of Detail to **0.2917**" and set the **Alternate Back Color** property to **No Color**.
6. One by one select CourseName Header, SessionID, and CoureName Footer heading and make sure that the **Alternate Back Color** property for each of these sections is set to **No Color**.
7. Print Preview the report to check if there is any shading still left.
8. In the Print Preview use the Page controls at the bottom of the screen to scroll to the fifth page (see Figure 11.26).

   Look for Session 211. It appears that we have a problem with the EmployeeID 5 who registered for the same session on two different dates. We should flag these rows for the decision-maker who will review the report.

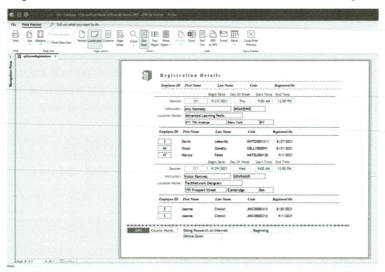

FIGURE 11.26 Reviewing the report in the Print Preview can help us identify issues we may want to flag for others to see.

9. Switch to the Report Design view and add a text box control to the right of the **RegisteredDate** text box. Delete the label for this control and align the Unbound text box to the Bottom of the RegisteredDate control.

10. Set the following properties for the text box:

Property Name	Property Value
Width	**1.9583"**
Name	txtPossibleError
Border Style	Transparent
Font Size	10
Font Italic	Yes
Fore Color	Accent 5

11. Save the changes you made in this report.

USING AN IMMEDIATE IF FUNCTION

In Chapter 9, while working with form controls, you learned about the `DLookUp` function that can be used to create expressions that return a single value from a field in a table or query. Another useful function to use in expressions is the Immediate IF function (`IIF`). This function allows you to test a condition without writing programming code. It works like the `IF...THEN...ELSE` statement in a Visual Basic procedure. The `IIF` function returns one of two values depending on the evaluation of a condition. Its syntax requires three arguments:

```
IIF (expr, truepart, falsepart)
```

`Expr` is the expression to be evaluated, `truepart` is the value or expression returned if expr is true, and `falsepart` is the value or expression returned if `expr` is false. Be aware that a comma separates each argument.

For example, if you want to check if the ID = 5 and return "Found" or "Not Found," you would write the following expression:

```
= IIF ([ID] = 5, "Found", "Not Found")
```

This will display the string "Found" if the ID field is equal to 5, and the string "Not Found" if the ID is not 5.

You can also evaluate multiple conditions by nesting `IIF` functions. A nested IIF is an expression that uses the IIF function multiple times to evaluate different conditions and return different values. For example, examine the following nested IIF:

```
= IIF(Year([RegistrationDate]) > 2023, "Future",
IIF(Year([RegistrationDate]) = 2023, "Current",
IIF(IsNull([RegistrationDate]), "Blank", "Past")))
```

This expression will return the string "Future" if the Year of the Registration-Date field is greater than 2023, the string "Current" if it is equal to 2021, the string "Blank" if it is null (empty), and the string "Past" if it is any other value. The Year function returns the year part from the specified date.

The Intermediate IIF can be quite slow as it does not stop evaluating an expression as soon as the result is determined. In more complex expressions that require the IIF you can use the Switch function instead. This function is much faster as it avoids unnecessary calculations.

The Switch function has the following syntax:

```
Switch (expr1, value1, expr2, value2, ..., exprn, valuen)
```

The expr1, expr2, ...exprn are expressions that are evaluated in order, and value1, value2, ..., valuen are values or expressions that are returned if the corresponding expression is true. The Switch function stops evaluating as soon as it finds a true expression and returns the corresponding value. You can rewrite the previous nested expression using the Switch function like this:

```
Switch (Year([RegistrationDate]) > 2023,
"Future", Year([RegistrationDate]) = 2021, "Current",
IsNull([RegistrationDate]), "Blank", True, "Past")
```

The True after "Blank" in the Switch expression is a way of specifying a default value or a catch-all case. It means that if none of the previous expressions are true, then the Switch function will return the value associated with True, which is "Past" in this case.

The True expression is always evaluated last, so it will only be used if none of the other expressions are true. If you omit the True expression, and none of the other expressions are true, then the Switch function will return Null.

⊚ Hands-On 11.1   Creating a Course Registrations Report

(Part VIII—Detail Section—Adding an Expression to an Unbound text box Control)

1. In the Report Design view, select the Unbound text box control you previously added to the Detail section.

2. In the Property Sheet, activate the Control Source property for the Unbound text box which you previously named **txtPossibleError** and click the ellipsis (…) button to display the Expression Builder dialog.

3. Enter the following expression (see Figure 11.27):

```
=IIf(IsNull([RegisteredDate]),Null,IIf([ID]=DLookUp("[Employee
ID]","[Registration]","[EmployeeID] = " & [ID] & " AND
[RegisteredDate] <> #" & [RegisteredDate] & "#" & " AND
[SessionID] = " & [SessionID]),"Possible duplicate
record",Null))
```

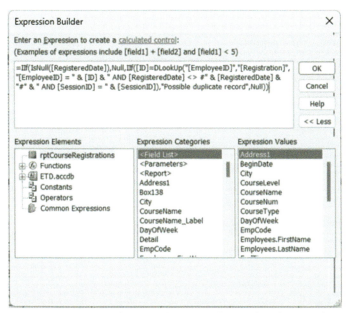

FIGURE 11.27. You can draw attention to specific records in the report by writing an expression using the IIF function.

The preceding expression uses the IIf and DLookUp functions to check if a record is a possible duplicate based on some criteria. The first IIf function checks if the [RegisteredDate] field is null, which means that the employee has not registered yet. If this is true, then the expression returns null. If this is false, then the expression evaluates the second IIf function.

The second IIf function compares the [ID] field with the result of the DLookUp function. The DLookUp function looks for the [EmployeeID] field in the [Registration] table, where the [EmployeeID], [RegisteredDate], and [SessionID] fields match the values of the current record. If the DLookUp function finds a matching record, then it means that there is another record with the same employee ID, registered date, and session ID, which indicates a possible duplicate. In this case, the expression returns "Possible duplicate record". If the `DLookUp` function does not find a matching record, then it means that there is no duplicate, and the expression returns null.

In summary, the expression we wrote returns one of these three values:

- Null, if the employee has not registered yet.
- "Possible duplicate record", if there is another record with the same employee ID, registered date, and session ID.
- Null, if there is no duplicate.

Using the intermediate IIF function in a report control, you can draw attention to specific records in the report.

4. Click **OK** to close the Expression Builder dialog.

Now in the Report Design view the text box control displays the expression we wrote (see Figure 11.28).

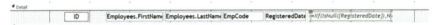

FIGURE 11.28. An example of an Unbound text box control containing an expression.

5. Open the report in the **Print Preview** and scroll to **page 5**.

Notice that problem records are now flagged with the message displayed in red (see Figure 11.29). No other records are affected.

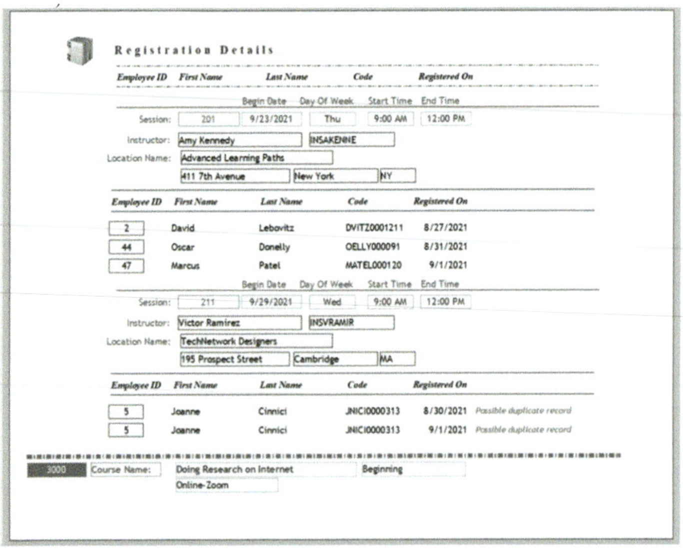

FIGURE 11.29. This report shows how using expressions in report controls can bring more value to your report by drawing attention to areas that should be reviewed.

6. Close the Print Preview and return to the **Report Design** view.

7. Save the changes in your report.

Our report needs other formatting adjustments that we will apply at the end after we are finished working with the remaining three sections: CourseName Footer, Page Footer, and Report Footer.

PREPARING THE COURSENAME FOOTER

The CourseName Footer is the only Group Footer that we've added to this report. This section will appear at the end of each group of records in the report. We will use it to display information about the number of employees who registered for a particular course or who have not registered for any course. We will use an Unbound text control with an expression. This should be quite simple considering that we just went over the previous section that also used a calculated control and explained the use of the Intermediate IIF function. Figure 11.30 shows the Design View with two controls: custom formatted line that was copied from the CourseName Header section and an Unbound text box with an expression. The complete expression, assigned to the Control Source property of this text box, is as follows:

```
=IIf(Not IsNull([RegisteredDate]),"Summary for " & [CourseName]
   & " ( Registered Employees: " & Count([ID]) & " ) ","
   ( Unregistered Employees: " & Count([ID]) & " )")
```

FIGURE 11.30. The CourseName footer will calculate the number of employees who registered for a course or not registered for any courses.

(⊙) Hands-On 11.1   Creating a Course Registrations Report

(Part IX—CourseName Footer Section—Summarizing the CourseName Group Data)

1. In the Report Design view, copy the horizontal line from the CourseName Header to the CourseName Footer section placing it at the top of the section.

2. Add a Text Box control to the CourseName Footer and delete its label, and then reselect the text box.

3. Working with the text box in the Property Sheet, set the **Width** property to **5.9167"** and the **Border Style** to **Transparent**.

4. Assign the expression shown earlier to the **Control Source** property of the text box.

5. Verify the output, by reviewing the report in Print Preview (see Figure 11.31).

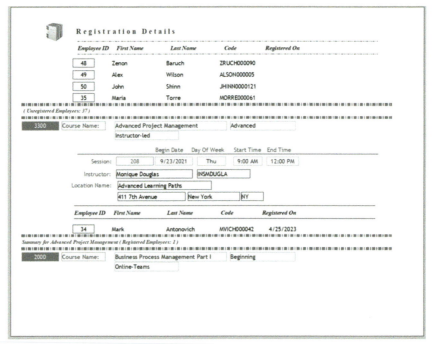

FIGURE 11.31. The CourseName footer displays the count of employees in each course name group.

6. Return to the Report Design view and save the changes you made in this report.

Now, let's proceed to the last two footers in the report: Page Footer and Report Footer.

PREPARING THE PAGE FOOTER AND REPORT FOOTER

The Page Footer section which appears at the bottom of every page of report is a great place to display information that you want to repeat on each page, such as date and page number. Like any other section, you can beautify it by adding lines, boxes, and images. A quick way to complete the Page Footer section is to copy it from another report that was created by Report Wizard and may already have the controls you need.

The Report Footer section appears at the very end of the report, after all other sections, and is printed only once per report. It can be used for summarizing the entire report, like displaying grand totals and other relevant information. We will use this section to display the report name, the current username, and the contact phone number.

Hands-On 11.1. Creating a Course Registrations Report

(Part X—Page and Report Footer Sections—Adding and Formatting Controls)

1. Open in Report Design the **Employees by Department Name** report that you created in Chapter 10.

    Notice that this report (see Figure 11.32) contains the footer section with two controls: one displays the current date and the other shows page number of the total number of pages. We can easily copy these controls to our rptCourseRegistration report.

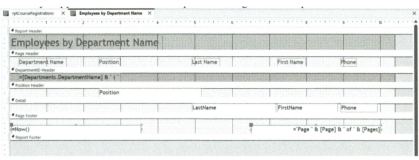

FIGURE 11.32. You can copy the required controls from one report to another.

2. Select both text box controls located in the Page Footer section of the Employees by Department Name report, right click on the selection, and choose **Copy**. Switch to your other Report Design view, right click the Page Footer section and choose **Paste**.

3. Close the Employees by Department Name report.

4. In the Design View of the rptCourseRegistration report, increase the width of the Page Footer section and bring the pasted controls a bit down.

5. Copy the horizontal line from the CourseName Footer section and position it at the top of the Page Footer section. In the Property Sheet, set its **Border Style** to **Solid**.

    The completed Page Footer is shown in Figure 11.33.

FIGURE 11.33. The completed Page Footer report contains information about date and number pages in the report and is separated from the preceding section with a horizontal line.

6. Expand the Report Footer by dragging down the lower edge of its band to the position of 3 inches on the vertical ruler.

7. Click the Course Registration Report label in the Report Header and, in the Property Sheet, set its **Name** property to **ReportTitle_Label**. We need to name this control so we can refer to it in an expression from a different control.

8. Add three text boxes to the Report Footer section and format them as shown in Figure 11.34.

The controls are surrounded by a rectangle with a solid red border that was positioned on top of them and then sent behind them by using the Send to Back button in the Sizing and Ordering group of the Arrange tab.

FIGURE 11.34. The completed Report Footer section.

9. Switch to the Print Preview and examine the last page of your report which now displays the report information.

10. Return to the Report Design view and save the changes you made in the report.

The completed design view of this report is shown in Figure 11.35.

Now that the design of the report is finalized with the controls placed in the desired sections, we need to address some bothersome issues that prevent this report from looking its best. For example, if you preview the report, its first page displays a list of unregistered employees. These employees did not sign up for any courses, therefore the controls placed in the CourseName Header and SessionID Header appear on the report blank, which does not look very professional. We must hide these sections for those employees. If you go to the third page of the report you will notice that it lists the remaining employees who did not register, then there are sections for two courses and the sections are running into each other. We can fix this by telling Access to move the CourseName and SessionID Header sections to a new page when the course name changes. Some changes can be made by setting section properties, others will require using event procedures.

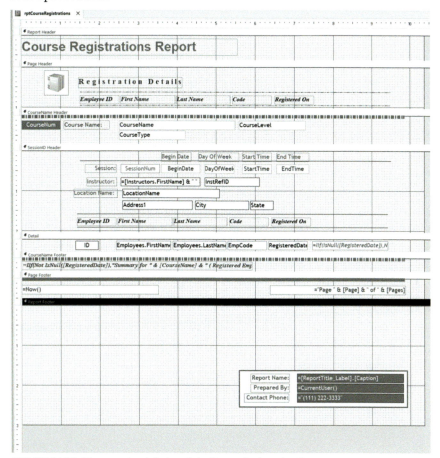

FIGURE 11.35. The completed design of the Course Registration Report.

ADDING PAGE BREAKS

In our report design, we would like to have a page break after the CourseName Footer so that each course begins on a new page. We can get this done quickly by using the Force New Page property in the CourseName Footer. This property will force a page break every time there is a new group. We've already seen this property at work in the previous chapter and we know that it offers four different settings: None, Before Section, After Section, and Before & After. The setting we need is "After Section." After we display the count of the employees that registered or not registered for a course, we want to start a new page.

(⊙) Hands-On 11.1   Creating a Course Registrations Report

(Part XI—CourseName Footer Section—Forcing a Page Break)

1. In the Report Design view of the rptCourseRegistration report, select the **CourseName Footer** section and, in the Property Sheet, on the Format or All tab, set the **Force New Page** property to **After Section**.
2. Save the report and preview it to verify that each course starts on a new page.

EVENTS IN ACCESS REPORTS

Like forms, Access reports respond to various events that occur when you open, close, print, or view a report in Access. You can use macros or VBA code to respond to these events and perform custom actions such as formatting a report, filtering data, or displaying a dialog box.

There are two types of report events:

- *Report-level events*:

  These events apply to the whole report, such as Open, Close, Activate, Deactivate, and Print.
- *Section-level events*:

  These events apply to each section of the report, such as Header, Footer, Detail, GroupHeader, and GroupFooter. Each section has its own Format and Print events that occur before and after the section is formatted or printed.

Events occur in a specific order:

- When you open a report, the Open and Activate events occur for the report.
- When you print or preview a report, for each section of the report, the Format (section) and Print (section) event occurs. Except for headers and footers, sections also respond to Retreat event that occurs when Access returns to a previous report section during report formatting.
- When you close a report, the Deactivate and Close events occur for the report.

The detailed coverage of report events is beyond the scope of this book. Depending on the type of report you are preparing, and its complexity, various events may be needed.

FORMAT EVENT (SECTION FORMATTING)

The formatting issues that remain in our report can be addressed by using the Format event for the following sections: Page Header, CourseName Header, and SessionID Header. The Format event occurs when the section is preformatted in memory before it is sent to the printer. You can use the Format event to apply special formatting to controls within a section before a section is printed. For example, we can hide controls we don't want to print based on some conditions. In the final part of Hands-On 11.1, we will write Format event procedures for three sections to clean up the appearance of our report. Let's get started.

(◉) Hands-On 11.1   Creating a Course Registrations Report

(Part XII—Page Header on Format Property: Hiding Specific Controls Based on a Condition)

1. In the Report Design view, select all the controls in the Page Header section except for the image and Registration Details label. All column heading labels and both line controls should be selected.
2. In the Property Sheet of Multiple selection, click the All Tab, and set the value of the **Tag** property to **PageHeader_Heading**.

    Access will assign the specified string to all the selected controls so we can refer to them easily in code. The Tag property is used to assign an identification string to an object without affecting any of its other property settings. In the Format event procedure for a section, we can loop through the Controls collection and perform some action based on the Tag property of each control. In our case, we want to control the Visible property of these controls so we can either display them or hide them.
3. Click the Page Header section and, in the Property Sheet for the PageHeaderSection selection, select the Event tab, and click the **On Format** property. Click on the ellipsis (…) button and select **Code Builder** and click **OK**.

    Access displays the stub of the PageHeaderSection_Format subroutine procedure that you need to complete by writing VBA statements that will tell Access to perform the actions you specify.

4. Complete the event procedure as follows (see also Figure 11.34):

```
Private Sub PageHeaderSection_Format(Cancel As Integer,
    FormatCount As Integer)
    Dim ctl As Control

    'Check if the value of the CourseName field
    'in the CourseName_GroupHeader section is empty or null
    If IsNull(Me.CourseName) Or Me.CourseName = "" Then
        ' iterate through all controls in this section
        For Each ctl In Me.Controls
          ' check if the Tag property is set to the specified string
            If ctl.Tag = "PageHeader_Heading" Then
                ' show the control
                ctl.Visible = True
            End If
        Next
    ' run this code if the CourseName has value
    Else
        For Each ctl In Me.PageHeaderSection.Controls

            If ctl.Tag = "PageHeader_Heading" Then
                ' don't show the control
                ctl.Visible = False
            End If
        Next
    End If

End Sub
```

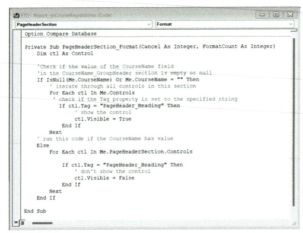

FIGURE 11.36. This Format procedure for the PageHeaderSection works like a toggle button; it hides or unhides the specified controls based on a condition.

The purpose of the code we wrote is to set the visibility of the controls in the Page Header section which were assigned the string PageHeader_Heading in their `Tag` property.

The first statement in the procedure is a declaration line which specifies that we will use the string `ctl` to store a control object. In programming parlance this string is referred to as a variable. A variable is a way of storing information in the computer memory that can be used in your VBA code. A variable can store a number, a text sting, a date, a logical value, or an object. In VBA there are different types of variables to store these values. In this code, we have a variable called `ctl` that is an object variable. It refers to a control in your report section. We use the `Dim` keyword to declare variables in VBA.

The first line after the declaration of the variable uses the VBA If conditional statement to check if the CourseName control value in the current section is null or empty. We refer to the current section using the keyword `Me`.

If the condition is true, that is there is no data in the CourseName field, we want to loop through all the controls in this section and check if the `Tag` property of the control is set to the string "PageHeader_Heading", and if this is true then we want to set the `Visible` property of that control to `True`, so it is shown when we Print Preview the report.

The `Else` part (known as `ELSE` clause) does the same, but when the condition if false it will hide the specified control.

The looping (or iterating) through the controls is done with the special VBA construct `For...Each...Next`. The statement `For each ctl in Me.Controls` reads as follows: For each control object in the current section's collection of controls, do something. Because what we want to do depends on a satisfaction of a specific condition you must start with the `If` keyword to state the condition. If the condition is true then we tell Access what to do: `ctl.Visible = True`. If the `Tag` is not what we are looking for, then we don't do anything, but continue looping; that is why we have the Next statement that sends us back to the beginning of the loop which accesses the next `ctl` variable in the collection of controls of the current section and we are going through the same process of checking the `Tag` property and perform the action based on the result of that check.

5. Save the changes in the Visual Basic screen by clicking the **Save** button on the toolbar, close this screen, and return to the report.
6. Print preview the report and examine each page.
   The Heading in the Page Header Section should not appear for courses with registrations (see Figure 11.37).
7. Return to the Report Design view.

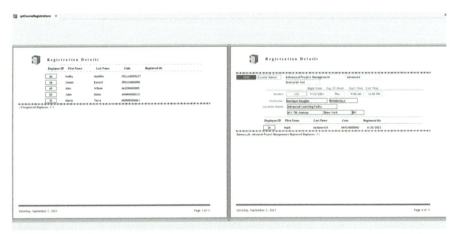

FIGURE 11.37. The report after implementing custom formatting procedure in the Page Header section.

Hands-On 11.1   Creating a Course Registrations Report

(Part XIII—CourseName Header on Format property: Hiding an Entire Section Based on a Condition)

1. In the Report Design view, click the CourseName Header section and in the Property Sheet, click the All tab and set the name property of the section to **CourseName_GroupHeader**.

   When you add sections to your report, Access assigns default names to the sections and it is recommended to change the default name into something meaningful when you are planning to refer to it in code.

2. In the Property Sheet for the CourseName_GroupHeader, select the Event tab, and click the **On Format** property. Click on the ellipsis (…) button and select **Code Builder** and click **OK**.

   Access displays the stub of the CourseName_GroupHeader_Format subroutine procedure that you need to complete by writing VBA statements that will tell Access to perform the actions you specify.

3. Complete the event procedure as follows (see also Figure 11.38):

```
Private Sub CourseName_GroupHeader_Format(Cancel As Integer,
FormatCount As Integer)
    If IsNull(Me.CourseName) Or Me.CourseName = "" Then
        Me.CourseName_GroupHeader.Visible = False
    Else
```

```
            Me.CourseName_GroupHeader.Visible = True
        End If
End Sub
```

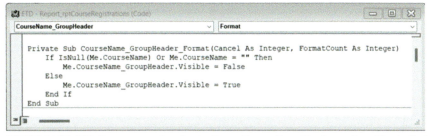

FIGURE 11.38. This Format procedure for the CourseName_GroupHeader section will only display when there is a value in the CourseName control on the form.

4. Save the changes in the Visual Basic screen by clicking the **Save** button on the toolbar, close this screen and return to the report.
5. Print Preview the report and examine each page.

     The entire CourseName_GroupHeader section is now hidden for the unregistered employees (see Figure 11.37). There is still the Session information section that needs to be handled in a similar way for our report to pass the grade.
6. Return to the Report Design view.

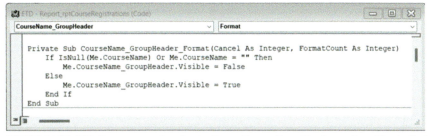

FIGURE 11.39. The report after implementing custom formatting procedure in the CourseName_GroupHeader section.

◉ Hands-On 11.1　Creating a Course Registrations Report

(Part XIV—SessionID Header on Format property: Hiding an Entire Section Based on a Condition)

1. In the Report Design view, click the **SessionID Header** section and in the Property Sheet, click the All tab and set the name property of the section to **SessionID_GroupHeader**.

   When you add sections to your report, Access assigns default names to the sections and it is recommended to change the default name into something meaningful when you are planning to refer to it in code.

2. In the Property Sheet for the CourseName_GroupHeader, select the Event tab, and click the **On Format** property. Click on the ellipsis (…) button and select **Code Builder** and click **OK**.

   Access displays the stub of the CourseName_GroupHeader_Format subroutine procedure that you need to complete by writing VBA statements that will tell Access to perform the actions you specify.

3. Complete the event procedure as follows (see also Figure 11.40):

```
Private Sub SessionID_GroupHeader_Format(Cancel
   As Integer, FormatCount As Integer)
   If DCount("*", "Registration", "EmployeeID=" & Me.ID) > 0 Then
      Me.SessionID_GroupHeader.Visible = True
   Else
      Me.SessionID_GroupHeader.Visible = False
   End If
End Sub
```

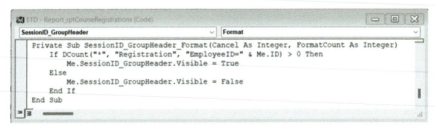

FIGURE 11.40. This Format procedure for the SessionID_GroupHeader section will only show up when there is a value in the CourseName control on the form.

The purpose of the preceding code is to set the visibility of the `SessionID_GroupHeader` section based on a condition.

The `DCount()` function is a built-in function that returns the number of records in a specified set of records and is used here to count the number of records in the `Registration` table where the `EmployeeID` field is equal to the

ID control on the report. If the DCount result is greater than zero, it means that there are some records that match and we set the Visible property of the SessionID-GroupHeader section to True, which means that the section will be shown on the report. If the result of the DCount function is not greater than zero, it means there are no records that match, so we set the Visible property of the SessionID_GroupHeader section to False, which means that the section will be hidden on the report.

4. Save the changes in the Visual Basic screen by clicking the **Save** button on the toolbar, close this screen and return to the report.

5. Print Preview the report and examine each page.

   The entire SectionID_GroupHeader section is now hidden for the unregistered employees (see Figure 11.41). This report is now finished.

6. Return to the Report Design view.

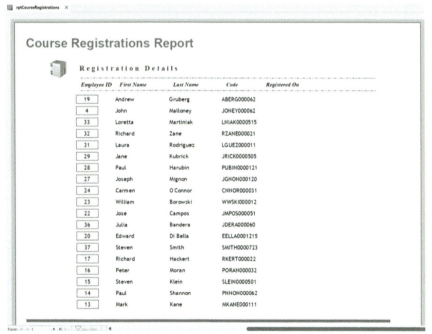

FIGURE 11.41. The report after implementing custom formatting procedure in the SessionID_ GroupHeader section. Notice that the CourseName Header and SessionID Header controls are not visible.

This report is now finished. You can spend additional time with it if you'd like to add your own enhancements, for the saying goes "Practice makes perfect." Report writing skills are high in demand and your extra efforts can be rewarded in a career as a Report Writer.

PUBLISHING THE REPORT

Access provides several options in the Print Preview Data group (see Figure 11.42) and in the Export menu (accessible from the Database Navigation pane), to output the report into different formats.

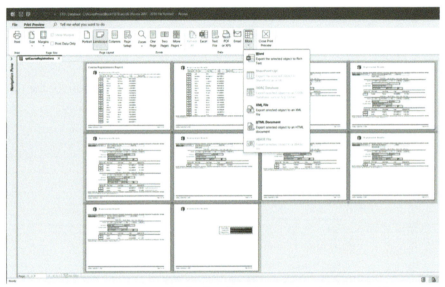

FIGURE 11.42. An Access report can be distributed to other users in various ways and formats.

Action Item 11.1

Save the report you just created in every available format and review how it was rendered in the chosen format. The Companion files contain the PDF version of this report as well as HTML files for each page of the report that were generated by Access. The HTML files have hypertext links to help you navigate from one page to another. If you are familiar with HTML programming, you can create a template that will apply desired formatting to your report. When you choose the HTML document from the More button in the Print Preview, Access gives you an option to choose and apply your own template. The same goes for the XML files. However, a report cannot be saved as an XML file from the Print Preview. You must close the report, right click its name in the Database Navigation pane, and choose Export | XML File. Other Export options listed in the Print Preview are also available in the Export menu.

CREATING A REPORT SELECTION FORM

For most users, navigating to the available reports from the Database Navigation pane is not very convenient. Users like to work with forms, and an Access form can be easily created to display your selection of reports including the buttons for previewing and printing. In the remaining sections of this chapter, we will be working with Hands-On 11.2 building the form depicted in Figure 11.2 at the beginning of this chapter.

The Option Group Control

The form that we will be creating utilizes the Option Group control for the selection of reports. This group contains a Frame control and four Option Button controls. Instead of option buttons you can use check boxes or toggle buttons depending on your preference. In the Option Group control, only one option can be selected at a time. Each control in an Option Group has a numeric value that you can set with the Option Value property. When you select an option in an option group, Access sets the value of the field to which the option group is bound to the value of the selected option's Option Value property. Note that an Option Group can be bound to a field, set to an expression, or unbound. If the Option Group is bound to a field, only the group frame itself is bound to the field, not the individual controls inside the frame.

In Hands-On 11.2, you will use the Option Group Wizard to create an Option Group control. The Wizard will walk you through the steps required to set the Option Value property for each control in the Option Group.

(◉) **Hands-On 11.2   Creating a Report Selection Form**

(Part I—Creating a Form With an Option Group Control)

1. In the ETD database window, click **Create | Form Design**.
   Access creates a blank form for you.
2. Select the Option Group control in the Controls Section of the Form Design tab. This is the control illustrated by a frame with XYZ letters. With this selection, draw a frame in the Detail section as shown in Figure 11.43. When you release the mouse button the Option Group Wizard will appear. Enter the labels for each report option as shown. When done entering labels, click **Next** to continue.
3. In the second screen of the Option Group Wizard, **click No, I don't want a default** (see Figure 11.44) and click **Next**.

4. In the third screen of the Option Group Wizard (see Figure 11.45), Access assigns the values to each option. Click **Next** to accept the default values.

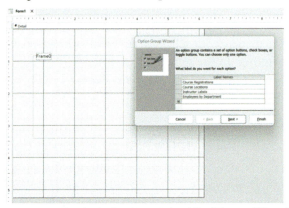

FIGURE 11.43. The Option Group Wizard (1 of 5)—specifying a label for each option.

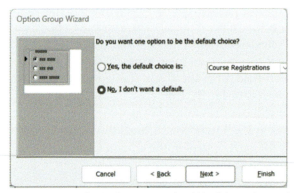

FIGURE 11.44. The Option Group Wizard (2 of 5)—setting up the default option.

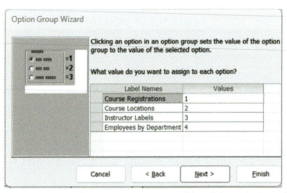

FIGURE 11.45. The Option Group Wizard (3 of 5)—assigning values to each option.

5. In the fourth screen of the Option Group Wizard, choose **Option buttons** as the type of controls for the option group and a **Shadowed** style to use as shown in Figure 11.46, and click **Next**.

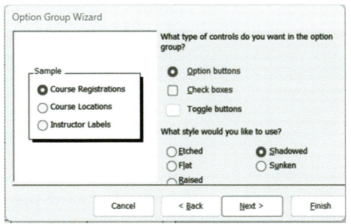

FIGURE 11.46. The Option Group Wizard (4 of 5)—styling the Option Group—selecting type of controls and the frame style.

6. In the fifth screen of the Option Group Wizard (see Figure 11.47), delete Frame0 and enter **Choose Report** for the Option Group caption, and click **Finish**.

FIGURE 11.47. The Option Group Wizard (5 of 5)—Specifying a caption for the Option Group.

Access creates the Option Group as shown in Figure 11.48.

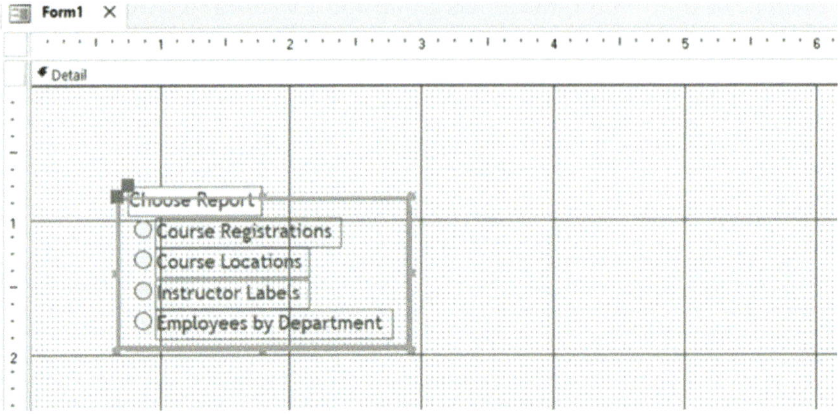

FIGURE 11.48. The Option Group control created by the Option Group Wizard.

7. While the entire Option Group Frame is selected, use the Property Sheet to set the **Name** property of Frame0 to **ChooseReport** (no spaces).
8. In the Form Design view, select all the labels in the form and use the Property Sheet to set the **Font Name** property of the multiple selection to **Arial Narrow**.
9. Click the first option button (circle) and in the Data tab of the Property Sheet, notice that the Wizard assigned the value of 1 to this option button. The second option button has 2 in the Option Value property, and so on.
10. Click the report frame surrounding the option buttons and notice that in the Data tab of the Property Sheet, the Default Value property is blank, as we did not ask the Wizard to set it. Let's do it now. You can enter a value from 1 to 4 to indicate which option should be selected when the form is loaded.
11. Enter **1** in the **Default Value** property.

The Option Button Group is completed with the required property settings, and we will return to it later because we still need to program these buttons to get the reports we need. But first, let's complete the form design by adding the required command buttons.

⊙ **Hands-On 11.2   Creating a Report Selection Form**

(Part II—Using Command Button Wizard to add buttons to the Form)

1. In the controls section of the Form Design tab, select the **Button** control and click to the right of the Option Group. Access displays the Command Button Wizard (see Figure 11.49).

2. In the Command Button Wizard, select **Report Operations** in the Categories box and choose **Preview Report** in the Actions box (see Figure 11.49) and click **Next**.

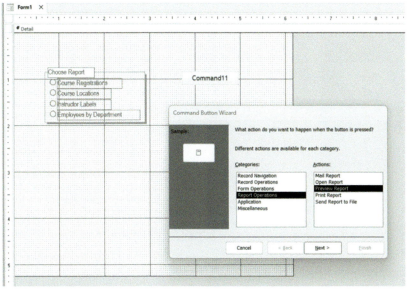

FIGURE 11.49. The Command Button Wizard (1 of 4)—Specifying the type of action the selected button will perform.

3. In the second screen of the Command Button Wizard, choose **rptCourseRegistrations** report as shown in Figure 11.50 and click **Next**.

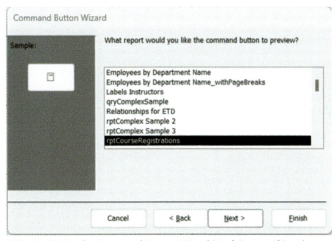

FIGURE 11.50. The Command Button Wizard (2 of 4)—Specifying the report name to preview.

4. In the third screen of the Command Button Wizard (Figure 11.51), choose the **Text** option button to display the text and enter **Preview** as shown and click **Next**.

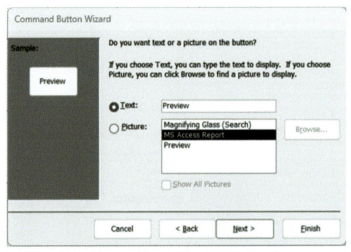

FIGURE 11.51. The Command Button Wizard (3 of 4)—Specifying a text or picture on the button.

5. In the fourth screen of the Command Button Wizard, assign the name to this button as **cmdPreview** as shown in Figure 11.52, and click **Finish**.

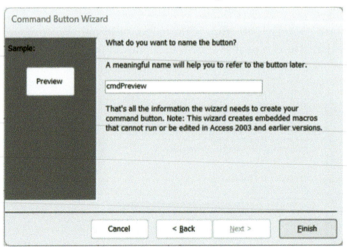

FIGURE 11.52. The Command Button Wizard (4 of 4)—Assigning a name to the button. This is the same as setting the Name property of the button.

The Wizard had completed its task, and our form design displays the Preview button. Let's test it out.

6. Switch to the Form view. The Course Registrations option button should be selected as we set earlier the default option button to 1. The other option buttons have not been programmed yet. Click the **Preview** button to load the **Course Registrations** report that we created in Hands-On 11.1. Access should load the report in the Print Preview.

7. Close the report, return to the Form, and switch the Form Design view.

We tested the button and it is working just fine. Let's examine what specific settings make it work.

MACROS: A BRIEF INTRODUCTION

Macros are a very powerful feature of Access as they can perform just about any task you can do with the Access user interface using the keyboard or the mouse. They provide an easy way of opening and closing various Access objects (tables, queries, forms, and reports) and they are behind the command buttons created with the Command Button Wizard. You can use them to automate repetitive tasks, execute commands on the Access Ribbon, set values for form and report controls, import and export spreadsheet and text files, display informative messages, or even sound a beep. A special category of macros can also enforce business rules at a table level. These are just a few examples of what macros can do. Macros, however, cannot create and manipulate database objects; these tasks require the use of the Visual Basic for Applications (VBA) programming language.

Microsoft Access supports three types of macros:

- *Standalone macros* (also used in versions of Access prior to 2007)
  The standalone macros are the named macros that are visible in the Database Navigation pane under the Macros category.

- *Embedded macros* (introduced in Access 2007)
  The embedded macros are a part of an object in which they are embedded (form, report, or control) and therefore are not visible in the Database Navigation pane.

- *Data macros* (introduced in Access 2010)
  Data macros allow developers to implement business rules in an Access database application. These macros do not have a user interface, they are applied at a table level and cannot be used to open a form or a report.

Macros have their own Macro Designer that you can use to create and modify simple and more complex standalone macros and edit the embedded macros created by Access wizards.

Due to the publishing page constraints, this book does not include a dedicated chapter on macros. However, ignoring them is practically impossible, as Access built-in Wizard tools, rely heavily on macros to automate forms, reports, and controls. You will come across embedded macros every time you request help from the built-in Access tool. We saw it already in Chapter 8 when we examined the OK and Cancel buttons on the Modal Dialog form. Your second encounter with an embedded macro took place in this chapter when you enlisted the Command Button Wizard's help in creation of the Preview button for your form.

Let's look at what's behind that button. What makes it work?

Hands-On 11.2   Creating a Report Selection Form

(Part III—From the Embedded Macros to the VBA Code)

1. In the Form Design view, click on the Preview button to select it and click the Event tab in the Property Sheet.

    Notice that Access created an embedded macro [**EmbeddedMacro**] in the On Click property (see Figure 11.54 later).

2. Click the **ellipsis** (…) button next to the **On Click** property, to activate the Macro Design Screen (see Figure 11.53).

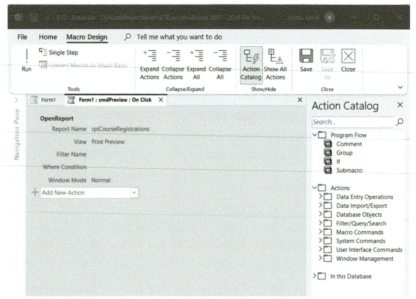

FIGURE 11.53. When you use the Command Button Wizard Access creates an embedded macro that will run the specified action when you click the button.

The Macro Design screen consists of the Action Catalog pane on the right and the macro design grid on the left. The Action Catalog displays all the available macro actions organized by type and searchable. You can drag and drop actions from the Action Catalog to the macro design grid. The grid is a collapsible area that contains various Access commands such OpenReport and specific properties that these commands have and which you can modify to suit your need.

In the macro shown in Figure 11.53, we are simply telling Access to execute the OpenReport command for the report that is specified in the Report Name property, and we provide the type of view to open the report in, using the View Property. You could also include the Filter Name and Where Condition. This report will be opened as a normal window, but you can change this by selecting another choice from the drop-down menu, that will be available upon clicking the OpenReport command. You can try it now to see how it works. Many properties can be chosen from drop-down boxes, and you can add new actions and different program flow to the macro by clicking the plus button (+) and choosing an action from a drop-down menu or by dragging it directly from the Action Catalog. To collapse the macro, simply click anywhere in the gray area.

If you are new to this type of interface, it will feel awkward at the beginning, but you will soon get used to it if you work with it enough. Many templates that you can download from Microsoft include embedded macros, some of them with advanced complexity; you should study them carefully to find out how they are put together. For someone who have already tasted the power of VBA programming language and is used to writing code, this macro interface may seem a bit limiting. Therefore, for users who prefer to work with VBA editor, Microsoft has provided a way to convert the embedded macros to event procedures. We will see how this process works in the next steps.

3. Close the Macro Design screen and in the Tools group of the Form Design tab, click the Convert Form's Macros to Visual Basic (see Figure 11.54).

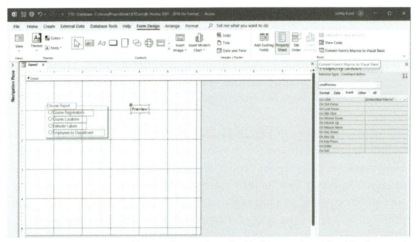

FIGURE 11.54. You can quickly turn the Form's Embedded Macros into Visual Basic procedures using a button on the Tools group of the Form Design tab.

Access displays a Convert form macros dialog where you can choose to add error handling and macro comments to generated functions (see Figure 11.55).

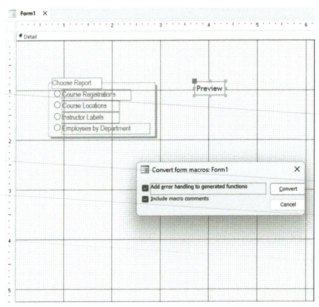

FIGURE 11.55. When converting macros, you can add to generated functions error handling and macro comments.

4. Click the **Convert** button to begin the conversion process.
5. When Access notifies you that the conversion is finished, click **OK**.
   Notice the changes in the Property Sheet shown in Figure 11.56. The On Click property is now set to [Event Procedure] instead of [Embedded Macro].

FIGURE 11.56. The cmdPreview button's On Click property indicates that the button is driven by [Event Procedure] instead of the initially created [Embedded Macro].

6. Click the ellipsis (…) button in the On Click property to activate the Visual Basic screen.
   Access displays the converted Macro in the VBA language as shown in Figure 11.57.

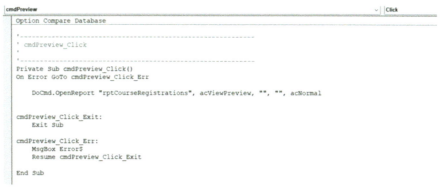

```
cmdPreview                                                      ∨  Click

    Option Compare Database

    '--------------------------------------------------------------
    ' cmdPreview_Click
    '
    '--------------------------------------------------------------
    Private Sub cmdPreview_Click()
    On Error GoTo cmdPreview_Click_Err

        DoCmd.OpenReport "rptCourseRegistrations", acViewPreview, "", "", acNormal


    cmdPreview_Click_Exit:
        Exit Sub

    cmdPreview_Click_Err:
        MsgBox Error$
        Resume cmdPreview_Click_Exit

    End Sub
```

FIGURE 11.57. The cmdPreview_Click procedure was generated by Access from a macro embedded in a Command button.

This code tells Access to open the report named rptCourseRegistrations in full view of the Print Preview screen:

```
DoCmd.OpenReport "rptCourseRegistrations", acViewPreview,
    "", "", acNormal
```

The preceding statement is a VBA code that uses the `DoCmd.OpenReport` method to open a report in Access. The statement has the following arguments:

- ReportName: This is the name of the report to open. In this case, it is "rptCourseRegistrations," which is a string expression that's the valid name of a report in the current database.

- View: This is the view in which the report will open. In this case, it is `acViewPreview`, which is an `AcView` constant that specifies the Print Preview view.

- FilterName: This is the name of a query in the current database that will be used to filter the records in the report. In this case, it is an empty string, which means no filter will be applied.

- WhereCondition: This is a SQL `WHERE` clause without the word `WHERE` that will be used to further restrict the records in the report. In this case, it is also an empty string, which means no additional condition will be applied.

- WindowMode: This is the mode in which the report window will open. In this case, it is `acNormal`, which is an `AcWindowMode` constant that specifies the normal window mode.

The other statements in this code are comments and error handling that we specified to include during the conversion process. Comments are indicated by lines in green font that begin with a single quote. These are the lines that provide additional information about the procedure. Comments are ignored when the procedure runs and can be added for each line of code to provide detailed explanations on how the procedure works.

Let's modify this code so it can handle not one, but all the option buttons in the Option Group on the form.

7. Modify the cmdPreview_Click procedure as shown in Figure 11.58.

```
ETD - Form_Form1 (Code)
cmdPreview                                              Click

Option Compare Database

'------------------------------------------------------------
' cmdPreview_Click
'
'------------------------------------------------------------
Private Sub cmdPreview_Click()
On Error GoTo cmdPreview_Click_Err

Select Case ChooseReport
    Case 1
        DoCmd.OpenReport "rptCourseRegistrations", acViewPreview, "", "", acNormal
    Case 2
        DoCmd.OpenReport "TrainingCourseLocations", acViewPreview, "", "", acNormal
    Case 3
        DoCmd.OpenReport "Labels Instructors", acViewPreview, "", "", acNormal
    Case 4
        DoCmd.OpenReport "Employees by Department Name", acViewPreview, "", "", acNormal
End Select

cmdPreview_Click_Exit:
    Exit Sub

cmdPreview_Click_Err:
    MsgBox Error$
    Resume cmdPreview_Click_Exit
End Sub
```

FIGURE 11.58. The cmdPreview_Click procedure has been modified to handle all option button controls in the form's Option Button Group.

The cmdPreview_Click procedure is a type of procedure called a subprocedure, which means it does not return any value. It is also an event procedure, which means it is triggered by an event, such as clicking a button or opening a form.

The purpose of this procedure is to open a report in preview mode, depending on the value of a variable called ChooseReport. The code of the procedure is written between Private Sub and End Sub keywords that mark the beginning and end of the subprocedure. The word Private means that the procedure can only be called from within the same module, in this case this is a Form1 module as you can see in the title of the code window in Figure 11.58.

The first statement (line) in the procedure On Error GoTo cmdPreview_ Click_Err enables error handling in the procedure. It means that if an error occurs during the execution of the code, the program will jump to the label cmdPreview_Click_Err and execute the code there.

The second statement, Select Case ChooseReport, starts a conditional block that evaluates the value of the variable ChooseReport and executes different actions depending on the case.

The statements beginning with `Case 1`, `Case 2`, `Case 3`, and `Case 4` specify the possible values of `ChooseReport` and the corresponding actions to take. In this case, each value corresponds to opening a different report using the `DoCmd.OpenReport` method. This method and its various arguments were explained earlier in this section.

The `End Select` statement marks the end of the `Select Case` block.

The `cmdPreview_Click_Exit:` is a label that marks a location in the code. The program will jump to this label when it reaches the `Exit Sub` statement or when it finishes executing the `Select Case` block without errors.

The `Exit Sub` statement exits the subprocedure and returns control to the calling procedure or macro.

The `cmdPreview_Click_Err:` is another label that marks the location where the error handling code begins. The program will jump to this label when an error occurs in the `Select Case` block.

The `MsgBox Error$` displays a message box with the error message that occurred.

`Resume cmdPreview_Click_Exit` resumes execution at the label `cmdPreview_Click_Exit`, which exits the subprocedure.

8. In the Visual Basic Editor menu, choose **Debug | Compile**.

   This tells Access to check the VBA code you've written for syntax errors and compile it into a more efficient format. If any errors are found, they will appear in red. You can then correct the errors and run the command again until no errors are found.

   By compiling your code, you can improve the performance and speed of your code execution, reduce the size of your database, and make your code less prone to corruption. It is recommended that you compile your code regularly, especially before distributing your database to other users.

9. Exit the Visual Basic Editor screen; if asked to save changes to the module, click Yes.

10. Switch to the Form view and test the button by selecting an option for each report.

    All your option buttons should open the specified report in the Print Preview.

11. Close all the reports you opened and return to the Form switching to the Design View.

12. Now that you've made so many changes in your form and its code, save the form as **frmChooseReport**. The form should now appear in the Forms group of the Database Navigation view.

13. In the Design View of this form, create another button that will be used for printing the reports without previewing them.

The simplest way to create another button is to copy the existing button (Preview) and change some of its properties:

- In Design view, click the Preview button to select it and press **Ctrl+C** to copy it to the clipboard.
- Click in the empty spot in the form and press **Ctrl+V** to paste it.
- The button appears in the top left corner of the Detail section.
- In the Property Sheet, change the **Caption** property of the copied button to **Print**, and set its **Name** property to **cmdPrint**.
- In the Design view, drag the button and position it just below the Preview button.

14. With the Print button selected, select the **Event** tab in the Property Sheet, click the **On Click** property and click the ellipsis (…) button. Select **Code Builder** and click **OK**.

15. Enter the code shown in Figure 11.59 for the cmd_Print_Click procedure.

```
ETD - Form_frmChooseReport (Code)

cmdPrint                                    Click


    Private Sub cmdPrint_Click()

    On Error GoTo cmdPrint_Click_Err

    Select Case ChooseReport
        Case 1
            DoCmd.OpenReport "rptCourseRegistrations", acViewNormal, "", ""

        Case 2
            DoCmd.OpenReport "TrainingCourseLocations", acViewNormal, "", ""

        Case 3
            DoCmd.OpenReport "Labels Instructors", acViewNormal, "", ""

        Case 4
            DoCmd.OpenReport "Employees by Department Name", acViewNormal, "", ""

    End Select

    cmdPrint_Click_Exit:
        Exit Sub

    cmdPrint_Click_Err:
        MsgBox Error$
        Resume cmdPrint_Click_Exit

    End Sub
```

FIGURE 11.59. The cmdPrint_Click procedure will print a report based on the Option Group selection.

This procedure looks almost identical to the one that handles the Preview button, except that it uses the acViewNormal constant instead of acViewPreview. The acViewNormal constant means that the report will be sent to the current default printer queue, without displaying it on the screen. This is useful if you want to print the report immediately, without previewing it or modifying it. Therefore, the statement,

```
DoCmd.OpenReport "rptCourseRegistrations", acViewNormal
```

will print the report named `rptCourseRegistrations` using the default printer settings.

> **NOTE**   *You can check your default printer settings by selecting* **File | Print** *and choosing* **Print** *as shown in Figure 11.60.*

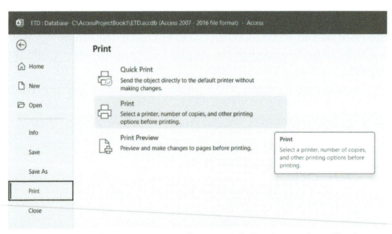

FIGURE 11.60. Use the Print option to select your default printer and specify other printing options.

If your default is printing to PDF files, when you click the form's Print button, you will be asked for the folder and file name where the report should be saved.

Notice that in the preceding statement I have omitted some arguments. The `DoCmd.OpenReport` statement has six arguments, but only one is required. You must specify the report name that you want to open. The other five arguments (`View`, `FilterName`, `WhereCondition`, `WindowMode`, `OpenArgs`) are optional and you can omit them if you don't need to specify them. To omit any of the optional arguments, you can either leave them blank or use a comma to separate them from the other arguments. The `DoCmd.OpenReport` statement can also be written as follows:

```
DoCmd.OpenReport "rptCourseRegistrations", acViewNormal,,,,
```

All statements will have the same effect.

16. Verify that your code does not contain any errors (**Debug | Compile**) and if all is OK, exit the Visual Basic screen.

17. Test the Print button by printing one of the reports. I suggest you first check the printer settings and set the default printer to Microsoft Print to PDF, so you don't waste any paper for this test.

There is still one button left to create and program.

18. Create a button with the **Caption** property set to **Cancel** and the **Name** property set to **cmdCancel**. This button will be used to cancel the form. Use the Copy & Paste method as described earlier in this Hands-On. Move the button under the Print button. Set the On Click property of the **cmdCancel** button to [**Event Procedure**] and enter the following code in the Visual Basic Editor screen:

```
Private Sub cmdCancel_Click()
On Error GoTo Cancel_Click_Err

    ' Closes popup form.
    DoCmd.Close acForm, "frmChooseReport"

Cancel_Click_Exit:
    Exit Sub

Cancel_Click_Err:
    MsgBox Error$
    Resume Cancel_Click_Exit
End Sub
```

19. Save and compile your code and close the Visual Basic Editor screen.

20. Switch to the Form view and test the Cancel button.

All the buttons are working, but we still need to make changes to the form itself, so it looks exactly like the one in Figure 11.2 in the beginning of this chapter.

⊙ Hands-On 11.2   Creating a Report Selection Form

(Part IV—Adjusting the Form Properties)

1. Open the frmChooseReport in the Design View and, in the Property sheet, ensure that **Form** is selected from the drop-down box. In the All tab, change the following properties as follows:

Property Name	Property Value
Caption	Report Selection
Pop Up	Yes
Width	5"
Fit to Screen	No
Border Style	Dialog
Record Selectors	No
Navigation Buttons	No
Scroll Bars	Neither
Min Max Buttons	None

2. In the Design view, set the form's height to 3 inches on the vertical ruler.
3. Switch to the Form view and test your form.

    This form is now a Pop Up form, and it can be moved anywhere on the screen without interfering with other database window selections that you may want to make while this form is open.

4. Save the changes in your form and close it.

SUMMARY

Kudos to you if you were able to complete all the steps in both Hands-On projects without pulling your hair out or getting frustrated as much as I did while preparing this chapter. Working with reports is very interesting and exciting work, but we tend to underestimate how much time it takes to get those complex reports up and working properly.

In this chapter, you worked with numerous report and control properties and learned quite a bit about report sections and their customization. You created a report completely from scratch and went through various stages of report design process step by step. This process may have been challenging with so many details and steps to keep track of, but by following this process you are now more in control of database reporting than someone who relies strictly on the built-in wizards to generate so-called canned out-of-the-box reports.

In this chapter, you also saw how forms can provide a handy user interface for your reports. You've converted the Wizard-generated embedded macro into Visual Basic and learned how to modify it to extend it to other form controls quickly. You learned new VBA keywords and constructs like Select Case and advanced your knowledge of building more complex expressions using functions such as Intermediate IIF and Switch. I hope that all the practical skills you now possess in Access reporting can be put to good use in your future endeavors by enabling you to deliver reports that are customized and fine-tuned and that meet the expectations of your audience.

The next and final chapter of this book is Chapter 12. This is where we split this database into two pieces and learn about the advantages you can gain from doing so. You also find out how to use linked tables and perform some database maintenance tasks.

Part VI

COMPACT, SPLIT AND SECURE THE DATABASE

P art VI focuses on the steps you need to follow to maintain a stable and secured Access desktop database that can run well in a network environment.

Chapter 12   Compacting, Splitting, and Securing an Access Database

Chapter 12 COMPACTING, SPLITTING, AND SECURING AN ACCESS DATABASE

ach database you create will require regular maintenance tasks that can keep it running smoothly, securely, and efficiently. Some of these tasks include compacting, repairing, backing up, splitting, and securing the database. In this chapter, we discuss and apply each of these tasks to our ETD database in Hands-On projects.

COMPACTING AND REPAIRING YOUR DATABASE

You may have already noticed the growing size of the ETD database. When you add, delete, or modify data and objects in an Access database, the database file grows larger which eventually can slow it down and make it unstable. If you notice that queries you run take longer than normal, and users start complaining about the slowness of various processes, it's time to compact and repair your database.

When you delete records and objects from your database Access does not automatically release the space these records and objects occupied. To reclaim unused space, reduce file size, and ensure optimal performance of your database, you must regularly compact your database. Another important reason for compacting your database is to ensure that the information that Access stores about database objects in system tables is consistent with the actual objects in your database, such as tables, queries, forms, and reports. Any inconsistency in this area can cause errors and corruption in the database. Also, when Access crashes due to some unexpected error, it may leave some locks on the database that prevent other users from accessing it. Compacting the database will remove these locks so users can access the database again. Also, an unsuccessful insert, update or delete operation often results in an incomplete transaction that must be cleaned up.

The File | Info and Compact and Repair (see Figure 12.1) will help you prevent and correct various database file problems. You can use this command to manually compact a database file that is open.

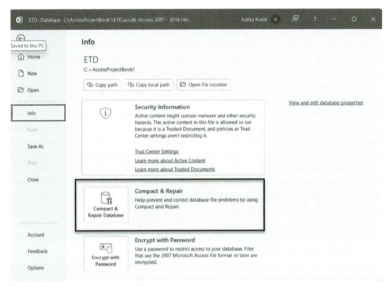

FIGURE 12.1. Compact and Repair an open Access database.

You can also compact and repair the database that is not currently open as demonstrated in Hands-On 12.1.

Database Compact and Repair: Precautions

Before compacting an Access database, always start with the following:

- Make a backup copy of your database.
  This ensures that if something goes wrong during the process you will still have a working database.
- Make sure no one is using the database you plan to compact.
  Compacting requires exclusive access to the database while the operation is in progress.
- Ensure that you have appropriate file permission to the database.
  You must have the right to access and modify the database file to compact and repair it. If you don't have this right, you will not be able to perform the

operation and you may see an error message. The system administrator is the person who manages the network and the permissions of the users. You can contact them and ask to grant you the permission or to compact and repair the database for you.

The compact and repair process eliminates unused space in the database, reorganizes the data in a contiguous way, deletes no longer needed temporary objects, and fixes any errors that may have occurred. It is a good practice to compact and repair regularly to ensure optimal performance and reliability of your database.

(●) Hands-On 12.1   Compact & Repair a Closed Access Database

1. Use the File Explorer to create a copy of your ETD database. Name the file **ETD_Backup_BeforeCompact.accdb** and store it in another folder of your choice.
2. Open **Microsoft Access** and do not open any database.
3. Click **Options**, and when the Options dialog appears, choose **Cancel**.
4. Click the back button (<) in the top left corner of the Access application window.
5. Choose the Ribbon's **Database Tools** tab and click the **Compact and Repair Database** button.

   Access displays the Database to Compact From dialog as shown in Figure 12.2.
6. Choose the **ETD.accdb** database and click **Compact**.

FIGURE 12.2. Compact and Repair a closed Access database.

Access performs the Compact and Repair Database operation and displays the Compact Database Into window. The time it takes to compact and repair the database depends on the size of the database, the resources available on your computer and how long it has been since you last ran this command.

7. In the File name box, enter **ETD_Compacted_After_Chap11.accdb** and click **Save**.

Access saves the file and may display the message that the active content in this file is blocked. This simply tells you that Access has detected some code or macros in the database that could potentially harm your computer if they are not from a trusted source. As you created this database by yourself, there is nothing to worry about.

8. Click **OK** to dismiss the message box.

Access saves the file, and you are returned to the empty database window. Your AccessProjectBook1 folder should now contain your database compacted under a different file name.

Action Item 12.1

Open the ETD database in Access and use the Compact and Repair Database button shown in Figure 12.1.

NOTE	*When you compact an open database, Access creates a new compacted file and then deletes the original database. However, this process may not be visible to you, as Access automatically renames the new file with the original name and reloads it into Access.*

Using the Compact on Close Option

You can have Access automatically compact and repair your database when it closes, using the following steps:

1. Select **File | Options**.
2. In the Access Options dialog, choose **Current Database** (see Figure 12.3).
3. Under Application Options, select the **Compact on Close** check box.

This option must be set separately for each database you want to automatically compact and repair on close.

4. Click **OK**.
5. Close the database for this option to take effect.

> | NOTE | *The Compact on Close option is not recommended in a multi-user database as compacting makes the database unavailable while the compact operation is in progress.* |

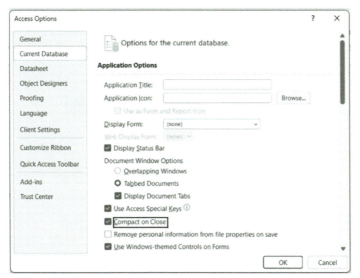

FIGURE 12.3. The Compact on Close option will perform the Compact and Repair process every time the database is closed.

BACKING UP AND RESTORING YOUR DATABASE

Corruption in a database often occurs when you least expect it. To protect your data from accidental loss or damage, you should back up your database regularly. To create a backup of your Access database, you can use the built-in backup feature that is available in Access or use a third party backup software.

Using Access to Back Up a Database

When you back up a database, Access creates a copy of the database file that can be used to restore the data or specific database objects in case of a system failure or a human error.

⊚ Hands-On 12.2   Backing up the ETD Database.

1. Open Access and load the database you want to back up.
2. Choose **File | Save As**.

3. Under the File Types, choose **Save Database As** (see Figure 12.4).

NOTE	*This option will be selected by default if there are no open objects in the database. If an object is open, for example, the Employees table, you could create a standalone backup of this table using the Save Object As option in the File Types.*

4. In the Save Database As area, under the **Advanced** section, choose **Back Up Database**.
5. Click the **Save As** button.

FIGURE 12.4. Using the built-in database backup feature in Access.

6. In the Save As dialog box, select the location for your database backup and specify the backup name.

   The default name includes the name of the original database file and the date that you make the backup, for example, ETD_2023-09-12.accdb. Note, that you shouldn't store your database backup on the same drive as your original database.

7. Click **Save**.

   Access goes to work and creates the backup file. When the backup is completed, you may see the message that the active content in this file is blocked.

Restoring a Database From a Backup Copy

To restore a database from a backup copy, simply replace the original database file with the backup file. You can also restore individual objects from a backup copy by importing them into the current database. The following are the import steps:

1. Choose **External Data | New Data Source | From Database | Access**.
2. In the File name box, enter the name of your backup database or click the Browse button to select the file.
3. Click the first option button to **import tables, queries, forms, reports, macros, and modules into the current database**.
4. Click **OK**.
5. If Access flashes the database window, click inside the window to acknowledge the message about the active content.
6. In the Import Objects dialog box, choose the objects you want to restore and click **OK**.

   You can specify additional import options by clicking the Options button (see Figure 12.5).

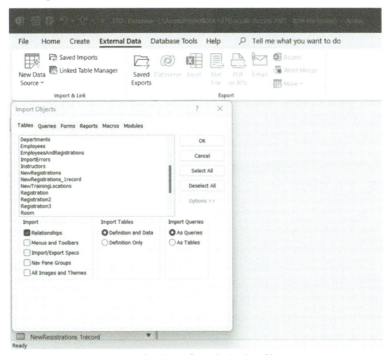

FIGURE 12.5. Restoring specific objects from the backup file.

SPLITTING YOUR DATABASE

So far in this book project you were the only developer and a sole user of the ETD database. Most databases, however, are developed and accessed by multiple users over a network. If you give the current database file to several users, you can expect the following problems:

- Reduced performance
  Every time a user opens the database and accesses an object all the database objects (tables, queries, forms, reports, etc.) will be sent across the network. This drastically slows down the network and the database operations.

- Increased risk of database corruption
  If multiple users attempt to change the same data at the same time, data conflicts or errors will occur. If a user opens the database in exclusive mode, other users will not be able to access it. A power outage or a network failure while using a database can corrupt the entire database file.

- Limited functionality
  Some features or capabilities of Access are not available or are restricted when you share a single database file with multiple users. For example, you cannot compact and repair the database, change the database password, or modify the design of the database objects unless you have exclusive access to the file. Exclusive access means that only one user can open the file at a time. If other users are using the file, you must wait until they close it or ask them to close it. This can be inconvenient and inefficient for your work.

The way to avoid all these issues is to split the database into two files: a *front-end file* that contains the forms, reports, queries, and other objects that you use to interact with the data, and a *back-end file* that contains only the tables that store the data. You can then distribute the front-end file to each user's local computer and link it to the back-end file that is stored on a shared network folder. This way, each user can work with their own copy of the front-end file and access the same data in the back-end file. Because only the data will be sent across the network, this can improve performance, reduce corruption, and provide more functionality.

In the following Hands-On project, we will go through the steps required to separate the data in the ETD database from the rest of the database. We will use the Access Database Splitter wizard to move tables from the ETD database to a new back-end database. In a multi-user environment, this will help reduce network traffic, and will allow continuous front-end development without affecting data or interrupting users. Let's get started.

⊙ Hands-On 12.3   Splitting the ETD Database

1. Create a backup copy of the ETD database and save it as **ETD_BeforeSplit.accdb**.

2. Open the **ETD.accdb** database in Access and ensure that only the following tables are present (see Figure 12.6). Delete all the other tables that you may have in the database that were used for backup or testing.

FIGURE 12.6. Leave only the tables that provide data for forms and reports and are referenced in queries. Delete all the other tables that were used for testing and are no longer needed.

3. In the Move Data group of the Database Tools, click **Access Database** (see Figure 12.7).

FIGURE 12.7. Selecting the Access Database will begin the process of splitting a database into two files.

The Database Splitter Wizard will appear (see Figure 12.8).

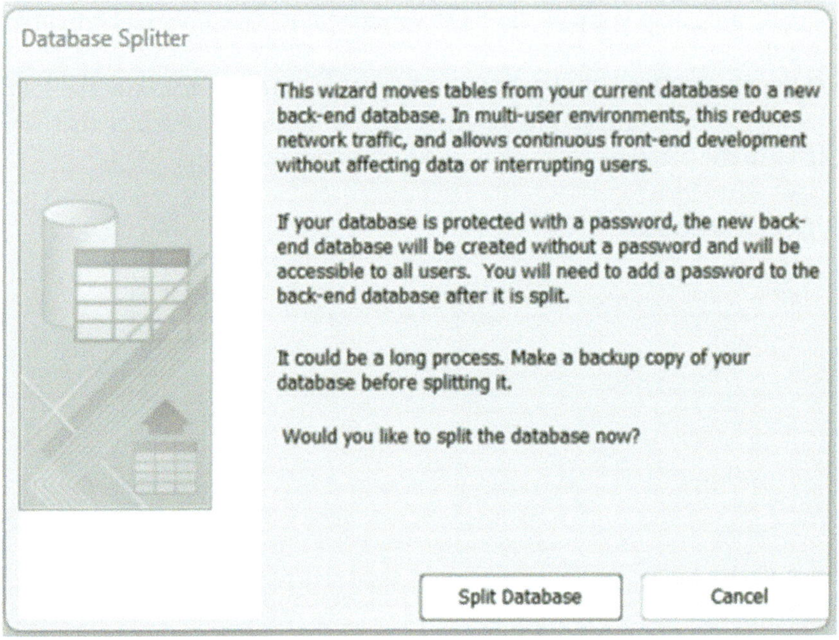

Database Splitter

This wizard moves tables from your current database to a new back-end database. In multi-user environments, this reduces network traffic, and allows continuous front-end development without affecting data or interrupting users.

If your database is protected with a password, the new back-end database will be created without a password and will be accessible to all users. You will need to add a password to the back-end database after it is split.

It could be a long process. Make a backup copy of your database before splitting it.

Would you like to split the database now?

Split Database   Cancel

FIGURE 12.8. The Database Splitter Wizard.

4. Click **Split Database**.

Access displays the Create Back-end Database dialog box and proposes the name for your back-end database (see Figure 12.9). The _be suffix indicates that it is the back-end file.

NOTE	*You can change the location of your back-end database to a shared network folder to which all users will have access. For example, if the network location is \\MyNetServer\Share1\ you can enter \\MyNetServer\Share1\ETD_be.accdb in the File name box. When creating a back-end database you should specify the Universal Naming Convention (UNC) path because UNC paths are the same for all computers on the same network. Note that a UNC path starts with two back slashes, and is followed by the name of the server, a slash, and the path to the network location.*

The Tools drop-down menu to the left of the Split button has an option to Map Network drive. You can use this option when you want to assign a drive letter to the network location where you'll store the back-end database. This can make it easier for users to access the back-end database without having to browse for its network path each time. However, keep in mind that mapped drives are unique to each computer, and there is no guarantee that the mapped drive will be available to everyone who uses the database.

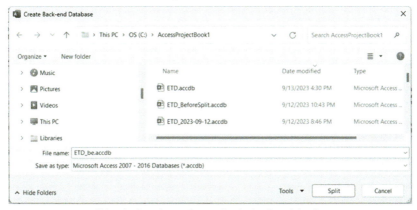

FIGURE 12.9. Specifying the location and name for the back-end database.

5. Click the **Split** button to accept the default name and location for the back-end database.

   Access starts the process of exporting the tables, deleting the tables in the local database, and creating links to the back-end tables.

6. When the process is completed, you should see the message "Database successfully split." Click **OK** to close the Database Splitter.

UNDERSTANDING LINKED TABLES

Notice that after splitting the database into a front-end and back-end file, the front end-file (ETD.accdb) shows different icons in front of each table name (see Figure 12.10). These table icons with arrows next to them indicate that these are linked tables. Before splitting the database all the tables were local to the database, now they are pointing to tables in the back-end database.

Linked tables are tables that are stored in a different database than the one you are working on but can be accessed and manipulated as if they were local tables. After splitting a database, you need to know how to manage the linked tables in the front-end database, such as how to refresh, relink, find, edit, add, or delete them. You can use the Linked Table Manager tool in Access to perform these tasks. You also need to know how to write queries that use linked tables, such as how to join them with other tables, how to filter and sort them, and how to update or insert data into them. You can use the Query Design tool in Access to create and modify queries that use linked tables.

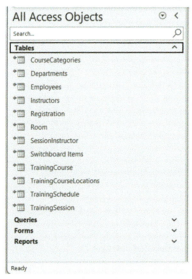

FIGURE 12.10. The Database Navigation pane shows linked tables in the front-end file after the database was split.

When you work with a front-end database that contains links to data in a back-end file, and the back-end file resides on a network, you need to consider that the performance of your database will depend on the speed and reliability of the network connection. If the network is slow or unstable, you may experience delays or errors when accessing or updating the data in the back-end file. To improve performance, you can try optimizing your queries, use local tables for temporary data, and minimize network traffic. When creating queries, avoid using aggregate functions such as DCount, which retrieve all the records from the linked table before performing the calculation. To view data from external (linked) tables, use the query criteria wisely, by limiting the number of records that are displayed at one time. If you retrieve lots of records to display in a datasheet, moving from the first to the last record in the datasheet using page down and page up may become very slow. By specifying in your query, the exact set of records you want to preview, you will get better performance. Earlier in this book we created a data entry form for the Employees table. When working with a split database, if you are planning to add new records to the linked tables, it is recommended that you create data entry forms to avoid loading existing data just to enter a new record.

When Access split the database into two files, all the relationships between the tables that we established earlier in this book project were preserved in the front-end database.

Any linked table reference you see in the Navigation pane can be deleted from the database by selecting it and pressing the Delete key. Deleting a linked table will only delete its name from the database objects. The actual data will still be available in the source (back-end) file.

Using the Linked Table Manager

Sometimes the links to the external tables get broken and you need to fix them. Access has a handy utility known as a Linked Table Manager that allows you to view and manage all the data sources and linked tables in your Access database. You can Access the Linked Table Manager by right clicking any linked table in the Navigation pane and choosing Linked Table Manager or use the Linked Table Manager button in the Import & Link group of the External Data tab (see Figure 12.11).

FIGURE 12.11. Accessing the Linked Table Manager via the External Data tab.

Use the Linked Table Manager regularly to perform the following tasks:

- Refresh a data source and its linked tables to ensure that they are working properly and up to date.
- Relink a data source or a linked table if the location, name, or schema of the source has changed.
- Find a linked table by searching for its name, data source, or connection string.
- Edit a data source if you need to change its location, name, password, or connection string.
- Add a new data source and link to its tables if you want to use external data in your database.
- Delete a data source or a linked table if you no longer need them in your database.

⊙ **Hands-On 12.4   Working With the Linked Table Manager**

1. In the ETD database, which is now your front-end file, choose **External Data |
   Linked Table Manager**.
2. Access displays the dialog box that shows the data Source information, and
   that is the name of your back-end database (see Figure 12.12).

FIGURE 12.12. Linked Table Manager (collapsed view).

3. Click the **Expand All** button and when Access displays the list of tables, click
   Select All (see Figure 12.13).

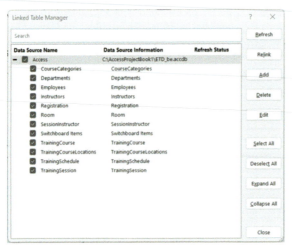

FIGURE 12.13. Linked Table Manager (expanded view).

4. Click the **Refresh** button.

When you use this button Access refreshes the data source and its linked tables to ensure that they are working properly and are up to date. You should use this button when you want to check the status of your linked tables or when you make changes to the data source or the linked tables.

Access refreshes the data and enters Succeeded in the Refresh Status column (see Figure 12.14).

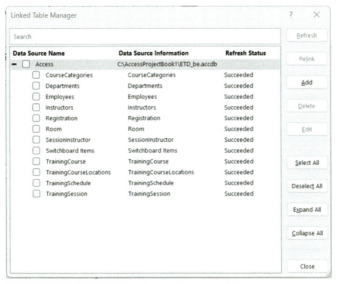

FIGURE 12.14. Linked Table Manager (after refresh).

Notice that there are other action buttons in the Linked Table Manager (Relink, Add, Delete, and Edit), and they are described in the following list:

- **Relink**: This button relinks the data source or a specific linked table if the location, name, or schema of the source has changed. You should use this button when you want to update the connection information of your linked tables or when you move or rename the data source or the linked tables.

- **Add**: This button allows you to add a new data source and link to its tables if you want to use external data in your database. You should use this button when you want to create a new linked table from SQL Server / Azure, Access, Excel, Text, Dynamics, SharePoint List, or ODBC.

- **Delete**: This button allows you to delete a data source or a linked table if you no longer need them in your database. You should use this button when you want to remove unnecessary or obsolete linked tables from your database.

- **Edit**: This button allows you to edit the data source of a linked table if you need to change its location, name, password, or connection string. You should use this button when you want to modify the properties of your data source or when you change the credentials or settings of your data source.

Also notice, at the top of the Linked Table Manager, there is a Search area where you can search for a linked table by its name, data source, or connection string. You should use the search if you have lots of linked tables in the database and you want to find them quickly.

5. Click the **Select All** button, and then click **Edit**.

Access displays the Eidt Link dialog as shown in Figure 12.15. If you ever rename your back-end database or replace it, you must specify the new file name for your data source using the Edit Link dialog.

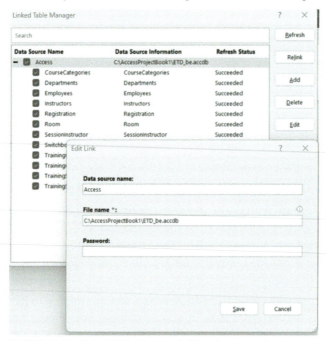

FIGURE 12.15. Linked Table Manager (editing data source).

6. Click **Cancel** to dismiss the Edit Link dialog.
7. Click **Close** to exit the Linked Table Manager.

	If you rename your back-end database, and then try to access any tables in the front-end database, Access will display the message that it cannot find the source file. You will then need to use the Link Table Manager to relink your tables to the new data source.
NOTE	

Access does not automatically synchronize the data in linked tables with the data in the back-end database. Rather, it refreshes the data in linked tables whenever you open them or run a query that uses them. This means that you can see the latest changes made to the data in the back-end database, as well as any changes made by other users who are connected to the same data source. However, this also means that if you make changes to the data in linked tables, you need to save them to the back-end database before closing Access or switching to another object. Otherwise, your changes will be lost and not reflected in the back-end database or other linked tables. To save your changes to the back-end database, you can use the Save command on the Quick Access Toolbar, or press Ctrl+S. Alternatively, you can use the Linked Table Manager tool to refresh or relink your data sources and linked tables manually.

Let's look at the ETD_be.accdb back-end file that Access created.

REVIEWING THE BACK-END DATABASE

Notice that the back-end file (ETD_be.accdb) contains only the tables (see Figure 12.16). From now on, if you need to modify the table structure or add new tables to your ETD database you need to open the back-end file exclusively and make the necessary changes. You also need to refresh or relink the tables in the front-end database using the Linked Table Manager tool.

To open a back-end file exclusively in Access, perform the following steps:

- Start Access and click **Browse** to locate your back-end file in your computer or network folder.
- Select your back-end file, and in the Open drop down, choose **Open Exclusive**.

  This will open the back-end file in a mode that prevents other users from accessing it at the same time.

Keep in mind that you cannot use the front-end file when you open the back-end file exclusively. When you open a database file in exclusive mode, you prevent other users from accessing it at the same time. This means that the front-end file cannot link to the tables in the back-end file, and you will not be able to view or edit the data in the front-end file. You should only open the back-end file exclusively when you need to perform certain tasks that require exclusive access, such as setting a database password, compacting, and repairing the database, or modifying the table structure.

If you want to protect your data from unauthorized access or modification, you can encrypt the back-end database with a password. To do this, you need to open the back-end database exclusively and set a database password. You also need to update the connection information of the linked tables in the front-end database with the new password. You will encrypt both database files with a password in the next section.

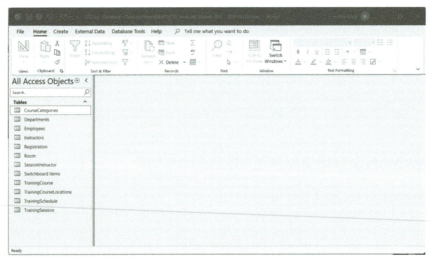

FIGURE 12.16. Access application with the back-end file open.

SECURING AN ACCESS ACCDB DATABASE

To secure an Access ACCDB database that was split into front and back end is to encrypt both parts by using a database password. This will make your data unreadable by other tools and require a password to use the database.

When you encrypt a database with a password you can use the same password to decrypt the database and remove its password. It is important that you keep this password secure; if you forget it, you will not be able to use or decrypt the database. You can only encrypt a database that is in the ACCDB file format.

Encrypting a Database With a Password

In this section, we create and apply a password to our Access front-end and back-end databases. The encryption of a split database consists of three parts as demonstrated in Hands-On 12.5.

⊙ Hands-On 12.5   Encrypting a Database

(Part I—Encrypting a Back-End Database)

1. Choose **File | Open**.
2. In the Open dialog box, browse to your back-end database (ETD_be.accdb) file and select it.
3. Click the arrow next to the Open button and choose **Open Exclusive** (see Figure 12.7).

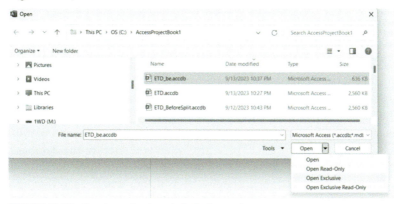

FIGURE 12.17. Opening a database in Exclusive mode.

4. Choose **File | Info**, and then click **Encrypt with Password**.
5. In the Password box, type your password, and then type it again in the Verify box. For this exercise let's enter **Trainer21**.

NOTE	*Password Rules* *It is important to use strong passwords that combine uppercase and lowercase letters, numbers, and symbols. Password should be at least 8 characters long but the longer the password the better. Write down your password and store it in a secure place and remember that if you lose or forget it, there is no way to retrieve it (you cannot reset it by using your Microsoft account or another tool).*

6. Click **OK** to exit the Password dialog.

7. Access displays the message shown in Figure 12.18.

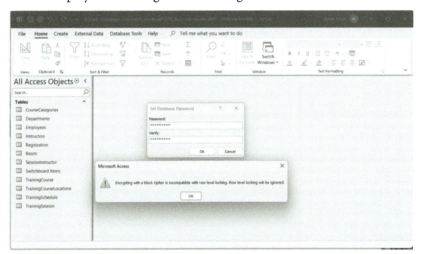

FIGURE 12.18. When setting the database password, Access informs you that row level locking will be ignored.

When you encrypt a database with a password, a block cipher method is used. This is a type of encryption that encrypts the whole database file, not just individual records, or rows. Row level locking that allows you to lock only the record that you are editing, not the whole page or table, is incompatible with block cipher encryption. Therefore, when you encrypt the database with a password, row level locking will be ignored, and page level locking will be used. This means that when you edit a record, the whole page that contains that record will be locked, and other users will not be able to access it. This can cause conflicts or delays if multiple users are trying to access the same data.

8. Click **OK** to dismiss the message box.

9. Close the back-end file and reopen it. When prompted for a password, enter **Trainer21** and click **OK**.

10. Now that you know that the password is working, close the back-end file.

⊚ Hands-On 12.1   Encrypting a Database

(Part II—Relinking Tables)

Before you can apply a password to a front-end database you need to delete the links to the tables in the back-end database, and then link to them again. Access will prompt you for the back-end database password when you relink.

1. Close the ETD.accdb front-end database.

2. Reopen the ETD.accdb database in exclusive mode.
3. Delete all the links to the tables in the back-end database. To do this, right-click each linked table in the Navigation pane and select **Delete**. Or select the first table, hold down the Shift key and click the last table in the list, then right click the selection and click Delete.

   Access will ask you to confirm the deletion.
4. Click **Yes**.

   The tables are deleted, and we need to reconnect them.
5. In the External Data tab, click the New Data Source, choose **From Database | Access**.
6. In the Get External Data – Access Database, use the **Browse** button to browse to your back-end file, choose the second option button (**Link to the data source by creating a linked table**), and then click **OK** (see Figure 12.19).

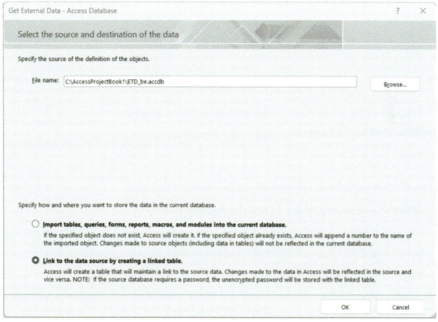

FIGURE 12.19. Creating linked tables in the front-end database.

7. Enter the password to the back-end file **Trainer21** and click **OK**.

8. In the Link Tables dialog box, click **Select All** and then click **OK** (see Figure 12.20).

FIGURE 12.20. Access displays a list of tables that can be linked.

All the links to the back-end tables should now appear in the Navigation pane.

⊙ Hands-On 12.1   Encrypting a Database

(Part III—Encrypting a Front-End Database)

After relinking tables to the back-end database, you are ready to encrypt the front-end database. The steps to encrypt a front-end database are the same as for the back-end database.

1. With the ETD.accdb database still open in the exclusive mode, choose **File | Info**, and then click **Encrypt with Password**.
2. In the Password box, type your password **Trainer21fe**, and then type it again in the Verify box, then click **OK**.

NOTE	*You should use a different password for the front-end database than the one you used for the back-end database. Make sure you don't forget it.*

3. Click **OK** again to dismiss the informational message about ignoring row level locking.
4. Close the database and reopen it in a normal mode.

   Access should prompt you for the password.

Decrypting Database

If you know the password to the encrypted database, you can remove it from a database and replace it with another password at any time. Simply repeat the steps 1–3 that were given in Part I of the previous Hands-On. In step 4, choose the Decrypt Database after selecting File | Info (see Figure 12.21). The Unset Database Password dialog will appear where you should enter your password in the Password box, and then click OK.

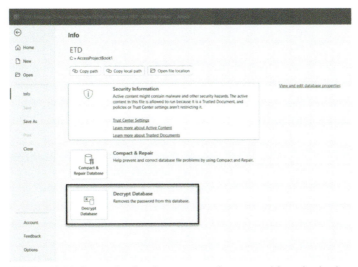

FIGURE 12.21. Decrypting Database removes the password from the database.

USER-LEVEL SECURITY IN ACCESS DATABASES

A user-level security is a feature that allows you to create user accounts and passwords and assign permissions to different database objects for each user or group of users. To implement this feature Access relies on a special database, called a *workbook information file*. When you install Access, a default workbook file called *System.mdw* is automatically created for you. This file includes two built-in groups: the Users group, which contains every user, and the Admins group, that is used for users who have been given special permissions to administer the database.   A built-in user, called Admin, is available in the Admins group to act as a default administrator. Working with different dialog boxes, you can remove the default Admin from the Admins group and designate another user as an administrator, as well as assign different permissions to every user in your database. Working with user-level security is beyond the scope of this book because this type of security only applies to Access database files created in the older MDB file format. I have dedicated a whole chapter to this topic in my book titled *Access 2021 / Microsoft 365 Programming by Example, with VBA, XML, and ASP* (Mercury Learning and Information, 2022).

The ACCDB database file format that we have been working with does not have a user-level security feature. Microsoft removed this feature because it was not very secure; it allowed people to bypass it by using a different workgroup information file or by opening the database in another program. The ACCDB file format was designed to be compatible with other Microsoft products, such as SharePoint and SQL Server, that have their own security mechanisms. In short, if your ACCDB database needs to be accessed by multiple users in a network environment and you need to limit access to its data so that some users can read it but can't change it, and others can modify the data, Microsoft wants you to use other more secure options, such as encryption, database server, or SharePoint site.

As mentioned earlier, encryption makes your data unreadable by other programs or tools, and it forces users to enter a password to use the database.

By using a database server, such as Microsoft SQL Server, to store your Access data, the server can manage your user security, and you can still use Access to build your queries forms and reports by linking to the data on the server. This works on databases saved in any Access file format.

Access and SharePoint are two Microsoft products that can be used to create and manage data and content. While they have different features and capabilities, they can also work together to provide a more secure and integrated solution. Some SharePoint integration features are available only in Access databases that use one of the new file formats (ACCDB, ACCDE, ACCDC and ACCDR).

MIGRATION PROCESS: FROM ACCESS TO SQL SERVER

To use SQL Server more advanced security features, such as encryption, authentication, authorization, and auditing, you should migrate your data from Access to SQL Server.

- Encryption is used to protect sensitive data from unauthorized access or tempering. SQL Server supports several encryption options, for example, you can encrypt the entire database or specific columns in a table.

- Database authentication is used to verify the identity of users who connect to your database. You can use Windows authentication that uses the existing Windows user accounts and groups, or SQL Server authentication.

- Database authorization is using database roles and permissions to grant or deny access to specific database objects (tables, view, stored procedures, etc.) for each user or group of users.

- Auditing allows you to track and log events that occur in your database, such as login attempts, data modifications, and deletions. You can monitor user activity and detect potential security breaches.

There is no tool in Access to migrate your database to SQL Server. The Upsizing Wizard, which was a tool to automate the migration process in earlier versions of Access, is no longer available. However, you can use the Microsoft SQL Server Migration Assistant (SSMA) for Access, which is a free tool that was specifically designed to automate the migration process from Microsoft Access 97 and higher to all editions of SQL Server 2012 through SQL Server 2022, Azure SQL Database and Azure SQL Database Managed Instance. You can download the SSMA tool from: *https://www.microsoft.com/en-us/download/details. aspx?id=54255*.

The migration process from Access to SQL Server using SSMA involves several steps that are described in the following article: *https://support.microsoft. com/en-us/office/migrate-an-access-database-to-sql-server-7bac0438-498a-4f53-b17b-cc22fc42c979*.

After the migration, if you want to use your existing Access application with SQL Server, you can link your original Access tables to the migrated SQL Server tables. Linking modifies your Access database so that queries, forms, and reports use the data in the SQL Server database instead of the data in your database.

You can download SQL Server 2022 Developer, which is a full-featured free edition, licensed for use as a development and test database in a nonproduction environment from: *https://go.microsoft.com/fwlink/p/?linkid=2215158*.

SUMMARY

In this chapter, you were introduced to topics that allow you to run your Access database in a multi-user environment. You learned the steps involved in the process of splitting an Access database into front-end and back-end databases, and you learned how to work with the Linked Table Manager to manage the linked tables in the front-end database. You also learned how to use the Compact and Repair Database, Database Backup, and Encrypt with Password features that are built into Access. I explained why you cannot use the User-Level security in the ACCDB databases and recommended resources to use if you decide it's time to migrate your database back-end to an SQL Server.

I hope you have learned a great many useful and interesting database skills and techniques while working with this book. The ETD database is by no means completed. There is so much more you can do with it. We've added many fields that require data and were not filled in. You can get more practice by creating data entry forms for all the tables and use them to enter new data manually. Or you can create action queries that load your own data from various sources like we did in this book. The more data in the database, the more complex and interesting queries, forms, and reports you can create. Your learning process is not finished, continue it by exploring more Access design and development topics and resources that interest you. You can use Bing powered AI or other ChatGPT engines to help you with your learning goals. There has never been a better and easier time to learn than now.

Appendix

MICROSOFT
ACCESS FILE FORMATS

This appendix provides information about various file formats supported in Access 2007–2021.

TABLE A.1 File Formats Supported in Access 2007–2021

File Format	Description	Additional Notes
.ACCDB	File format first introduced in Access 2007 (default). This file format is not readable by Access versions prior to 2007. DO NOT use this file format if you need to support: • Replication • User-level security	*Note:* Access versions 2013–2021 do not support replicated databases. Use Access 2010–2007 to create a replica of an MDB database formatted in Access 2000–2003 file format.
.ACCDE	File extension for Access 2007–2021 .ACCDB files that are in execute only mode. These files have all VBA programming source code removed. This file extension replaces the .MDE file extension used in earlier versions of Access.	Users can only execute VBA code; they cannot view or modify it. In addition, users do not have permission to make design changes to forms or reports. If you need to save the Access 2021 database in .ACCDE format, open the database and choose File | Save As | Save Database As. Select Make ACCDE and click the Save As button.
.ACCDT	This is an Access Database template file. Access 2007–2021 all come with professionally designed database templates.	Templates provide you with predefined tables/table relationships, forms, reports, queries, and macros. To save the Access 2021 database as a template, open the database and choose File | Save As | Save Database As. Select Template (.ACCDT) and click the Save As button.
.ACCDR	This file extension denotes an Access 2007–2021 database functioning in runtime mode.	To create a "locked-down" version of your Access 2021 database, simply change the file extension from .ACCDB to .ACCDR. To restore the full database functionality, do the reverse: change the file extension from .ACCDR to .ACCDB.

File Format	Description	Additional Notes
.MDB (Access 97, Access 2000, Access 2002, Access 2003)	Access database file format used in versions prior to 2007. *Note:* In Access 2007–2021, you can create files in either the Access 2000 format or the Access 2002–2003 database format. These files will have the extension .MDB.	Use the .MDB file format if the database will be used in earlier versions of Access to: • Support replication • Support user-level security
.MDE (Access 97, Access 2000-2003)	An .MDE file is a compiled version of an .MDB database without any VBA code. This change prevents a database user from reading or changing your VBA code. Users cannot edit the design of forms, reports, or modules.	An .ACCDE file is the Access 2007–2021 version of the .MDE file in earlier versions of Access.
.ADP	This is a file extension for a Microsoft Access Data Project file that lets you connect to an SQL Server database or the Microsoft Data Engine (MSDE) on your PC and create client/server applications. A project file does not contain any data or data definition objects such as tables, views, stored procedures, or user-defined functions. All database objects are stored in the SQL server database. An .ADP file stores only database front-end forms, reports, and other application objects (macros, modules).	Access 2013–2021 does not support the .ADP file format. If you need to open and edit an existing ADP database that was created in an earlier version of Access or create a new ADP database, use Access 2007–2010.
.ADE	This is a file format for a Microsoft Access project (.ADP) file with all modules compiled and all editable source code removed. Like .MDE files, projects stored in the .ADE file format prevent users from making design changes to the frontend and gaining access to your VBA source code.	Access 2021 does not support the .ADE file format. To create an .ADE file from your Access Data Project (ADP), use Access 2007–2010.

(Contd.)

File Format	Description	Additional Notes
.MDW (Access 97, Access 2000, Access 2002, Access 2003)	This file format is used by a Workgroup Information File. The .MDW files store information for secured MDB databases.	There are no changes to the .MDW file format in Access 2016–2021. The .MDW files created in earlier versions of Access (2000 through 2003) can be used by Access 2016–2021. When an MDB database is opened, you can choose File | Info | Users & Permissions | User-Level Security Wizard to create a new Workgroup Information File (.MDW).
.LDB	This is a locking file extension for the MDB database. This file prevents users from writing data to pages that have been locked by other users and lets you determine which computer/user has a file or record locked. The .LDB file keeps track of usernames/computer names of the people who are currently logged into the MDB database.	A locking file is created automatically when the database is opened and is deleted automatically when the last user closes a shared database. *Note:* You can view the information stored in this file by opening it with Windows Notepad.
.LACCDB	This is the file extension for a locking file used by the .ACCDB file format in Access 2007–2021.	As with the .LDB file, the .LACCDB file is created automatically when the database is opened and is deleted automatically when the last user closes a shared database. *Note:* Because different locking files are created for MDB and ACCDB databases in Access 2007–2021, .MDB and .ACCDB files can be open in Access 2007–2021 without causing conflicts in the locking file.

Index